Postdisciplinary Studies in Discourse

Series Editors
Johannes Angermuller
University of Warwick
Coventry, United Kingdom

Judith Baxter
Halsecombe House
Minehead, United Kingdom

Postdisciplinary Studies in Discourse engages in the exchange between discourse theory and analysis while putting emphasis on the intellectual challenges in discourse research. Moving beyond disciplinary divisions in today's social sciences, the contributions deal with critical issues at the intersections between language and society.

More information about this series at
http://www.springer.com/series/14534

Jan Zienkowski

Articulations of Self and Politics in Activist Discourse

A Discourse Analysis of Critical Subjectivities in Minority Debates

Jan Zienkowski
Institute for Culture and Society
University of Navarra
Pamplona, Navarra, Spain

Postdisciplinary Studies in Discourse
ISBN 978-3-319-82159-7   ISBN 978-3-319-40703-6 (eBook)
DOI 10.1007/978-3-319-40703-6

© The Editor(s) (if applicable) and The Author(s) 2017
Softcover reprint of the hardcover 1st edition 2016
This work is subject to copyright. All rights are solely and exclusively licensed by the Publisher, whether the whole or part of the material is concerned, specifically the rights of translation, reprinting, reuse of illustrations, recitation, broadcasting, reproduction on microfilms or in any other physical way, and transmission or information storage and retrieval, electronic adaptation, computer software, or by similar or dissimilar methodology now known or hereafter developed.
The use of general descriptive names, registered names, trademarks, service marks, etc. in this publication does not imply, even in the absence of a specific statement, that such names are exempt from the relevant protective laws and regulations and therefore free for general use.
The publisher, the authors and the editors are safe to assume that the advice and information in this book are believed to be true and accurate at the date of publication. Neither the publisher nor the authors or the editors give a warranty, express or implied, with respect to the material contained herein or for any errors or omissions that may have been made.

Cover image © Yagi Studio/ Getty images

Printed on acid-free paper

This Palgrave Macmillan imprint is published by Springer Nature
The registered company is Springer International Publishing AG Switzerland
The registered company address is: Gewerbestrasse 11, 6330 Cham, Switzerland

Introduction

Discourse is a slippery thing. The range of theories and disciplines that try to explain how it functions, what its basic elements are and how we may objectify it is wide and full of contradictory positions. At the same time, it is agreed that discourse is ultimately about meaning. The discourse we use informs the way we conceptualise and create the contexts in which we move, as well as the outlook with which we approach these realities. It not only tells us what objects we can speak about, it also provides us with the semiotic options and strategies that allow us to articulate who and what we are ourselves. Discourse, I will argue, is first and foremost a multilayered practice of articulation.

The concept of articulation has a long history in the English language. Throughout this history some meanings have been forgotten and others have been recently recovered and reconceptualised in social and political theory. At times, the concept is used in order to designate a practice of linking discursive elements to each other. In this sense, articulation consists of practices such as linking vowels, words, sentences, narratives, texts, identities and ideologies to each other. But the concept of articulation can also be regarded as a notion of performativity. It is a particular *way* of quilting such elements together in a poetic and public performance. We all perform both types of articulation simultaneously when we talk about our world and about ourselves.

When studying political discourse, it is therefore important not to lose track of these two aspects of articulation. Meaning is not produced in a mechanical way. It is not a matter of encoding and decoding messages as if the message itself can be abstracted from the context in which it was produced, mediated and interpreted. Language is not a puzzle that guarantees only one possible outcome as long as some uniform rules of interpretation and construction are followed. On the contrary: the various ways in which we perform the practice of linking elements to each other impact on the way we construct meaning. In this book, the focus will be on the relationship between politics and subjectivity as articulated in activist discourse.

Human beings define a great deal of who and what we are through discourse. We constantly renegotiate and appropriate the way we can and should interpret each other's words and practices by rearticulating voices, statements and stories that are not our own. In the context of political communication this principle becomes especially relevant. We rely on the discourse of others in order to position and define ourselves. Entire debates can be described in terms of discursive processes of rearticulation. Debates about issues such as migration or financial debt are about the way we connect societal elements, functions and meanings to each other. Social actors struggle over the power that allows them to reshape societies in the image of a preferred sense of self and other. They articulate categories such as 'politics', 'culture', 'ethnicity', 'community', 'integration' or 'neoliberalism' accordingly in political debates and performances.

The use of such abstract categories is not a prerogative of academics and politicians. Such notions also figure in everyday language use. This can be exemplified with reference to the Flemish debates on integration and minorities discussed in this book. Even critics of hegemonic interpretations of concepts such as identity or integration are not always able to avoid using such notions altogether. Critique does not so much rely on a strict refusal to use problematic terms altogether as on the capacity to undermine the logics informing hegemonic understandings of terms that support the current status quo.

Public debates are inherently multilayered. They take place in a variety of institutional settings and involve a multiplicity of actors. However, this variety is not completely eclectic. It is always possible to discern recurring arguments. Some arguments will be valued over others and some voices will be granted more authority than others. There are regularities in the dispersion of statements within every public debate. These regularities can be described in terms of logics. This does not mean that large-scale debates are completely predictable or static. They are not. But it is not easy to influence them as an isolated citizen. The political success of a counter discourse can be assessed with reference to the extent to which it manages to be articulated with and within competing discourses in the public realm.

Anyone who follows up on a mediatised topic for some amount of time will notice that similar actors make similar arguments time and time again. Some aspects of a discourse may change—for example, its expressions, slogans or metaphors—but quite often there is an adaptive interpretive logic that structures a debate and that resists true change in the sense of a restructuration of social and political relationships. Most contemporary theories of discourse agree that there is no one-to-one relationship between a linguistic form and its meaning. A new metaphor may signal a change in the large-scale interpretive logic structuring a particular discourse, but it may also perform an equivalent political function.

Whether the discourse of a person, an organisation or a movement can be labelled as critical or counter ideological depends not so much on the specific characteristics of a particular signifier within the discourse, but on the question whether the interpretive logic performed and articulated in a concrete discourse challenges hegemonic understandings of a society or a sociopolitical relationship. Throughout this book, I will provide a heuristic for analysing the logics of large-scale public debates, as well as for analysing the large-scale interpretive logics of language users who seek to challenge the dominant logics of the debates they are involved in. I chose to focus on the way Flemish, Belgian and/or Moroccan intellectuals and activists—they articulated such labels in different ways—established critical modes of subjectivity while engaging with hegemonic voices and statements in interviews on Flemish minority debates in Belgium.

In preparing this book, I was frequently asked to provide some reasons for people to be interested in the minority discourse of a small country such as Belgium. I was also asked to explain why my readers should be interested in the discourse of a minority of activists, within a Moroccan minority, within the Flemish region, within Belgium. After the terrorist attacks in Paris and Brussels, I think it is less likely that I will receive such questions in the near future. Many international commentators turned their attention to this tiny country in the heart of Europe, wondering why Belgium has the largest percentage of foreign fighters in Syria per capita, why there were so many terrorists with proven links to the Brussels district Molenbeek and—to a lesser extent—why Belgium ranks so badly in international and national reports on the integration of minorities into the labour market, the education system and other important areas of life.

My book does not answer these questions. But it may provide some context. I conducted all of my interviews in what may seem to be more innocent times. The interviews presented here were conducted before the rise of ISIS, before Europe's 'refugee crisis', before Trump made his bid for the presidency, at the beginning of Obama's post-Bush era in American politics. It was only after I conducted my last interview that a radical Islamist group called Sharia4Belgium started to profile itself publicly and gained mainstream media attention. However, a closer look at my interviews shows that these were not innocent times at all. Homogenising and neo-racist statements have been alienating Flemish/Belgian guest workers, migrants, Muslims and other 'allochthons' for decades, while international research reports continue to address exclusion mechanisms and outright discrimination in schooling, in real estate and in the labour market.

This book focuses on Moroccan/Flemish intellectuals and activists engaging in democratic forms of social and political activism. It is not about Islamism, terrorism or non-democratic forms of radicalism but constitutes an attempt to approach a dense network of issues related to integration, racism, discrimination and migration from the point of view of a politicised minority within a minority. By focusing on the way Flemish/Moroccan activists talk about their preferred and disavowed modes of political engagement, it becomes possible to come to grips with the intricate relationship between self and politics as marked in discourse. As such, I would like to argue that any understanding of the logics that structure our societies should involve an understanding of the pragmatic and interpretive processes that allow us to articulate a more or less coherent sense of self.

In reaction to the recent Brussels attacks, Flemish homogenising and nationalist discourses on integration are back in full swing—even though they never really went out of fashion. The far right is on the rise all across Northern and Eastern Europe and attacks on Muslims and refugees are becoming ever more frequent. At the same time, many Europeans see their neo-racist discourses and attitudes justified by horrible acts committed by terrorists who claim to act in the name of Islam. It does not take a lot of imagination to realise that such developments are likely to fuel feelings of alienation and misrecognition upon which terrorist recruiters capitalise. It is therefore important to steer clear of sensation-driven stereotypes and to listen to the way critical minority members think about themselves, about politics and about the societies they live in. Maybe I did conduct my interviews in more tranquil times, but the statements made by my interviewees have gained rather than lost political significance.

Chapter 1 of this book problematises the relationship between self and politics as articulated in activist discourse with reference to concrete interview data. As such, it sets the stage for the two theoretical chapters that follow. By focusing on the way my interviewees dealt with abstract categories such as politics and identity, I will show that the barrier between academic and political discourse is extremely fuzzy. Abstract categories such as politics and identity are not merely analytical categories for social scientists. They also function as social values that allow my interviewees to distinguish between preferred and disavowed modes of politics. With respect to the self, Chap. 1 shows that language users attempt to articulate some degree of coherence with respect to the multiplicities they are. It offers an initial delineation of the object of investigation and a list of desiderata for a perspective that allows for an empirical discourse analysis of large-scale interpretive processes and political debates such as the minority debate in Flanders.

I will present the theoretical elements for my perspective on self and politics in activist discourse in Chaps. 2 and 3. Chapter 2 deals with the practice of articulation from the point of view of poststructuralist discourse theory. Here, I will focus especially on the ways in which the meanings of self, society and politics can be partially and temporarily fixed. As such, I will focus especially on the ways in which equivalence, difference, fantasy, power and critique function in relation to subjectivity and politics. Another point to be made is the fact that the very process of doing research involves a multilayered process of articulation. Throughout Chap. 2, I will argue that the poststructuralist notion of articulation provides us with a rich conceptual framework for thinking political subjectivity. However, I will also argue that there is a methodological deficit that needs to be addressed.

Chapter 3 of this book offers a pragmatic approach to articulatory practice. It articulates poststructuralist discourse theory with pragmatic perspectives on language, communication and discourse. This not only enables us to address the methodological deficit of discourse theory, but it also allows us to come to grips with the in situ ways in which people manage the complex links between self and politics as marked in discourse. By linking discourse theory, linguistic pragmatics and pragmatist accounts of the self, I seek to contribute to a post- or transdisciplinary concept of discourse that accounts for power and domination as well as for creativity and emancipation. Chapter 3 focuses on the pragmatic ways in which subjects articulate reflexive, metapragmatic and critical awareness in the face of powerful discursive logics that inform their very sense of self and politics.

Chapter 4 provides an introduction into the key features of hegemonic discourses on minority-related issues in Flanders. It focuses on the discourse of integration and on the allochthony/autochthony distinction—a binary pair that is unique to minority-related debates in Flanders and the Netherlands. This discussion of hegemonic integration discourse serves as a background for the critiques formulated by my interviewees. Even though almost all of my interviewees criticised at least some aspects of integration-related policy and discourse, it is important to bear in mind that my interview questions focused first and foremost on the political ideas and engagements of my respondents. The counter-hegemonic discourses of the intellectuals and activists I talked to should therefore not be interpreted as a mere anti-integration discourse.

As we will see in Chap. 5, my interviewees construct a more or less coherent sense of self and politics by articulating complex patterns of statements, subject positions, practices and institutions they may positively, negatively or partially identify with. It analyses the intricate logics of political and self-awareness as marked in discourse. I will demonstrate the value of a pragmatic perspective on discourse, subjectivity and critique with reference to a series of case studies that focus on the sense of self and politics articulated by my respondents. As such, this book constitutes an attempt to go beyond stale oppositions between agency and structure in the study of discourse. Chapter 5 focuses on the way activists and intellectuals respond to discourses and policies that do not correspond to their preferred modes of politics and subjectivity. It explores their feelings of misrecognition as well as the creative and reflexive ways in which they dealt with interpellations that conflicted with their preferred mode of politics and subjectivity. It is also worth noting that this book contains a glossary of frequently used concepts.

Acknowledgements

This book could not have been written without the intellectuals and activists who shared their time, their insights and their experiences with me.

Some of my interviewees preferred me to use pseudonyms: Bassim W., Amane X., Fatima Y. and Issam Z. Others preferred to use their own names: Karima Adouiri, Abdellatif Akhandaf, Abied Alsulaiman, Samira Azabar, Nadia Babazia, Bilal Benyaich, Naima Charkaoui, Mohamed Chakkar, Najib Chakouh, Najim Einauan, Brahim Harchaoui, Karim Hassoun, Mohamed El Khalfioui, Hicham el Mzairh, Nadia Fadil, Mohammed Ihkan, Mohamed Ikoubaan, Zohra Othman, Youssef Souissi, Sami Zemni and Ahmed Zizaoui.

I would like to thank all of these interviewees for their help and for the trust they placed in me. All of them were given the opportunity to read and to comment on the analyses presented in this book. Some of them did. Their comments have been integrated in the final version of the manuscript. Nevertheless, I would like to ask the reader to consider that political views shift and change. My interviewees do not necessarily still hold the views expressed in this book at the time of reading.

I would also like to thank Brigitte, my family, my friends and my colleagues for their love, support and help. Special thanks should go to Jef Verschueren, Marie-Claire Foblets, Henk de Smaele, Manuel Casado, Johannes Angermuller, Jan Blommaert, Sarah Scheepers, Ico Maly, Roel Coesemans, Inés Olza, Matylda Weidner, Stefanie Peeters, Liesbeth

Michiels, Nancy Decloux and Jo Bogaerts. The same goes for Nadia Fadil, Delphine Hesters, Iman Lechkar, Pieter Maeseele, Michiel van Oudheusden, Benjamin Decleen and Annelies Decat. Their feedback, questions and critique have been invaluable. I would also like to thank Jens Maesse, Paul Sarazin, Norah Karrouche, Eline Versluys, Frank Brisard, Anabela Carvalho, Tinne Kenis, Lutgard Lams, Bram Vertommen, Dorien Baelden, Alfonso del Percio, Katrijn Maryns, Meryem Kanmaz, Yannik Porsché, Felicitas Macgilchrist, Sigurdt d'Hondt, Paul Sambre and Jason Glynos.

All of them have contributed in one way or another to the book that lies in front of you. In this sense, I would also like to thank Lieslotte, Liesbeth, Herman, Alex, Seppe, Jan, Tom, Jan, Geoffrey, Egon, Annelies, Sigrid, Farid, Marie, Michiel, Manu, Karolien, Karolien, Steffi, Leen, Pieter-Jan, Jeffrey, Wouter, Toon, Dries, Jef, Kathrien, Isabelle, Mieke, Suus, Anna, Ximena, Daniel, Paul, Gabriel and Jessica for their friendship along the way.

Contents

1 **Problematising Self and Politics in Activist Discourse**   1
  1.1 Multiplicity and Coherence in Critical Subjectivities   3
  1.2 Abstract Categories as Embodied Values in Political Discourse   9
  1.3 Rethinking (Research About) Politics   18
  1.4 Unifying the Subject of Investigation   28
  1.5 Research Goals and the (Re-)Articulation of a Problematic   30

2 **Discourse Theory on the Logics of Articulation, Politics and Subjectivity**   35
  2.1 Structuralist Semiotics and the Double Articulation of Language   39
  2.2 Articulation in Poststructuralist Discourse Theory   42
  2.3 A Poststructuralist Ontology of Discourse and Politics   46
  2.4 Fixing Meaning Through Equivalence and Difference   51
  2.5 Fixing Meaning Through the Logic of Fantasy   56
  2.6 Fixing Meaning Through Social Logics, Counter-Logics and Self-interpretations   59
  2.7 Destabilising and Politicising Social Logics Through Critique   62

2.8 Fixing Meaning Through Performativity and Subjectivity 67
2.9 Fixing Meaning Through Power, Domination and Subjectivation 73
2.10 Fixing Meanings Through the Self-technique of the Interview 77
2.11 Methodological Deficits and Challenges in Poststructuralist Discourse Theory 83

3 The Pragmatic Dimension of Discourse as Articulation 91
3.1 Pragmatically Established Boundaries for Interpretation in Talk About Integration 98
3.2 Linguistic Pragmatics as a Poststructuralist Perspective on Discourse 103
3.3 Articulatory Practice as a Variabale, Adaptable and Negotiable Performance 108
3.4 Fixing Meaning by Adhering to the Pragmatic Maxim 114
3.5 Early Pragmatist Understandings of Self and Subjectivity 121
3.6 Fixing Meaning Through Performative Language Games 133
3.7 Fixing Subjectivity Through Practices of Enunciation 144
3.8 Articulation as a Metapragmatic Negotiation of Interpretive Context 152
3.9 Articulating Political Awareness in the Public Realm 166

4 Articulating the Problematic of Integration in a Minority Debate 175
4.1 Integration Between Science and Politics 179
4.2 On the 'Failure' of Integration and Integration Policy in Flanders 189
4.3 The Rise and Fall of a Dutch Binary Pair: Allochthons versus Autochthons 196
4.4 Hegemonic Logics of the Migrant Problem 205
4.5 Integration in Counter-Discourse 210
    4.5.1 Contradictory Logics of Integration Articulated by a Single Individual 214

		4.5.2 Logics of Integration and the Imagination of Social Ontology	223

        4.5.2 Logics of Integration and the Imagination of Social Ontology   223
        4.5.3 Integration and Imaginations of the Public Realm   230
        4.5.4 Integration as a Natural Phenomenon and Integration as a Political Process   239
        4.5.5 The Failure of Integration Processes and the Failure of the Integration Industry   243
        4.5.6 Integration as an Accomplishment and Integration as an Unfinished Process   249
        4.5.7 Indexing the Location of Integration   255
   4.6 Integration in a Politicised and Polyphonic Public Space   261

5 Self and Politics in Activist Discourse   267

   5.1 Research Questions and the Use of CAQDAS in Discourse Studies   269
   5.2 Observations on Ambivalence in Political Discourse and Subjectivity   280
        5.2.1 Being Dragged into the Stories and Debates on Islam   283
        5.2.2 The Search for a Platform for Public Engagement   290
        5.2.3 Intellectual Engagements with Culturalist and Neoliberal Logics   295
        5.2.4 Issues of a Young Intellectual 'Allochthon' in the Public Sphere   298
   5.3 Identifying Large-scale Logics in the Public Realm   301
        5.3.1 Countering Patronising Logics in the Political Game   303
        5.3.2 Staying True to Oneself in the Face of a Politics of Assimilation   312
        5.3.3 Pragmatic and Humane Politics in an Open Dialectic of Dissent   318
   5.4 Recognition and Misrecognition in Political Discourse   328
        5.4.1 On the Desire for Recognition and the Pain of Exclusion   330

	5.4.2 Building Bridges and Crossroads in Response to Misfiring Interpellations	337
	5.4.3 Common Logics for Dealing with Feelings of Misrecognition	346
5.5	Establishing a Coherent Sense of Self: The Case of Zohra Othman	350
	5.5.1 Opening One's Eyes to the Film of One's Life	354
	5.5.2 Objectifying the Systemic Logic of Capitalism	357
	5.5.3 Lightening Up the Dark Space in One's Inner Centre	361
	5.5.4 Towards a Preferred Mode of PvdA Politics After Resist	364
5.6	Activism as a Self-Technique: The Case of Nadia Fadil	368
	5.6.1 Shaping the Self at the Crossroads of Class, Ethnicity and Religion	370
	5.6.2 Eye-Openers and Shifting Subjectivities	378
	5.6.3 Shifting Modes of Politics and Self-Awareness	386

6 Conclusion   393

Glossary   399

Bibliography   411

Index   435

List of Figures and Tables

Fig. 3.1   Discourse studies as theory and analysis (Angermuller
           2014a, 26)   92
Fig. 3.2   Contextual correlates of adaptability (Verschueren 1999, 76)   162
Fig. 5.1   Screenshot of coded topics and subtopics of the interview
           conducted with Sami Zemni   277
Table 3.1 Indicators of metapragmatic awareness (Verschueren 2004)   155

1

Problematising Self and Politics in Activist Discourse

This book is as much about politics as about selves engaged in political practice. In many respects, self and politics are two sides of a coin called subjectivity. We all talk about ourselves to our family, to our online and offline friends, to our doctors and psychologists, and sometimes even to an unidentified audience of hundreds or millions of people. There is an incitement to talk about and to perform oneself, and we have a whole range of techniques at our disposal that allow us to do this. Through talk and practice, we can project authenticity as well as irony. But in both cases, we objectify ourselves as beings that have at least some degree of control over who and what we are and want to become in specific contexts.

The contexts through which we move provide us with the communicative options we can use to articulate and to perform a specific sense of self. But this sense is never completely stable. Books on identity and identification processes are filled to the brim with examples and case studies that illustrate this basic principle of subjectivity. They illustrate that every human being performs a balancing act between multiplicity and coherence. Our bodies, emotions and feelings change and shift. We perform very different social roles and identities as we move through time, space and context. Even the concepts we use in order to define ourselves are open to negotiation. And still, this multiplicity does not seem to impede the possibility of constructing a more or less coherent sense of self.

Our selves can be viewed as working frameworks. We proceed on the assumption that there is something continuous about the way we think and move. But this sense of continuity requires a great deal of work. We may not always be aware of the fact that we are protecting ourselves against a regression into a nightmarish personality disorder, or of the fact that a great deal of our talk performs an anchoring function that prevents exactly this. Through a myriad of routine communications as well as through strategic acts, we provide each other with clues and pointers that are meant to guide both self and other to particular modes of understanding. At the same time, there is no guarantee that we really understand each other, even if we claim and think we do. A reasonably satisfying outcome is the best one can hope for.

Embodied language use is the most important tool we have at our disposal for establishing a more or less satisfactory sense of coherence. But language is not a private matter. It only exists in communication and is therefore dependent upon the words and discursive strategies of others. As such, discourse is never only a social but also a political phenomenon. The way we talk and write is always normatively loaded and hierarchically valued. This principle holds for the language we speak as well as for the categories we deploy. But it also goes for the way we talk, the register we draw upon and the communicative rules we follow or flaunt with respect to grammar, genre, narrative or any other dimension of discursive organisation.

At each level of discursive structure, we can make a multiplicity of choices. But not every discursive choice carries the same weight in any given context. Choices are always valued and evaluated and this entails that the range of acceptable choices will always be limited. It is not only the case that the acceptability of specific descriptors may vary across time and space. The basic categories in which these descriptors are placed may be problematic as well. For instance, many of my interviewees did not only criticise specific identity constructs such as 'white', 'liberal', 'allochthon' or 'Moroccan'. They also commented upon the way people talk about general categories such as 'culture', 'politics' or 'identity'.

In the upcoming sections, I will offer a discussion of the way my interviewees articulated critical attitudes with respect to the multiplicities they are and of the way they were able to communicate a more or less coherent sense of self. I will then move on to demonstrate how abstract categories such as identity and politics function as discursive values in political discourse. This allows for a discussion of the ways in which we have to rethink (research about) politics and for a critical evaluation of the subject under investigation. All of this will then result in a list of features that specifies the qualities of an adequate approach for dealing with self and politics in activist discourse and in a rearticulated problematic.

1.1 Multiplicity and Coherence in Critical Subjectivities

During one of my first interviews with a former activist in the Flemish minority debates, I was asked what my research was about. This was a question asked by virtually all respondents, but at that time, I found it rather difficult to give a straightforward answer. The project proposal stipulated that I should investigate Islamic political identities in Flanders. However, I was feeling increasingly uncomfortable about this initial framing. I felt that the emphasis put on a potential Islamic aspect of political engagements of intellectuals and activists with a Moroccan background in Flanders could easily lead to a misrepresentation of the way these people think and talk about politics.

Of course, the topic of Islam plays a big role in European debates about migration, integration and (super) diversity. But after some basic fieldwork and desk research, it became evident that political engagements of intellectuals and activists with a Moroccan background in Flanders could not be reduced to a matter of Islam. Even though many of my interviewees considered themselves to be Muslims, this did not necessarily mean that they would use theological arguments or analogies in their political discourse. In fact, this hardly ever happened. Moreover, when interviewees did rely on an Islamic frame in order to construct or explain the evolution of their political engagement or awareness, this did not imply that Islam was the *only* way of giving meaning to one's political engagement.

It may be useful to take a closer look at the way Fatima Y. described the role of Islam in relation to her world view. She told me that "Islam" and its "central figure"—"the prophet Mohamed"—constituted her greatest "source of inspiration" even though she also pointed out that her "entire education" impacted on her "way of thinking". Immediately after this, she set out to explain what the word Islam meant to her and how her relationship towards the Koran and to the Hadith influenced her general attitude towards people. The signifiers "peace" and "tolerance" emerge as universal values linked to her experience and interpretation of Islam.

> FY: ... well uhm ... basically my entire education has uhm, has had an impact upon me, on my way of thinking. But my greatest source of inspiration is Islam itself uhm, ... well, the central figure over there, is the prophet Mohamed eh, uhm, ... I got a lot of inspiration out of this, and strength, ... Especially uhm, ... because of the fact that ... the word 'Islam' itself means peace, and within this peace there is also very prominently this word 'tolerance', ... And because of this I really learned, and uhm, also, uhm 'istislam' means surrender to God. Well, God asks you to be able to live with people, very literally in the Koran, *people*, not Muslims, *people*. So, to me this meant like "I just have to open up myself, also towards others, and I have to learn a lot about these things".
> **excerpt 1 – 01/02/2008**

Islam as a whole is framed as a "surrender to God". To Fatima, this surrender implies a non-discriminatory attitude towards "people" and an incitement to "open" herself "towards others". In the excerpt below, she goes on and illustrates how a story from the Hadith inspires her to be "tolerant" of other human beings no matter their cultural or religious background.

> FY: For instance, there's this story about the prophet Mohamed that, a Hadith, one says it's said about the prophet that he used to have a Jewish neighbour. And this Jewish neighbour uhm, ... he uhm, ... well, he didn't want to have anything to do with the prophet, so each morning, he threw his garbage in front of his door. And the prophet uhm, always simply cleaned this garbage away, very, very patiently, never said anything about it ... .
> Until one day, he came out with his broom in order to wipe it away, and he

1 Problematising Self and Politics in Activist Discourse

didn't see any garbage. The second day, still no garbage, the third day, no garbage … . Well, something must be off … . So he went to knock on the door of his Jewish neighbour, and his son opened the door, and he said "well, I noticed your father hasn't thrown his garbage at my house, how come?". And he's like "well, uhm, I have, … well, they, uhm, my father is sick, he's really very sick, and that's why he can't stand up, and so on, he, well", "ah, would you please go to your father and would you ask him whether I could visit him, because that's a duty in our religion as well, if someone is ill, you go and visit him". And he's like "okay, I'll ask him", and he asked, and he was allowed inside … . And he came inside, and this Jewish neighbour was so amazed about him, like "yes, but didn't I always treat you very badly? And still, you're here?", and he's like "well, you're a human being, and I respect you, and you may have another opinion, but this doesn't mean I have to hate you because of this, on the contrary, I am very tolerant towards you", and ever since, they became very good friends.
excerpt 2 – 01/02/2008

Even though many of my interviewees explained that the Islamic cultural and/or religious values of their parents impacted on their way of thinking, hardly anyone relied on religious arguments in order to advocate a particular standpoint. Even in the case of Fatima, it is important to point out that the Islamic aspect of her subjectivity should not be considered in isolation of the remainder of her sense of self and politics.

At the time of our talk, Fatima was working at my university as a student counsellor. But this is not where I met her. We met at an information booth of an organisation called BOEH! at a Ramadan market organised by the Federation of Moroccan Associations in the Antwerp district Borgerhout. BOEH! is an acronym for a slogan that translates as *Boss Over One's Own Head* (Dutch: *Baas Over Eigen Hoofd*). This acronym is an adaptation of the older feminist slogan *Boss Over One's Own Belly* that was used in order to argue in favour of women's integrity and autonomy with respect to sexuality and reproduction. On its website, BOEH! describes itself as follows:

BOEH! (Boss Over One's Own Head) is an activist platform with members of various allochthon and autochthon women's organisations. BOEH! originated in January 2007 in response to the intention of the new city government of

6 Articulations of Self and Politics in Activist Discourse

> *Antwerp to institute a ban on headscarves for city personnel performing public functions. BOEH! wants women to decide for themselves what they are wearing on their heads without any interference by governments or anyone else. It advocates equal rights for men and women. The choice to wear a headscarf is a human right, so is the right to exercise a job and to get a diploma. BOEH! therefore opposes this measure that disfavours women – as accepted in the Antwerp governmental agreement for 2007-2012 – and forces them to deny their individuality[1] when performing a municipal occupation.*

Municipal authorities framed the ban on headscarves as a ban on all religious and political symbols for people performing a public function. Antwerp was the first Belgian city to institute such a ban. Since 2007, many other municipalities have followed its lead. This policy is usually defended on the basis of a neutrality principle whereby neutrality is conceptualised as a matter of impression management. According to this logic, symbols indicative of the religious and political orientations of civil servants, teachers and judges are inherently problematic, disregarding the actual ideas or the actions performed by the individual in question. BOEH! opposed this logic and the associated concept of neutrality.

In mainstream discourse, the practice of wearing a headscarf is frequently associated with religiously informed practices of gender-related discrimination and oppression. It is also frequently linked to radicalisation and fundamentalism. It is therefore interesting to note that most people who publicly argue in favour of the right to wear headscarves in Flemish schools and public institutions do not rely on a religious mode of argumentation in order to advance their case. The BOEH! discourse as articulated by Fatima is a case in point. As we noticed before, Fatima is a pious Muslim who wears a headscarf and considers Islam to be an important factor in her life. Nevertheless, her mode of argumentation is based on the principle of *freedom of choice* and not on theological argument. In the excerpt below, she argues in favour of a rather liberal and feminist re-interpretation of the neutrality principle that has informed the ban.

---

[1] The translation of the Dutch word *eigenheid* into *individuality* is somewhat inaccurate. The word connotes a sense of uniqueness and particularity. The most literal translation would be something like *own-ness*, that which is particular to one's self.

1 Problematising Self and Politics in Activist Discourse

FY: It's a social uhm, ... perhaps, I would dare to call it a social calling, like uhm, ... you discriminate, by introducing a [policy] measure [like the ban on headscarves] you make the life of a minority very difficult, ... a minority that would like to contribute to society but that remains discriminated like this. For instance, our standpoint is uhm, concerning the headscarf, uhm, forbidding the headscarf is the same as obliging the headscarf, and we are against both. We believe in freedom of choice, the woman chooses herself eh, and this was our slogan back then as well, with this poster campaign, headscarf or not, the woman decides. And so, 'Boss Over One's Own Head' [Dutch: *Baas Over Eigen Hoofd*, i.e. BOEH!], that's the name of a strictly feminist thing, whereas it used to be 'boss over one's own belly'. We said no, no, right now, it's 'boss over one's own head' eh, I choose what's in my head, and how I want to express this. But I can also be neutral in the way I function, by uhm, simply by being very kind, and by doing my job.
excerpt 3 – 01/02/2008

Ideologies are never strictly delineated semiotic networks. Fatima's discourse is filled to the brim with intertextual links through which she positions herself ideologically. As such, her creative re-contextualisations of BOEH! statements rearticulate large-scale processes of ideological positioning that constitute the debates that structure the public sphere. This implies a considerable degree of creativity and critical awareness. Note how Fatima distinguishes between the dominant interpretation of 'neutrality' and her own pragmatic re-interpretation. Her discourse is marked by a valuation of individuality and autonomy: "I choose what's in my head, and how I want to express it". She is aware of the feminist historical undertones of the BOEH! slogan and considers the mainstream definition of neutrality to be discriminating. Her usage of the pronoun "we" clearly testifies to a positive identification with the BOEH! project.

It should also be noted that Fatima displays a high degree of awareness with respect to the voices active in the debate. In the excerpt below, she recounts some typical interactions she had with people dropping by at the BOEH! information booth at the Ramadan market where we met.

FY: On this Ramadan market a lot of people came over to say like "I'm against this eh, what you're doing", and "we don't agree at all", and, and "you should simply take it off, what were you thinking", and that sort of

thing, and uhm, ... And then, well, we tried to explain like "but don't you think it's bad that we simply cannot participate because you think that I am sort of like [standing] in your way with my headscarf? Because [what] you're telling me, this is exactly the same thing as if you would tell a black person like 'you're black, I don't like you, get out of here'". So I say, "that's the same signal you're giving to us eh". "Yes, but you can take off that headscarf and you can't take off that black colour, and of course, I think it's bad, ... I think, I have nothing against it eh". They always say this, "I don't have anything against your headscarf, but when you're behind a counter, when you have to service me, I prefer you not to put it on" ... . It's almost as if it's a hat that you can put on or off, and one does not realise that there really is an identity, an experience of religion attached to it eh.
excerpt 4 – 01/02/2008

Using subtle changes in intonation, tonality and tempo, Fatima distinguished between her own voice and the voices of her conversational partners. She used both direct and indirect reported speech in order to recount a type of interaction that is indicative of the structure of the Flemish debates on neutrality and Islamic veiling practices. Doing so, she rearticulated a chorus of voices saying they "*don't agree* with BOEH! *at all*" and that Muslim women should simply unveil themselves. Fatima's response consists of two strategies. She embeds her stance on the headscarf within a larger discussion on participation and discrimination. As such, she equates racial and cultural discrimination. But she also mentions and criticises a common response to her line of argumentation: "I don't have anything against your headscarf, but if you're behind a counter, when you have to service me, I prefer you not to put it on." According to Fatima, such responses are informed by people's inability to distinguish between a common piece of clothing and an object linked to "an identity" and "an experience of religion".

Within the context of my corpus, Fatima's discourse was exceptional because of its explicit references to religious sources. But in spite of the fact that Islam proves to be very important for the way she constructs meaningful relationships towards herself and towards others, there are also other ideological elements at play that are just as important for an adequate understanding of her preferred mode of socio-political engagement. Such ideological practices of *bricolage* are the rule rather than the exception in political discourse. All of my interviewees rearticulated a multiplicity of ideological elements in their discourses because they need to mark their relationships with respect to a variety of social and political actors in order to provide some indication of what their world view looks like. They integrated a polyphony of voices and identities into their discourse—an observation that triggers a whole set of questions about the way we manage to experience and to articulate some degree of coherence.

It was not uncommon for me to identify over 150 identity labels articulated in the course of a two-hour interview. A single interviewee may positively, partially or negatively identify with a multiplicity of genders, classes, ethnicities, religions, political parties, intellectual positions and ideologies. And at the same time, my respondents were usually able to trigger a sense of understanding and coherence on my part. The complexity of the discursive strategies they deployed in order to achieve this only became apparent upon a closer investigation of the interview transcripts. It therefore made no sense to carry out an investigation of the political engagements of intellectuals and activists with a Moroccan background on the presumption that these engagements would be Islamic per se. However, this multiplicity of voices is not the only aspect of discourse that complicates an analysis of political subjectivity and engagement. The fuzzy barrier between academic and political discourse is another issue one should not ignore in this type of work.

1.2 Abstract Categories as Embodied Values in Political Discourse

Categories such as identity, politics and culture frequently come to us in very mundane ways. We often use them as if they were mere descriptors. In a lot of contexts, people do not reflect upon the fact that such notions are extremely abstract categories functioning as under-defined values in social and political debates. Definitions and theories about the meaning of such terms are usually left to academics and to the politically correct. But this does not stop people from using such terms as if one does know what they mean. People often use such notions in 'straightforward' ways because they link notions such as diversity or integration with particular images and experiences. Public usage of politico-academic terms therefore tends to gravitate towards hegemonic modes of understanding. It should therefore not come as a surprise that mainstream usage of such notions is frequently criticised by people at the margins of the public debate.

Tensions between different uses of abstract categories can be observed within the context of a single interview or text. This makes sense, since large-scale social and political debates do not exist independently of concrete speech events. When one of my first interviewees—I will call him Bassim W.—asked me what my research was about, I wanted to be honest with him. I decided to tell him that my research was supposed to be about "Islamic political identities". His immediate response was a rather spontaneous "ouch" immediately followed by laughter. Responding to his laughter and to my own discomfort with this way of framing my research, I told my interviewee that I wanted "to get away" from this angle. In the conversational turns following my confession—because that is what it felt like—it became clear that my interviewee did not only have a problem with the Islamic aspect of my description but also with the category of identity as such.

> JZ: and I am also completely I want to get away from that completely
> BW: yes yes it does not even (laughs) it does not exist
> JZ: no that's why ... that impression well I had that impression as well
> BW: there is not even a Moroccan identity or Belgian identity, come on (laughs)
> **excerpt 5 – 20/05/2008**

In the excerpt above, Bassim denies the validity of researching Moroccan or Belgian identities. At this point, things become interesting. As I explained above, I was growing increasingly sceptical about a research project based on the assumption that the political engagements of Muslims and/or Moroccans in Flanders were necessarily Islamic. I therefore assumed that Bassim took issue with the politico-Islamic link. However, it was the category of identity itself that was problematic to him. The excerpt below is a continuation of the excerpt above. Bassim links the notion of a singular Belgian, Moroccan or Islamic identity with "hotheads" who (literally and/or figuratively) "go to war" over this and argues that the minority of people that pushes the Islamic element to the foreground triggers the construction of a faulty image of "the remainder of the community" in the eyes of "public opinion".

> JZ: No, I am noticing that more and more, so I have, if I would be allowed to change the title I would definitely take out the Islamic ... also because when I talk to those people, actually ... Sometimes Islam is discussed as a political topic actually sometimes it does happen in those conversations but that is definitely not the only thing that comes up uhm also quite often it is not the most important or the
> BW: no ... it's unfortunate that a number of hotheads put that to the fore as the most important element and that, because of that, in the end, public opinion gets the wrong image of the remainder of the community
> JZ: yes
> BW: But the largest part of the community uhm is may be pious may be Islamic may ... but will not go uhm to war over it [laughs] or uhm
> **excerpt 6 – 20/05/2008**

I proceeded by telling Bassim what I would prefer to do. I wanted to talk to "people with a Moroccan background" who "engage themselves in various ways". I also explained that I would like to focus my analyses on the variety of ways in which such people talk about politics. This meant that Islam should be discussed whenever it proves to be relevant to the political engagements and world views of my respondents. But it also meant that the *a priori* focus on Islam would be abandoned. Moreover, such an approach implies paying attention to the variety of ways in which people use abstract signifiers as analytical categories and values to infuse their political views and practices with meaning.

The importance of this last point should not be underestimated. In a context where academic, political and everyday discourses share a common terminology, one cannot assume that the same words mean the same things to everyone. For instance, not everyone is as reluctant to use the category of identity as Bassim is. Many of my respondents used the notion of identity in order to articulate a preferred sense of self and politics. As such, the concept of 'identity' may be embedded in sociopolitical or philosophical theories about human subjectivity. It may also be used rather intuitively since it is frequently linked to a whole set of other categories such as 'culture' or 'individuality'. Moreover, individualised usage of such politico-academic categories does not come out of nowhere.

Utterances are always embedded in histories of use through which individuals link up with others and organise themselves ideologically. This can be illustrated with reference to an interview I conducted with former Arab European League (AEL) activist Issam Z. During our interview, Issam used the notion of identity in a way that cannot be understood without analysing his usage of a set of related categories such as individuality or culture. At first sight, his discourse may seem to be highly particular. It can easily be interpreted as a very personal philosophy. However, his views on identity can also be found among other AEL activists. For instance, the distinction between Islam as a culture and Islam as a religion constitutes a sophisticated response to a discourse that has been problematising and/or vilifying Islam and Muslims in Flanders for decades.

One of the main goals of the AEL was to provide legitimacy for anti-discriminatory actions by migrants and for the public performance of Islamic identities in various locations of the public sphere. AEL arguments frequently revolve around notions of citizenship. The organisation can be described as a left-wing identity political movement. It would be a serious mistake to confuse this project for an Islamist political ideology. Most of its activists were Muslims, but their views on what this meant tended to vary. As we will see, the AEL developed a distinction between Islam as culture and Islam as religion that accommodates for this tension. The organisation focused on issues such as racial discrimination, police brutality, political representation, Palestine and Iraq. It attracted sympathy from radical leftists, anti-racists, Islamic progressives and even Islamists who criticised mainstream discourse on diversity and integration (Jacobs 2005, 104–105).

The unifying element between AEL activists was a stress on the opposition between the excluded and the included in Flanders and in the international arena. According to Jacobs, '*there is no gain for the AEL in having a "pure" ideological line and thus exclusively defining themselves as Arab nationalists or Islamists*' (Jacobs 2005, 105). Note that the US-styled hyphenated identity 'Arab-European' is quite uncommon in Flemish hegemonic discourse. Jacobs concluded his study by pointing out that '*The bulk of its followers are mainly attracted by its firm stress on the opposition between the excluded and the included, of which AEL defends the underdog position of the excluded population of immigrant (Muslim) background*' (Jacobs 2005, 112–113). There is a lot more to be said about the AEL. However, for current purposes, it suffices to focus on the fact that 'identity' was one among many other empty signifiers in its discourse. I will now turn to an illustration of the way the concept of 'identity' functions as a politico-theoretical building block in the construction of a more or less coherent sense of self and politics in an interview conducted with an AEL activist.

There was a set of topics I raised in all of my interviews. No matter the specific type of organisation and/or politics my interviewees were engaged in, I asked everyone about the way their political awareness was triggered and how it developed from that moment on. This always resulted in complex discourses in which a multiplicity of concrete topics (e.g. unemployment, international relations or experiences with authoritative figures such as teachers) and abstract categories (e.g. diversity, liberalism, ethnicity) were linked to concrete narratives about experiences and emotions in the public sphere. It is through the establishment of such links between embodied socio-political experiences and an individual's metalinguistic awareness of the usage of abstract categories that we become able to *value* specific modes of being over others. Through such discursive acts and processes, we imbue empty signifiers with concrete experiential contents and emotional values that are powerful enough to propel us towards the project of articulating ourselves with respect to the public sphere through various modes of political engagement.

All of this may seem rather abstract. Let us therefore take a look at the way such principles function in a concrete interview context. In the excerpts below, former AEL activist Issam Z. articulates a notion of identity that is closely intertwined with a preferred mode of individuality and politics. His usage of such categories is at once very particular and deeply ideological. He explains how he had been living with a "concept of fighting for your individuality" since the age of 13. At the time, he felt rather inarticulate about this. His first response consisted of a search for identity in Islamic religion and culture. But what attracted him to the discourse of Dyab Abou Jahjah and his AEL was the fact that this activist and his organisation were able to articulate "a clear view" on identity and individuality.

When I asked him about the way he felt before he got to know the AEL, Issam explained how he experienced "a pressure" to assimilate and to eradicate his "eigenheid" or "individuality". In this context, it should be noted that there is no fully adequate English translation for "eigenheid". The word may be translated as "individuality" but also as "particularity" or "selfhood". The most literal translation would probably be something like "own-ness". The word has a reflexive connotation that highlights an idea of uniqueness. When Issam read my analyses and my transcriptions, he remarked that my translation of "eigenheid" into "individuality" should not be mistaken for a "liberal" or "autonomous" concept of the self. This was important to him since his notion of "eigenheid"—henceforward translated as "individuality"—implied an acceptance and a reflexive stance with respect to one's socio-cultural heritage. A non-recognition of this heritage would therefore lead to a loss of "individuality".

IZ: Well, my feeling before was, … you are thirteen fourteen years old. And then it starts. You feel something isn't right. You are completely different and you feel, on the other side there is a pressure to be like them, and you have to give up your individuality in order to go along with, … jokes about Moroccans, with a certain perspective on life, with a certain lifestyle. And very early I have, resisted might not be the right word, but my way of dealing with this, I had discovered being a Muslim very early, and I started to read a lot about Islam. And there, for the first time, I got another representation of Islam than what you hear all of the time, even back then eh, I am talking about '95 '96.
JZ: By the way, how old are you?
IZ: 28, so, I was fourteen fifteen years old when I started to read about this. Everything I started to read about Islam back then basically gave me some kind of self-esteem eh. Because, we have had a history that you can definitely be proud of, with a lot of positive aspects connected to it. It's a civilisation with a beautiful culture that has triggered a lot. And my way of dealing with it back then, … when you're being explicitly pushed into repression for being retarded or culturally backwards, … was to emphasise this. But thanks to the AEL, I was able to learn that you don't even need this. You don't need to be very pious in order to possess an individuality, (this turn continues in the excerpt below).
excerpt 7 – 03/09/2007

1 Problematising Self and Politics in Activist Discourse 15

The conceptual confusion surrounding "eigenheid" or "individuality" is indicative of the politically charged connotations such terms may have. Issam explains that he felt like he had "to give up" his "individuality" "in order to go along with" racist "jokes about Moroccans, with a certain perspective on life", and "with a particular lifestyle" in his teenage years. He also explained that this pressure prompted him to start reading about Islam and to discover his Islamic identity. When he was 14–15 years old, his explorations of literature about Islamic civilisation and culture allowed him "to emphasise" the positive aspects of this "beautiful culture" whenever he was "being explicitly pushed into repression for being retarded and culturally backwards". Nevertheless, his confrontation and involvement with the AEL would change his views considerably.

Issam explains that the AEL allowed him to make a distinction between a pious and a cultural mode of being a Muslim. The AEL framework allowed him to look for a sense of uniqueness or "individuality" that was not necessarily religious. This did not mean that the AEL was an anti-religious organisation. Rather, it provided an ideological framework in which several modes of political subjectivity and "individuality" were legitimised. In the excerpt below, Issam continues by pointing out that one "can be a Muslim" for religious reasons, but that one "can also be a Muslim" because of one's "culture". An inability to make such a distinction in a societal context that exerts an assimilatory "pressure" on minorities can cause one "to derail" and to "start living in complete discord" with one's "culture" and "religion".

> IZ: (this turn is a continuation of the turn above) and to have a clear separation like 'I can be a Muslim and I can be proud of this', but I can also be a Muslim because of my culture. And this is something I continually, ... something I saw ... . For instance, I had a friend in Leuven who was very rigorously involved with Islam. And at a certain moment he got into a crisis of faith, and this has caused him to derail to such an extent, he saw no way out. He did feel like a Muslim, but at the same time, this Flemish society had marked him, and he simply couldn't find a way out. I think the AEL could have given an answer to this, like "look, that's normal, when you study here, you start to think, you start to ask critical questions, and your faith may succumb to that. But you have to be able to distinguish between

your individuality, identity on the one hand, and being pious, faith, on the other hand. When you have this [faith], that's a nice extra. But it's not because you lose your faith, that you have to start living in complete discord with your culture and with your religion". And this is what you see happening with a lot of allochthons today eh. Today, you see a lot of allochthons, this is my opinion about it, when you see that a lot of Muslims are actually becoming more pious, this is a search for individuality, a search for identity, a search for a place you can conquer in this society. A place of your own without giving up too much of oneself. But of course, the question is … it's a bit unfortunate that you need a religion to do so. Why isn't this possible just like that, why can't you just, with your individuality as identity … (this interaction continues in the excerpt below)
excerpt 8 – 03/09/2007

According to Issam, the AEL had an answer to identity crises triggered by the emotional tension between the demand to "become more like them" and one's sense of "individuality". He argues that the AEL dissociation between a cultural "identity" or "individuality" on the one hand and religious "faith" on the other constituted "a way out" and an alternative for a mode of subjectivity that requires one either to become ever more pious or to start living in discord with one's cultural or religious heritage. He argues that it is important to find "a place" within society "without giving up too much of oneself". One can do this by becoming ever more pious, but he also suggests that one does not necessarily "need a religion to do so". One can also claim "a place" on the basis of one's "individuality as identity".

Issam paints a complex intellectual canvas and articulates multi-layered relationships between politico-academic signifiers such as culture, identity and individuality into a narrative about a preferred mode of subjectivity and politics. His notion of conquering "a place" in society on the basis of one's "individuality as identity" confused me though. I therefore asked him what he meant by "identity". His answer frames the AEL project as a struggle for a particular mode of political subjectivity.

> JZ: (this interaction is a continuation of the excerpt above) What do you mean with identity?
> IZ: Well, simply, as a Moroccan, simply living in a society, a society where people simply take you as you are.

1 Problematising Self and Politics in Activist Discourse

JZ: Why do you think this type of individual identity development is less attractive than …
IZ: Because you are being repressed. Exactly because of your being a Moroccan in this society. What choice do you have left?
JZ: And is it about being Moroccan, or Muslim, or a combination, … ?
IZ: A combination. I don't think you can separate this that strictly. Being a Moroccan partially means speaking Arabic or Berber. I'm not so much in favour of drawing a line, … . But I do know that among the group of Muslims who are pious, they will always try to distinguish like "on the one hand there is traditional Islam, but we are different, we are modern Muslims, we are a renewed Islam …".
JZ: And what do they consider to be traditional Islam?
IZ: Well, the Islam of their parents from Morocco, people who didn't enjoy any education, whose Islam was inherited by their parents and village imam. "but we are not like this, we are more modern", this is supposed to be some sort of legitimation of them being Muslim, something I consider to be bullshit. Because, in the end you succumb to the same mechanism, because you are different you will have to do your best, you will have to show something that proves you are civilised nevertheless. And their way of doing so is to say like "look, we are going back to the basis of Islam, and if you take a look at this, there are some scientific arguments that are being confirmed by science". And I think this is a step too far. It's still a type of mea culpa one does. This other who is demanding like "you're not good enough, show me something". Whereas I'm like, "whether you're a Muslim or not, whether you experience this actively or not, you are who you are, including your cultural heritage, …". According to me, this was the struggle of the AEL.
excerpt 9 – 03/09/2007

In the excerpt above, Issam explains that his notion of identity implies a notion of selfhood that includes ethnic and/or religious markers of identity. His struggle for a "place" within society boils down to a struggle for "a society where people simply take you as you are". For Issam and the AEL, this means that such a society should also accept Moroccan and Islamic identities as being part and parcel of people's identity or individuality. The struggle for identity or individuality is therefore always and necessarily a struggle for being "who you are, including your cultural heritage". Issam is sceptical about looking for one's individuality in a so-called modernised or "renewed Islam". According to him, there is an apologetic element to such a quest that he cannot reconcile with his preferred mode of politics and subjectivity.

Not all of my interviewees shared Issam's views or used categories such as identity or individuality in the same way he did. There are also differences between his discourse and some of the statements made by other AEL members. But this interview is certainly representative in terms of its complexity. All of my interviewees displayed high degrees of metalinguistic awareness with respect to the usage of abstract categories. All of them forged complex links between politico-academic concepts, theories and embodied experiences. And last but not least, they all made systematic distinctions between preferred and disavowed modes of subjectivity and politics. It therefore became necessary to rethink the epistemological status of what I actually investigated.

1.3   Rethinking (Research About) Politics

I already mentioned that I reframed my research as an investigation into the political engagements of intellectuals and activists with a Moroccan background in Flanders. But the concept of politics is at least as problematic as 'selfhood' or 'identity'. Interviewer and interviewee understandings of what 'politics' means may be quite different. Moreover, people frequently deploy different notions of politics within the context of a single interview. A neglect of these observations leads to a warped understanding of political awareness and engagement. It should also be noted that I was not a blank slate either. My own understanding of politics informed a specific mode of questioning and influenced the way my interviewees articulated themselves.

My understanding of politics was—and still is—informed by poststructuralist writings on identity, ideology and hegemony. Politics can be thought of as a dimension of social and discursive reality. It is an analytical category that designates those public and discursive acts through which we challenge and install (un-)equal relationships in the public sphere and distribute various forms of capital. Politics functions as an umbrella term that designates all practices implying a reconfiguration of (our imagination of) identities and relationships. In this sense, social reality is fundamentally political. Even though our awareness of the political nature of specific identities, practices, institutions and discourses may fade into the hegemonic background, it can always be reactivated at times of instability.

Seeking to understand the Flemish minority debates from the point of view of activist minority members, I did not want to focus on traditional forms of politics alone. I interviewed party politicians, but also activists, journalists, academics and various other people engaging themselves within the context of various non-governmental organisations (NGOs) or even on a more individual basis. My goal was to investigate the diversity of world views among people voicing their opinions on minority-related issues in the Flemish public sphere. Considering the variety of people I talked to, I could not expect my interviewees to share my definitions, theories and views. Nevertheless, in spite—or because—of the varied usage of the abstract category of politics, this notion functioned as a major tool for establishing coherence, both within and between individual interviews. I therefore decided to focus on (the signifier of) politics as a key object of investigation.

Every interview was explicitly framed as an interaction within the context of a research project in which the political world views, ideas, discourses, identities and/or engagements of the respondents would be analysed. My interviewees generally accepted my broad understanding of politics, but it should also be noted that our conversations frequently focused on particular modes of politics that were valued and disqualified in different ways. An example that illustrates the compatibility of my own notion of politics with the concept of politics articulated by one of my interviewees can be found in an interview conducted with Mohamed Ikoubaan. At the time of our interview, Mohamed was president of Moussem, a nomadic art centre that seeks to provide a framework for intercultural interaction between Arab, Berber and Moroccan artists on the one hand, and the Antwerp, Flemish, Belgian and European artistic scene on the other hand. Among other things, Moussem organises exhibitions, performances and concerts.

I suggested to Mohamed that his engagement for Moussem might be framed as "a political project" and asked him whether it seemed "legitimate" to him to put it like that. He responded by stating that "almost everything is political" in one way or another. At the same time, he pointed out that his engagement for this project is not primarily politically motivated. Rather, he is "moved" by "the stories of these artists". Moreover, Mohamed seeks to "fill a void" that is "located within the artistic movement". And even though he argues that this artistic project should be understood in relation to a "political background" or "constellation", he locates "the essence" of (his engagement for) Moussem elsewhere.

> MI: Well, politics, I think almost everything is political eh (laughs)
> JZ: Yes. I was wondering about this, I also see it this way, but I was wondering whether you agreed with this.
> MI: No, I, ... I think ... . No, I don't do it because it, actually uhm. In the first place, I meant that I do it because I think it's beautiful eh, because I am basically moved by it, by those things eh, by the, the stories of these artists. This is basically the first reason, I think. And I think that in the second place, it's in order to basically fill a void basically located within the artistic landscape ... . So, basically, well, ... there is a ... the genesis of uhm, of this movement, ... is also informed by a political ... uhm background so to say. But this isn't ... the essence ... It's essentially about artists who can tell something ... about, about themselves, uhm about their country, about their situation, and so on eh ... . But, ... within the context, the political constellation wherein we find ourselves, it gets, it always has a political
> JZ: indeed
> MI: charge to it, I think. But this isn't essential to the project, ... so, not uhm
> JZ: No, I was just wondering how you thought about this yourself ...
> **excerpt 10 – 08/04/2008**

To Mohamed Ikoubaan, the "genesis" or "essence" of his "movement" is partially informed by "the political constellation wherein we find ourselves" and will "always" have "a political charge". But it is ultimately the beauty of "artists" telling "stories" about themselves, their countries and their situations that motivates (his engagement for) Moussem. The idea that such "stories" may be more or less political depending on the political situation in which they are told rhymes very well with my own understanding of politics. In this sense, politicisation becomes a matter of degree rather than a question of absolutes.

But even if my interviewees did not object to my rather open and vague concept of politics, they did tend to distinguish between various modes of political activity. When I asked filmmaker Mohammed Ihkan about the sort of political issues that interested him at the time of our interview, he remarked that I talked "a lot about politics" and prompted me to elaborate what I meant by this term. I told him that I thought "everything can be political" in principle and that the issue boils down to the "the question ... what people consider to be worth foregrounding". I also told him that I wanted to talk to him because of the documentary he made about the life stories of two Moroccans who migrated to Belgium in the 1960s and who built a life for themselves and their families in the Antwerp region. His film is called *My Story* and was screened at various cultural events, institutions and universities.

Considering the fact that Mohammed did not work as a professional filmmaker but as a maintenance technician, and considering the fact that he made the documentary in his free time, I suggested that this "time and energy" consuming project must "testify to some sort of engagement" in a societal context where such documentaries are rarely screened in public media. I said all of this as part of an answer to his question what I considered to be political about him and his activities. Mohammed told me that I wasn't wrong but that his movie should be interpreted as a "very small engagement" on his part. To him, "making a movie" involves a practice of "giving an opinion". It is a matter of articulating people's stories "about social interaction" in the public sphere. In the excerpt below, Mohammed discusses his engagement as a filmmaker in more detail.

> MI: ... Making documentaries, I want to make documentaries, documentaries about social interaction, people, their stories, uhm, and so on. Because I personally think that I can make myself useful by means of this contribution. This is what it's all about, making oneself useful for uhm, for the community, uhm, for all communities that are here. And this is my conviction, this is my political conviction, if you're talking about politics.

This is my politics, because I don't really have an orientation, I don't have a colour in politics. Today, uhm, I might vote for SPa, tomorrow for Groen, uhm, and the day after that for the uhm liberals. Yes, to me, it's the person who is important, whether he (s)he did something, this is what I'm voting for, not, not in order to have a political colour. I don't have a political colour. Yes, this is, this is also my, yes, politics is about being there for people. That's it, being there for people, giving them a lot of information, we're very happy there's a pedagogical package being made, uhm, which is basically part of the film. The film is a part of this pedagogical project, and we're going to try to bring this to several schools. Because the schools, it has a surplus value for the students as well. The history of the first generation of Moroccans is unknown. It isn't being talked about at all, whereas in most schools, especially here in the Antwerp region, there are relatively, relatively many Moroccan children. Yes. And these children do not know their origin. Yes, it's not written down in any books. You can't trace this back. Who are we? Yes, Moroccans. But how did we get here? And what happened back then? And so on. Yes. We don't know.
excerpt 11 – Summer 2008

Mohammed distinguishes his own mode of political engagement from party politics. At the same time, he underscores the fact that he wants to make himself "useful" to all communities including the Moroccan one. Note that this is another example of a person linking a preferred mode of political engagement with a preferred mode of subjectivity and politics. For Mohammed, "politics is about being there for people". This can take the form of a "pedagogical" practice whereby one provides people with information that is useful to them. He states explicitly that he doesn't have a "[party] political colour". When casting his ballot, the fact that a politician "did something" is more important to him than this person's party political "colour" or "orientation". Mohammed's own "politics" take the form of making pedagogic documentaries that are useful to people who are not yet familiar with the "history of the first generation of Moroccans" and who are questioning who they are and how they got here.

Many interviewees distinguished between different modes of politics. The establishment of an ethical hierarchy of modes of political behaviour is a key feature of political stance taking and struggle. It is therefore important to ask how a discourse, a person, a group or an institution can be labelled as *apolitical* when there is supposedly a political dimension to every social practice. Sometimes, individuals and groups are considered to be "depoliticised" by my interviewees. So, if an individual considers certain aspects of social reality to be non-political, would it not be a grave neglect on my part to ignore such interpretations of reality? It may be a good idea to take a brief look at such statements. In order to do this, I performed an automated search for all instances of "apolit*", "not polit*", "no political", "not politics" and "no politics" within my NVIVO 8 interview database.[2] The results showed that such notions perform two basic functions. Actors either used the notion of depoliticisation in order to differentiate and/or to disqualify a particular mode of discursive practice, or criticised the very possibility of something or someone being apolitical.

At the time of our interview, Mohamed Chakkar, chairman of the Federation for Moroccan Associations (FMV) argued that "ordinary Moroccans are not that politically aware". But this doesn't mean he considered them to be completely "apolitical". His point was that they display a negative and disinterested attitude towards politics characterised by a "liberal" and at times "egoistic" or individualistic attitude. Chakkar ironically remarks that many Moroccans have this "in common with the Flemings". To him, this can be problematic since he does not believe in a "purely individual emancipation". His preferred mode of political subjectivity entails a "group based emancipation". Chakkar explains that it has taken a while for his organisation to gain popular support among Moroccans because they considered his organisation to be "political" in a negative sense of the word. According to him, this attitude towards the political character of a civil society organisation such as his FMV tends to change when people become aware of the problems their children face "in school". At that point, they become more interested in politics and "civil society" can start "to bloom".

> MC: (this turn is a continuation of an ongoing turn) Look, ordinary Moroccans are not that politically aware. They really have a lot in common with the Flemings … . You can't say [they're] apolitical, but "politicians, all

---

[2] The search entries were formulated in Dutch. The Dutch queries identified all occurrences of "apolit*", "geen polit*" and "niet polit*". These queries correspond to the English search terms mentioned above.

of them, bullshitters" … . Today, we have a relatively big backing, but this took a long time, you know.
JZ: mmh
MC: "that's politics, leave me alone man" …
JZ: Do they consider FMV to be political then … ?
MC: Yes … . Politics like uhm. Until they come here. Their daughter or son in school. We get a lot of cases that are really uhm … . A question of teachers or allochthon students … . They say like "you have to stand up for … for your kids eh … and you have to organise yourself and and do something about education" and so on, and so on. And it actually works pretty fine. And then we can say like "right now, we are with, I think we've started with one hundred volunteers, and right now we have about a thousand … people who are coming", and all of them are members … . This is why I say civil society grows and blooms, and this is important … . This is important, because this way you can [establish] a group based emancipation … . I don't really believe in a purely individual emancipation, that's kind of, I consider this to be a bit too liberal … . Whereas individuals, we should place them within a group, but this liberal idea sometimes leads to egoistic uhm, and this is what Moroccans have in common with the Flemings. Moroccans are basically all individualists.
excerpt 12 – 27/06/2008

Mohammed Chakkar may not consider the average Moroccan to be completely apolitical but it is clear that his concept of depoliticisation performs an important function in his definition of a preferred mode of emancipatory politics. Many of my interviewees seem to consider political awareness to be a matter of degrees. But it can also be a question of modality, a matter of fundamentally different practices and techniques for articulating one's sense of self and politics. For instance, sociologist Nadia Fadil pointed out that a collaboration between "religious" and "sociocultural" minority organisations is "rather exceptional" in the Flemish public sphere. According to her, the reasons for this are "ideological" and "religious" even though the actors involved may not describe their differences in this way.

In the excerpt below, Nadia distinguishes between a typically sociocultural association such as Mohamed Chakkar's FMV on the one hand and a religious organisation such as Youngsters for Islam (JVI) on the other hand. JVI has been labelled as a salafist, fundamentalist, extremist

1 Problematising Self and Politics in Activist Discourse

and Islamist organisation in mainstream media (e.g. Bossche 2008, 59, 69, Cattebeke 2008). However, the organisation publicly refused such labels (JVI 2009). I do not wish to pass judgement on this organisation considering the fact that I did not talk to any of its members. At this point, I merely wish to point out that different types of politics tend to be associated with different practices and organisations.

> NF: ... for instance, concerning JVI ... they are a lot less involved in citizenship issues and so on. They are really uhm involved in uhm the type of uhm the type of personal uhm ... personal politics between quotation marks ... . I don't think they are apolitical. They are also very political, but it is actualised by the reshaping of uhm one's uhm yourself. The reshaping of ... life in accordance with the prophet, to follow the life according to the principles of ... . And out of that, there does emerge ... you can construct a certain community of believers .... So that is a very different way of doing politics than uhm take FMV for instance ... . So I really think ideological differences ... . But I would, well, according to me it can be named like that. That way it becomes visible, [the fact] that there are differences within the community ... . Also for that youngster ... because it's not that obvious you know ... who thinks "yeah we're all the same and there is just one Islam and there are ...", while that's not the case eh.
> **excerpt 13 – 22/08/2008**

Nadia describes the type of subjectivity developed within the context of JVI in terms of "a type of ... personal politics between quotation marks". By hedging her usage of this category, she provides us with a first indication that people engaging themselves in civil society organisations may develop very different modes of politics. In spite of the fact that JVI members are less involved in "citizenship issues", she does not consider JVI members to be "apolitical". Even though citizenship is a key concept to many civil society organisations, Nadia believes that a religious practice aimed at "reshaping" one's "life in accordance with [the life of] the prophet" may also lead to the construction of a "community of believers" that deploys a different mode of politics.

The excerpt also provides us with a very good example of the way philosophy and academic discourse may inform particular utterances on the relationship between self and politics. Nadia's statement on the possibility of "reshaping" oneself is part and parcel of a world view influenced by the writings of Michel Foucault. At the time of our interview, Nadia had finished her PhD on *Submitting to God, submitting to the Self*. She agrees with Lois McNay who argued that "Foucault's conception of the self ... represents an attempt to attribute a degree of agency and self-determination to the individual without jettisoning his anti-essentialist view of the subject" (McNay 1992: 62 cited in Fadil 2008a). Following this line of reasoning, she argues that one can only become a meaningful subject to oneself through a set of techniques inscribed in discursive and non-discursive power relations that do not exist independently from historical stratifications, institutions and discourses.

Because Nadia and myself were thoroughly familiar with each other's ideas on Foucault before the interview took place, a whole set of ideas could be left to function in the background of our conversation. Nevertheless, she frequently marked her intellectual orientations by means of particular jargon and intertextual references. Her discourse on the transformation of the self through religious practice carries heavy Foucaultian undertones. In the excerpt above, Nadia thus distinguished between two types of subjectivity. On the one hand, there is a citizenship-based mode of subjectivity she associates with socio-cultural organisations such as the FMV and with political movements such as the AEL. On the other hand, one can also make reflexive use of religious self-techniques in order to transform one's sense of self.

Whenever someone or something was considered to be apolitical, the operative definition of politics was narrowed down to a problematic political practice or discourse. AEL activist Mohamed El Khalfioui asked himself "what's political" and replied to this rhetorical question by stating that "it's all relative". In the interaction below, Mohamed paraphrases a conversation with Karim Hassoun who succeeded Dyab Abou Jahjah as chairman of the Belgian AEL.

MEK: (laughs) So uhm, yes, ... that's my motto. I also say this to Karim Hassoun, and to others, I say "everything is political" ... "everything is political" ... . Merely saying "well, I have my religion, it's Islam" or "I'm Moroccan" is a political statement as well. Because you're located within a

1 Problematising Self and Politics in Activist Discourse 27

political climate eh. You say "I'm a Moroccan, ... I'm a Belgian, a Fleming", "ah, why don't you say Belgian, or Fleming, or, ...". And this is a political statement eh. But I know what you mean, apolitical in the sense of, well, activism.
JZ: organised, or, or activism, or
MEK: activism yes, ... Our community isn't that active here in Belgium. [It] isn't uhm politically active, or aware, or uhm, ... I think it's going to take generations, well, two generations before, ... The AEL took the first step eh, but uhm, but uhm, ... It's still just a first step eh, so, ...
JZ: yes, yes
MEK: the second and the third step still have to be made, so uhm, but our community isn't politically active.
excerpt 14 – 30/06/3008

In the excerpt above, Mohamed points out that generally speaking, the Moroccan or Islamic "community" is not "politically active" or "aware" in spite of the fact that we live in a "political climate" in which basic identifications along ethnic, national and religious line constitute political statements. The only way to consider people and groups to be apolitical is to restrict the meaning of politics in a particular way. In the excerpt above, this is achieved by narrowing the definition of politics to activism. In an AEL context, being associated with a lack of political awareness or inactivity does not exactly count as a compliment.

It should be clear by now that the discourses of my interviewees testify to a high degree of reflexivity and metalinguistic awareness. The conversational structure of the interview is multilayered and draws upon identities, topics, jargons, genres, narratives and ideologies that may or may not be marked explicitly in discourse. I already mentioned that my interviewees were active in very different organisations and institutions. They identified themselves and others in ways that were never completely the same. And even though most of my respondents have Moroccan parents or grandparents, this neither means that they (always) identified themselves as such or that this identity necessarily informed their discourse on politics. It didn't mean that I investigated a so-called *community* either. People hedged this notion as well, displaying their awareness that this term is by no means less problematic than categories or values such as *politics* or *identity*.

1.4 Unifying the Subject of Investigation

There was not a single signifier in the debates about migration, diversity and integration that has not been questioned by one or more of my interviewees. Culture, neutrality, citizenship, identity, assimilation; the list is endless. At the same time, the intellectuals and activists I talked to occupied various social, cultural, economic and ideological positions in the public sphere. Their usage of some of these terms varied accordingly. The unity of my object(s) of investigation can therefore not be found in the identifications of my respondents. It does not reside in the topics raised or in the discourses my interviewees used in order to frame their thoughts and experiences either.

Traditional ethnographic research entails an investigation of the local behaviours, beliefs, customs, social life, economic activities, politics, religions and discourses of groups and communities. However, neither the identifications, the practices, the beliefs or the organisational affiliations of my interviewees allowed me to talk about a uniform community. Nevertheless, a great deal of them knew each other and/or each other's organisations. Such organisations included government agencies, socio-cultural minority associations, universities, political movements, pressure groups, political parties and/or other civil society organisations. Some of my respondents also recommended me to talk to people who engaged themselves within the context of mosques and other religious organisations.

As I mentioned before, I initially selected people on the basis of their Moroccan background and on the fact that they publicly voiced a political opinion or an analysis about an aspect of the Flemish minority debates. At the end of every interview, I always asked who else I should contact in order to shed some light on the "diversity of opinions" among people active in the minority debates. After a while, the same names of people and organisations started to pop up again and again. However, this does not mean that all of my interviewees necessarily agree with each other. Many respondents criticised each other's politics, engagements, practices, tactics, strategies and/or discourses. Some of my respondents saw each other socially while others merely knew each other's organisations and opinions through public media and hearsay. At public events such as a fundraiser for Palestine, a debate on Islam or allochthons in education, or at an event such as a presentation of a book on Flemish and minority identities, I could expect at least a handful of my interviewees. Nevertheless, it was clear that my interviewees were not part of a homogeneous community.

Neither the self-identifications, the practices, the convictions or the organisational affiliations of the people I talked to allowed me to talk about a uniform community in any unproblematic sense of the word. The fact that my respondents hardly constituted a community in any objectifiable way—be it in imagined, in organisational, in ideological or in practical terms—forced me to look for a different way of conceptualising the links between these people. Moreover, if I was to understand their relations to one another, I needed to make sure that I included a great variety of voices into this project. For that reason, I chose to add an additional selection criterion, namely that of maximum variety sampling (see Morse 1994 cited in Powell 1997, 148)[3] with respect to types of engagement in the Flemish public sphere.

I was faced with a complex intertextual network of people discursively constructing their political engagement with reference to a great variety of concepts, texts, individuals, organisations, practices and myself. These and many other observations prompted me to abandon my research as an investigation into a Moroccan *community* in favour of an investigation into the discourse of activists and intellectuals with a Moroccan background in Flanders. Similar to the abandonment of the notion of identity as an analytical category, this decision was informed by a close and problematic articulation of political and academic discourse about the notion of community. If there was a unity to be found among my respondents, it resided in the intertextual links that were created through speech events such as the interview practice itself. This proved to be a far more productive and far less deceptive category for analysis than the notion of community.

---

[3] Maximum variety sampling seeks to maximise heterogeneity in the sample. This method is useful if one seeks to identify patterns and commonalities that exist across otherwise divergent individuals. I sought to achieve maximum variety with respect to types of political engagement among intellectuals and activists with a Moroccan background in Flanders.

1.5 Research Goals and the (Re-)Articulation of a Problematic

My main goal was to understand the political engagements of intellectuals and activists with a Moroccan background in Flanders. In order to achieve this, I came to realise that I had to reconstruct an entire debate as perceived by this minority within a minority. It would not suffice to discuss the way these people positioned themselves with respect to mainstream ideas on issues such as migration, integration and diversity. I would also have to investigate their usage of abstract categories relevant to their understanding of preferred and disavowed modes of politics and subjectivity. Put differently, if I was to understand the complexities of the minority debate as interpreted and dealt with by my interviewees, I had to take their interpretive analyses into account.

Such an individualised approach to political engagement and public debate is not easy to carry out. It is certainly easier said than done. At the beginning of this chapter, I suggested that the self could be considered in terms of a working framework. This framework is at least in part oriented towards the establishment of a sense of coherence with respect to itself and with respect to the discursive world surrounding it. There is little doubt that the self is a discursive construct. But this statement only prompts more questions. What is discourse? What are its elements? And how do they function in relation to the self and to the way we infuse our words and actions in the world with meaning? Every theory of discourse is also a theory of subjectivity. It involves implicit and explicit ideas on who and what we are as language users and as human beings. In the upcoming chapters, I will deal with these questions by relying on poststructuralist and pragmatic insights into the functions of discourse and subjectivity.

The humanities are littered with concepts of the self. Some of these concepts may be at odds with each other. At other times, the theories involved display a surprisingly high degree of similarity in spite of some important terminological, conceptual and disciplinary differences. The variety of answers to the question of self and subjectivity can also be observed in the interdisciplinary field of discourse theory and analysis.

The self has been discussed in terms of an internalised conversation with others (Mead 1967; Thayer 1970). Others have discussed human subjectivity in terms of stage metaphors such as roles and various types of onstage and backstage behaviour (Goffman 1959). The self can also be considered in terms of a polyphony of voices or in terms of an intertextual network of utterances (Wiley 2006). It has been described as a narrative practice and as a performance (Bamberg et al. 2007, Holstein and Gubrium 2000; Schiffrin 2000). But what is striking about most discursive approaches to subjectivity is the fact that they all highlight the social, process-based and decentred aspects of selfhood.

The observations made in this introductory chapter highlight the need for such perspectives. I have tried to show that a study of ideologies requires more than an understanding of the big 'isms' such as socialism, liberalism or pluralism. We also need to understand how individuals deploy such notions as values in order to invest their political practices and world views with meaning. From an analytical standpoint, it is rather dangerous to attribute too much unity to the big 'isms', frameworks or ideologies that one may rely upon in one's philosophies. The boundaries of discourse and ideology are never clearly delineated. In fact, the establishment of such boundaries is an ideological practice itself. It involves an act of imagination that allows us to develop a specific mode and sense of social and political awareness.

Based on the analyses presented above, we may conclude that an adequate framework for analysing self and politics in activist discourse should meet a specific set of requirements. As such, we are in need of a perspective that allows for an analysis of non-unitary objects of investigation. An analysis of the political engagements of intellectuals and activists in a particular set of debates cannot pretend to be an investigation of a single community, identity or mode of politics. We need an approach that recognises the inherent multiplicity of subjectivity and debate. Moreover, whatever approach one comes up with, it should allow researchers to flesh out the intricacies of a complex and ever-shifting network of relationships between positions, identities, texts, concepts, practices and institutions. This involves a thorough understanding of the way contexts are defined and negotiated.

Secondly, our perspective should allow us to recognise that the people we investigate may deploy categories of their own that may or may not contradict our own perspectives. Consequently, we need a mode of analysis that allows us to recognise potential contradictions and conflicting definitions of reality. This is important to avoid the risk of overpowering the voices of the people one investigates. In the upcoming chapters, I will demonstrate that such an attitude requires a high degree of sensitivity for the metalinguistic features of the discourse one investigates. Discourse is never completely original. Especially in political discourse, people engage in practices of *bricolage* whereby discursive elements derived from various contexts are articulated with each other. As I have demonstrated above, my interviewees frequently mark their awareness of problematic usage of categories such as identity and politics in discourse. In this sense, ideological and political awareness does not contradict reflexivity but presupposes it.

Thirdly, it is important to realise that the categories deployed in social and political discourses perform important functions in the discursive construction of one's sense of self and one's sense of politics. Abstract notions such as democracy of freedom need to be articulated with concrete experiences and images if they are to be valued enough to effect and affect political engagement. The third requirement of our desired perspective is that it enables us to analyse the ways in which individuals personalise their relationships towards signifiers and practices they may or may not share with others. This involves an understanding of the way individuals order various modes of subjectivity ethically. An understanding of processes of subject-formation is key to such an endeavour.

An understanding of the way people deal with the complexities of large-scale political debates also involves an understanding of large-scale processes of interpretation. Of course, we have no direct access to the interpretative worlds of individuals. Nevertheless, individuals do engage in discursive strategies in order to trigger a sense of coherence with regard to their political subjectivities and world views when they communicate about politics. They do so by articulating preferred and disavowed modes of interpretation in empirically observable ways. Consequently, our analytical framework should allow us to recognise and investigate the way individuals mark large-scale processes of interpretation.

1 Problematising Self and Politics in Activist Discourse

Taking these concerns into account, this book will be about the way people articulate a more or less coherent sense of self in relation to preferred and disavowed modes of political engagement. It is about the discursive construction of political awareness and about the way we make sense of ourselves and of our political realities. On a topical level, I will investigate the way individual activists and intellectuals articulate their sense of self in relation to large-scale social and political discourses on integration and diversity in the Flemish public sphere. This implies a close analysis of the way they position themselves with respect to adversarial and antagonistic actors, practices, discourses and institutions. It also involves an understanding of the categories language users deploy in order to articulate a particular sense of self.

2

Discourse Theory on the Logics of Articulation, Politics and Subjectivity

The approach to political engagement and subjectivity outlined in this book is grounded on a multidimensional notion of articulation. Like many other notions in the humanities, 'articulation' finds itself at the crossroads of academic, political and everyday discourse. In this sense, it is not that different from notions such as 'culture', 'politics' or 'identity'. Articulation is a polysemic concept with a rich etymological and theoretical history that makes it very suitable as a framework for analysing political subjectivity and debate in a way that takes the self-interpretations of individuals as marked in discourse into account.

Articulation has two primary senses in the English language. On the one hand, there is a sense of articulation as a connection or movement as developed in the context of biology and anatomy. On the other hand, articulation refers to the interpretive and performative aspects of speech and other modes of expression. Contemporary academic usage of the concept in the humanities has evolved from the biological and anatomical senses that consider articulation in terms of a physical connection. For instance, in the context of zoology, the notion has been used since the fifteenth century to designate a connection of bones or skeletal segments through joints. Articulation can also refer to a specific *manner* of jointing.

In botany, an articulation refers to the place where leaves are connected to the stem of a plant. In dentistry, it designates the place of contact between upper and lower teeth or the movement of the jaw (OED 2010).

From the nineteenth century on, one started to use the notion of articulation in order to refer to man-made structures and mechanisms. Metaphorical usage of articulation as a connection or linkage in the context of social science only emerged in the twentieth century. In this context, the notion designates a conceptual relationship or a point of juncture between social or discursive entities (OED 2010). As such, it becomes possible to talk about the articulation of individuals to their societies or about the articulation of identities, social classes and/or political parties into a single political project or discourse. This is the dominant sense of articulation one may encounter in cultural studies (Grossberg 1986; Daryl Slack 1996) and in poststructuralist approaches to social reality and politics such as those developed within the context of Essex style discourse theory (Torfing 1999; Howarth 2000). In this book, I will elaborate on the pragmatic, artistic and/or performative dimensions of articulatory practice.

The first usage of the term articulation in the field of phonetics can be traced back to the late sixteenth century. Here, articulation commonly refers to the formation of speech sounds by the control of airflow in the vocal tract by means of vocal organs. It may also refer to the particular way in which this is done. Another phonology-related usage of articulation links the concept to the very faculty of speech and the expression of thought. This can be exemplified with reference to a sentence such as "The declarant has been without the power of articulation". Moreover, the notion can be used to designate manifestations and expressions of abstract things such as emotions or ideas. Consider the following examples: "all aspects of the self share in the generalization and articulation of character effected by interpersonal intercourse" or "for the moderately conservative spirit ... a vigorous articulation of their viewpoints was offered" (OED 2010).

In the sphere of artistic expression, the notion was first observed in 1870 within the context of discourse on music. Here, the signifier designates the separation of successive notes from one another, individually or in groups, regarded as an aspect of a performer's technique or interpretation. This sense of articulation refers to the interpretive processes and techniques related to the expression of successive musical elements by an individual performer. For instance, "one cannot imagine a performance more remarkable for attack, verve, clarity of articulation and gradations of tone colour" (OED 2010).

All of these uses still occur today. For instance, I used the concept of articulation in order to raise some analytical problems resulting from the high degree of overlap between political and academic discourse. As such, I pointed out that people articulate a multiplicity of abstract categories such as identity and politics in relation to preferred and disavowed modes of politics and subjectivity. I have also demonstrated that these categories cannot be taken at face value since they simultaneously perform descriptive, analytical and evaluative functions in the discourses of researchers *and* interviewees. The concept of articulation I have in mind is grounded both on the concept of articulation as a connection and on the idea of articulation as a performance. Articulation is the performative and interpretive practice through which we link the discursive elements of our realities to each other. But there is more to this principle than meets the eye.

If we are to understand the discursive strategies and mechanisms through which we develop, express and practice our political awareness and engagements, we need to be more explicit about *the way* we link discursive elements to each other at various levels of discursive organisation. A systematic investigation of political subjectivity requires insight into the performative dynamics of articulatory practice. A more accurate understanding of what it means to articulate one's political awareness in the public sphere also implies an understanding of the strategies we deploy while considering the communicative options at our disposal. These strategies have not always been discussed under the header of articulation. Within discourse studies, it is more common to write about speech acts, statements, enunciations, utterances or narratives in order to describe such phenomena. One exception can be found in studies that rely on the notion of articulation as developed within the Essex approach to discourse and subjectivity (see: Jørgensen and Philips 2002; Fairclough and Chouliaraki 1999).

The most influential theory of articulation in the field of critical discourse studies is without a doubt the poststructuralist discourse theory set out in *Hegemony and socialist strategy* (Laclau and Mouffe 1985). Laclau and Mouffe are poststructuralists in the sense that they distrust and criticise the very possibility of centred and closed semiotic and sociopolitical systems. They accept the structuralist idea that meaning is differential and arbitrary but deny that discursive elements function within closed and centred wholes. According to them, it is not only impossible to fix the meaning of particular signifiers for once and for all but it is also impossible to draw fixed boundaries around identities, discourses or societies. The implications of this semiotic principle are fundamentally political.

The principle of articulation as developed by Laclau and Mouffe inspired an approach to political discourse and subjectivity that is frequently referred to as the *Essex school of discourse theory* (Laclau 2000, x). This school focuses on the articulation of identities, practices and processes in ideological discourse (Howarth et al. 2000). This includes academic discourse. Authors working with this framework have considered every stage of the research process—from data collection to the writing of reports—as an act of rearticulation (Howarth 2005, 318; Glynos and Howarth 2007, 180; Howarth 2000, 140–141). Academic practices always involve the establishment of new links between various types of texts and genres. Such links impact upon the meanings attributed to the objects and processes under investigation.

My own work draws upon many insights developed within the Essex school. At the same time, I will try to overcome some of its most important theoretical and methodological problems by linking up with approaches to discourse that focus on the pragmatic functions of language use. Of course, any attempt to combine elements of two or more theories or perspectives necessarily implies that a new perspective will emerge. I don't claim to stay true to one perspective or another for this would require an essentialist stance that is incompatible with what we know about the workings of discourse itself. In the sections below, I will therefore introduce a variety of approaches to articulation developed by poststructuralist authors.

After a brief discussion of the way the notion of articulation has been used in structuralist thought, I will introduce the poststructuralist concept of articulation as an attempt to partially fix the meanings of identity, politics, discourse and society. The different sections of this chapter focus on aspects of articulatory practice explored by discourse theorists such as Foucault, Laclau, Mouffe, Glynos, Howarth and Stavrakakis. As such, we will not only focus on the principles of equivalence, difference and fantasy but also discuss the way critique and counter-discourse can be conceptualised in relation to performativity, subjectivity and power. The last two sections of this chapter focus on the interview as an articulatory practice and on the methodological challenges that poststructuralist discourse theorists have to face.

2.1 Structuralist Semiotics and the Double Articulation of Language

If we are to understand poststructuralist theories of articulation, it is useful to understand in what ways they are influenced by structuralism. Within structuralist thought, the notion of articulation was used in order to refer to one of the most characteristic features of human languages: the property of double articulation. This structuralist notion is a theorisation of the linguistic structures and principles that allow us to link semiotic elements of speech to each other. The idea of double articulation is usually attributed to André Martinet and/or to Charles Hocket. Martinet was the first one who coined the notion in a 1949 article in order to identify the basic units of a string of speech. Any string of speech is simultaneously a string of words and a string of phonemes. Martinet argues that the first level of articulation takes place at the level of meaningful words or morphemes. The phonemic level being secondary. Both levels are first and foremost levels of analysis. Martinet seems to suggest that primacy should be given to the morphological level.

According to Hocket, however, there is no priority involved. This author used the notion of double articulation in order to designate what he called duality of patterning. He was interested in the question how human languages differed from non-human communication systems and argued that this duality was one of the unique design features of human language systems. He argued that the meaningful elements of language were composed of meaningless elements. He also pointed out that the articulation of phonemes and the articulation of words follow different rules and principles (Ladd 2012, 261–264). Hocket used the notion of double articulation to explain Hjelmslev's point that we can make use of a limited set of meaningless elements (phonemes) in order to create a virtually unlimited set of meaningful units (morphemes). From this point of view, the principle of double articulation lies at the heart of creative language use and the generation of meaning. Because of it, we do not need to learn an infinite number of words and an unlimited storage capacity to remember them (Ladd 2012, 261–264).

The idea that words are meaningful should be taken with a grain of salt though. The notion that there is no such thing as an independent meaning is a generally accepted principle in both structuralist and poststructuralist approaches to language, discourse and society. This idea can be traced back to the work of Ferdinand de Saussure who argued that meaning is generated by the very structure of language. To him, language was "form and not substance". He argued that language consisted of "differences with no positive terms". As such, he opposed referential theories in which words and concepts directly refer to objective and coherent entities in reality. Instead, he came up with a concept of meaning whereby the significance of a word depends upon its structural relationships towards other words within an over-arching language system (Chandler 2002, 6).

The meaning of the semiotic elements at the morphological level of articulation is never stable. I already exemplified this with respect to some of the categories used by my interviewees. There is nothing essential about notions such as identity, culture or politics. But the same may be said about every other word. As we will see, not even the referent of the pronoun 'I' is stable. We sometimes use this pronoun in order to talk about a specific role and at other times we use it to describe our sense of individuality as a holistic Gestalt. We may use it to describe past and future selves. It may even be deployed to take another person's viewpoint when we report someone else's speech in a re-enactment of an encounter with another person. For these reasons, I will refuse a notion of articulation built upon the premise that the units combined through articulatory practice have independent meanings at the morphological level.

What a particular word means is ontologically arbitrary. De Saussure conceptualised the sign in terms of a signifier (the sound/image) and a signified (the concept). According to him, signs consist of the unity of these two elements. Through arbitrary convention, we link particular sounds/images to particular concepts. From a structuralist point of view, the meaning of signs does not lie in the sign itself or in its relationship towards reality but in its relationship towards other signs within the language system. These relationships are structured according to different rules in every language. On the one hand, there are syntagmatic rules that prescribe how signs can be combined with each other in meaningful speech or *parole*. On the other hand, there is a paradigmatic axis that determines the range of words we have at our disposal and what words can function as equivalents for each other (Torfing 1999, 87).

Saussure claimed that the system conceptualised "as a united whole" should be "the starting point" to determine the relative meanings and values of signs towards each other. Herein lies the structuralist core of his perspective. The paradigmatic and syntagmatic structures of language (*langue*) supposedly pre-exists individual utterances (*parole*). It is the underlying structure of language that explains instances of use. Arbitrary as signs may be, once they are incorporated into a semiotic system, they become part of its history. Through convention, signs become part of social and cultural contexts and their meaning is fixed to a significant extent. Lévi-Strauss noted that the sign may be arbitrary *a priori*, but ceases to be so *a posteriori* (Gottdiener 1995, 6–7; Kress 2001).

Since the Saussurean sign does not have any inherent meaning, it is possible to extend the notion of double articulation to other levels and types of linguistic and semiotic organisation. Daniel Chandler claims that the principle of double articulation also functions at higher levels of linguistic organisation. He argues that we can generate an infinite number of sentences from a limited vocabulary. This principle allows us to communicate "the particularity of experience". Without the principle of double articulation, human communication and learning would be extremely limited (Chandler 2002, 22–28). Nevertheless, according to Ladd, this usage of the term double articulation is not what Hocket had in mind since the latter does not consider words to be meaningless elements (Chandler 2002, 6). Nevertheless, authors such as Susanne Langer tried to extend the principle of double articulation to other semiotic systems such as painting whereby lines, colours and shapes without independent meanings can be articulated in meaningful combinations (Ladd 2012, 264).

The structuralist notion of double articulation draws attention to the multiplicity of meanings we can generate with a limited set of signifiers and to the ontological arbitrariness of the sign. It also draws our attention to the idea that language is a question of connectivity and difference. Poststructuralists accept these principles while rejecting the ideas that language has a closed structure and that this structure is prior to discursive practice. Moreover, they tend to highlight the political aspects of articulatory practice and its implications for studies of subjectivity and hegemony. These dimensions of discourse become especially salient in the writings of Ernesto Laclau and Chantal Mouffe and in the Essex approach to discourse they initiated.

2.2 Articulation in Poststructuralist Discourse Theory

There are many approaches towards discourse across the disciplines. Some authors focus on small-scale utterances and linguistic phenomena whereas others focus on the narrative, ideological and/or power-related dimensions of language use. But there are also authors who study society as if it were a language itself and who refuse to make a distinction between discourse as language (use) and discourse as a broader set of semiotic practices. According to the latter, the political structure of identities and societies can only be known in and through categories of discourse. They argue that social and political processes should therefore be studied as such. This is a stance taken by many poststructuralist researchers that use linguistic concepts as metaphors in order to conceptualise and analyse social and political change.

The label discourse theory is often used to designate the approach that was first presented in *Hegemony and socialist strategy* (Laclau and Mouffe 1985). The authors of this book provided the groundwork for what would be known as the *Essex school* of *discourse theory*. But the label 'theory' may be somewhat misleading in this respect. It may give the faulty impression of a clear-cut binary opposition between theoretical studies of discourse on the one hand (Torfing 1999) and various analytical approaches such as conversation analysis (Sidnell and Stivers 2013),

2 Discourse Theory on the Logics of Articulation, Politics... 43

linguistic pragmatics (Cummings 2005) or critical discourse analysis (CDA) (Wodak 2013a) on the other hand. The work carried out within poststructuralist approaches is certainly characterised by a high degree of abstraction. It may even seem opaque or mystifying. But this binary opposition between discourse theory and discourse analysis does not do justice to the analytical practices of so-called discourse theorists. Neither does it justice to the theoretical endeavours undertaken in other approaches to discourse, subjectivity and politics. Nevertheless, for the time being, I will use this label in order to refer to the Essex approach to discourse and politics.

In the previous chapter, I already mentioned that my understanding of politics is heavily informed by poststructuralism. The perspective of Ernesto Laclau and Chantal Mouffe has been instrumental in this respect. It is therefore useful to take a closer look at the model of discourse involved. If one claims that subjectivities and societies function according to basic discursive principles, one needs to specify what these principles are and how they function. I will therefore start with an outline of the discourse theory of Ernesto Laclau and Chantal Mouffe. Their work has been seminal for a generation of discourse theorists who seek to build bridges towards empirically oriented discourse studies that are more explicit about their methodological principles and procedures.

Poststructuralist discourse theorists refuse to separate political theory from political practice at the conceptual level. In this context, Laclau points out that "theoretico-political categories do not only exist in books but are also part of discourses actually informing institutions and social operations" (Laclau 1994a, 55; Marchart 2004). This claim is closely associated with Laclau's reluctance to distinguish theory from analysis. The type of analysis proposed in *Hegemony and socialist strategy* was heavily informed by poststructuralist interpretations of post-Saussurean semiotics. But the goal of the book was first and foremost political. The subtitle is clarifying: *towards a radical democratic politics*.

The authors wanted to get rid of the essentialisms that haunted Marxist thought. In order to get away from reductions of reality to matters of class, state and economy, they set out to explain how and why political struggles and alliances proved to be more dynamic than orthodox and revisionist Marxists predicted. Also, they tried to articulate the conditions of emergence for a radical and democratic hegemonic project (Torfing 1999, 15–53). Their discourse theory was developed as a political theory of political subjectivity and struggle. Due to its high degree of abstraction, this framework would be adopted, adapted and used in order to explain a great variety of identities, struggles and processes of social change (Howarth et al. 2000; Howarth and Torfing 2005). Nevertheless, in order to understand poststructuralist discourse theory properly, one needs to understand its ontological and political claims.

For Laclau and Mouffe, a radical democracy is always plural. This means that the demands made in defence of one interest group—for example, workers—should not go at the expense of the rights of other groups such as women, immigrants or consumers. It also means that democracy cannot be restricted to the traditional field of citizenship. Rather, it involves an expansion of democratic activities to as many spaces of the social as possible (e.g. the home, the family, the workplace, the economy, etc.). Democracy comes in many forms. It can vary according to the identities involved (e.g. ethnic, cultural, gendered) or according to the contexts in which democracy is practiced (e.g. in the neighbourhood or at work).

The strengthening of specific democratic struggles requires, therefore, the expansion of chains of equivalence which extend to other struggles. The equivalential articulation between anti-racism, anti-sexism and anti-capitalism, for example, requires a hegemonic construction which, in certain circumstances may be the condition for the consolidation of each one of these struggles. (Laclau and Mouffe 1985, 96–97)

For Laclau and Mouffe, the political project of the Left "cannot be to renounce liberal-democratic ideology, but on the contrary, to deepen and expand it in the direction of a radical and plural democracy". They argue that the Left needs to construct a new hegemonic strategy whereby a multiplicity of political struggles and spaces can be linked to each other in a way that modifies the very identities of those involved. The authors explicitly frame their work as an attempt to come up with a concept of hegemony that could be "a useful instrument in the struggle for a radical, libertarian and plural democracy" (Laclau and Mouffe 1985, 3–4). Their notion of articulation performs a key function in this politico-theoretical endeavour.

In fact, the notion of articulation is one of the most important concepts in the Essex approach to discourse and subjectivity. It means more than merely adding signifiers, ideas and identities to each other. Laclau and Mouffe argue that whenever ideas, identities, social groups or ideologies are linked, a change in the meaning of these discursive elements occurs (Laclau and Mouffe 1985, 105). They claim that Marxist theory has been unable to explain contemporary societal developments because it always conceived of social and political identities as class-based. Consequently, no matter what alliances would be forged, the identities and interests of social actors were supposed to remain unmodified. And when something unexpected did happen, (neo-)Marxists invented new categories such as hegemony in order to explain why a particular development contradicted this basic idea (Laclau and Mouffe 2001). In this sense, the increasing centrality of hegemony in Marxist theory was a response to dislocations in Marxist orthodoxy.

Whereas the notion of hegemony initially referred to state dominance, Lenin started to use the concept of hegemony in order to designate the way his party was to establish a relation of political leadership with respect to a variety of classes in order to achieve short-term instrumental gains. Here, the establishment of a relationship did not impact on the identities of the classes involved (Howarth 2004, 257; Williams 1983, 144–145). This would change in Antonio Gramsci's concept of hegemony that was picked up and radicalised by Laclau and Mouffe. Howarth points out that Gramsci no longer thinks about politics as a zero-sum game conducted by classes with fixed identities and interests. Politics rather becomes a question of constructing relationships and agreements through the process of winning over agents and groups to particular ideological and political positions (Howarth 2004, 258).

For Gramsci, hegemony came to mean the creation of a collective will based on ideological unity among several groups and classes. It is no longer a matter of a purely instrumental alliance between classes that maintain strictly separate identities. Neither is it a matter of merely imposing one will onto all others. It rather involves the creation of a common sense and a collective will. Put differently, hegemony involves practices of disarticulation and rearticulation of ideological elements and the creation of new projects and subjectivities. Nevertheless, for Gramsci, these elements still had an ultimate class belonging. By rejecting this last idea on the basis of a poststructuralist theory of meaning and identity, Laclau and Mouffe would radicalise Gramsci's ideas on the contingency of hegemonic struggles (Mouffe 1979, 184–195; Laclau and Mouffe 1985, 66–71).

The emergence of new social movements focusing on feminism, environmental issues and ethnicities was difficult to grasp for orthodox Marxist theories. The big revolution did not occur and instead, a multiplicity of struggles emerged (Laclau and Mouffe 1985, 1–4, 1990, 97–98). In order to account for these developments, Laclau and Mouffe reconceptualised hegemony as a matter of (re-)articulation by drawing on poststructuralist concepts of language and society (Howarth 2004, 259). The reason for this linguistic turn is simple. If hegemony is about establishing some common sense with respect to a common will that alters the identities of the political actors involved, politics becomes a discursive struggle over meaning.

The model of meaning on which Laclau and Mouffe built their discourse theory is based upon a reading and critique of De Saussure. On the one hand, Laclau and Mouffe accept the idea that signs consist of signifiers and signifieds. On the other hand, they refuse the structuralist concept of language as a closed system. They also dismiss the rigid distinction between *langue* and *parole*. For Laclau and Mouffe, the meaning of semiotic elements is determined not by an over-arching system but by the relative positions these elements are allotted within particular discursive contexts. This has huge implications for the hegemonic war of positions they seek to understand (Jørgensen and Philips 2002, 10–12). It implies that politics can be understood as the whole of attempts to fix the meanings of identities, values, practices and society itself.

2.3 A Poststructuralist Ontology of Discourse and Politics

If all meaning shifts and if there is no necessary referential link between the signifiers we use and the objects and practices we designate, we need to ask ourselves how social and political life can be possible at all. How can we identify with anything if the ground on which we position ourselves is inherently imagined and unstable? The answer lies in the fact that meanings and identities can neither be fully fixed nor be completely arbitrary. Rather, they are partially and temporarily articulated with historically contingent discourses and ideologies. Discourse is all about a *relative fixation* of signifiers and signified (Laclau and Mouffe 1985, 106–107). In order to understand this, we have to return briefly to the field of semiotics and shed some light on the ontological dimension of the Essex school of discourse theory.

For Laclau and Mouffe, discourse designates the "relational totality resulting from articulatory practice" (Laclau and Mouffe 1985). This entails that the category of discourse is not reducible to textual or verbal exchanges. Rather, it captures the linguistic and non-linguistic aspects of language games. Also, Essex authors contend that a discourse can never be delineated or closed in any final sense. The principle of articulation prohibits this. But of course, we do attribute boundaries to discourse on a daily basis. We talk about medical, literary or architectural discourses. We distinguish between the discourses of liberals, anarchists and communists. And there seem to be recognisable differences between the discourses of various social groups and classes. In order to investigate what constitutes the unity of a particular discourse, Laclau and Mouffe turn to Michel Foucault's *Archaelogy of knowledge*. Following Foucault, they conclude that the unity of a discourse emerges through the dispersal of its elements (Laclau and Mouffe 1985, 105–106).

Foucault points out that the boundaries of discourses can never be captured by the topics they address or the objects they investigate. Neither can they be delimited on the basis of the form and type of connections between their statements. Moreover, the unity of a discourse does not reside in the permanence of the concepts involved. And not even the persistence of themes can account for the boundaries of a discourse. He therefore prefers to describe the unity of discursive formations in terms of the dispersion of their statements. It is useful to quote him at length (Foucault 1969, 40).

Whenever one can describe, between a number of statements, such a system of dispersion, whenever, between objects, types of statement, concepts, or thematic choices, one can define a regularity (an order, correlations, positions and functionings, transformations), we will say, for the sake of convenience, that we are dealing with a discursive formation *– thus avoiding words that are already overladen with conditions and consequences, and in any case inadequate to the task of designating such a dispersion, such as 'science', 'ideology', 'theory', or 'domain of objectivity'. The conditions to which the elements of this division (objects, mode of statement, concepts, thematic choices) are subjected, we shall call the* rules of formation. (Foucault 1969, 40–41)

Nevertheless, it is still possible to signify a discourse as a totality. Discourses can be signified *as if* they have clearly delineated boundaries. The structured totality of discourse or the discursive field must therefore be differentiated from necessarily incomplete and open discourses that attempt "to dominate the field of discursivity, to arrest the flow of differences, to construct a centre" (Laclau and Mouffe 1985, 110–113).

Laclau and Mouffe seek to go beyond a "banal constructionism" that merely states that reality is defined and framed by discourse (Glynos and Stavrakakis 2004, 204). They wonder why human beings engage in signifying practices in the first place. Why do we care so much about meaning in spite of the fact that no meaning will ever completely satisfy us? And why do we continue to identify ourselves with identities that can never be fixed in any final way? These questions about identity and meaning lead us to the ontological question about the nature of reality. Laclau and Mouffe contend that reality is not merely mediated or framed by discourse. It is not merely a matter of selecting and highlighting certain aspects of reality and/or downplaying others. Rather, it emerges through our attempts to create meaning. It is constructed through the organisation of discursive elements into moments of discourse through productive attempts to delimit identities and spaces of the social. In order to understand the way reality is structured, Essex authors frequently turn to Lacanian psychoanalysis.

A Lacanian description of reality involves a discussion of three dimensions: the Real, the Imaginary and the Symbolic. It also involves a description of the emergence of subjectivity whereby individuals gain an imperfect sense of being a unified self. According to Lacan, this type of awareness emerges in the last phase of a process called the *mirror stage*. He claims that prior to this stage, children have no sense of being separate

2 Discourse Theory on the Logics of Articulation, Politics...

from the whole of reality. At this point, the child has no awareness of the limits and unity of its body. Its own limbs are perceived as uncoordinated elements entering into its field of vision. During this period of its life, the child is immersed in the Real and has no awareness of the symbolic and imaginary dimensions of reality (Mansfeld 2000, 41–45). During the mirror phase, all of this changes radically.

From the sixth to the eighteenth month of the infant's life, the child's fragmented experience is transformed into a sense of wholeness through the assumption of its image in the mirror. But this sense of wholeness soon becomes alienating. The image is never the same: it is inverted, bigger or smaller and will always remain alienating. Moreover, there is a spatial gap separating the sense of 'I' from its mirror image. Even though the mirror image suggests the permanence of an 'I' and a Gestalt that functions as an alter ego, it is incapable of providing the emerging subject with a stable identity. The entry of the child into the order of the Imaginary seems to leave only one other option: an entry into the field of linguistic representation (Stavrakakis 1999, 17–19; Lacan 1994).

The entry into the Symbolic coincides more or less with the subject's entry into the Imaginary. As soon as we enter these dimensions of reality, our access to the Real is lost. At the same time, our subjectivity becomes decentred.

> *What is lost is all unmediated access to the real. Now we can only try to encounter the real through symbolisation. We gain access to reality, which is mainly a symbolic construct, but the signified of the signifier 'reality', the real itself, is sacrificed forever. No identification can restore it or recapture it for us. But it is exactly this impossibility that forces us to identify again and again. We never get what we were promised but that's exactly why we keep longing for it.* (Stavrakakis 1999, 34)

The above citation mentions a signifier and a signified. In order to account for our discursive separation from the Real, Lacan reinterprets the Saussurean sign by providing us with the following formula: S/s. The signifier 'S' is located over the signified 's'. And between them there is a bar that resists signification. It disrupts the unity of the sign that was posited in Saussure's model. For Lacan, the signifier does not represent a signified. The signified only exists because we like to believe in its existence, a belief that is crucial for our construction of reality as a coherent and objective whole that guarantees the validity of our knowledge. Nevertheless, the Symbolic is first and foremost the order of the signifier. The signified itself belongs to the order of the Real and can never be captured. Stavrakakis puts it as follows: "signification is articulated around the illusion of attaining the signified" (Stavrakakis 1999, 24–27). This model of reality has great implications for subjectivity and politics.

With respect to subjectivity, it implies that there is not a single signifier that will ever truly delimit and capture our sense of self. There is always a lack at the heart of every symbolisation and signification of the subject. As such, all identifications are ultimately doomed to fail. As a result of their insertion into language, individuals will try to adopt identities only to find out that identification will always be incomplete. But this does not prevent us from dreaming about a steady ground on which to base our identity. In this sense, the main function of the ego is to misrecognise "the impossibility of fullness" and to drive us towards attempts to fill the lack at the centre of subjectivity through practices of articulation (Laclau and Zac 1994, 35). In this sense, the basic function of the ego is misrecognition (Lacan 1994, 98).

With respect to politics, the implications are vast as well. Laclau and Mouffe posit the *primacy of the political* in understanding and instituting social relations and subjectivities. Ultimately, all social relationships have been shaped in and through political struggles understood as discursive practices of articulation. But over time, these relationships become less politicised as their political origins sediment and fade into the background. This does not mean that the political dimension of these relationships evaporates. Rather, it is repressed and can always be reactivated by discursively questioning the normative practices they are based upon (Torfing 1999, 70). The political is therefore "a dimension that is inherent to every human society and that determines our very ontological condition" (Mouffe 1993, 3). More specifically, it is a "particular modality of the real" (Stavrakakis 1999, 73).

In order to explain the emergence and contestation of political identities and struggles, Essex authors have developed an interpretive framework that seeks to name and identify various logics of critical explanation.

Logic should thereby not be understood in the formal sense of the word. Neither does it refer to the study of truth values of propositions, to the (in-)validity of inferences or to causal laws. In the context of the Essex approach to discourse theory, logic is first and foremost an analytical category that one can use in order to name and analyse social and political practices of identity formation and hegemonic struggle (Glynos and Howarth 2007). Essex authors seek to name and explain the rules or the grammar of a practice, as well as the conditions that make these practises possible and vulnerable (Glynos and Howarth 2007). In order to do so, they distinguish between political, fantasmatic and social logics of critical explanation. Together, they explain how meanings and identities are fixed through practices of articulation.

2.4 Fixing Meaning Through Equivalence and Difference

Political logics are all about the institution and de-institution of the social. The social and the political constitute two idealised sides of a coin. The social consists of all identities, relationships and practices that provide a more or less stable ground for our ideological presuppositions and daily practices. But as we noticed before, every aspect of the social has at some point been instituted by an act of political articulation into a pattern with some degree of stability. The political can therefore be described as all practices and performances that institute and challenge social practices and relationships. Laclau puts it as follows: "social logics consist in rule-following" while "political logics are related to the institution of the social" on the basis of social demands (Glynos and Howarth 2007, 134–142).

There are two basic political logics that account for processes of politicisation. Both of them involve processes of highlighting the contingency of the discursive identities and relationships involved: a political logic of equivalence and a political logic of difference. The logic of equivalence simplifies socio-political space through the establishment of a chain of equivalence that articulates various discursive elements or signifiers (e.g. identities, subject positions, practices) to one another. Logics of difference expand and complicate political space. This type of logic works through the decomposition of existing chains of equivalence and by rearticulating these elements in new differential orders (Laclau and Mouffe 1985, 130; Howarth 2000, 107). According to Howarth, political logics of equivalence and difference play a quasi-transcendental role in discourse theory since they are integral to the construction and contestation of social relations and practices (Howarth 2005, 328).

> *The dimension of equivalence captures the* substitutive *aspect of the relation by making reference to an 'us-them' axis: two or more elements can be substituted for each other with reference to a common negation or threat. That is to say, they are equivalent not insofar as they share a positive property (though empirically they* may *share something in common), but, crucially, insofar as they have a common enemy. The dimension of difference, by contrast, captures the* combinatory *or contiguous aspect of the relation, which accounts not simply for differences in identity among elements, but also for keeping elements distinct, separate, and autonomous.* (Glynos and Howarth 2007, 144)

Howarth and Glynos illustrate the operation of equivalence with reference to a national liberation struggle against an occupying colonial power. Such struggles typically attempt to cancel out particularities of class, ethnicity, region and/or religion in the name of a more universal nationalism that serves as a point of orientation for all the oppressed. For instance, the logic of difference is dominant in the age-old practice of 'divide and rule' through which occupying powers separate and oppose groups in order to hinder the articulation of a collective oppositional identity, demand and/or will. Discursive elements are always part and parcel of signifying networks that exhibit equivalential *and* differential relationships. But at any moment in time, one is always stronger than the other. Politics can be conceptualised as being informed by the dynamic interplay of both types of logic (Glynos and Howarth 2007, 144–145).

Chains of signifiers need to be quilted together in one way or another. This happens by means of a practice of privileging some signifiers over others. As such, some signifiers can become nodal points in a discourse. They function as *points de capiton* in which signifiers become temporarily attached to each other. These discursive nodal points function as common points of reference that allow political actors to unify a set of

2 Discourse Theory on the Logics of Articulation, Politics... 53

identities and demands. At this point, it is useful to recall that Laclau and Mouffe consider discourses in terms of attempts "to dominate the field of discursivity, to arrest the flow of differences, to construct a centre" (Laclau and Mouffe 1985, 110–113). The imaginary unity and coherence of a discourse is centred on such nodal points. In order to exemplify the functions of these *points de capiton*, Yannis Stavrakakis asks us to consider a group of 3000 people participating in a mass rally:

> *Suddenly they realise that their leader has disappeared. The question which is immediately asked is the following: 'Where are we going, 3,000 people alone?'. What creates the feeling of unity and collectivity is not reduced to the physical presence of 3,000 people. When the identificatory link with the leader is cut the illusionary character of collective identity and group power is uncovered. Without the intervention of a* point de capiton *(the leader in this case), instead of constituting a collectivity they are reduced to 3,000 individuals.* (Stavrakakis 1999, 78)

However, in most cases, *points de capiton* or *nodal points* have a strong linguistic dimension. Most examples and analyses of nodal points include rather abstract categories such as democracy or freedom. Such notions have no inherent meaning. Rather, their meaning emerges through the discursive practice of quilting them together. The resulting ideological quilt presupposes that the signifiers articulated with each other interpenetrate each other and thus effect each other's meanings. Žižek points out that the connection of a signifier such as ecology to other signifiers is never determined in advance:

> *one can be a state-oriented ecologist (if one believes that only the intervention of a strong state can save us from catastrophe), a socialist ecologist (if one locates the source of merciless exploitation of nature in the capitalist system); a conservative ecologist (if one preaches that man must again become deeply rooted in his native soil), and so on; feminism can be socialist, apolitical ...; even racism could be elitist or populist.* (Žižek 1995, 87)

Interestingly, if every political project requires the construction of a series of nodal points, this also goes for the project of a radical democratic imaginary as developed by Laclau and Mouffe. Žižek points out that the signifier 'democracy' functions as a nodal point in their discourse. According to these authors, a multiplicity of struggles—for example, feminism, ethnicity, socialism—can be articulated together and put into a chain of equivalence in a struggle for a more egalitarian society. Consequently, it is this more general struggle that provides particular struggles with meaning. Put differently, in the discourse of Laclau and Mouffe, 'democracy' functions as a nodal point that quilts a multiplicity of signifiers into a common hegemonic demand (Žižek 1995, 88). At this point, it is important to return to the issue of articulation. The final definition of articulation in *Hegemony and socialist strategy* reads as follows:

> *The practice of articulation therefore, consists in the construction of nodal points which partially fix meaning; and the partial character of this fixation proceeds from the openness of the social, a result, in its turn, of the constant overflowing of every discourse by the infinitude of the field of discursivity.* (Laclau and Mouffe 1985, 112)

It should be clear that this definition is an abstraction of the anatomical or biological sense of articulation as a connection. It does not refer to a node or joint in the stem of a plant but to a node in a chain of discourse that connects various discursive elements to one another. If we take a bird's-eye view of the various nodal points that we encounter in particular discourses, we will see that some signifiers are shared by a great deal of subjects. For instance, most political parties in Western societies will call themselves 'democratic' even though they may have very different ideas on what a democratic society should look like. Such nodal points can exert a strong mobilising force when they are (considered to be) unrealised, threatened or stolen.

In order to capture the antagonistic struggles that take place around certain nodal points, Laclau came up with the concept of the *empty signifier* (Laclau 1994c). Empty signifiers are so over-coded with meanings that they mean everything and nothing at the same time (Torfing 2005, 301). They mean everything in the sense that our identities seem to depend on their realisation. They propel us towards action and political mobilisation. And they mean nothing in the sense that they signify ideals that can never be fully realised. Moreover, if they are to perform

2 Discourse Theory on the Logics of Articulation, Politics... 55

their function as hegemonic nodal points, they will have to remain vague enough to allow for a multiplicity of identifications. Howarth and Glynos put it as follows:

> *Certain signifiers or linguistic expressions – 'sustainable environment', 'health', 'justice for all' and so forth – function as names that stand in for the absent fullness of a dislocated community or life. Though they are metaphors with no corresponding facts – they are moments of naming in a radical sense – they strive to represent the failure of a signifying system or language. At least in part, this is why Laclau calls these signifiers 'empty signifiers'.* (Glynos and Howarth 2007, 122)

Empty signifiers urge us to go look for something that is absent or lacking in our identity as well as in our society. They simultaneously promise meaning and withhold it (Glynos and Howarth 2007, 131). The enjoyment of fullness is thus placed beyond our reach. Consequently, the production of empty signifiers involves the construction of a constitutive outside that resists and threatens the political subjects engaged in their realisation.

For Laclau, the presence of empty signifiers constitutes the very condition of hegemonic projects. A hegemonic project involves the expansion of a chain of equivalence. An entity is hegemonic to the extent that it presents itself as realising the broader aims of emancipating or ensuring order for wider masses of the population (Laclau 1994c, 43). As we will see in greater detail later on, the notion of 'integration' has functioned as an empty signifier in Flemish debates about minorities for decades. In academic and political discourse, the integrated society frequently operates as a mythical ideal. A lack of integration supposedly leads to a lack of society. This way of thinking requires an externalisation of many issues and classes of people. It requires the construction of a constitutive outside that has fuelled many processes of exclusion and a great deal of political debate.

In Flanders, the groups held responsible for this lack of integration tend to be Moroccans, Turks, Musims or so-called allochthons. These groups are considered to be in most need of integration and usually share an Islamic background. Muslims often function as antagonistic others in nationalist or Eurocentric definitions of Flemish, Belgian and European culture and identity (Arnaut et al. 2009; Blommaert and Verschueren 1998). Antagonism implies that "the presence of the other prevents me from being totally myself" (Laclau and Mouffe 1985, 125). Through the attempts to cancel out antagonistic difference, society emerges. It institutes itself in opposition to entities that—supposedly—negate it. Internal differences are glossed over and the internal chain of equivalence expands. In the case of Flanders, a vague and under-defined demand for integration allowed for a great deal of political consensus on migration. It also allowed for the creation of integration policies and institutions. As such, the antagonist relationship with supposedly non-integrated elements became constitutive for a significant part of Flemish politics and identity.

Antagonisms and empty signifiers are present in every political project. The primacy of politics and the principles of discourse imply that the social is instituted through difference, conflict and antagonism. Difference, conflict and the choice between alternatives lie at the heart of liberal and plural democracy. Chantal Mouffe argues that "democracy is in peril not only when there is insufficient consensus and allegiance to the values it embodies, but also when its agonistic dynamic is hindered by an apparent excess of consensus, which usually masks a disquieting apathy". Consequently, democratic processes call for a "vibrant clash of political positions and an open conflict of interests" (Mouffe 1993, 6). The trick is therefore not so much to get rid of antagonism as such, but to allow for a distinction between antagonistic enemies and agonistic adversaries.

2.5 Fixing Meaning Through the Logic of Fantasy

A second dimension of articulatory practice one needs to consider is fantasy. Political logics of equivalence and difference allow us to understand the constitution and transformation of social norms and practices. Fantasmatic logics provide "the means to understand why specific practices and regimes 'grip' subjects" (Glynos and Howarth 2007, 145). In everyday discourse, fantasy is usually associated with some kind of flight from reality. In the Essex framework, it is the other way around. Here, fantasy is what drives us to undertake attempts to come to grips with reality and identity. Reality emerges through a futile but productive search for fixed meanings and truths. Following Lacan, Essex authors take the view that "fantasy supports reality" (Stavrakakis 1999, 62).

It may seem strange to claim that we can partially fix meaning through fantasy. Fantasy is usually associated with that which is not—and cannot be—real. It is often thought of as a pointless or irrelevant endeavour in the face of real problems and realistic politics. It may therefore seem awkward to link this notion to the logics of equivalence and difference that institute and challenge our social and political realities. But these latter logics do not explain why people invest their affective energies into politics. People are gripped emotionally by some discourses and feel appalled by others. Their experience of identity is *felt* and their demands are infused with emotions. Politics is not merely about linking signifiers into arbitrary formations. The value of these signifiers is also a matter of affective investment.

If certain signifiers become more central than others and if some signifiers function as nodal points or as empty signifiers in a particular discourse, this is possible because we *feel* some signifiers are more important than others. This valuation can be understood in terms of fantasy in the sense that the ideological function of fantasy is "not to set up an illusion that provides a subject with a false picture of the world, but to ensure that the radical contingency of social reality – and the political dimension of a practice more specifically – remains in the background" (Glynos and Howarth 2007, 145). Authors working in poststructuralist discourse theory argue that fantasy is characterised by a logic that allows for an explanation of emotional investments in political processes. Glynos highlights three key aspects of the logic of fantasy:

> *first, it has a narrative structure which features, among other things, an ideal and an obstacle for its realisation, and which may take a beatific or horrific form; second, it has an inherently transgressive aspect vis-à-vis officially affirmed ideals; and third, it purports to offer a foundational guarantee of sorts, in the sense that it offers the subject a degree of protection from the anxiety associated with a direct confrontation with the radical contingency of social relations.*
> (Glynos 2008, 287)

The failure of the—realisation of—horrific and/or beatific aspects of fantasies leads to the experience of affect and emotion. This can be illustrated with reference to workplace fantasies of leadership. When leaders fail to live up to their imputed omnipotence, contempt and sarcasm lurk around the corner. And when leadership fantasies are structured around the ideal of a caring, rewarding and/or accessible boss, anger or injured pride may arise when these leaders fail to exhibit these characteristics in an adequate way. Failure to live up to the beatific ideals provided by ideological fantasy and fear for its horrific imaginary can easily lead to frustration and depression (Glynos and Stavrakakis 2008, 258–259).

Fantasy provides us with the possibility to imagine a different future that goes beyond the hegemonic norms of the social reality in which we find ourselves. It is in this sense, that fantasy is transgressive. But it also allows us to think about our ideals as if they are achievable and to imagine our identities as objects of desire that can be filled with concrete contents. In this sense, fantasy keeps the Real at bay and covers over the lack within the subject and within society. Put differently, fantasy structures our *relation* to social norms and the force with which we pursue them. The logic of fantasy thus explains our ideological attachment to particular identities and narratives. It also explains why a destabilisation of an ideological fantasy can lead to feelings of anxiety and danger (Glynos 2008, 289).

Interestingly, there are different modes of attachment to ideological fantasies conceivable. When subjects are in the thrall of ideological fantasy, they become rather insensitive to contingency. Even though they may be able to imagine an alternative to their current condition, alternative futures are either rejected or embraced completely. But it is also possible for a subject to be more oriented towards the contingency of the social (Glynos and Stavrakakis 2008, 265). To the extent that political subjects embrace this type of openness and the contingency of making political choices, they can be said to enter into an ethical mode of enjoyment. For David Howarth and Jason Glynos, ethics and ideology refer to two different modes of affective investment in political identities: discourses and projects (Glynos and Howarth 2007, 291).

An 'ethical' detachment with respect to 'ideological' fantasies does not involve the abandonment of fantasy as such. Rather, it allows for the idea that particular practices, signifiers and identities can be re-signified. It is a matter of taking a critical distance with respect to essentialist imaginaries and relationships towards the Real. Politics consists of a struggle between competing fantasies (Glynos 2008, 291). However, an ethical critique as imagined by Glynos involves that one does not only criticise the fantasmatic modes of ideological investment of others but that one also struggles with the dynamics of fantasy of such (Glynos 2014, 9).

Of course, this does not imply that one can—or should—escape ideology altogether. Rather, it means that one can loosen its grip on oneself in order to avoid a pathological overinvestment in a particular type of discourse. The more invested one becomes in a particular discourse, the more vehement one will become in guarding and delineating the boundaries of the associated sense of self. The more overinvested one is in a particular discourse, the higher the probability that a—perceived—threat to its structure will be interpreted in antagonistic terms. In turn, this may lead to pathological splitting tendencies whereby one un-reflexively externalises one's own dreams and desires on antagonistic enemies.

In contrast, one might imagine an ethical mode of subjectivity in which one may not escape ideological discourse as such, but in which one can take a different attitude with respect to the way we function. One might imagine a subjectivity in which the fantasmatic relationship of the self to the self and to others is treated with a higher degree of reflexivity, suspicion or awareness. So, even though ethics and ideology are two sides of the coin called subjectivity, the development of an ethical attitude requires that one trains oneself in recognising and dealing with the ontological contingencies of social and political reality. Moreover, this type of ethical attitude does not only imply that one questions the way particular identities are construed. It also involves a critical stance with respect to the mode of ideological investment one might have with respect to the discursive elements that fix the meanings of life.

2.6 Fixing Meaning Through Social Logics, Counter-Logics and Self-interpretations

Most of the meanings of life surround us in a rather unobtrusive manner. They are part and parcel of everyday social relationships and practices. The operation and dispersion of the rules informing their articulation can be described in terms of social logics. Once such rules become normalised through fantasy, they start to function according to logics of their own and become part and parcel of a hegemonic background (Glynos and Howarth 2007, 139). But this does not imply that they become less powerful in the process. They continue to structure the sense(s) we attribute to each other's practices and subjectivities.

Social logics can take many forms. They structure the interpretive realities that subjects engage in through everyday practices: "social logics of competition, for example, might describe the way that actors interact with, and understand, each other as competitors. Or social logics of 'individualization' might capture those patterns of discursive articulations which, in the self-understanding of actors, individuate persons, isolating them from each other" (Glynos and Howarth 2007, 139–140). By naming and describing social logics, one characterises the particularities of the rules and regularities informing a social practice or regime.

This involves a process whereby researchers articulate self-interpretations to contexts by means of theoretical concepts and ontological assumptions. Doing so, such researchers articulate some kind of unity to the heterogeneous discursive elements that inform particular interpretive practices. Moreover, the process of naming involves a redescription of the discursive elements under investigation. This description may be grounded in the self-descriptions of those we study, but it is certainly not reducible to it. Identifying social logics can be thought of as an act of judgement that opens up possibilities for epistemological and ontological critique. It also allows for the articulation of counter-logics—alternative ways of conceptualising and organising socio-political space (Glynos and Howarth 2007, 183–189). Let us turn to an example.

> *Now consider the 'logic of the market'. Clearly, the way we conceptualize the market depends on whether it is a supermarket, a market in energy supply, a market in educational goods, and so on. In other words, the meaning of expressions such as 'the efficient allocation of resources', 'fair price', or 'supply and demand' depends on the way we understand the key actors and terms associated with the specific paradigm we have adopted. There is a clear relational network at stake here which the concept of logic must try to capture and name. Crucial in this respect is the way actors themselves interpret their roles and activities.*
> (Glynos and Howarth 2007, 136)

One might say that social logics are relatively concrete as compared to the logics of equivalence and fantasy. Naming them involves strategies of exemplification. For instance, the *logic of the market* described above can only be imagined with reference to concrete discursive elements such as subject positions (e.g. buyers and sellers), objects (e.g. commodities and means of exchange), practices and a system of relations that articulates objects and subjects with each other (e.g. a particular legal system). Moreover, the concept of logic captures the conditions that makes the continued operation of these practices, discourses and subject positions possible (Glynos and Howarth 2007, 136).

Naming involves an identification of patterns of coherence in a discursive practice. This attributed unity should be characterised by some degree of contingency. The regularity in the distribution of discursive elements has to be demonstrated empirically and needs to be conceptualised theoretically. It is equally important that the practice of naming a logic takes its cue from the self-interpretations of those one studies. One has "to pass through the self-interpretations of the social actors involved in the regime and practices under investigation". Logics may not be reducible to self-interpretations but they are not reducible to reified theoretical concepts that subsume social reality without any possibility for empirical feedback either (Glynos and Howarth 2007, 139).

Naming is basically an act of articulation whereby academic concepts and perspectives are linked with the discourses of research subjects. According to Howarth and Glynos, the labels of specific logics should take their cue from the languages and vocabularies through which subjects articulate themselves. At the same time, one should go beyond the self-interpretations of the subjects one studies by engaging in practices of contextualisation. But what does this mean exactly? In contrast to more traditional hermeneutic approaches, Essex authors do not understand contextualisation as a matter of putting things in a right or original context of enunciation. Interpretation does not consist of a hermeneutics of recovery. Neither does it imply a search for so-called hidden truths through a hermeneutics of suspicion (Howarth 2000, 128–129; Glynos and Howarth 2008). Like other hermeneutic thinkers, they underscore the importance of context (Glynos and Howarth 2008), but at the same time, they emphasise that the nature of this context should be conceptualised in terms of articulation.

Context is never simply given. Writing about articulation from the perspective of cultural studies, Daryl Slack points out that context is "not something out there within which practices occur or which influences the development of practices. Rather, identities, practices and effects generally constitute the very context within which they are practices, identities or effects" (Daryl Slack 1996, 124–125). But how does one delineate relevant contextual boundaries for interpretation and explanation? There is surprisingly little literature that addresses this question directly from an Essex point of view. One exception can be found in an exchange between Judith Butler and Ernesto Laclau. The latter states that "it is not possible to, strictly speaking, attribute closed boundaries to a context". Like any other aspect of discourse, "contexts are defined by their limits, and yet, these limits are impossible to fix". Unsurprisingly, the solution lies in a relative meaning of contextual boundaries (Butler and Laclau 2004, 335).

So, if the naming of social logics implies that one passes through the contextualised self-understandings of subjects, we need to ask what this implies at a lower level abstraction. Because even though it is impossible to delineate contexts in an ontological sense of the word, this is certainly feasible on a more pragmatic level. We do this all the time. A more fine-grained account of how social actors delimit each other's contextual boundaries for interpretation is therefore called for. I will explore this issue further during a discussion of the methodological issues the Essex approach to discourse is currently facing. For the moment however, it suffices to point out that the main Essex strategy for delineating interpretive contexts in terms of social logics consists of the practice of naming itself.

2.7 Destabilising and Politicising Social Logics Through Critique

The naming of logics is conceptualised as a critical practice. Like many other critical approaches to discourse, the Essex school positions itself in the critical field. It shares many issues (e.g. ecology, racism, inequality), concepts (e.g. identity, ideology, hegemony and power) and goals (raising critical awareness, combating discrimination and racism, contributing to a more just and democratic way of life) with other approaches to discourse such as CDA, DHA (Discourse Historical Analysis), the ethnography of communication and critical modes of linguistic pragmatics. But considering the polysemy of the concept of critique, it is important not to gloss over these differences all too readily. Ignoring these conceptual differences easily leads to confusions regarding the role of the discourse analyst and the question "what if any political stance she ought to take" (Breeze 2011, 499–500).

For Kant, the articulation of critique implied a rational enterprise on the basis of a priori principles that would provide an alternative for uncritical dogmatism. Authors of the Frankfurt school used the notion of critique in order to designate a capacity to evaluate society from a particular—neo-Marxist—point of view. More generally, across a range of disciplines, the term is used today in order to conceptualise a mode of subjectivity that is critical with respect to the status quo or critical of liberal humanist perspectives, "with a view to highlighting commitment to social change". The notion can also refer to an intellectual skill that does not presuppose any particular ideological affiliation at all (Breeze 2011, 498–502). Most critical approaches to discourse are quite eclectic with respect to the philosophical and sociological grounds on which they base their (concepts of) power, emancipation and critique (Forchtner 2011; Forchtner and Tominc 2012). However, in order to come up with a more accurate description of the goals and functions of critical modes of analysis, it is important to be more precise about what we mean by critique.

Many authors in the field of critical discourse studies tend to justify their critique with reference to a set of basic convictions such as the idea that hidden power structures should be uncovered, that inequality and discrimination should be fought, that analysts should be self-reflexive with respect to their own positions and be frank about their standpoints (see Forchtner 2011; Breeze 2011). But on a theoretical level, they may use elements of very different theoretical frameworks without considering the different ontological and ethical stances these imply. Nevertheless, it makes a huge difference whether one grounds one's sense of critique in a Marxist or in a post-Marxist ontology and epistemology.

Whether one relies on Foucault or on Habermas impacts on the type of critique one can—or should—articulate as an analyst. Even though it may be rather popular to think about theories as toolboxes, this metaphor is rather inadequate because any combination of theoretical elements entails a change in perspective. In this book, I have selected elements from various theoretical traditions, the most important ones being poststructuralism, philosophical pragmatism and various modes of linguistic pragmatics. The selection and articulation of particular concepts and methods has led to something that is different from the sum of its parts.

It might be argued that the practice of critique involves different practices depending on its aims. As such, Reisigl and Wodak distinguished between three modes of critique: (1) immanent critique highlighting objectively observable contradictions within the internal structure of a text or discourse; (2) socio-diagnostic critique in which the critic takes a normative point of view in order to demystify propagandist discursive practices; and (3) prognostic or retrospective critique that seeks to transform a current state of affairs through an engagement linked to guiding principles such as human rights (Reisigl and Wodak 2001, 88). In the case of the Essex framework, critique is inseparable from analysis. It involves a mode of subjectivity that challenges the social logics that support relationships of power and domination in particular social and historical contexts.

> *The very naming of a social logic already involves critical judgement. First, as we explained above, it serves to gather together – understood in terms of articulation – what is ultimately a heterogeneous field of elements that have no 'objective' or 'necessary' connections. Second, this process of naming enables us to conjure alternative names and accompanying socio-political visions, if only because the significance of atomization in this context derives from those names and reaggregations to which it can be opposed.* (Glynos and Howarth 2007, 194–195)

A logic can function as a mode of critical explanation as it moves "between the world of self-interpretations and practices on the one hand, and our social science explanations and critiques on the other" (Glynos and Howarth 2007, 157). It is important to realise that logics—abstract as they may sound—do not function in an automatic way. They can only function in and through performative practices to the extent that they operate at the level of value rationality and self-interpretation mediated by some degree of reflexive awareness (see Flyvbjerg 2001, 42–43, 47). This goes for everyone involved in acts of self-interpretation, including social scientists themselves. By naming social logics, researchers can engage in a critique of established norms in specific social and historical contexts. But their critique can also be ethical in the sense of an orientation towards the fantasmatic operations that lead to an ideological over-identification with discourses that support or institute practices of domination.

It may be useful to provide an example. I already mentioned that a social logic of integration has characterised mainstream discourses and policies of migration in Flanders for decades. Nevertheless, most of the intellectuals and activists I interviewed proved to be highly critical of the culturalist and essentialist premises on which the dominant logic of integration was based. As we will see, the ways in which they challenged the hegemonic discourses of integration varied strongly depending on their ideological standpoints and theoretical backgrounds. But whether they articulated their preferred mode of migration politics with reference to liberal, Marxist or poststructuralist perspectives on identity and society, their struggle was always oriented towards a weakening of the homogenising premises and concepts that informed dominant thinking about diversity.

From the point of view of a perspective supportive of a radical and plural democracy, this multiplicity of critiques can only be welcomed and described in terms of various attempts to construct society and identity around an alternative set of democratic and emancipating counter-logics. Nevertheless, there are also some voices that may be critical of 'integration', but that are at least as homogenising and antagonising as the voices they challenge. Even though such discourses are relatively rare, they are relevant for purposes of illustration. In the context of Flanders, an example can be found in the discourse of *Sharia4Belgium*, an Islamist organisation whose spokesman claimed that "one is either a Muslim or a democrat" and that the "only law" he respects is "the law of Allah". Arguing for a Sharia-based state in Belgium, its spokesman Fouad Belkacem—aka Abou Imram—articulated the following message:

I say to you the audience, *I say to Filip Dewinter* chairman of the far right and racist party Vlaams Belang, *and I say to any Westerner who does not agree with Islam or with Muslims, 'Adapt or get out!'* (Fouad Belkacem cited in Vlaams Belang 2011)

A video recording of the 2011 debate in which this statement was made is still to be seen on the YouTube channel of the far right Vlaams Belang. The imperative to 'adapt' or to 'get out' is usually addressed to migrants and uttered by far right politicians such as Dewinter himself. However, this ironical usage of a far-right discursive element does not turn Belcacem's discourse democratic. I do not want to go into the logics that give rise to this particular statement. Neither do I want to suggest that this is a dominant discourse among Muslims in Flanders. I merely want to make clear that counter-logics can take many forms. Some of them may be compatible with pluralist and democratic principles while others undermine equality and difference. The opposition to dominant ideas about integration that we see in the quote above is oriented towards the myth of a totalitarian political project grounded on an essentialist and undemocratic interpretation of Islam. Democracy is an obstacle to be overcome in the struggle for a state in which this interpretation of Islam acquires a completely hegemonic status.

But I cannot stress enough that critique of mainstream discourses of integration usually takes very different forms. One can oppose homogenising logics of integration by articulating an alternative political project informed by socialist, liberal, pluralist, citizenship-based concepts of political subjectivity. For instance, instead of a homogenising and assimilatory logic of integration, it is possible to identify logics of integration based on liberal and pluralist principles. Some interviewees rejected the notion of integration altogether whereas most reformulated it in accordance with their preferred modes of subjectivity. And sometimes they did both things at the same time, refusing the notion in some contexts and using it in others. At any rate, even though all types of critique are meant to challenge and dislocate the status quo, there is a great difference in terms of the extent to which subjects mark their awareness of the contingent nature of their own project and the validity of the existence of political adversaries and alternative projects.

It is also important to emphasise that my interviewees did not merely articulate very different counter-logics in relation to the dominant concept of integration than the one informing an undemocratic organisation such as *Sharia4Belgium*. Their mode of ideological investment is different as well. All of my interviewees reflected upon their own words and thus highlighted the contingency of their standpoints. At the same time, they invested their subjectivities with ethical considerations and a great deal of affect. They questioned the discourses of others and their relationships to themselves, while rearticulating a multiplicity of voices echoing in the public sphere. I will provide many examples of such statements in the chapters to come. As such, the question of critique will pop up regularly throughout this book as a quintessential political and intellectual praxis.

2.8 Fixing Meaning Through Performativity and Subjectivity

Researchers are certainly not the only actors capable of articulating patterns of coherence in the discourses that surround us. In fact, the identification of large-scale social and political patterns—theorised here as logics—is a key requirement for the development of any form of political awareness. In this sense, logics are always interpretive. The subject that articulates such logics is constituted through this very practice. The ability of human beings to partially fix meanings is co-dependent with their ability to achieve some degree of discursive coherence and a corresponding mode of self-understanding.

Logics can therefore be defined as interpretive patterns that inform and shape one's sense of self. They do so by establishing relationships with preferred and disavowed mode of subjectivity. They also inform the mode of relationships one establishes with others and with oneself. Logics are basically configurations of articulatory practices that establish functional relationships between subject positions, statements, practices, topics and other discursive elements relevant to an understanding of self and other. As such, they positively and negatively define preferred and disavowed modes of political subjectivity.

Glynos and Howarth argue that the naming and description of social logics of critical explanation should be based—partially—on the self-understandings of one's research subjects. But the subject is not a straightforward entity with nicely delineated boundaries. From a poststructuralist perspective, subjects are neither transparent nor unified. We may come to ourselves in and through discourse, but we also have the potential to act reflexively upon ourselves and upon others. We can lie, cheat, joke, exaggerate, be ignorant, naïve or paranoid, withhold information or tell a euphemistic version of what we consider to be the truth about ourselves. To complicate things further, we all have concepts of the self that function as working frameworks of what and who we are. And these frameworks are always incomplete and may or may not be compatible with academic modes of explanation.

Within poststructuralist thought, the concept of a 'subject' has always been a very tricky notion, subject to a great deal of debate and misunderstanding. On the one hand, there is a notion of the subject as "subject to someone else by control and dependence". On the other hand, one can be a subject in the sense of someone who is "tied to his own identity by a conscience or self-knowledge" (Foucault 1982b). This ambiguity also pops up in the linguistic senses of the word. The subject of a sentence can be performing an action but can also be subjected to it. This observation leads us to questions about the relationship between subjectivity on the one hand, and power, subjugation, domination and violence on the other hand. But before we go into these notions, it is important to focus on the Foucaultian concept of a subject position and on the concept of 'the death of the subject'.

At first sight, the notion of a subject position may seem rather static. The spatial metaphor of a position suggests the existence of a sociodiscursive field in which one can occupy specific locations that determine one's outlook as well as one's action radius. Nevertheless, subject positions are more dynamic than this. In the archaeological framework of Michel Foucault, subject positions are first and foremost functions of so-called 'statements'. Statements are the basic units of analysis in Foucault's concept of discourse. Foucault emphasises that the statement or the *énoncé* cannot be reduced to a speech act, a sentence, a sign, a logical proposition or any other aspect of language use. All of these linguistic and semiotic elements may function *as* statements to the extent that they establish functional relationships between objects and subjects. A statement is characterised by its objectifying and subjectifying functions. The analysis of statements therefore involves a functional analysis of so-called subject positions.

Contradicting the idea that his theory of subject positions constitutes a static and deterministic view on individuality, Foucault explains that he tried to demonstrate "how it was possible for men, with the same discursive practice to speak of different objects, to have contrary opinions, and to make contradictory choices". His "aim was also to show in what way discursive practices were distinguished from one another". Put differently, he "wanted not to exclude the problem of the subject, but to define the positions and functions that the subject could occupy in the diversity of discourse" (Foucault 1969, 221). The differentiation between the Foucaultian statement (*l'énoncé*) and the linguistic utterance (*énonciation*) is at least partly motivated by a functional relationship that the statement possesses vis-à-vis the subject; "to describe a formulation qua statement does not consist in analysing the relations between the author and what he says (or wanted to say, or said without wanting to); but in determining what position can and must be occupied by any individual if he is the subject of it" (Foucault 1969, 107).

Foucault emphasised that the subject of the statement should not be confused with the grammatical subject of the sentence. The subject of the statement is labelled as a vacant place that may be occupied by different individuals. At odds with a more structuralist conceptualisation of the subject position, he points out that this place is "variable enough to be able either to persevere, unchanging, through several sentences, or to alter with each one" (Foucault 1969, 107). A Foucaultian analysis of statements thus involves a functional analysis of subject positions. But we are dealing with a very specific concept of function that is not to be confused with some trans-historical systemic or structural functionalism (see Brenner 1994). In contrast, we are dealing with a historicised and relational concept of function that may be described in terms of articulation and pragmatic effect. Functions can be thought about as temporary and flexible relationships between discursive elements that establish contexts for interpretation and positioning. To produce a statement involves a functional articulation of the self with multiple subject positions. And this is never an entirely un-reflexive process, no matter how static the idea of a subject position may seem.

My emphasis on the reflexivity and flexibility of Foucault's subject may be rather atypical. It goes against the grain of a more popular interpretation whereby Foucault is said to be celebrating the so-called 'death of the subject' in a way that "amounts to nothing short of a wholesale repudiation of the concept of subjectivity". Adherents of this anti-subjective reading accuse him of ignoring the self-reflective understandings of individuals. They claim that Foucault's subject is nothing more but an arbitrary effect of discourse and power. Different variations of this critique can be found in the works of authors as varied as Jürgen Habermas, Axel Honneth, Thomas Mccarth, Michael Walzer, Nancy Hartsock and Linda Alcoff. But there are also supporters of Foucault who defend the latter's work by acknowledging that the anti-subjective hypothesis may hold for Foucault's archaeological and geneaological work but is overcome in later writings. Amy Allen refers to Richard Bernstein as a case in point (Allen 2000, 115–117):

> *One might think ... that Foucault is heralding the death of the subject, that he is claiming that the subject itself is only the result of the effects of power/knowledge regimes, that he completely undermines and ridicules any and all talk of human agency. There is plenty of textual evidence to support such claims. But it is also clear, especially in his late writings when he deals with the question of the self's relation to itself and the possibility of 'the man who tries to invent himself', that he is not abandoning the idea that 'we constitute ourselves as subjects acting on others'.* (Bernstein quoted in Allen 2000, 218)

In contrast, Allen argues that the anti-subjective hypothesis does not apply to any phase of Foucault's work. I agree with her. It is true that Foucault designed his genealogical work as a mode of analysis that aims to "dispense with the constituent subject" and as an approach that does not need to make "reference to a subject which is either transcendental in relation to the field of events or turns in its empty sameness throughout the course of history" (Foucault cited in Allen 2000, 121). Foucault also acknowledged that his early archaeological analyses begin at the level of discourse rather than at the level of individual subjects or agents. Nevertheless,

2 Discourse Theory on the Logics of Articulation, Politics... 71

this should not be taken as a denial of the possible efficacy of any subject centred account (Allen 2000, 122). Foucault put it as follows:

> *If I suspended all reference to the speaking subject, it was not to discover laws of construction or forms that could be applied in the same way by all subjects, nor was it to give voice to the great universal discourse that is common to all men at a particular period.* [...] *I wanted not to exclude the problem of the subject, but to define the positions and functions that the subject could occupy in the diversity of discourse.* (Foucault 1969, 220–221)

Even in his early work, Foucault addressed the double-edged issue of reflexivity and consciousness directly. At the end of the *Archaeology of knowledge*, he explicitly denied that his theory condemns subjects to conformity and obligation: "I have not denied –far from it– the possibility of changing discourse: I have deprived the sovereignty of the subject of the exclusive and instantaneous right to it" (Foucault 1969, 228–230). If there is one stance shared by all poststructuralist authors, it is probably this sceptical attitude with respect to the idea of man as a unified and centred structure that functions as the centre of knowledge, reason, experience and discourse. Poststructuralists take a critical stance with respect to the idea that man has always functioned in the same way across various social, political and historical contexts. As such, they reject any transcendent understanding of subjectivity as a basis for analysis.[1]

It is important to understand that the metaphorical 'death' of the subject refers to the end of a particular *mode, model, and understanding* of the self in terms of a transcendental and ahistorical subjectivity. It does not refer to the disappearance of subjectivity as such. What had to be dispensed with was not the subject in its generality but the constituent subject as a monocausal explanation for historical development.

---

[1] The transcendental self is a philosophical figure that has occupied a central place in philosophy ever since Descartes wrote: "I think, therefore I am." This self was conceptualised as a rather abstract and singular entity that functioned in a timeless and universal way, independent of "the artifices and superficialities of the social whirl" (Solomon 1988). It was transcendent because it was to be distinguished from individual particularities. The transcendental self—whether conceptualised as the Cartesian cogito or as the soul of humanity—has informed claims for radical egalitarianism and for global sensitivities, but it has also justified paternalism and self-righteousness with respect to Western superiority over non-Western ideas, practices and concepts of the self (Solomon 1988, 1–4; Holstein and Gubrium 2000, 18–20).

Structuralists (Saussure, Lévi-Strauss, Althusser) and poststructuralists (Lacan, Foucault, Derrida, Laclau) have undermined the idea that human beings are completely sovereign in relation to their own rationality and authenticity (Hall 2004, 87). They have demonstrated that subjectivity and individuality do not originate in the individual but emerge in and through relationships of discourse and power. Such observations do not pre-empt the possibility of some degree of reflexivity. But it does imply a movement of the subject "from the position of that which explains to the position of that which must be explained, from *explanans* to *explanandum*" (Allen 2000, 120–121).

Authors such as Michel Foucault and Judith Butler have come to think about the subject as an effect of both discourse and power. But they also considered the subject as being constituted through the practice of concrete techniques and performances. Butler points out that speech is always produced through bodies. As such, it is not merely a matter of linguistics but also a matter of embodiment (Rothenberg 2006). The sense of coherence and integrity characteristic of human subjectivity comes to us through the performative practices of the body. Like all poststructuralists, she takes an anti-essentialist view on subjectivity. Her statements about the gendered body shed some interesting light on subjectivity as a performative effect.

> *That the gendered body is performative suggests that it has no ontological status apart from the various acts which constitute its reality. This also suggests that if that reality is fabricated as an interior essence, that very interiority is an effect and function of a decidedly public and social discourse, the public regulation of fantasy through the surface politics of the body, the gender border control that differentiates inner from outer, and so institutes the "integrity" of the subject. In other words, acts and gestures, articulated and enacted desires create the illusion of an interior and organizing gender core, an illusion discursively maintained for the purposes of the regulation of sexuality within the obligatory frame of reproductive heterosexuality.* (Butler 1990, 185–186)

Butler draws our attention to a dimension of articulation that is often overlooked or left implicit in Essex discourse theoretical work. Her emphasis on the performative dimension of articulatory practices allows us to theorise the under-theorised artistic and/or musical senses of the word. The production of discourse and subjectivity is never a matter of linking elements to each other alone. Any (linguistic or non-linguistic) practice of articulation is an embodied act that is performed in a particular way: "the speech act is at once performed (and thus theatrical, presented to an audience, subject to interpretation), and linguistic, inducing a set of effects through its implied relation to linguistic conventions" (Butler 1999, xxvii). Every articulation requires acts that link various non-linguistic and linguistic elements to each other. Such acts are performed through embodied practices that can be observed empirically.

The status of the speech act as word and deed is necessarily ambiguous. The same should be said about the principle of articulation. The articulation of a series of musical notes is always more than a connection of successive elements. They are always also articulated in a particular mode. Relying on Austin's speech act theory, Butler highlights the performative power of speech. Some words, uttered in specific contexts, have the power to change or redefine social identities and realities. Through embodied discursive acts and performances, one can also reshape and rearticulate one's embodied and performed subjectivity.

2.9 Fixing Meaning Through Power, Domination and Subjectivation

To say that the subject is an effect of discourse and power does not necessarily mean that the subject is a structural dupe. This depends entirely on the concepts of discourse and power involved. The idea that power is everywhere does not mean that it only comes to us in a form we cannot grasp or that it determines every aspect of saying, doing and/or being in a way that precludes the possibility of reflexivity and change. Rather, both power and discourse can take many contingent and historical forms that allow us to shape who and what we are. It is anything but stable. I have tried to show that Foucault's concepts of discourse and subjectivity are relational and functional. The same goes for his concept of power. Foucault recommends us not to look for an essentialist definition of power but to wonder *how* power is exercised in concrete relationships:

To put it bluntly, I would say that to begin the analysis with a "how" is to introduce the suspicion that power as such does not exist. It is, in any case, to ask oneself what contents one has in mind when using this grand, all-embracing, and reifying term; it is to suspect that an extremely complex configuration of realities is allowed to escape while one endlessly marks time before the double question: what is power, and where does power come from. The flat and empirical little question, "What happens?" is not designed to introduce by stealth a metaphysics or an ontology of power but, rather, to undertake a critical investigation of the thematics of power. (Foucault 1982b, 336–337)

Foucault warns us against reifying power. One cannot analyse it in the abstract, as if power can be understood independently from the concrete relationships in which it manifests itself. He points out that any analysis of the laws, institutions, ideologies, structures or mechanisms of power is based on the premise that "certain persons exercise power over others". In this sense, "the term power designates relationships between 'partners' (and by this I [Foucault] am not thinking of a game with fixed rules but simply, and for the moment staying in the most general terms, of an ensemble of actions that induce others and follow from one another)" (Foucault 1982b, 337). As a consequence, power itself can never be analysed. We have to content ourselves with an analysis of historically grounded power relations between concrete actors (Foucault 1982b, 339).

Foucault investigated various modes of power such as pastoral power (see: Foucault 1979b, see: Foucault 1982b, 333–335), juridico-discursive power (see: Foucault 1976, 82–91), power as strategy and tactics (see: Foucault 1976, 100–102), biopolitics or biopower (Foucault 1979a), power as war (see: Foucaultet al. 1997, 1–23) and governmentality (see: Foucault 1979a). The institution of a specific type of power relationship in a particular historical period is always intertwined with a specific form of rationality. For this reason, "those who resist or rebel against a form of power cannot merely be content to denounce violence or criticize an institution". Rather, "what has to be questioned is the form of rationality at stake" (Foucault 1979b, 324). Every concept of power named and described by Foucault therefore involves a mode of rationality that articulates individuals as subjects and objects in an unequal and ever-changing world.

In the light of our discussion on the (death of) subjectivity, it is important to realise that Foucault distinguishes between power on the one hand

2 Discourse Theory on the Logics of Articulation, Politics...

and domination or violence on the other hand: "what defines a relationship of power is that it is a mode of action that does not act directly and immediately on others. Instead, it acts upon their actions: an action upon an action, on possible or actual future or present actions." A relationship of violence does not work in this subtle way: it "acts upon a body or upon things; it forces, it bends, it breaks, it destroys, or it closes of possibilities" (Foucault 1982b, 340). To Foucault, "the exercise of power is a 'conduct of conducts' and a management of possibilities". It is here that he links up with the notion of government in a very particular and broad sense of the word and where he distinguishes power from something like slavery:

When one defines the exercise of power as a mode of action upon the action of others, when one characterizes these actions as the government of men by other men – in the broadest sense of the term – one includes an important element: freedom. Power is exercised only over free subjects, and only insofar as they are "free". By this we mean individual or collective subjects who are faced with a field of possibilities in which several kinds of conduct, several ways of reacting and modes of behavior are available. Where the determining factors are exhaustive, there is no relationship of power: slavery is not a power relationship when a man is in chains, only when he has some possible mobility, even a chance of escape. (Foucault 1982b, 342)

In an interview on *Sex, power, and the politics of identity* (Foucault 1982a), Foucault described power relations as strategic relations towards one another. It is in this sense that "power is always there" and that we cannot get away from it. Practices of resistance thus never involve positioning oneself outside of power, since this would involve a retreat from the relationship(s) we hold towards others—an impossibility. Nevertheless, this does not mean that there is no room for agency. Even though "there is no point where you are free from all power relations", "you can always change" the power relations you are involved in (Foucault 1982a, 167). For Foucault, the exercise of power is not a matter of mere obedience:

You see, if there was no resistance, there would be no power relations. Because it would simply be a matter of obedience. You have to use power relations to refer to the situation where you're not doing what you want. So resistance comes first, and resistance remains superior to the forces of the process; power relations are obliged to change with the resistance. So I think that resistance *is the main word,* the key word, *in this dynamic.* (Foucault 1982a, 167)

Thomas Lemke points out that to Foucault, the concept of domination refers to a rather stable, hierarchical and fixed power relationship that is difficult to reverse. He uses the term domination to designate "what we ordinarily call power" (Foucault cited in Lemke 2002). We should therefore keep in mind that Foucault's notions of power differ from this more common meaning of power. With respect to domination, Foucault acknowledges that:

states of domination do indeed exist. In a great many cases, power relations are fixed in such a way that they are perpetually asymmetrical and allow an extremely limited margin of freedom. […] *In such cases of domination, be they economic, social, institutional, or sexual, the problem is knowing where resistance will develop.* […] *In such a situation of domination, all these questions demand specific answers that take account of the kind and precise form of domination in question. But the claim that "you see power everywhere, thus there is no room for freedom" seems to me absolutely inadequate. The idea that power is a system of domination that controls everything and leaves no room for freedom cannot be attributed to me.* (Foucault 1989, 292–293)

For Foucault, "nothing, including the exercise of power, is evil in itself – but everything is dangerous" (Faubion 1994, xix). If we are to understand how the subject is constituted as an effect of power, knowledge and discourse, we have to investigate the specific techniques that shape our sense of self as well as the conduct of our conduct. Such techniques are relatively autonomous and can be transposed between various historical periods and social institutions. For instance, we can think of the techniques employed in slave colonies in Latin America which turn up later in nineteenth-century France or England (Trombadori and Foucault 1980, 293). Other examples include interactional practices such as the confession or the interview that can be conceptualised as technologies that allow us to generate a particular relationship towards ourselves. Considering the centrality of interview data in this book about self and politics in activist discourse, it is useful to discuss the function of the interview as an articulatory technology of the self.

2.10 Fixing Meanings Through the Self-technique of the Interview

The analysis of self-interpretations marked by individuals in discourse requires that we analyse the articulation of selves to themselves as well as to others. In this sense, a focus on self-techniques becomes a useful heuristic guideline. Nicolas Rose thinks of these articulations in terms of 'assemblages'. He claims that all of the effects of psychological interiority—thoughts, emotions and the like—as well as other capacities and relations are established through the linkage of humans into other objects, practices and forces. As such, subjects are assembled or articulated entities that come to themselves as desiring selves, as sexed selves, as labouring selves or as intending selves capable of acting as subjects. To Rose, subjects are nothing more or less than the changing connections into which they are associated (Rose 1998, 172). Such a concept of the self rests on a process of reification of various processes.

To Foucault, the self is form rather than substance. It is not always identical to itself. Foucault points out that you do not have the same type of relationship to yourself when you vote, when you speak at a meeting or when you try to fulfil your desires in a sexual relationship: "Undoubtedly there are relationships and inferences between these different forms of the subject; but we are not dealing with the same type of subject. In each case, one plays, one establishes a different type of relation to oneself. And it is precisely the historical constitution of these various forms of the subject in relation to the games of truth which interest me" (Foucault 1989, 290–291). The idea of the self as a form that takes the shape of its assemblage rhymes nicely with the idea of the self as a multidimensional process of articulation. Perhaps, the self can be viewed as a reification of the processes that allow individual bodies to reflexively position themselves as more or less coherent mind/bodies in relation to spatial, temporal, social and (inter)textual aspects of (contextual reality). The self is just as stable as the self-techniques, performances and relative fixations of meaning we use to give ourselves the semblance of substance. Our selves may be relatively unified and centred, but only to the extent that our interpretive logics and self-techniques enable us to be.

One of the most widely distributed self-techniques in the social sciences is without a doubt the interview. At first sight, the interview may seem to be an unproblematic and transparent activity with clearly defined roles for interviewers and interviewees. Interviewees have traditionally been conceptualised as rather passive vessels of answers or as repositories of facts, feelings and experiences. They hold answers about demographic questions related to age, gender, race, occupation, social networks, circles of care and other aspects of human relationships. Interviewees are thereby often considered to possess *a priori* opinions and knowledge that can be extracted by researchers as long as they stick closely to a set of pre-defined rules that define the interview situation. Such rules supposedly ensure the neutrality and authenticity of the interaction and are meant to avoid the generation of data characterised by bias and contamination (Gubrium and Holstein 2003b, 30–32). Interestingly, these rules can be reframed in terms of technologies of power and subjectivity.

When Foucault writes about techniques, he does not refer to hard technologies such as wood, fire or electricity. His notion of technology relies on Aristotle's idea of *techne* as a practical rationality governed by a conscious goal. This notion of *techne* implies the performance of practices that rely on intellectual virtue as well as on pragmatic and context-dependent knowledge. Governmental practices that regulate the conduct of conduct can be thought about as functions of technologies: for example, the government of individuals, the government of souls, the government of families, the government of children and—last but not least—the government of the self by the self (Flyvbjerg 2001, 364; Foucault and Rabinow 1982).

Nicolas Rose points out that human technologies are hybrid assemblages in which forms of knowledge, instruments, systems of judgement, buildings, spaces and persons ground "certain presuppositions and objectives about human beings" (Rose 1998). As such, the above-mentioned (model of) the interview supports and generates a particular relationship of the self to the self and to the public realm. Gubrium and Holstein consider the modern interview to be one of the most important technologies of the self of the twentieth century. The above-mentioned ideas on the practice of interviewing projected an aura of scientific and/or journalistic objectivity into the very concept of individuality while simultaneously generating a reified understanding of public opinion and the public sphere (Gubrium and Holstein 2003b).

However, if one considers the "pragmatic complexity of interview data" and the problematic assumptions underlying notions such as bias, distortion, reliability and validity of interactional data, it becomes necessary to rethink the interview. Doing so, Gubrium and Holstein argue in favour of a more active approach to interviewing that takes poststructuralist and pragmatist insights into the functions of subjectivity into account.

> *Interview roles are less clear than they once were; in some cases they are even exchanged to promote new opportunities for understanding the shape and evolutions of selves and experience. Standardised representation has given way to representational invention, where the dividing line between fact and fiction becomes blurred to encourage richer understanding. Reflexivity, poetics, and power are the watchwords as the interview process is refracted through the lenses of language, knowledge, culture, and difference.* (Gubrium and Holstein 2003d, 3)

The active approach to interviewing advocated by Holstein and Gubrium implies a rearticulation of the traditional relationship between interviewer and interviewee. It allows us to recognise the inter-subjective ways in which interviewers and interviewees generate and mark their reflexive, metalinguistic or metapragmatic awareness in discourse. Their postmodern view on the interview acknowledges the fact that interviews are constitutive not merely for the subjectivities of the conversational partners involved but also for their articulatory relationships with respect to other voices and practices in the public realm. They rearticulate the roles of interviewee and interviewer as follows:

> *Where standardised approaches to interviewing attempt to strip the interview of all but the most neutral stimuli (but see Holstein and Gubrium 1995 for a discussion of the inevitable failure of these attempts), the consciously active interviewer intentionally provokes responses by indicating – even suggesting narrative positions, resources, orientations, and precedents. In the broadest sense, the interviewer attempts to activate the respondents' stock of knowledge (Schutz 1967) and bring it to bear on the discussion at hand in ways that are appropriate to the research agenda.* (Gubrium and Holstein 2003a, 75)

As such, the interviewer may encourage the interviewee to shift positions in order to alternate perspectives and stocks of knowledge. He or she abandons the quest for authentic answers (Gubrium and Holstein 2003a, 77). The active interviewer considers the various discursive functions that the co-constructed discourse may have vis-à-vis the topic(s) under discussion. Such an approach impacts upon the type of data that are being generated as well as on the way these data can be analysed.

An analysis of active interviews should show the dynamic interrelatedness of the *whats* and the *hows* of communication. The focus should be as much on the assembly process as on what is assembled (Gubrium and Holstein 2003a, 79). Also, the multiple subject positions that may be activated throughout the interaction should be taken into account. This goes for both the interviewer and the interviewee: "the active subject behind the interviewer thus becomes a necessary, practical counterpart to the active subject behind the respondent" (Gubrium and Holstein 2003b, 33). Of course, this is not to say that there is some Cartesian puppeteer behind our subjectivity. This becomes clear when Gubrium and Holstein explicitly refer to the importance of analysing subject positions and voices in relation to issues of ownership and empowerment (Gubrium and Holstein 2003b, 35–42).

The issue of voice is important since it "references the subject position that is taken for granted behind speech". Gubrium and Holstein claim that "voice works at the level of everyday life, whereas subject positions are what we imagined to be their operating standpoints" (Gubrium and Holstein 2003b, 39). They are fully aware of the fact that both interviewer and interviewee continually shift between subject positions as the interview process proceeds. These shifts are not always made explicitly. Moreover, this shifting is a process that hinges upon reflexivity with respect to one's own sense of self and with respect to the perception of the other participant—interviewer and/or interviewee—engaged in the interview (Gubrium and Holstein 2003b, 39–40; Ellis and Berger 2003, 160–165). An active approach to interviewing implies a concern with empowerment and domination.

Many of my respondents displayed a high degree of metalinguistic or metapragmatic awareness of the fact that they entered into an unequal situation, asking for clear agreements with respect to my usage of their

2 Discourse Theory on the Logics of Articulation, Politics... 81

discourse and their names within the context of this research project. These concerns were indicative of the political dimension of the social-scientific interviews I conducted. Such speech events can therefore be conceptualised in terms of interactively established sites that enable participants to (re-)articulate a multiplicity of socio-political positionings and engagements. Since political engagement involves a rearticulation of socio-political patterns in a public sphere through (imagined) collective action, the interview can be constitutive of the public sphere as well as of the political engagement of the actors involved.

Charles Briggs points out that interviews are usually designed to produce information that will be recontextualised in books, articles, reports, media productions and so on. Interviews often serve as media or language games that provide the institutions of the nation state with representations of its marginalised populations. He points out that throughout this process, the possibility of constructing a minority voice that merely confirms the hegemonic status quo becomes acute (Briggs 2003, 244). Being "popular" as a research topic in the social sciences is therefore a "rather dubious honour", as one of my interviewees put it.

Like any other technology, the interview can function in emancipatory as well as in exploitative or dominating ways. Gubrium and Holstein emphasise its emancipatory or empowering potential. Their point is not that interviewers should seek to liberate or rearticulate a so-called authentic voice. Rather, the active interviewer promotes an approach that forces interviewers to "provide respondents with the opportunity to convey [their] stories to us [interviewers] on their own terms rather than deploy predesignated categories or other structured formats for doing so" (Gubrium and Holstein 2003b, 36). Put differently, when researchers recontextualise or rearticulate interview data, it is important that one devotes attention to the *how* as well as to the *what* of this process. This sensitivity with respect to the self-interpretations of research subjects should go hand in hand with an analysis of the relationship between the forms and functions of the discourse that interviewer and interviewee co-establish.

In a Foucaultian argument, Charles Briggs points out that the power of interviewers over interviewees does not merely lie in the control they exert upon the interaction itself but also in their ability to use the interview as a setting geared towards the creation of a field for the circulation of discourse. The power-related processes involved are often rendered invisible in order to seem unbiased or neutral. This involves various decontextualisations. Briggs refers to Atkinson and Silverman (Briggs 2003, 248):

> *Atkinson and Silverman (1997) observe that even many critical, revisionist approaches to interviewing attempt to empower individuals to create biographical, authentic voices, thereby reifying an individual and confessional approach to discourse that is also promoted by corporate media. The indexical signs that point, as it were, to the embedding of this process in larger social and material structures are thus largely erased.* (Briggs 2003, 248)

The issue of empowerment and the question who owns the voice(s) rearticulated in interview contexts is especially poignant to the question of minority discourse. Without a significant degree of metapragmatic awareness with respect to the way researchers deploy their categories, they run a serious risk of overpowering the voices of interviewees. The localised utterances articulated in interviews are valuable to researchers to the extent that they say something about wider patterns of signification that are distributed among a multiplicity of actors. Interviews can be used in order to tell us something about local, regional, national or supranational structures. Individualised utterances about social reality can index common attitudes, relationships, meanings and inequalities. But the interpretation of such utterances should be conducted with great care.

The classification of respondents as members of particular cultures, ethnicities or races can easily lead to the suggestion that an utterance performed by someone with a Moroccan background is uttered *as* someone with a Moroccan background, representing all members of a supposedly homogeneous community. The reduction of others to one-sided subjects is an analytical mistake that opens up the door to unwarranted generalisations and stereotypes. Moreover, the mere inclusion of minority voices in research projects does not necessarily entail an inclusion of these voices in national conversations and debates (see Briggs 2003, 249).

My interviewees proved to be very much aware of the dangers that Briggs warns us about. The interview excerpts in Chap. 1 exemplify that not every statement articulated by a Muslim constitutes an Islamic voice. Researchers permanently run the risk of creating an image of the public sphere that is not in sync with the self-representations and self-interpretations articulated by interviewees. It is for this very reason that I have been searching for a way of tackling interview data so that the voices of my respondents may be rearticulated in an empowering rather than in a dominating way. I believe that the type of interpretive functionalism outlined in this book provides a promising avenue for such an endeavour.

As such, I will think of interviews in terms of inter-subjective articulatory practices that can function as self-techniques that shape subjectivity. Interview practices involve a game of positioning whereby interviewers and interviewees position themselves in relation to themselves as well as in relation to an imagined public sphere and to the imagined entities that populate it. Such relationships may be characterised by solidarity, adversity, antagonism, friendship, love and/or hate. They can take as many forms as discursive creativity and reality allow for. As such, the interview can function as a site for the (re-)articulation of large-scale interpretive logics in a co-constructed public sphere. The interview is merely one potential site in which a partial fixation of self and society can be realised.

2.11 Methodological Deficits and Challenges in Poststructuralist Discourse Theory

The time has come to consider the heuristic challenges that a multidimensional concept of articulation presents for a research project about self and politics in activist discourse. More specifically, we need to explore its implications with respect to research conducted on the basis of interviews with intellectuals and activists engaged in minority politics.

In the first chapter of this book, I concluded by summarising some useful characteristics for an approach that allows us to deal with such complex discourse. I demonstrated how my interviewees used a multiplicity of abstract categories to give meaning to their lives and to their political projects. They articulated a multitude of identities with each other while simultaneously constructing relatively high degrees of cohesion and interpretive coherence. At the same time, the complexities of their discourse challenged any straightforward understanding of the unity of my object of investigation. In fact, even the most traditional categories that one would associate with research into the political world views of minority members—for example, culture, identity and politics—became refracted through the lenses of their political gaze.

I have tried to show that the concept of articulation allows for an understanding of such observations. The poststructuralist frameworks formulated above provide us with a vocabulary to think the complexity of the interpretive processes involved. Individual statements about integration, identity, self and politics can be interpreted as techniques that allow individuals to assemble and to articulate themselves as selves. Both subjectivities and large-scale debates can be discussed in terms of logics. Moreover, activist interview practices can be conceptualised as self-techniques through which such logics operate. The frameworks introduced above thus provide us with a vocabulary with which to think the complex imaginaries that structure our relationships towards ourselves as well as towards our engagements with each other, with society and with politics.

In the context of a discussion on methodological issues, it should be noted that Essex authors do not only write about abstract notions such as identity, hegemony or difference. Their analyses frequently focus on concrete issues such as the construction of a new airport runway (Griggs and Howarth 2000), the Israeli–Palestinian conflict (Bowman 1994), identity and hegemony in former Yugoslavia (Saleel 1994) or Peronist populism (Barros and Castagnola 2000). It would be incorrect to say that the empirical dimension of discourse is wholly ignored. Especially in more recent work, bridges between different approaches to discourse are being built (Glynos and Howarth 2007; Glynos et al. 2012; Dahlberg and Phelan 2011). Nevertheless, case studies in readers such as *Discourse theory and political analysis* (Howarth et al. 2000), *The making of political identities* (Laclau 1994b) or *Discourse theory and European politics* (Howarth and Torfing 2005) hardly ever detail how data were gathered or analysed.

The question how to investigate articulatory practices is usually met with vague answers about the relative fixation of meaning. But even more frequent is a general avoidance of methodological issues in general. In part, this lack of interest can be explained by the fact that most Essex

2 Discourse Theory on the Logics of Articulation, Politics... 85

authors refuse to distinguish between theory and method. But it is hard to see how this refusal could justify the lack of explicitness with respect to the heuristic, methodological, and/or analytical operations carried out in discourse theoretical studies. Many discourse theorists restrict themselves to illustrations of pre-established theoretical principles and arguments. According to Torfing, too many of them "have thrown the methodological baby out with the epistemological bath water" (Torfing 2005, 27). He therefore argues that discourse theorists should solve a number of issues.

First of all, poststructuralist discourse theorists need to demonstrate the analytical value of their perspective in empirical studies that go beyond mere illustrations of arguments and concepts. Secondly, core topics within social and political science should be addressed. This means that discourse theorists should not focus exclusively on issues such as gender, ethnicity and social movements. And thirdly, discourse theory needs to reflect critically upon questions of method and strategy without surrendering to a positivist obsession with method that is based on the belief that the observation of a set of methodological rules would somehow guarantee the truth or reliability of research results. More generally, Jacob Torfing states that "there is an urgent need for critical, explicit and context-bound discussion of what we do in discourse analysis, why we do it, and what the consequences are" (Torfing 2005, 25–28). The book *Logics of critical explanation in social and political theory* constitutes a direct response to this call (Glynos and Howarth 2007, 6–7).

In addition to relatively explicit discussions of practices of naming and critique in discourse theory, Glynos and Howarth reconsider every step in the research process in terms of articulation. Every stage of the research process—from the initial problematisation, over the generation of data (though interviews, focus groups, desk research, participant observation or data mining), to the presentation of research results (in the form of handouts, presentations, papers or books)—involves (re-)articulations of discursive elements that generate and modify the meanings of the phenomena under investigation (Howarth 2000, 140–141, Glynos and Howarth 2007, 180–181). As such, the production of scientific discourse is subject to the same principles of articulation as any other set of language games.

Howarth and Glynos provide us with heuristic recommendations concerning the naming of social logics and recommend us to go through the self-interpretations of subjects. And even though the exact manner in which this should happen remains rather vague, it should be recognised that their work constitutes an important step towards more explicitness about heuristic and methodological considerations in discourse theory. Method is thereby not conceptualised as a set of neutral rules or techniques that can be applied mechanically to all objects. Rather, "while discourse theorists ought to reflect upon and theorize the ways they conduct research, these questions are always understood within a wider set of ontological and epistemological postulates and in relation to particular problems" (Howarth 2005, 317).

Howarth considers poststructuralist discourse theory to be problem-driven and distinguishes it from method- and theory-driven research. Whereas method-driven approaches emphasise techniques of data-gathering and analysis over the empirical phenomena under investigation, theory-driven research tends "to vindicate a particular theory" rather than "illuminate a problem that is specified independently of the theory" (Shapiro 2002, 601 cited in Howarth 2005: 318). Moreover, Howarth argues that problem-driven research should not be confused with problem-solving theory. The latter generally "takes existing social structures as a given, as well as the assumptions of the dominant theories of such reality, and then addresses anomalies that arise within such frameworks". By contrast, problem-driven research begins with a set of pressing political and ethical problems in the present and seeks to analyse the historical and structural conditions that gave rise to them (Howarth 2005, 318).

My investigation of the subjectivities and engagements of activists and intellectuals with a Moroccan background in Flanders constitutes a rearticulation of a number of problems. The combined effect of the overlap between political and academic terminologies about minority issues, the problems pertaining to the presupposed unity of my object(s) of investigation, and the interlacing logics that complicated the discourse and the subjectivities of my respondents required a thorough reconsideration of my initial research topic. It forced me to rearticulate the original research topic—Islamic political identities in the Moroccan communities of Flanders—as an investigation into the subjectivities and logics of intellectuals and activists with a Moroccan background in Flanders. In this rearticulated research project, issues of self and politics would be foregrounded and constitute the basis for a critique of key features of the hegemonic discourse(s) on minorities and minority issues in Flanders.

In order to come up with a systematic approach that would allow me to name the logics that structure the discourses of hegemonic and counter-hegemonic forces in the Flemish minority debates, it had to tackle some of the remaining problems related to the methodological deficit. All of these problems touch upon the linguistic and inter-subjective aspects of self-interpretations and logics of critical explanation. We already noticed that discourse theorists are reluctant to draw a strict boundary between theory and analysis as far as their own approach is concerned. It is therefore all the more striking that they frequently label their own approach as 'discourse theory' while distinguishing it from other approaches that are lumped together under the header of 'discourse analysis'.

Poststructuralist discourse theorists don't like to reduce discourse to mere auditory or textual phenomena. Their category of discourse certainly includes spoken and written words, but it also includes identities or subject positions, socio-political practices and not merely their labels. They tend not to make an analytical distinction between the linguistic and the non-linguistic aspects of meaning while affirming that no objects are given to us outside of discursive conditions of emergence. To them, any analytical distinction between linguistic and behavioural aspects of social practice is either invalid or based upon a particular discourse itself. Referring to Wittgenstein, they argue that language and action are part and parcel of the same language games (Laclau and Mouffe 1985, 107–108). Critique with respect to the methodological vagueness of the approach is often pre-empted with reference to the claim that Essex authors are more interested in the ontological and epistemological status of political identities and projects than in their linguistic or inter-subjective manifestations.

Nevertheless, a rigid distinction between discourse theory on the one hand and more 'linguistic' or 'textual' approaches on the other hand does not make sense if one takes the concept of articulation as a social scientific principle seriously. Such a distinction leads to a demarcation along disciplinary lines that severely limits the impact of poststructuralist discourse theory on linguistic, textual and ethnographic approaches to identity, ideology and hegemony. It also leads to an attitude whereby (critical) textual or discourse analytical approaches are considered in terms of toolboxes rather than as approaches in their own right with particular epistemological and ontological claims of their own. As a consequence, the reduction of the field of discourse studies to a binary opposition between discourse theorists interested in the ontological aspects of discursive reality on the one hand, and analytically oriented researchers interested in the inter-subjective, linguistic and multimodal dimensions of discourse on the other hand, protects discourse theory against ontological challenges posed by researchers that are more explicit about their analytical practices.

The very principle of articulation implies that a combination of particular concepts and perspectives impacts on the meanings of the elements involved. This means that an articulation of discourse theory with 'tools' provided by other approaches should go hand in hand with a reconsideration of its basic theories and claims. It could even lead to a modification of the concept of articulation itself. If we are to tackle the methodological deficit in an adequate way, this implies that we do not only look for linguistic, textual or other resources with which to 'apply' discourse theoretical principles and concepts, we also need to consider the implicit and explicit theoretical claims of the associated perspectives in their own right. As such, I subscribe to the claim that "in practice", the "ontological presuppositions do not always act as the rigid barriers to inter-approach conversations that they are often made out to be, these barriers being subject to productive articulation when the problem areas are more explicitly foregrounded" (Glynos et al. 2009, 7). With respect to the status of the ontological, Glynos and his co-authors adopt a stance that I would like to embrace wholeheartedly in the remainder of this book:

> *Indeed, while ontological presuppositions often function as the 'hard core' of an approach, we could argue that even these cannot be said a priori to be immune from contestation, though of course the degree of such contestation would very much depend upon the extent to which researchers adopt what Conolly (2002: xx) calls an ethos of 'presumptive generosity'.* (Glynos et al. 2009, 6)

In the upcoming chapters, I will demonstrate how a more detailed understanding of the inter-subjective, process-based and linguistic dimensions of communication could impact on the ontological assumptions of

2 Discourse Theory on the Logics of Articulation, Politics... 89

the discourse-theoretical framework. By integrating linguistic pragmatic and pragmatist perspectives on language and subjectivity with the Essex approach to discourse and subjectivity, I seek to enrich the concept of articulation with a more detailed understanding of the way articulatory practices function at the level of empirically observable discourse.

More specifically, I seek to clarify how the principle of articulation functions at the linguistic level and in what way we may specify some of its operations by relying on contemporary insights into the way social actors use language in concrete contexts. This implies a more detailed understanding of the way we delineate relevant contexts for interpretation and of the way we mark our preferred and disavowed interpretive logics through concrete texts and interactions. In poststructuralist discourse theory, articulation is at the same time a discursive, a political and an analytical practice. I would like to expand our understanding of its interactional and linguistic dimensions, while modifying the concept where necessary. This implies a more accurate understanding of the way we mark our interpretive logics and partially fix meaning through empirically observable cues and strategies that are performed with varying degrees of metalinguistic or metapragmatic awareness.

3

The Pragmatic Dimension of Discourse as Articulation

The slippery character of the term 'discourse' is a consequence of the wide range of theories and disciplines in which the concept has been defined, explained and operationalised (see Gee and Handford 2012; Angermüller et al. 2014a; Wetherell et al. 2003). Authors working in the trans-disciplinary field of discourse studies proceed on the idea that meaning is a social phenomenon. Discourse is thereby considered in terms of context-dependent practices that are socially constituted as well as socially constitutive. Most contemporary discourse analysts argue that discourse cannot be reduced to language alone (Angermüller et al. 2014b). Discourse analytical data may therefore include (transcribed) verbal and/or textual language use, but can also include multimodal data (sound and imagery) as well as observations about the practices that allow for their articulation. The category of discourse can be used in order to describe various levels of linguistic, textual, semiotic and socio-political organisation.

The multidimensional perspective on discourse as articulation developed in this book allows us to address these different levels and to blur the boundaries between discourse theory and discourse analysis (Angermüller et al. 2014b, 5–7; Zienkowski 2014, 283–285). Articulation and

© The Author(s) 2017
J. Zienkowski, *Articulations of Self and Politics in Activist Discourse*,
DOI 10.1007/978-3-319-40703-6_3

92 Articulations of Self and Politics in Activist Discourse

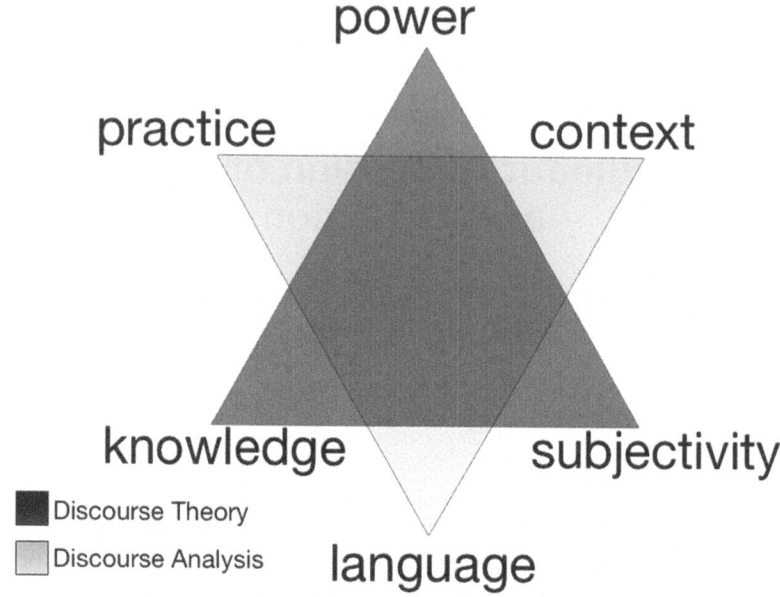

Fig. 3.1 Discourse studies as theory and analysis (Angermuller 2014a, 26)

discourse should therefore be thought of as multimodal and multidimensional categories of analysis (Fig. 3.1).

Schematically speaking, this project can be located in the overlapping field of the two triangles in Fig. 3.1. The triangle pointing downwards represents what is commonly understood by discourse in fields such as conversation analysis (Sidnell and Stivers 2013), the ethnography of communication (Gumperz and Hymes 1972), discursive psychology (Edwards 2005; Wetherell 2007) or pragmatics (Blommaert 2011; Cutting 2007; Wodak 2007; Zienkowski et al. 2011b). The other triangle represents poststructuralist understandings of discourse such as the ones discussed in the preceding chapter. Both sets of approaches deal with the question how meaning is partially fixed. Seeking to answer this question, discourse 'analysts' tend to focus on praxis, language and context while discourse 'theorists' prefer to focus on knowledge, subjectivity and power (Angermüller 2014a, 22–26). The approach to discourse presented in this book recognises the relevance of both fields of inquiry.

Articulation is a multilayered process that functions at multiple levels of abstraction. Consider the data presented in the first chapter of this book. Explaining their preferred and disavowed modes of politics, my interviewees made choices at all levels of language use in order to (re-)articulate their interpretive relations with a multitude of identities, abstract categories, arguments and narratives. One could point at the choices they made at the level phonemes, tonality, pitch or tempo. But one could also focus on body language, morphology, grammar, speech acts, argumentation, topic, narrative, genre, ideology and/or any other aspect of communication (Verschueren 1999, 120–146). I do not claim that we are aware of everything we do while we communicate but language does provide us with an array of options for negotiating, rearticulating and re-imagining—the meanings of—our social and political relationships. It allows us to index, mark and shape our interpretive relations towards ourselves, towards each other and towards contextual reality with varying degrees of reflexivity in multimodal ways.

The logics that provide our understandings of self and politics with some degree of coherence operate through concrete texts, interactions and institutions. We mark our limited awareness of such logics through linguistic and non-linguistic discursive forms that allow us to guide and influence each other's (self-)understandings (Zienkowski 2013, 2014). It is therefore useful to recall that naming, describing and analysing large-scale interpretive patterns such as logics requires a 'passage' through the self-interpretations articulated by subjects (Glynos and Howarth 2008, 2007, 51, 157–159). This 'passage' should not be taken literally. Subjectivity is always an opaque phenomenon. Consequently, the study of self-interpretations can never be more than a mode of analysis that takes the functional and metapragmatic aspects of language use and communication into account. People use discourse in order to link themselves interpretively and functionally with others. Language allows them to orient themselves inter-subjectively towards the temporal, spatial, social and intertextual contexts they engage in by provisionally fixing the meanings that allow them to make sense of the world.

Language use is interpretive in the sense that it involves a continuous making of choices that requires at least some mode and some degree of awareness about the communicative options and constraints we have at our disposal. It is functional in the sense that it operates through a process whereby relationships between discursive elements belonging to various levels of linguistic organisation and context—for example, labels, concepts, metaphors, arguments narratives, genres and/or language games—are linked with each other (Verschueren 2009, 19–22; 2004). Consequently, if we are to understand the meaning of one specific linguistic element—for example, pronoun, a concept, an argument or a narrative—we need to interpret its form and its functions in relation to an ever-shifting context of interpretation.

Not unlike poststructuralist authors (Butler and Laclau 2004, 335), scholars of linguistic pragmatics argue that contextual boundaries are never simply 'out there'. Contexts do not function as fixed structures that surround us. Rather, they emerge and take shape as they are made (relevant) through discursive de-, en- and re-contextualisation processes that generate provisional boundaries for communication and interpretation (Auer 2009; Blommaert 2001; Duranti and Goodwin 1992; Gumperz 1992b; Verschueren 2008). Nevertheless, a combination of pragmatic and poststructuralist discourse theories does imply a change of perspective. The very principle of articulation implies that any combination of theories will alter the identities of the theories involved. An integration of pragmatics understood as "the study of linguistic phenomena from the point of view of their usage properties and processes" (Verschueren 1999, 1) with Essex style discourse theory will therefore involve more than a mere addition of two sets of statements. Among other things, it requires a reconsideration of 'articulation' along the following lines:

> *An articulation is a temporary and partial linkage between semiotic forms and pragmatic functions. These functions include processes of awareness, ideology and hegemony. Articulations between signifiers, identities, narratives and/or political projects imply linguistic and/or non-linguistic performances that render them material and allow them to emancipate themselves from the domain of interpretive and discursive imagination. By means of the practice and principle of articulation, we can index semiotic forms and performances as traces of wider interpretive and political processes that allow for reflexive modes of subjectivity.*

Poststructuralist discourse theorists tend to focus on the social and political dimensions of discourse from a macrosocial and historical point of view. They tend to use the notion of discourse in order "to account for the symbolic constitution of society" (Angermüller et al. 2014b, 5) and consider discourse as a relational and "structured totality resulting from articulatory practice" (Laclau and Mouffe 1985, 105). Considering their approach to articulation, this means that the boundaries of discourse(s) can never be closed and can only be temporarily fixed. Nevertheless, most poststructuralist theorists tend to remain silent and/or vague about the interactional and empirical features of the way(s) in which meanings are fixed in concrete interactional contexts. This problem is related to the poststructuralist methodological deficit.

Linguistic pragmatics teaches us that articulation and contextualisation are not only about the discursive construction of identities through difference and equivalence. It shows us that articulatory practices involve a generation of indexical and interpretive boundaries. It is as much about forging alliances and hegemonic discursive practices as it is about the development and performance of particular modes of selfhood. Through practices of (re)articulation, we adapt our self-definitions and world views to ever-changing discursive realities. The pragmatic point of view allows us to consider varying degrees of reflexivity with respect to the communicative possibilities we have at our disposal for negotiating (the relative fixation of) the adaptable connections between semiotic forms and functions (Verschueren 1999, 59, 69).

Pragmatics offers more than a mere set of tools that can be used to operationalise discourse theoretical concepts. It provides a non-foundational and anti-essentialist perspective on language use marked by an empirical stance towards subjectivity. Its empirical focus forces us to pay attention to the way relationships between forms and functions of communication shift in observable ways. The pragmatic perspective forces us to pay attention to the way discursive elements are linked to each other in discourse at multiple levels of abstraction. It incites us to explore the functions of utterances and statements in concrete performances. The pragmatic principle that there is no one-to-one correspondence between a discursive element and its function is invaluable to the multidimensional notion of articulation outlined in this book.

A linguistic pragmatic perspective on discourse involves a study of the various functions that signs have in relation to each other, to language user(s), to the speech event(s) under investigation and to any other intertextual, social, cultural or ideological dimension of reality. If we think of these relationships in terms of a multimodal concept of articulation, it becomes possible to examine the large-scale logics that structure the way we mark our understanding(s) of self and other in large-scale social and political debates. In contrast to some pragmatic linguists, I will not restrict the notion of discourse to mere language use. I would like to stress that a pragmatic study of subjectivity and political language use should include a study of the way we mark our orientation to linguistic as well as non-linguistic dimensions of reality.

Most of the time, I will use the term 'discourse' in order to refer to concrete utterances made by interviewees. But the meaning of the term will also widen and shift in order to include societal debates about specific issues (e.g. discourse about discrimination on the labour and housing markets), specific ways of talking about a particular discourse (e.g. a homogenising or culturalising discourse) or semiotic practices and policies articulated by specific (types of) actors and institutions (e.g. the discourse of the integration sector). The boundaries of what I mean by 'discourse' at any one time will have to be determined pragmatically and *in situ*. Like Foucault, I will allow the 'boundaries' of discourse to shift in correspondence with the focal points of the analysis. The boundaries that constitute the unities of discourse are always shifting because its basic elements—statements or articulations—are defined by their functions rather than by their forms.

Foucault taught us that a statement "is not in itself a unity, but a function that cuts across a domain of structures and possible unities, and which reveals them, with concrete contents in time and space" (Foucault 1969). Any statement can appear in a multiplicity of forms. An anti-racist statement may come to us in the form of a proposition, a (speech) act, an argument, a narrative or a movie. Statements may operate through text and talk but they do not necessarily do so. They are functions established through performances that may take many forms. And it is through their (re-)articulation in orders of discourse that we become subjects and objects of knowledge to each other. Some of these functions can be described in terms of subjectivity whereas others can be described in terms of power and technology. In all cases, however, we are dealing with a pragmatic notion of discourse.

3 The Pragmatic Dimension of Discourse as Articulation

The pragmatics-infused notion of discourse I argue for embraces the messiness of discourse and considers communities, languages, discourses, ideologies and identities in terms of non-unitary objects of investigation (Bublitz and Norrick 2011, 4). It focuses on meaningful communication in terms of an ever-shifting interpretive network of discursive performances that establish functional relationships between subject positions, identities, texts, concepts, practices and institutions. It is true that some pragmatic authors tend to focus on a relatively small set of phenomena such as speech acts, code-switching and/or inference (e.g. Huang 2007). But this observation should not obscure the fact that linguistic pragmatics can help us to understand how power, ideology and subjectivity function at an empirically observable level of reality (Angermüller 2011; Blommaert 2011; Verschueren 2011; Zienkowski 2013).

My emphasis on the pragmatics of discourse should not be read in opposition to (other) critical approaches to discourse. Ideology, inequality and power are categories for analysis that highlight important dimensions of human experience. I subscribe to the emancipatory agenda of CDA and consider the discursive construction of relations of domination, discrimination and oppression to be legitimate objects of investigation (Breeze 2011; Fairclough and Wodak 1997; Wodak 2013b). I also recognise the relevance of research on problematic constructions of gender, culture, ethnicity, minority politics, religion and class in dominant media, discursive formations, ideologies and hegemonies. But it is equally important to understand the way counter-ideological projects and critical discourses function in the political praxis of activists and intellectuals.

This book includes an analysis of the dominant Flemish discourses about integration. However, the major part of this study focuses on the way intellectuals and activists critically (re-)articulate, politicise and critique such discourses. In this sense, my approach constitutes a rather atypical mode of critical discourse studies. It includes a strong emphasis on the articulation of critical awareness and agency in and through discourse. Contrary to critical approaches that seek to 'unveil' dominant ideologies and to 'uncover' 'hidden' structures of domination, I seek to understand the ideological logics that inform the critical discourses of my interviewees. I do not consider their discourses to be any less ideological than the discourses they criticise. Their mode of fantasmatic involvement with respect to their identifications is frequently marked by an awareness of the contingency of their claims, but this awareness does not place them outside of the realm of ideology.

In the next section, I will illustrate the need for a pragmatic perspective on articulation with reference to concrete interview data. I will then move on to discuss linguistic pragmatics as a poststructuralist perspective on discourse. This will clear the ground for a discussion of articulatory practice as a variable, adaptable and negotiable performance on the basis of linguistic pragmatic principles. In order to explore linguistic pragmatics as a perspective on meaning and subjectivity, I will explore different sources of pragmatics such as early pragmatist philosophy, philosophy of language and French enunciative linguistics. This discussion allows for an understanding of linguistic pragmatics as an interpretive and functional approach to discourse, reflexivity and critical awareness. The last section of this chapter explores the implications of a linguistic pragmatic perspective on the articulation of political awareness in the public realm.

3.1 Pragmatically Established Boundaries for Interpretation in Talk About Integration

It is useful to illustrate the need for a pragmatic take on articulatory practice with reference to an interview conducted with a civil servant working in the Antwerp integration service called DIA (*Dienst Integratie Antwerpen*) in Flanders, Belgium. At the beginning of our interview, civil servant Amane X. explicitly told me that her statements should be interpreted as personal opinions rather than as representative samples of official DIA discourse. Amane resorted to a footing strategy that allowed her to communicate a reflexive attitude with respect to a—partially—fragmented discourse and subjectivity. Moreover, by distancing herself from her DIA-related subject position, she was able to open up a discursive space in which she could pragmatically challenge and politicise hegemonic boundaries for interpretation regarding Flemish integration policy.

3 The Pragmatic Dimension of Discourse as Articulation

One of Amane's most important claims was that a "true integration policy" should take the principle of the "transferability of dreams from older generations to younger generations" into account. She pointed out that people often seek to realise the unfulfilled dreams of their parents and that this principle also holds for children of migrants. This "transferability" of dreams may take the form of children pursuing "the job dad or mum dreamt about". But it may also lead later generations to dream of a return to the home country of their parents. According to Amane, the danger of ignoring the principle of the transferability of dreams in integration policy lies in the emotional turmoil that may result from one's inability to realise these dreams.

> AX: And some will dream and it will always remain a dream ... yes ... and there are two consequences to that: bitterness, you'll have a big unhappy group who is embittered because their dream was never realised, or people themselves, that also happens eh, like 'that dream did not turn into reality no problem I'll deal with it like this', very healthy, but I don't think we can allow this to happen. I don't think this is a good thing.
> **excerpt 15 – 04/10/2007**

Amane argues that "in an integration policy, in a diversity policy, one not only needs to take needs and values into account, but also and especially the expectations of people". She deplores the fact that dreams and expectations tend to be ignored by those who draft integration policies. Amane goes on and exemplifies the problem with reference to the interview itself. This requires a high degree of metalinguistic and political awareness. The excerpt below illustrates the negotiable character of contextual boundaries. It shows that language users adapt their awareness of self and other as their interpretive gaze shifts and new contexts for interpretation are generated.

In order to highlight the importance of human dreams and expectations in discussions about integration, Amane presented me with a scenario that was meant to challenge any stereotypical expectations I might have had about the way she wants to grow old. At the same time, by turning her gaze to the identities within the language game of the interview, she set out to challenge expectations about migrants as constructed in society-wide debates about integration and diversity.

AX: [...] I can only present arguments to make sure that the other sees this too: that in an integration policy, in a diversity policy, one not only needs to take current needs and values into account, but also and especially the expectations of people. There is too often an expectation like ... [turns her body to face me more directly and addresses me in a more informal tone] you see me sitting here on a chair and I guarantee that your image about me and about how I will grow old does not include a headscarf. In my image about how I will grow old whether ... whether this is really the case or not it does not matter, these expectations are there but are not being articulated ... in my expectation there is not a hair on my head that thinks about growing old without a headscarf. One day I will wear the headscarf because it makes me trigger an association of growing old in a respectable way. Islam and culture aside, merely a woman, that does a 'watergolfke'¹ with the hairdresser every week, perhaps that's a familiar image to you, but maybe eh

excerpt 16 – 04/10/2007

In the excerpt above, Amane explains that the legitimacy of integration and diversity policies depends on the extent to which one can accommodate for the dreams, "expectations" and the associated—fantasmatic— "image" an individual may have about "growing old in a respectable way". She knows that her views on integration are not commonly shared in Flanders. Nevertheless, she hopes that "the other" can see the need for an approach to integration and diversity in which the expectations and dreams of migrants and their children are calibrated with the expectations of 'others' in society. In order to make her point, she reframes the issue by problematising the context of the interview itself and by pointing at a potential mismatch between my expectations as a majority member on the one hand, and her personal dreams on the other hand. She constructed an interpretation of the interview setting in which my perception of her would be in line with a dominant logic of integration that does not recognise the dreams and expectations of (children of) migrants.

---

¹ A *watergolfke* (literally: a little water wave) is an Antwerp dialect word for a haircut that involves artificial curling. Amane uses the term in order to construct a stereotypical image of the way in which elder—Antwerp—women mark their dignity at a certain age. The code-switch to the Antwerp dialect (through the diminutive 'ke') performs an important indexical function that marks her local Antwerp identity.

Whether this representation is accurate or not "does not matter" to Amane in this particular context.

By changing her bodily posture and changing her tone of voice, she addressed me directly: "you see me sitting here on a chair [without a headscarf or other Islamic cultural markers] and I guarantee that your image about me and about how I will grow old does not include a headscarf". She then contrasted this image with her own ideas about dignified seniority. This contrast allowed her to rearticulate the headscarf debate as a universal issue of dreams and expectations with respect to the question how to grow old in a dignified way. This contextual reframing provides an alternative for a cultural logic that has been the hallmark of hegemonic discourses about integration in Flanders for decades. We will focus on such hegemonic logics later on. Right now, it suffices to point out that Amane does not consider the issue of integration to be about "Islam and culture" but about enabling people with migration trajectories to realise their dreams and expectations within the countries in which they reside.

It is possible to describe this type of interview discourse in terms of logics. The political logics of equivalence and difference are at play in the binary opposition between two sets of identities. On the one hand, there are the dreams and expectations associated with migrants and their descendants. And on the other hand, there are the dreams of others who expect these people to integrate themselves by leaving their dreams behind. Both sets of identities can be associated with particular practices, discourses and identities. It is also possible to read Amane's analysis of dreams and expectations as a critique of the fantasmatic logic of hegemonic discourses about integration. By highlighting the contingency of the expectations that minority and majority members may have towards each other and towards themselves, Amane distanced herself from a dominant understanding of integration. Instead, she imagined an alternative integration policy that takes dreams and expectations into account. As such, she lessened her degree of ideological investment in hegemonic integration discourse.

All of this is achieved pragmatically. The 'logics' described here do not simply exist 'out there' but were activated and (re-)articulated through an inter-subjective exchange in a concrete interview context. Logics exist through the performances of those who (re-)enact them. In this sense, they do not pre-exist interaction. Their histories are first and foremost histories of practice. The need for a pragmatic understanding of context and discourse becomes pressing when we take a closer look at the way interviewees distinguish between preferred and disavowed modes of politics and subjectivity. Amane articulated a particular type of politics—the current variety integration policy—with a mode of subjectivity marked by unfulfilled dreams and desires. A more dignified mode of subjectivity requires a politics of recognition that does acknowledge the dreams and desires of those it seeks to 'integrate'.

Logics are always articulated, maintained and challenged by human beings that exhibit some degree of reflexive awareness. Their discursive operation hinges on the human capacity for metapragmatic awareness. Logics cannot operate without some awareness of the normative patterns through which semiotic forms and functions are linked to each other. These forms can be linguistic (e.g. accent, dialect, intonation, vocabulary) and/or non-linguistic (e.g. physical appearance, stance, symbolic attributes). At the same time, it is important to keep in mind that metapragmatic awareness also includes an awareness of the way unequal power relationships impact on the articulation of identity and discourse. Without such basic (meta-)pragmatic knowledge about the way (political) discourse functions in Flanders, it would not have been possible for Amane to (re-)articulate and problematise the Flemish minority debates in the way she did.

In order to make sense of the world, we need to construct and index relevant contexts for interpretation. The aspects of reality we draw upon in processes of contextualisation do not simply surround us but need to be (re-)articulated and oriented to in the course of discursive interaction. Every person with a minimal degree of reflexive awareness can find numerous examples of the way shifts in contextually established boundaries for interpretation impact on the ways we fix the meanings of self, discourse and reality. One of the main tools at our disposal is language use itself. Any attempt to understand the pragmatic dimension of a multimodal notion of articulation therefore requires insight into the negotiable, adaptable and variable features of discourse.

3.2 Linguistic Pragmatics as a Poststructuralist Perspective on Discourse

Pragmatic linguists provide us with theoretical and empirical support for the idea that the meanings of self, politics and society can only be partially fixed. They do not understand language and discourse in terms of unified and closed structures. The more integrated perspectives in the field can even be interpreted as attempts to understand the partial fixation of meaning in terms of reflexive processes of articulation whereby others, selves and a limited set of contextual and discursive elements are linked with each other. During my discussion of poststructuralist discourse theory, I relied mostly on Essex school authors. Now I will consider the articulation of self and discourse from a pragmatic point of view. I have no intention of providing an extensive overview of the field. I rather seek to present the reader with a (meta-)pragmatic understanding of discourse in terms of negotiable, adaptable and variable language use (Verschueren 2009). This entails an understanding of pragmatics as an inter-subjective perspective on the interface between discourse, context and subjectivity.

The poststructuralist thrust of the type of pragmatics presented below is grounded on three types of sources. Pragmatics can be traced back to North American varieties of pragmatism as developed by authors such as James, Cooley and Mead. But it is also indebted to the British tradition in analytical philosophy. The work of authors such as Wittgenstein, Austin and Searle triggered a wealth of studies in which language was understood in terms of a multiplicity of language games through which we perform and (re-)articulate rules for generating meaning. Language philosophy stimulated an increasingly empirical focus on phenomena such as speech acts, presuppositions and other pragmatic phenomena. The field of linguistic pragmatics is heavily indebted to both types of philosophy (Angermuller et al. 2014c, 17–19). Thirdly, the type of pragmatics presented below draws on dialogic, polyphonic and/or enunciative understandings of discourse and subjectivity (Angermuller 2011).

Linguistic pragmatics originated in the seventies and eighties as a reaction against the formalism and structuralism dominating linguistics in the middle of the last century. It posited a reconsideration of language in terms of "an agentive, active and dynamic object which operates between people in particular activity patterns (the interactional dimension), where such patterns are socially, culturally and politically constituted" (Blommaert 2011, 123). Pragmatism, ordinary language philosophy and polyphonic approaches to discourse provided a new generation of researchers with ammunition to challenge formalist and structuralist understandings of language and subjectivity.

The pragmatic turn in linguistics implied an increasingly interdisciplinary point of view whereby discourse became an object investigation for combined linguistic and social scientific modes of inquiry. It involved a shift of perspective from *langue* to *parole* and enunciation (Blommaert 2011, 123; Angermuller 2014b, 10–11). One could use the image of a pragmatic dam-burst in order to imagine the changes in the linguistic landscape. Ideas that had been piling up for decades were now combining into a strong current that would break through in the seventies and eighties (Nerlich and Clarke 1996, 375–376). Pragmatics now incorporates elements of rhetoric, semiotics, stylistics, narrative analysis, linguistic anthropology, the ethnography of communication, literary studies and cultural studies. The pragmatic agenda is informed by the double question what people do with language and what language use does to them (Koyama 2011, 140).

The metaphor of a pragmatic 'dam-burst' can be used in order to highlight the idea that pragmatic concepts and theories started to cluster together as if they were water molecules that aggregated into clouds of contextualism and functionalism. Authors became increasingly interested in the complex dynamics between context and language use. Instrumental and goal-directed functions of language were attended to as well. And many pragmatically oriented scholars would come to embrace the principle of reciprocity when dealing with speakers and hearers, while considering language in terms of indexicality, dialogue and conversation (Nerlich and Clarke 1996, 375–376). At the same time, it is important to recognise the heterogeneity of the field from the outset. The image of one single burst should therefore be taken with a grain of salt.

Right now, the field is so interdisciplinary that any attempt to order it neatly along disciplinary lines would grossly oversimplify the process of its constitution (Verschueren 1999, 256). One of the earliest ways to describe pragmatics made use of a metaphor that highlighted its topical heterogeneity. Since pragmatics frequently looks like "a repository of extremely interesting but separable topics such as deixis, implicature, presupposition, speech acts, conversation, politeness and relevance" (Verschueren 2009, 9), it has been described as a ragbag or as a wastepaper basket designed to absorb those phenomena that could not be explained with reference to semantics and syntax alone (Mey 1998). As we will see, this idea of pragmatics as a repository is closely associated with the idea that pragmatics is merely a component of semiotics (Verschueren 2009, 12).

In the context of this book, pragmatics will be understood as an interdisciplinary perspective on language use in context. A widely accepted definition of pragmatics along these lines describes it as "a general cognitive, social and cultural perspective on linguistic phenomena in relation to their usage in forms of behaviour (where the string 'cognitive, social and cultural' does not suggest the separability of what the terms refer to" (Verschueren 1999, 7). As an area of study, pragmatics is not so much defined by its objects of investigation as by a point of view that considers meaning in terms of a process that cannot be grounded either in individual consciousness or in language as a closed and centred system.

Of course, the question whether the notion of pragmatics as a perspective does not include almost all human activity is valid and one might wonder if it leads to a conceptualisation of pragmatics that incorporates the whole of social science (Verschueren 2009, 14). Nevertheless, it is possible to avoid the Scylla of confining oneself to a strict linguistic definition of pragmatics, and the Charybdis of developing impossibly vague definitions that incorporate as much social context as possible, thus blurring the boundaries between linguistic disciplines and approaches (Mey 1999). As we will see, practitioners of linguistic pragmatics do not try to analyse the whole of reality, but trace the processes through which language users provide each other with indexical pointers that help them to delineate relevant contexts for interpretation.

The increasing popularity of the pragmatic perspective can be understood in terms of a 'turn' in the study of language. Social scientific turns occur when an object of investigation becomes the lens through which we look at reality in general. Categories that were previously used in order to designate objects of investigation become analytical categories and metaphors to know the world. All turns rely on metaphors. After an initial linguistic turn whereby social, cultural and political phenomena were increasingly understood in terms of linguistic processes, we have seen a series of partially overlapping turns in the study of culture: interpretive, semiotic, dialogic, spatial and translational turns that have made us think of society in terms of dialogues, performances, spaces, translational practices (Bachmann-Medick 2016, 16–29) and articulations.

By relying on interpretive, dialogical, performative and translational perspectives on discourse and subjectivity, linguistic pragmaticians have developed a multiplicity of perspectives for analysing the inter-subjective and indexical processes through which interlocutors partially fix meaning in empirically observable discourse (Zienkowski et al. 2011b). The pragmatic turn can therefore be understood as a meta-turn that systematically redirects attention to the reflexive and inter-subjective processes that lie at the heart of communication.

It is true that a great deal of linguistic pragmatic research focuses on a limited number of topics such as speech acts, presuppositions, inferences or indexicals, but if we consider pragmatics as a perspective on context, meaning and subjectivity, linguistic pragmatics reveals itself as a general outlook on meaning, discourse and subjectivity. As we will see, pragmatics is especially valuable for those researchers who are interested in the way subjects engage in ideological processes of self-interpretation while dealing with each other and with the world in general. Linguistic pragmatics can be understood as a perspective for analysing the way subjects mark their (self-)interpretations in empirically observable discourse. It allows researchers to consider subjectivity and discourse as phenomena over which humans can always exert a limited amount of reflexive control.

Most pragmatic scholars are very sceptical about thinking about language and language users as unified objects of investigation. This sceptical attitude with respect to reified understandings of the world parallels poststructuralist understanding of meaning whereby there is no one-to-one relationship between a linguistic form and its function or meaning. Especially the non-Cartesian varieties of linguistic pragmatics can be understood as poststructuralist perspectives on language and subjectivity. From the sixties and seventies on, more and more linguists would consider language use in terms of narrative, enunciative, polyphonic and intertextual processes whereby interlocutors seek to establish some degree of interpretive cohesion and/or coherence. Studies of figures of speech, genre, public discourse and the question of context would become increasingly pragmatic and interdisciplinary (Zienkowski 2011b, 7–8).

If we are to understand the way people articulate preferred and disavowed modes of politics in relation to their sense of self, we need to understand self and discourse as working frameworks and as an unfinished, decentred and reflexive processes. A lot of the boundary work through which we inter-subjectively articulate a more or less coherent sense of self is performed through concrete language use marked by some degree of reflexive awareness. Linguistic pragmatic perspectives allow us to recognise the creative ways in which we deal with the messiness of everyday communication in concrete embodied contexts (Bublitz and Norrick 2011, 4). Subjectivity and debate are marked by a degree of heterogeneous multiplicity that fluctuates along the extremes of utter chaos and relative order. From a pragmatic perspective, the notion of 'language' is merely a shorthand for a vast range of linguistic options we have at our disposal in order to generate meaning in inter-subjective ways within the context of concrete language games.

Language provides us with a wide range of options for communicative behaviour. We have no choice between choosing or not choosing to use language in the production and interpretation of utterances. Even silence is a communicative option. Moreover, when we do use language, a whole set of other options emerges. As soon as we decide to use—a—language, we also need to make a multiplicity of decisions at nearly every level of discursive structure. Moreover, speakers do not only choose linguistic forms, they also opt for particular communicative strategies to achieve specific ends. This is not to say that language use is all about voluntarianism and goal-directed action. Not every choice is made with the same degree of awareness and we do need structure in order to make sense of reality. Meaningful language use is, to a large extent, a matter of delimiting the range of possible interpretations (Verschueren 1999, 55–59).

When my grandparents—who have no background in the humanities—ask me to explain what my research is about, I usually make a conscious choice to explain myself without words such as 'discourse theory', 'discourse analysis' 'poststructuralism' or 'pragmatics'. I mostly explain myself by telling them that I seek to understand how people use language in order to make sense of themselves and their world. I may also add that I do so by focusing on the way activists and intellectuals with a Moroccan background in Flanders talk about politics. Some of these choices are reflexive and strategic. In this particular situation, I tend to be aware of the fact that I opt for a discursive strategy aimed at reaching understanding and retaining face. But it is impossible to monitor every aspect of discursive choice-making with the same degree of reflexivity. Many choices are made in the background.

I may be unaware of the fact that my physical posture is very different from the posture I may take with a colleague. I may be oblivious to aspects of tonality, articulation, eye movement or grammatical structuring. And in more general terms, it may not even cross my mind that many of my choices are made according to the conventions associated with the language game of small talk. Many choices are made with a very low degree of conscious consideration. Any conscious choice made at one level of discursive structure implies a multiplicity of choices that are made with a lower degree of salience. At the same time, it is important to emphasise that this pragmatic take on language as choice-making should be understood in relation to a pragmatic—and therefore dynamic—understanding of structure. From a pragmatic perspective, the structures of language are established through the ongoing pressures of language use itself. Language use involves the making of choices between options for communication provided by variable structures of language (Verschueren and Brisard 2009, 29).

3.3 Articulatory Practice as a Variabale, Adaptable and Negotiable Performance

My poststructuralist understanding of pragmatics has to be understood with reference to Verschueren's conceptualisation of language in terms of variability, adaptability and negotiability (Verschueren 2009, 20).

Let us start with variability. The notion of linguistic variation was originally developed in the field of quantitative sociolinguistics but has undergone a development that is indicative of changes in the study of linguistics as a whole (Fried et al. 2010; Gumperz 1982, 23–29). Studies of linguistic variation have homed in on different aspects of linguistic structure leading to a clear shift in focus: "from the early interest in sounds, morphological structure, and word etymologies as manifestations of speaker-independent systems to gradual inclusion of syntactic patterning in texts to, most recently, incorporating patterns of language use and the speaker's role in language change" (Fried 2010, 1).

The pragmatic idea of variability can be described as "the property of language which defines the range of possibilities from which choices can be made". Choices at the structural levels of morphology, grammar, discourse strategy, textual structure or genre impact on the range of possibilities for consequent choice-making. Every choice we make rules out alternatives and creates new ones for the current purposes of the exchange (Verschueren 1999, 58–59). For instance, my choice to address my grandparents with a non-academic vocabulary when explaining my research has implications with respect to the ongoing interaction. A sudden decision on my part to draw on a more academic register is likely to be noticed. There is even a high level of probability that such a breach of expectations would mark my academic identity. It could even lead to an evaluation of my utterances as a 'pedantic' instance of 'ivory tower' discourse. Every communicative choice introduces expectations and possibilities in the ongoing context. At the same time, these choices are never completely equivalent to each other.

The pragmatic notion of variability does not allow for an analysis of language and discourse as a static or closed totality. Whenever pragmaticians talk about so-called *things* as phonetic, syntactic or narrative structures, they are very much aware of the fact that they are reifying complex and variable processes that have no independent existence from actual language use. In fact, the pragmatic notion of variability was explicitly developed in opposition to both Saussurean and Chomskyan assumptions about the uniformity of grammatical systems that was unable to account for individual and social variations of empirically observable speech diversity (Gumperz 1982, 24–29). The structures pragmatic authors write about have nothing to do with the closed and centred totalities criticised in poststructuralist thought. Instead, the pragmatic idea of structure can best be thought about in terms of structural objects of adaptability. It is useful to quote Verschueren at length:

> Any (combination of) element(s) at any layer or level of linguistic organisation or form at which choices can be made, *constitutes a structural object of adaptability or, for short, an element of 'structure'.* Thus, languages, codes, and styles are objects of adaptability albeit at a high level of structuring. So are all utterance-building ingredients, from sounds, over morphemes, words, clauses, sentences and propositions all the way to supra-sentential units. Also utterancs and utterances clusters (from the exclamation of "Ouch" to a full conversation or an entire novel) fit in here, as well as utterances-building principles such as coherence, relevance, information structuring, foregrounding, backgrounding, and the like. Usually, choices are not isolated, but rather part of an integrated process of choice-making that interrelates phenomena at different structural levels. (Verschueren 2008, 18)

The notion of structure thus functions as a shorthand for the range of potential options available to the discursive practices of a particular actor. Poststructuralist and pragmatic perspectives on discourse converge in the idea that any structure is always a reification of a multiplicity of inter-related and inter-subjective processes. Every discursive structure functions as a structuration through which rules and resources for communication are being (re-)articulated. As such, the structural objects of adaptability provided by language are the linguistic 'elements' we combine in linguistic practices of articulation.

The second principle of language we need to deal with is its *negotiability*. Negotiability can be defined as "the property of language responsible for the fact that choices are not made mechanically or according to strict rules or fixed form-function relationships, but rather on the basis of highly flexible principles and strategies" (Verschueren 1999, 59). In order to understand this point, we have to take a closer look at the notions of form and function involved. As we noticed before, the practice of articulation can be defined as a linkage of semiotic forms and their pragmatic functions. A semiotic form can be defined as (the empirically observable result of) a performance. Semiotic forms such as utterances, words, images, works of art, dance and literature provide us with the means to establish—our relationship to—relevant contexts for interpretation that help us to imagine a common ground for constructing meaningful interpretations of inter-subjective processes.

The meaning of discursive elements cannot be located *within* semiotic forms. Meaning emerges in interpretive and interactive processes whereby actors map particular functions onto specific forms of discourse. The notion of function advocated by Verschueren is grounded in the related traditions of pragmatism, social behaviourism and British functionalism. He advocates a relational notion of functionality that should not be confused with systemic or structural functionalism. In the social sciences, functionalism is usually associated with the tradition of Parsonian sociology whereby functions are conceptualised as links between relatively stable structural categories and/or as relatively mechanical processes. This type of functionalism is frequently contrasted with interpretive approaches in social science that supposedly deal more with 'meaning' rather than with 'functions' (Verschueren 2009, 19).

Verschueren refuses to distinguish between meaning and function in this simplistic way. And even though he does not provide us with a clear-cut definition of functionality, he is clearly arguing for a concept of discourse marked by interpretive functionality. This type of relational functionality can also be found in the work of Foucault who defined the basic units of discourse—statements—in functional terms. Nevertheless, Verschueren refers to another author who abandoned the Saussurean distinction between *langue* and *parole* in order to develop a functional perspective on communication—Bronislaw Malinowski (Verschueren 1999, 75).

In his attempt to write a grammar of the language of the Melanesian tribes of Eastern New Guinea, Malinowski realised that grammar can only be understood in relation to meaning and that meaning can only be understood in relation to concrete contexts (Nerlich and Clarke 1996, 320; Korta 2007, 1647–1648). Malinowski first equated meaning with pragmatic function in his *Argonauts of the Western pacific*. Here, he developed the idea that words are no receptacles of thought but that language is first and foremost a matter of action. Malinowski distinguished various functions of language in his work: "the active use of language to co-ordinate actions and make things happen, the narrative use of language, which is ultimately derived from action, and the ritual use of language, which includes phatic language use and creates the ties of human society" (Nerlich and Clarke 1996, 324). To him, speech in action underlies all forms of language.

Malinowski would later turn to pragmatism and social behaviourism in his search for an alternative to the functionalist sociologies of Durkheim and Radcliffe-Brown (Nerlich and Clarke 1996, 319). Borrowing from the pragmatist William James—whose work we will discuss below—he came to re-interpret the sociological notion of function as effect or purpose. His colleague Firth would go as far as to equate British contextualism with pragmatism and (social) behaviourism. Malinowski's pragmatist-inspired approach to functional meaning can be summarised as follows: "just as meaning is the function of a word, that is, the effect it produces in context, so the function of a custom or institution is the effect it produces" (Nerlich and Clarke 1996, 326–328). The negotiability of meaning and discourse rests upon the idea that any semiotic form can perform different functions and generate different meanings depending on its usage.

The principle of negotiability accounts for indeterminacy in the choice-making of language users. Once choices are made, the interpretive functions of these choices can always be renegotiated (Verschueren 1999, 58–61). Verschueren follows Malinowski because his notion of meaningful language use emphasises the functional relatedness of language with other facets of human life. In this sense, pragmatics should ultimately deal with the function*ing* of language use in context (Verschueren 1999, 9–10). Malinowski's notion of context anticipated most context-related questions that are currently being studied under the header of pragmatics. These include the physical setting of the utterance; the gestures of the speaker; the referents for indexicals; the speech previous to and after the utterance; and the activity in which the speech is embedded. Pragmaticians also focus on all sorts of implicit meaning; the rhetorical relations between sentences; the total cultural setting of the utterance that helps explain how certain perlocutionary effects are achieved; as well as the conversational implicatures generated in the process of contextualisation (Korta 2007, 1650–1652).

This brings us to the third characteristic of language use: its adaptability. If language use is characterised by shifting form–function relationships and choices that can be permanently renegotiated, it is necessary to ask how we can create relatively stable meanings for purposes of communication. This is where adaptability comes in. This concept refers to "the property of language which enables human beings to make negotiable linguistic choices from a variable range of possibilities in such a way as to approach points of satisfaction for communicative needs" (Verschueren 1999, 62). Verschueren's notion of communicative needs can be conflated with his notion of function. Communicative needs arise in specific speech events, language games and contexts. They are always rather specific and may change as our—awareness of—contextual reality shifts.

Adaptability is not completely unrestricted. It is a two-way process. We make choices in order to adapt ourselves to needs that are inter-subjectively and interpretively established. On the other hand, our discursively performed choices become part and parcel of the very contexts in which we act. For instance, if two interlocutors opt for a system of politeness that stresses solidarity or informality (e.g. '*tu*', first-name form of address) over a system that stresses formality and deference (e.g. '*vous*', '*usted*', last-name form of address, titles) a shift in register is likely to be interpreted in terms of either playfulness or antagonism (Verschueren 1999, 62). This is what is meant with choices not being equivalent to each other. If language use is marked by adaptability, this does not preclude the possibility of serious non- or miscommunication. Quite the contrary, as we will see, the notion of reaching common ground is always—partially—fantasmatic or imaginary. Points of satisfaction can be reached by approximation only.

Verschueren relies on Vygotsky's 'mind in society' in order to conceptualise the medium that allows us to interpretively relate structural objects of adaptability such as sounds, gestures, contextualisation cues, speech act verbs, narratives and strategies in relation to interpretive functions and meanings. By adopting the notion of a 'mind in society', he rejects the idea of a clear-cut opposition between society and cognition in a way that is reminiscent of the early pragmatists. The mind in society Verschueren writes about is not a closed and centred totality. It should rather be understood in terms of a series of linguistic and non-linguistic processes that can be marked in discourse. Considering this multifunctional 'mind', it should be clear from the outset that we are dealing with a fragmented entity whose multiplicity of voices, roles and/or subject positions should be recognised from the outset (Verschueren 1999, 77–91, 173–175).

In fact, the notion of subjectivity entailed by the inter-related principles of adaptability, negotiability and variability comes very close to a notion of the self in terms of a reification of the processes that allow an individual body to reflexively articulate itself as more or less coherent mind/body in relation to linguistic, (inter-)textual, social spatial and temporal aspects of contextual reality. The real question thus becomes how to fix the boundaries of this self, a question that has been dealt with not only in poststructuralist discourse theory but also in the writings of the early American pragmatists.

3.4 Fixing Meaning by Adhering to the Pragmatic Maxim

Most introductions to linguistic pragmatics trace the origin of the term 'pragmatics' back to early pragmatists such as Charles Peirce (1839–1914), William James (1842–1914) and/or Charles Morris (1901–1979). Peirce is usually considered to be the first 'pragmatist' philosopher whereas James is credited for popularising, re-interpreting and broadening the pragmatist perspective along non-positivist lines. Morris is known to have conceptualised pragmatics as a subfield of semiotics. He distinguished between syntax, semantics and pragmatics as three dimensions of the study of linguistic and non-linguistic signs. As such, syntax focuses on the study of relations between signs, semantics on the study of the relationships between signs and their referents (i.e. the real-world things to which they refer) and pragmatics on the study of the relations between signs and their interpreters (Fetzer 2011; Mey 1999; Verschueren 2009).

Even though most introductions refer to the early pragmatist philosophers as important sources for linguistic pragmatics, they remain rather superficial with respect to pragmatist ideas on subjectivity and communication. This vagueness may result from the rather indirect ways in which pragmatist philosophy has impacted on studies of language use. Pragmatism frequently impacted on pragmatics via its influence on academic (sub-)disciplines such as ethnomethodology, conversation analysis, qualitative sociolinguistics, linguistic anthropology and social psychology. Generally speaking, pragmatist theories about inquiry, meaning and selfhood have shaped a great deal of constructivist social science and share many family resemblances with poststructuralist understandings of subjectivity. Pragmatist and poststructuralist authors share a common foe in the Cartesian view on knowledge, discourse and subjectivity. Grand narratives and systems, foundationalism, and spectator theories of truth are popular objects of critique in both approaches. Moreover, both pragmatists and poststructuralist have argued in favour of decentralised notions of subjectivity as alternatives for transcendental understandings of the self (Bernstein 2010).

The linguistic pragmatic agenda is marked by pragmatist orientations. In philosophy, semiotics and linguistics alike, the label 'pragmatic' designates those approaches that seek to explain reality and experience with reference to use and context rather than with reference to an abstract system. This does not mean that a pragmatic orientation stands in opposition to an understanding of the systematic features of communication or that one shies away from theoretical abstraction. In the domain of linguistics, pragmatic scholars believe that the primary focus should be on language use and on language users if one seeks to understand how (linguistic) communication functions. They argue that we need to focus on the way extralinguistic aspects of context and reflexive awareness operate in tandem with the linguistic options for action at our disposal. This implies a thorough theorisation of language, context and structure (Bublitz and Norrick 2011, 3–5).

The field of linguistic pragmatics inherited more than its name from pragmatist philosophy. In its legacy, we find a dialogical notion of the self and a contextual understanding of meaning (Wiley 2006). And even though the field of pragmatics has many roots, pragmatist themes and orientations continue to shape the field. The current tendency among linguistic pragmatic scholars to look into empirically observable language use and to focus on the way language users make sense of the contexts in which they move is a continuation of early pragmatist concerns. As such, most authors that work with a pragmatic perspective argue in favour of a non-foundational and anti-essentialist theory of meaning that is grounded in an empirical and process-based understanding of communicative behaviour that takes varying degrees of reflexive awareness into account. Pragmatic and poststructuralist concerns converge on these issues.

We already noticed that the origin of the label 'pragmatic' as used within linguistics should be located in the classic pragmatist philosophies of Peirce, James, Dewey and Mead. In everyday language use, the expression 'to be pragmatic' designates a problem-solving attitude that can be contrasted with 'useless intellectualism'. It is also used to refer to the type of shallow opportunism associated with what William James called "the exclusive worship of the bitch-Goddess SUCCESS" (James 2003, cited in Campbell 2011, 69). The philosophical understanding of pragmatism cannot be reduced to either interpretation. Rather, we are dealing with a series of inquiries into the nature of truth, the possibility of knowledge and the demands of moral and political life. These inquiries are pragmatic to the extent that they draw on experiences, empirically observable practices and the practical consequences of actions on our lives (Bacon 2012, 1).

Because of their focus on dialogic practice and reflexive agency, some pragmatist authors provide us with elements that allow us to bridge contemporary linguistic pragmatics and poststructuralist perspectives on discourse and subjectivity. Both pragmatist and poststructuralist approaches to the partial fixation of meaning share an opposition to the Cartesian view on man and meaning. In this context, the 'non-Cartesian' thrust and the 'pragmatic maxim' of pragmatism deserve closer attention. Pragmatism originated in direct opposition to a way of thinking that can be traced back to Descartes. As such, Charles Peirce formulated pragmatism as an alternative to what he called the Spirit of Cartesianism. Richard Bernstein summarises this notion as follows:

> *By this* the Spirit of Cartesianism *Peirce meant a framework of thinking that had come to dominate much of modern philosophy – where sharp dichotomies are drawn between what is mental and physical, as well as subject and object; where 'genuine' knowledge presumably rests upon indubitable foundations; and where we can bracket all prejudices by methodical doubt. This way of thinking introduces a whole series of interrelated problems that preoccupied philosophers: the problem of the external world, the problem of our knowledge of other minds, and the problem of how to correctly represent reality.* (Bernstein 2010, ix–x)

Peirce's pragmatic maxim was formulated in direct opposition to the foundationalism advocated by Descartes who understood the mind as a private sphere separate from the external world and knowledge as a matter of accurate representations. In order to solve the question whether we can know external reality, he claimed that we have to found our knowledge on something that is free from doubt. This foundation was the *Cogito*. Descartes believed that we can have knowledge before experience in the form of clear and distinct perceptions of the cogito (Bacon 2012, 14–15). This cogito was a model of subjectivity marked by an indivisibility of consciousness. According to Descartes, the mind or cogito could not be broken down into compartments as the body could but should be thought of as a unified and centred whole. Atkins summarises the reasoning behind the Cartesian statement *cogito ergo sum—I think therefore I am*—as follows: "[…] even if I can call into doubt everything I perceive or believe, including my very existence, I cannot doubt that I am doubting". Any amount of doubt reiterates the truth that the cogito—the I as a thinking thing—exists (Atkins 2005, 8).

Peirce refused the idea that we can found knowledge on absolute doubt. There are always beliefs that we consider to be certain and beyond doubt. Also, individuals are not the absolute judges of truth and knowledge. According to Peirce, the pursuit of knowledge is practiced within a community of inquirers. He argued in favour of an inter-subjective or social understanding of inquiry, knowing, communication and logic. His notion of knowledge is therefore a public one and can be summarised as follows:

It is only in and through subjecting our prejudices, hypotheses, and guesses to public criticism by a relevant community of inquirers that we can hope to escape from our limited perspectives, test our beliefs, and bring about the growth of knowledge. (Bernstein 2010, 32–38)

Peirce argued that we fix our opinions and beliefs through the social practice of inquiry. Inquiry is thereby understood as a process whereby fallible human beings have to revise their beliefs about themselves and about the world when our habitual actions lead to unexpected consequences. The resulting doubt and the need for action lead to a response in the form of inquiries that allow us to establish new habits, actions and beliefs (Eldridge and Philström 2011, 33–34). Pragmatists reject the very idea of immediate knowledge. They also refuse the Cartesian image of the mind and its relation to the world. Peirce argues that all knowledge presupposes interaction with the external world and that no knowledge is immediately given to us through our intuitions, not even knowledge about ourselves and our own doubts (Bacon 2012, 16–17). In this context, Peirce formulated a principle for formulating clear ideas that would become known as the *pragmatic maxim*. It goes as follows:

> *Consider what effects, which might conceivably have practical bearings, we conceive the object of our conception to have. Then our conception of those effects is the whole of our conception of the object.* (Peirce 1970b, 88)

While considering this maxim, it is important to bear in mind that Peirce claimed that all thought functions in and through signs, and that signs do not represent objects in any direct way. To Peirce, the sign is a triadic unity of what is represented (the object or the signified), how it is represented (the representamen or the signifier) and how it is interpreted (the interpretant). The representamen is the sign vehicle that can be compared to Saussure's signifier. It is the form that the sign takes. The interpretant can be roughly compared to the latter's signified since it is itself a sign in the mind of the interpreter. The interaction between all three components of the sign is what Peirce called semiosis. Between the object and the representamen, there is no direct connection though. Objects cannot be known directly, if that would be the case, we would not need signs at all (Chandler 2002, 29–31).

At first sight, the idea that one sign or thought always leads to another one implies an infinite regression of meaning. Signs can only function within networks of other signs, a principle that could throw us into an endless process of interpretation. But the pragmatic maxim shows us a way out. We can stop this regression by partially fixing (the meaning) of our beliefs, habits and discourses through an imagination of the conceivable practical bearings of the concept at hand. Herein lies the value of the pragmatic maxim. Peirce's model of the sign implies that there is no single interpretant or signified of a given sign. The meaning of a sign can therefore never be established for once and for all. (Bernstein 2010, 44–45). It can only be partially fixed by a community of inquirers that adheres to a scientific method (Peirce 1970a, 74–78).

3 The Pragmatic Dimension of Discourse as Articulation

Consequently, both Cartesian certainty and Cartesian doubt become pragmatic impossibilities.

Peirce was not a naïve realist and pointed out that signs can be classified according to the specific ways in which objects relate to signifiers (representamens) and signifieds (interpretants). His symbolic signs are marked by a purely arbitrary and conventional link between signifier and signified. Languages, alphabets, numbers, traffic lights and national flags exemplify signs in which the symbolic dimension semiosis prevails. Signs can also function iconically when signifiers and signifieds are perceived as resembling each other. This is the case with portraits, onomatopoeia or imitative gestures. And last but not least, signs can be indexical. Indexical signs signify through a non-arbitrary connection between signifier and signified based on contiguity. This link can be observed in the case of natural signs such as smoke or medical symptoms. But indexical signs also function by means of personal trademarks such accents or catch-phrases, by pointers such as index fingers or directional signposts (Chandler 2002, 36–37).

It is certainly true that Peirce's pragmatism opened up a path towards the explicit anti-representational stances taken by William James, John Dewey and Richard Rorty. But if we take a closer look at Peirce's scientific method, it becomes clear that he believes that following a scientific method could lead to one final conclusion about how things really are.

> *the* scientific *method must be such that the ultimate conclusion of every man shall be the same, or could be the same if inquiry were sufficiently persisted in. Such is the method of science. Its fundamental hypothesis, restated in more familiar language, is this: There are real things, whose characters are entirely independent of our opinions about them; those realities affect our senses according to regular laws, and, though our sensations are as different as our relations to the objects, yet, by taking advantage of the laws of perception, we can ascertain by reasoning how things really are, and any man, if he have sufficient experience and reason enough about it, will be led to the one true conclusion.* (Peirce 1970a)

The idea that we could arrive at one single truth through a rigorous scientific method of inquiry would be rejected by other pragmatists (Buekens 1995). For Peirce, a statement is true if it stands firm against all conceivable objections and criticism, thus becoming part of the imagined final opinion of a community of truth-pursuing researchers. James refuses the idea that in order for a concept to be clear or true, it has to be backed by an entire community of inquirers. For him, truth can never be thought about in terms of a fixed and static property. What matters to him is the role truth plays in our lives and his version of pragmatism seeks to answer the question what its cash value is in experiential terms. Consequently, he defines a true belief as a reliable action that enables us to successfully pursue a course of action (Bacon 2012, 33–35).

William James broadened and popularised the notion of 'pragmatism' by taking a pragmatic stance towards truth itself. He understood truth as a way to cope with experience and claimed that beliefs can be held to be true only if they confirm to the totality of experience. Richard Bernstein explains that James was attracted to the British empiricists because of the down-to-earth quality of their philosophy and because of their insistence on experience as the touchstone of all knowledge, their abhorrence of jargon and their habit of explaining whole by parts. At the same time, James rejected the empiricist idea that experience consists of an aggregate of discrete units of sensation. For like Peirce, James rejected the Cartesian distinctions between subject and object, consciousness and content (Bernstein 2010, 55–58). James' radical empiricism would lead him to formulate an empirical and pragmatic alternative to the Cartesian cogito and to make room for a radically empirical understanding of the self.

What is important here is that authors in the field of linguistic pragmatics do not seek to ground truth in an ultimate foundation either. On the contrary, they are interested in the way we inter-subjectively make sense of ourselves and our world by following each other's linguistic and non-linguistic cues as to how to interpret this world. In linguistic pragmatics, meaning is a practical communicative achievement. Scholars in this field seek to investigate the traces of meaning that interlocutors leave behind on the surface of discourse. In this sense, the pragmatic principle as interpreted by William James is alive and kicking in linguistic pragmatic approaches in how to investigate partial fixations of meaning and to leave speculation aside. James reformulated Peirce's maxim as follows:

> *What difference would it practically make to anyone if this notion rather than that notion were true? If no practical difference whatever can be traced, then the alternatives mean practically the same thing, and all dispute is idle. Whenever a dispute is serious, we ought to be able to show some practical difference that must follow from one side or the other's being right.* (James 1947, 199)

According to James, pragmatism involves an attitude whereby one turns away from verbal solutions, from fixed principles, closed systems and pretended absolutes and origins. He argues that ideas become meaningful to us as we link them to conceivable outcomes in reality. We 'ride' ideas until they bring us in a satisfactory relationship with our experience (James 1947). This also goes for ideas on self and politics as we deploy them in the context of our political engagement. A great deal of political debate is centred around a struggle over the definition of abstract signifiers that play a role in the establishment of political subjectivities and alliances that strive for hegemony. Any understanding of the particularities of notions such as 'integration' or 'identity' as deployed by specific actors needs to be based on an analysis of the way usage of such terms impacts on all other aspects of (discursive) practice.

One can think of the field of discourse studies as a way to investigate the way we ride ideas as marked and constituted in and through language and other semiotic systems. To put it in linguistic pragmatic terms: we frequently mark our identities and ideas linguistically. This does not mean that ideas stand in an unproblematic relationship to discourse. We cannot use discourse in order to identify someone's 'true' outlook on the world or to identify a person's 'real' and 'ultimate' identity. Pragmatically oriented discourse analysts don't even look for such things. Instead, they ask how our interactive usage of language allows us to generate and mark meaningful identities and contexts for interpretation in ever-shifting ways. Pragmatically oriented discourse analysts refrain from uncovering 'real' or 'ultimate' meanings. They merely seek to understand what practical and interpretive difference it would make to make one communicative choice rather than another. This mode of inquiry is radically empirical and operates on the basis of the pragmatist maxim as interpreted by James.

3.5 Early Pragmatist Understandings of Self and Subjectivity

There is a thematic continuity in pragmatism that can be described in terms of a focus on a process-based self that functions on the basis of interactional or dialogical principles. In fact, pragmatist ideas and tropes provided an important basis for the dialogical self of symbolic interactionism, constructivist sociology and social psychology (Wiley 2006, 14–19). Since all of these approaches are important sources for linguistic pragmatics, many pragmatic linguists have implicitly inherited the legacy of Peirce's rejection of the *Cartesian Spirit*. Of course, one cannot define the entire field of linguistic pragmatics as a non-Cartesian enterprise. In fact, this philosophical position is hardly ever mentioned in introductions to the field. And it is certainly possible to encounter varieties of pragmatics that exhibit Cartesian tropes (Kopytko 2000). Both Cartesian and non-Cartesian tropes tend to establish themselves rather implicitly in linguistic pragmatic literature. Nevertheless, pragmatically inclined authors who consider pragmatics in terms of a holistic perspective on language use tend to gravitate towards non-Cartesian positions.

Cartesian variants of pragmatics present us with a language user that functions on the basis of individual, rational, context-free, abstract and universal acts of cognition. Non-Cartesian perspectives consider the agent as marked by a cognition that is "social, context dependent, interactive, collective, dynamic and embodied" (Kopytko 2000, 796–798). I will subscribe to this latter perspective and argue that the compatibility of poststructuralist discourse theory and linguistic pragmatic approaches to discourse hinges on a shared refusal of the *Spirit of Cartesianism*. The Cartesian model of selfhood presents us with a unified and fully coherent whole whose existence could be established by thought and doubt alone. This self stands above the social whirl. The idea was that in knowing itself, it could know all other possible selves. Such transcendental notions of selfhood imply that human beings function in the same way across time and space, irrespective of the particular self-techniques, social relationships, cultural configurations that characterise specific settings (Holstein and Gubrium 2000, 19):

> *The transcendental self was* the *self – timeless, universal, and in each one of us around the globe and throughout history. Distinguished from our individual idiosyncrasies, this was the self we shared. In modest and ordinary terms it was called "human nature". In much less modest, extraordinary terminology, the transcendental self was nothing less than God, the Absolute Self, the World Soul.* (Solomon 1988 cited in Holstein and Gubrium 2000, 19)

Transcendental notions of selfhood do not help us to understand the varieties of the self that we encounter in social life. They do not allow us to explain the shifting sense of self that my interviewees perform and describe when they articulate their relationships to dominant actors and discourses that constitute the Flemish minority debates. The transcendental self is not the self they talk about when describing the difficulties of drawing a line between their sense of self and the engagements they are involved in. Neither is it the self that emerges in interview-settings or therapeutic couches. It is rather a hypothesis that was severely challenged by both poststructuralist and pragmatist thinkers. As a conceptual tool to explain the fact that individuals articulate their self-interpretations with various degrees and modes of coherence, the transcendental model of subjectivity is inadequate.

Pragmatist authors offer a more useful point of entry based on the idea that the self does not exist separate from or above communication. As such, William James offered a radically empirical alternative to the Cartesian model of selfhood. Moreover, James, Cooley and Mead would highlight the multiplicity of selfhood as well as its social grounding. Interestingly, like many poststructuralist authors, they emphasised the key role of pronouns in the emergence of subjectivity. They all distinguish between the 'I' and the 'me' and consider the self as a process-based entity that functions through the establishment of a relatively high degree of coherence in conscious, unconscious, linguistic and non-linguistic ways. The specifics of their models vary, but in all cases we are dealing with "a distinct version of the 'decentred self'" which is a central idea of postmodernism (Wiley 2006, 19).

The pragmatist notion of the empirical self paved the road for the self as an object of investigation in social science. It involved a shift from an analysis of the subject in the abstract to an analysis of the self in the context of everyday living. The definition of the 'empirical self' as posited by William James is deceivingly simple: "The empirical self of each of us is all that he is tempted to call by the name of me" (James 1981, 279). The problem is that the distinction between 'me' and 'mine' is very difficult to draw. James pointed out that:

We feel and act about certain things that are ours very much as we feel and act about ourselves. Our fame, our children, the work of our hands, may be as dear to us as our bodies are, and arouse the same feelings and the same acts of reprisal if attacked. And our bodies themselves, are they simply ours, or are they us? Certainly men have been ready to disown their very bodies and to regard them as mere vestures, or even as prisons of clay from which they should some day be glad to escape. (James 1981, 279)

Because of the vague line between what men can call theirs and what they call their selves, James prefers to treat the self as 'fluctuating material' that consists of four constituents: a material self, a social self, a spiritual self and a so-called 'pure ego' that functions as a fluctuating stream of consciousness. The material self includes the body but also our immediate family and our homes. If a family member dies, a part of our self goes as well. Also, to varying degrees, our material collections become part of our empirical selves. Consequently, a loss of ownership can lead to a "sense of the shrinkage of our personality" (James 1981, 281, 292) on the condition that we have invested such objects with self-feeling and vice versa. The social self is the realm of multiplicity. We have as many social selves as we have relationships with individuals and groups. This results in "what practically is a division of the man into several selves" that may be either in discord or in accord with each other (James 1981, 281–283).

The third dimension of James' empirical self is the spiritual self. Note that this is *not* an inner core or an essence in any objective sense of the word. As James put it, it is "not the bare principle of personal unity, or 'pure' ego" (James 1981, 283). And as we will see, not even James' 'pure ego' presents us with a stable core for subjectivity. The notion of the spiritual self refers to a person's subjective being, his or her concrete psychic faculties and dispositions. It refers to things such as our ability to argue, our moral stances, or our will. It is what brings us to a subjective experience of having a centre around which our subjective life is construed. But interestingly, James is always careful to state that this is what it *appears* to be. Even though he considers the spiritual self to be "the most enduring and intimate part of the self", it should be understood in terms of processes and movements rather than as a stable entity (James 1981, 283, 288). Whether the spiritual self be "an indivisible active soul-substance" or a mere "personification of the pronoun I", or "any other of the guesses as to what its nature might be", it comes to us through the feelings, process

3 The Pragmatic Dimension of Discourse as Articulation

and movements through which we distinguish between I and me (James 1981, 292–293).

James argues out that we 'feel' a central sense of self, "no matter whether it be a spiritual substance or only a delusive word" (James 1981, 286). The pronoun 'I' refers to this reflexive feeling. The 'I' only 'exists' in our always momentary stream of consciousness. It is a Thought with a capital T. It refers to one's present mental state that binds individual past facts with each other and with itself. The Thought includes all past thoughts and experiences of the self that are quilted or herded together like wild cattle might be. The 'me' is the empirical aggregate of the things we know and experienced. There is no single shepherd that holds together all aspects and fragments of the 'me'. Rather, the stream of consciousness implies a long succession of herdsmen or selves that come rapidly into possession of each other's flock of experiences and thoughts. Throughout this process, they pass on to each other the title of 'self' (James 1981, 319–321). James claims that "Each Thought is thus born an owner, and dies owned, transmitting whatever it realised as its Self to its own later proprietor" (James 1981, 322). Concepts such as 'the soul' or 'the transcendental ego' are but hypotheses that seek to explain the unity of self and our stability in the face of our flock of thoughts and experiences.

Gubrium and Holstein point out that James' self arises through embodied interaction and functions as a working point of reference for ourselves as well as for the others we communicate with. As such, it is merely as stable as the patterns and material signs of our relationships (Holstein and Gubrium 2000, 23–24). Put differently, James' self is an interpretive function of the way we articulate experiences with each other and invest them with feeling. The analytical distinction between 'I' and 'me' would be adapted and adopted by other pragmatists such as Cooley and Mead and would subsequently impact on several variants of symbolic interactionism as well as on the dramaturgical approach to the self outlined by Erving Goffman (Meltzer et al. 1975). Pragmatist authors tend to consider pronouns as communicative markers of the experiencing self (Holstein and Gubrium 2000, 24). But these pronouns are not mere 'expressions' of a pre-existing unity. They are important not merely for communicating a sense of unity towards others but also for establishing this unity in relation towards oneself.

Referring to James, the pragmatist Charles Horton Cooley argued that pronouns function as names for a sense of appropriation that comes to us in the form of a my-feeling. For Cooley, "the self is that to which we have a my-attitude". This my-feeling can arise whenever an aspect the 'me' is attacked through theft, slander or ridicule. Self-feeling will automatically appear when such things occur. Moreover, Cooley pointed out that the mere pronunciation of pronouns such as 'I' or 'My' triggers (a sense of) self-feeling (Holstein and Gubrium 2000, 25–26). For Cooley, crude feelings of selfhood already exist at birth in an instinctual way. Nevertheless, this sense of self is altered, developed and changed over time along with our experiences in the world. It is in this sense that Cooley adds that the self, while rooted in self-feeling, operates in the imagination and always responds to real and imagined others. This last point is probably the most innovative aspect of Cooley's self (Holstein and Gubrium 2000, 26–27; Meltzer et al. 1975). Following the work of Baldwin, Cooley claimed that the entire empirical self is fundamentally social. This becomes very clear in his idea of the looking-glass self. Based on rather unsystematic observations of his own children, he came to the conclusion that human beings become aware of others before they become aware of themselves. Our very idea of self is an 'imaginative fact' that is established through "The imagination of our appearance to other persons; the imagination of his judgement of that appearance, and some sort of self-feeling, such as pride or mortification" (Cooley cited in Holstein and Gubrium 2000, 26–27).

George W. Mead thought that neither James nor Cooley went far enough in their social conceptualisation of the self. He pointed out that their emphasis on reflexive self-feeling did not account for the origin of the self. We may experience self-feeling if those around us are hurt, but the question to be asked is how this is made possible (Mead 1967, 173). Mead's entire endeavour was to show that "mind and the self are without residue social emergent" and that "language, in the form of the vocal gesture, provides the mechanism for their emergence" (Morris 1963, xiv). With this goal in mind, he developed a notion of the self in terms of a linguistic internalisation of a conversation of gestures. For Mead, the self does not exist at birth but emerges through the use of language:

3 The Pragmatic Dimension of Discourse as Articulation

I know of no other form of behaviour than the linguistic in which the individual is an object to himself, and, so far as I can see, the individual is not a self in the reflexive sense unless he is an object to himself. (Mead 1967, 142)

Mead points out that the word 'self' indicates the possibility of reflexivity. It points towards "that which can be both subject and object" to itself (Mead 1967, 136–137). But this does not mean that consciousness constitutes the self in its own right as if it were some sort of *cogito*. In fact, it cannot exist without a linguistic integration of our communications of gestures with others. Like all interacting biological organisms, human beings are engaged in conversations of gestures with each other. Animals communicate with behavioural stimuli called gestures that elicit responses that can function as stimuli in their own right. In the context of dogfights for instance, we can identify gestures such as growls, movements, postures and the baring of teeth aimed at a back-and-forth adjustment of behaviour. But human communication is different because of the ability to use significant symbols. According to Mead, language allows human beings to function as minded entities that can convey shared meanings and to emancipate themselves from the rather un-reflexive conversations of gestures we see in animal behaviour (Watson 2010, 305). This is made possible because of the fact that language allows us to integrate the points of views and the roles of others. It allows us to integrate the conversations of gestures within ourselves. Thought itself thus comes to function as an internalised conversation with real or imagined others. The self arises in the process (Mead 1967, 141–142).

Even though children start their communicative life with an imitation of the gestures they notice around them, at some point they will enter a stage of play whereby they take on the roles of others without others being present by means of language. This can be observed in acts of so-called doubling whereby the child takes on the roles of others such as policemen or parents and can provide itself with "a set of stimuli that will call out in itself the responses that they would call out in others". In response to the adopted role and the associated set of gestures, an organised structure of the self arises. However, the child also needs to learn how various roles in society relate to each other. According to Mead, the child needs to learn the structure of the social as an organised game with rules that structure the relationships between these roles. The difference between 'play' and 'game' is that in the latter, "the child must have the attitude of all the others involved in the game" in the form of a 'generalised other' (Mead 1967, 152–156).

In a way that is reminiscent of James and Cooley, Mead points out that there can be no clear line between our own selves and those of others. His reasoning is that our own selves only enter into our experience in so far as the selves of others do the same thing. (Mead 1967, 164). Also, he argues in favour of the normality of the multiple personality even though he acknowledges that pathological forms exist as well:

We carry on a whole series of different relationships to different people. We are one thing to one man and another thing to another. There are parts of the self which exist only for the self in relation to itself. We divide ourselves up in all sorts of different selves with reference to our acquaintances. We discuss politics with one and religion with another. There are all sorts of different selves answering to all sorts of different social reactions. It is the social process itself that is responsible for the appearance of the self; it is not there as a self apart from this type of experience. (Mead 1967, 142)

Mead uses similar terminology as James and Cooley in order to describe the different experiential 'phases' of the self while providing them with different meanings. As such, he defines the 'I' as a response of the individual to the attitude of the community as it appears in his own experience. At the same time, the 'I' of this moment continually turns into the 'me' in the next moment. As Mead puts it, "I cannot turn around quick enough to catch myself." To Mead, the 'I' is always a functional relationship that we can only access indirectly through memory. Consequently, the 'I' is responsible for the fact that we are never fully aware of what we are and that we are able to surprise ourselves with our own actions (Mead 1967, 174).

There is an element of uncertainty tied to the 'I'. Whereas the 'me' is constituted by the internalisation of conversations of gestures through language, the 'I' is our response to this conversation. Mead associates the possibility of freedom and initiative with the 'I' because the 'I' can never completely control and calculate the experience of its future-oriented actions. Consequently, even consciously considered behaviour leads to novel experiences that will impact on the way 'me' and 'self' are structured. For Mead, the self is not so much a substance as a process whereby the conversation of gestures is internalised in an organic form. (Mead 1967, 176–178).

To say that the 'I' and the 'me' are phases of the self means that they are parts or dimensions of the same entity or process. But there are situations and individuals in which the 'me' is foregrounded and there are other types of subjectivity where the 'I' seems to take the upper hand. People who tend to gravitate towards convention and conformity with roles belong to the former type. In contrast, for those who reply to the incorporated attitudes of others in a way that makes a social difference, the 'I' is the more important phase of experience. Such persons are more likely to be credited with a 'definite personality' (Mead 1967, 200). This should not be taken to mean that the 'I' is a unified and centred whole. Rather, Mead's model—like the models of Cooley and James—implies that consciousness is always consciousness of something else. It is an interpretive and functional process relative to experience, a notion that we will retain throughout this book with the caveat that reflexive consciousness is always mediated discursively.

Nevertheless, in spite of their focus on interaction, symbols and conversations (of gestures), the early pragmatists did not focus on discourse in its own right. And even though contemporary approaches to discourse would not reject any of the pragmatist ideas, discourse analysts stress that meanings do not come to us in the abstract. They always involve an articulation of experiences and concrete signifiers, labels, utterances, arguments, narratives and/or genres that are given to us in various empirical forms. All discourse functions on the basis of dialogical principles. We all use or internalise the words and actions of others into our own subjectivities in order to make sense of ourselves and of the world. However, the specific modes that such awareness can take are not analysed or explained by the early pragmatists by means of systematic investigations of particular ways of speaking and/or writing. The input of the pragmatists lies elsewhere. Mead and his predecessors provided an important basis for early interactional sociology that in turn allowed for the development of various modes of discourse analysis and linguistic pragmatics.

Approaches such as symbolic interactionism, ethnomethodology, labelling and role theory are immediate heirs to the pragmatist tradition. Pragmatism gave rise to a social science that stresses the agentive and reflexive dimensions of subjectivity without falling into the trappings of solipsism. The Chicago and Iowa schools of symbolic interactionism are respectively interpretive and positivist continuations of Mead's pragmatism (Meltzer et al. 1975, 55–67). Likewise, Garfinkel's ethnomethodology can be linked to one of the main themes in classical pragmatism: "The relevance of real lived experiences, habitual practices and language with its indexically and socially constitutive characteristics." By focusing on the everyday methods through which society members structure, interpret and perform their activities, ethnomethodology seeks to uncover the interactional structure of everyday practices (Domke and Holly 2011, 263).

Pragmatism also provided an important basis for Erving Goffman's dramaturgical approach to interaction. His book on *the presentation of self in everyday life* provides us with a metaphorical analysis of subjectivity as established through performative interactions that define the situations in which we act and come to understand ourselves. Goffman is first and foremost concerned with the impressions we *give off* and that enable others to make inferences about the way they should define the context of interaction and the practically established identities involved (Goffman 1969, 14–15). He explicitly takes "a functional and pragmatic view" and posits that individuals communicate impressions in conscious and unconscious ways in order to score the pragmatic effect of letting others act *as if* we have conveyed a particular impression (Goffman 1969, 18).

Goffman argues that we rely on social roles in order to present ourselves in public life. These roles are conceptualised as enactments of rights and duties linked to a given status in society. They consist of different parts or routines that function as pre-established patterns of action that generate social relationships when systematically performed for particular audiences (Goffman 1969, 27). Goffman builds upon William James' idea that an individual "has as many social selves as there are distinct groups of persons about whose opinion he cares" (James cited in Goffman 1969, 57). Roles thus function as idealised versions of the fragmentary group-identities we care about and that make up our social selves. As such, we may invest our roles with various degrees and modes of belief (Goffman 1969, 77).

Some people may reduce their selves to the roles they perform. Such self-understandings involve the sort of fantasy, repression, association and dissociation described by psychoanalysts (Goffman 1969, 86–87). We may also treat others as if there is nothing more to them than the particular role they are enacting. At the same time, it is possible to be cynical and to enact roles in performances in which we don't believe at all. Individuals invest their roles and practices with different types of affect because their relationships to particular identities are supported by ideological fantasies that allow us to invest our normative practices and values with emotional force (Glynos 2008, 289). We may be aware of a certain role distance but no matter our degree of reflexivity, "appearances still have to be managed" and marked in interaction (Goffman 1969, 77).

It is important to stress that role performance is a social accomplishment. It requires a team effort and it is therefore important to keep in mind that role performance can never be reduced to an "expressive extension of the characteristics of the performer" (Goffman 1969, 83). This is not to say that the self is 'a scam' or 'deception'. Rather, it is a complex interactional achievement. Even 'sincerity' has to be performed somehow if it is to be interpreted as such. Goffman's self is both a psychological and a social reality (O'Driscoll 2009, 81). Goffman does not belittle human agency. He merely points out that individuality is constituted *through* the complexity of performative and inter-subjective practices (O'Driscoll 2009, 85). A successful definition of a situation always requires an audience, even if this audience is entirely imagined (Goffman 1969, 86–87).

The irony of the social self lies in the fact that the processes that allow for self-constitution frequently generate roles and identities that are deemed socially undesirable (Holstein and Gubrium 2000). In *Asylums,* Goffman writes that stigmatised persons tend to incorporate the dominant beliefs regarding their stigmatised roles. This incorporation enables them to become "intimately alive to what others see a his failing, inevitably causing him, if only for moments to agree that he does indeed fall short of what he really ought to be" (Holstein and Gubrium 2000, 54). Totalising institutions such as prisons or asylums are very good at this according to Goffman. Here, an individual's sense of self can be mortified through ritualised interactions that screen out the rest of the world and that enclose individuals in an identity-trimming environment (Elliott 2009, 41–42).

Goffman's influence on pragmatics was both great and small. He broadened the social awareness of many linguists and a lot of his concepts were taken up by pragmatically oriented authors seeking to understand the complicities of linguistic interaction. Goffman's work on face, relevance and conversation was of special relevance here. Nevertheless, Goffman was no linguist. And even though he provides us with many examples of linguistic interaction in order to substantiate his claims, he considers language as merely one type of interaction. Broadly speaking, Goffman's value to pragmatic authors lies first and foremost in his contribution to the performative turn that pragmatics has taken in recent decades. At the same time, he reminds us that the rules of interaction should be understood in relation to the way we perform and understand ourselves (O'Driscoll 2009, 92–94; Domke and Holly 2011, 277–278).

In his work on participation frameworks, Goffman describes the various interactional roles people can occupy with respect to their statements. A speaker can perform the role of animator. The animator is the entity that actually communicates. It can be a person but it may also be a person mixed with some type of technology such as a cell phone. The animator is the sounding box through which utterances are made. Secondly, there is the author who composes the words uttered by the animator. The author and the animator are not necessarily the same person. For instance, a speech-writer can be the author of a politician's speech. Thirdly, there is the role of the *principal* who is responsible for the utterance. For instance, a politician's speech may be attributed to her political faction or party even though the animator and author roles attributed to this speech are different entities. As we will see, this differentiation between various ways in which subjects can be articulated with the discourses they perform is also a key theme in enunciative pragmatics.

For now, it suffices to know that the pragmatist notion of the empirical self gave rise to interpretive and functional approaches to human interaction whereby both multiplicity and coherence function as key principles of subjectivity. Moreover, this double function of subjectivity is intertwined with the principles of adaptability, negotiability and variability. Like language, all identity is adaptable, negotiable and variable. Pragmatism is not a form of discourse analysis in itself but it does provide an important background for the emergence of interactional and pragmatically oriented understandings of discourse. Moreover, it reminds us of the fact that our limited awareness of the fragmented dimensions of selfhood goes hand in hand with our attempts to reach a more or less coherent sense of self and context.

3.6 Fixing Meaning Through Performative Language Games

Ordinary language philosophy is the second pillar of linguistic pragmatics. Its most important contributions to the field can be found in Wittgenstein's programme of relating meaning to language use, in Austin's speech act theory and in Grice's ideas on the logic of conversation (Verschueren 2009, 4). It is often said that the linguistic and analytic turns in philosophy displaced pragmatism. Alternatively, Bernstein points out that philosophers such as Wittgenstein advanced themes that were already anticipated by the classical pragmatists. Wittgenstein responded to some of the same problems in modern philosophy as the pragmatists did before him and as the (post-)structuralists would do after him (Bernstein 2010, x, 14–15). Wittgenstein shares with the early pragmatists "a central – perhaps the central – emphasis with pragmatism: the emphasis on the primacy of practice" (Putnam 1995, 52 in Bernstein 2010, 21).

Within the context of linguistic pragmatics, most authors refer to the later work of Wittgenstein as written down in his *Philosophical investigations* (Wittgenstein 1967). This work can be read as a critique of the views he held as an ideal-language philosopher. In his renewed philosophy, ordinary language use would come to occupy a place of honour. Moving away from the idea that meaning is truth-conditional and that philosophy should seek to develop a language that is as representational as possible, he developed an understanding of language in terms of rules, games and family resemblances (Sbisà 2011a). As such, Wittgenstein developed a practice-based and non-representational theory of meaning that has informed a great deal of linguistic pragmatic research.

In his *Philosophical investigations*, Wittgenstein explains why it makes no sense to look for something like an essence of human language or a general characteristic that language must have in order to function and to be meaningful. He moved away from his earlier view that meaning results from a correspondence between logical forms and the shape of reality. Instead, he argued that language can become meaningful in a variety of ways. Wittgenstein's renewed concept of language is based on an analogy with a concept of 'games' that can be summarised as follows (Leilich 2011):

> *If one would ask what a game is, one would have difficulties to give a general definition, because each definition would let out some activity we could call a game. There is no collection of necessary features such as an adversary or a board, which all games would have to share in order to be games. Instead of general features which are common to all games we find family-resemblance, a network of overlapping and criss-crossing similarities.* (Leilich 2011, 203)

The analogy goes further. Both games and languages are rule-guided activities. Rules should not be thought about in terms of prescriptions for behaviour. It is rather the other way around. Something becomes a rule because we establish social practices without which such rules would not exist. Moreover, such regulated language games are always practiced within contexts that Wittgenstein describes in terms of forms of life (Kopytko 2007, 794–797). The name of Wittgenstein frequently pops up in anti-essentialist arguments within linguistic pragmatic as well as within poststructuralist perspectives on discourse. In fact, the very concept of logic outlined by Glynos and Howarth is constructed with reference to Wittgenstein's understanding of language games:

> *Like Wittgenstein's 'game', the term* logic *connotes a range of grammars in which 'logic' is uttered, articulated, implied, and so on. However, from a Wittgentseinian point of view, the identification of all these grammars as grammars* of logic *does not mean that we have to isolate a feature or set of features they all have in common. Of course, they may happen to share some feature(s), but this is not what is responsible for such a gather under 'logic'. Rather, again following Wittgenstein, they share a set of* family *resemblances.* (Glynos and Howarth 2007, 134)

The embrace of Wittgenstein by pragmatic linguists is based on a shared observation that meaningful language can take an almost unlimited number of forms. Pragmatically oriented linguistic anthropologists such as Alessandro Duranti prefer Wittgenstein's concept of language games over speech act theory because it provides a rich framework for analysing language as a contextualised social activity. Also, the notion of language games puts less stress on the role of individual intention in the generation of meaning then speech act theory (Leilich 2011). Roman Kopytko goes as far as to label Wittgenstein as "the first pragmatician" because of his anti-essentialist stance on language, his rejection of representationalism, his idea of meaning as use, his flexible understanding of rules and his rejection of Cartesian dualism in general (Kopytko 2007, 807). This may be an exaggeration though. Similar things may be said about the early pragmatists.

The second big contribution of ordinary language philosophy to linguistic pragmatic and poststructuralist approaches to discourse is the concept of the speech act. Like Wittgenstein, Austin reacted against ideal-language philosophies that reduced language to the function of making statements about true or false states of affairs. He also rejected the formal and truth-conditional semantics that supported such reductionist views. Austin wrote that real languages have few if any explicit conventions, no sharp limits to the sphere of operation of rules and no clear distinctions between syntax and pragmatics. Implicitly, he argued in favour of an integration of syntax and semantics into pragmatics (Nerlich and Clarke 1996, 366–368).

Even though he did not rely on the notion of pragmatics in order to make his point, he admitted to Pitcher that he chose the title for his contribution to the William James lecture series "for its pragmatic ring, to honour the man for whom the lectures were named" (Nerlich and Clarke 1996, 368). His contribution was titled *How to do things with words* (Austin 2011) and offered a distinction between performative and constative utterances. In contrast to constatives, performatives don't just 'state' things but 'do' things to the world and to the language user. Ritual speech acts such as 'I now pronounce you man and wife' or 'I christen this ship the Mr Stalin' wed people and baptise boats. Performative statements transform reality whereas constative statements merely convey information and state things (Robinson 2006, 43–45).

Later on, Austin would abandon this distinction and advocate the idea that *all* saying is doing. This involved an abandonment of the performative/constative opposition. Instead, Austin came to view every utterance as a simultaneous performance of locutionary, illocutionary and perloctionary acts. The performance of a locution involves the utterance of a string of (phonetic) sounds according to particular (phatic) conventions with a certain (rhetoric or semantic) meaning. The illocutionary dimension refers to the way in which utterances are used. This dimension of the speech act can be designated with speech act verbs (e.g. to thank, to promise, to insult) and/or their nominalisations (e.g. lies, denials, warnings, congratulations). The illocution is what one might call the force we attribute to an utterance (Sbisà 2009, 231–232). Nevertheless, the illocutionary force of an utterance does not necessarily score the desired effect upon the feelings, thoughts or actions of our interlocutors.

What is done by saying something is referred to as a perlocution. Perlocutions can be described by completing the utterance 'I got him/her to'. For instance, by producing a warning, we may score the perlocutionary effect of alarming someone; the utterance of a command may lead to a persuasion to act in a particular way; or an argument may or may not convince someone. It should be noted that there is a difference between the take-up and the taking effect of an illocution. We are able to recognise the illocutionary force of an utterance as an argument without being convinced by the utterance itself. Perlocutionary effects may include verbal and non-verbal responses or sequels. As such, a warning may score the perlocutionary effects of deterring someone to do something and/or prompt this person to alarm others (Austin 2011, 23–25). Austin named the conventional conditions under which speech acts are carried out successfully 'felicity conditions': participants and circumstances have to be appropriate to the invocation of the procedure. Such procedures have to be carried out completely and correctly in a manner whereby participants are expected to appropriate inner states and attitudes in accordance with which they act (Sbisà 2009, 232–233).

Speech acts can be performed implicitly or explicitly. Explicit speech acts involve an explicit articulation of what one does in using language. Examples include Austin's 'I promise that' or 'I pronounce you man and wife'. However, language contains a whole range of devices that can communicate illocutionary force such as certain adverbs (e.g. frankly, seriously, briefly, confidentially), aspects of word order, stress and intonation.

A question such as *Can you call me a taxi* is more likely to be a request than a question about one's ability to call a taxi (Verschueren 1999, 25). Implicit speech acts are never completely implicit. The conveyance of implicit meaning always relies on the negotiable and adaptable usage of linguistic and non-linguistic contextualisation cues that allow for processes of inference. Even the most implicit messages require indexes and some degree of metapragmatic awareness with respect to the contextualised (conventional and non-conventional) usage of semiotic forms.

Austin's speech act theory is relevant for discourse studies for a number of reasons. First of all, it draws our attention to the fact that performative language use can transform the world. It does not merely reflect or represent states of affairs but impacts on—our imagination and experience of—reality. Secondly, to say that language can transform reality implies that performative language use entails the exercise of power. The force of an utterance lies in its power to change things. Thirdly, speech act theory has important implications for our understanding(s) of self and subjectivity. It can be argued that the principle of performativity does not apply to linguistic speech acts alone but to action in general. This means that our linguistic and non-linguistic performances impact on the way we shape and transform our sense of self and identity (Robinson 2006, 60–69). It also means that the consequent possibilities for agency interface with social conventions and relations.

From a performative perspective, the possibility of agency lies in the possibility to play with the rules and regulations that structure discourse and subjectivity. Performativity is an important principle in the partial fixation of meaning. It gives substance to our reflexive senses of self, other and world. Judith Butler points out that subjectivity may be an effect that is generated, produced and performed through discourse and that this effect opens up possibilities for agency that are foreclosed by fixed and foundational categories of identity and the self (Butler 1990, 198, 201). Her reading of Austin's speech act theory (as interpreted by Derrida) is decidedly non-Cartesian and compatible with notions of the self informed by James' pragmatic maxim. Butler's take on performativity directs our attention to the political dimensions of self and subjectivity. If subjectivity is inscribed on the performative surfaces of the body, it cannot be considered in terms of mere 'expression' of an inner core or essence. Also, it is important to realise that both linguistic and non-linguistic practices have a performative and embodied dimension that can alter the subjectivity of the performer (Butler 1999, xxvi–xxvii).

Consider the language game of a political debate. Quite often, debates are not—exclusively—about the propositional 'content' of what is said. They are also about what is done by saying something. Do politicians argue or insult each other? Is a statement a racist remark or an objective description of some social reality? How does one perform a democratic image? How does one perform legitimacy or trustworthiness? Political identities, discourses and ideologies are not challenged by means of arguments alone. A great deal of metapragmatic efforts are put into negotiations over the force that needs to be attributed to specific utterances. For instance, if Angela Merkel says that 'multiculturalism has failed', this speech act can be construed as an objective statement, as a racist slur or as a populist manipulation. Performance is always an inter-subjective phenomenon and the value attached to an utterance impacts on the way identities are construed, performed and negotiated.

Grice's theory of speech acts and conversational implicatures constitutes the third main contribution of ordinary language philosophy to pragmatics. In contrast to Wittgenstein, Grice developed a view that meaning was based first and foremost on speaker's intentions. He observed that there are two competing notions of 'meaning' to be explained. What a speaker means with an utterance and the meaning of a sentence do not necessarily coincide. According to Grice, speaker meaning is prior to sentence meaning (Sbisà 2009, 231, 2011b, 6–7). Of course, the idea that we can ground meaning—primarily—in individual intentions runs against the views on discourse, performativity and (inter-)subjectivity outlined thus far. It is certainly true that language users tend to attribute intentions to their interlocutors. But this does not entail that meaning is a matter of accurately identifying intentions in individual minds.

It should be clear that I do not subscribe to the rather unified understanding of self and subjectivity that underlies the notions of intentionality advocated by Grice and Searle. As we will see, I propose an alternative understanding of subjectivity in which the functions of utterer, addressee, agent and observer do not simply correspond to individual participants in a language game. This will become very clear in the upcoming chapter on enunciative linguistics. Subjectivity is more complex and opaque a phenomenon than the intentional models proposed by Austin and Searle suggest (Sbisà 2011b). This being said, it is useful to take a closer look at the notion of conversational implicature proposed by Grice because it does provide us with important insights into the process of making inferences and into the way implicit meanings can be generated.

Like Austin, Grice presented his ideas on inference and conversation in a paper titled *Logic and conversation* at the William James lectures series in Harvard in 1967 (Grice 2011). His main claim was that there is an underlying principle that determines the way language is used in rational interaction with maximum efficiency and effectivity (Huang 2007, 25). And like Searle, Grice was interested in the problem of "how it is possible for the speaker to say one thing and mean that but also to mean something else" (Searle 2011, 28). Grice argued that speaker meaning refers to the intention of a speaker to produce an effect in the hearer by triggering a recognition on the part of the hearer of his intention to produce that effect (Sbisà 2011a, 18).

According to Grice, there is a logic to conversation that cannot be reduced to the study of validity and invalidity of inferences as conceptualised in formal logic (Mey 1998, 720–721; Vergauwen 1995). He argued that conversation has a logic of its own and should be understood with reference to an over-arching co-operative principle. According to him, speakers generally operate on the assumption that language use is co-operative and that a conversational contribution will be made in a way "such as is required, at the stage at which it occurs, by the accepted purpose and direction of the talk exchange in which you are engaged" (Grice 1975 cited in: Verschueren 1999). Within this framework, co-operation is a regulative principle that shapes the structure of our own conversational contributions as well as the way we set about interpreting the utterances made by others (Cummings 2005, 10).

Grice composed a list of four maxims accompanying the co-operative principle (Verschueren 1999, 32, Huang 2007, 25). These maxims do not present us with an account of what we actually do when we use language. Rather, they "specify what participants have to do in order to converse in a maximally efficient, rational, co-operative way: they should speak sincerely, relevantly and clearly, while providing sufficient information"

(Levinson 1983, 102). Grice's conversational maxims are usually presented in the following way (Cummings 2005, 11; Huang 2007, 25; Levinson 1983, 101–102; Mey 1999, 65; Robinson 2006, 161–162; Verschueren 1999, 32):

The maxim of quantity: try to make your contribution one that is true

a. Make your contribution as informative as is required for the current purposes of the exchange.
b. Do not make your contribution more informative than is required.

The maxim of quality:

a. Do not say what you believe to be false.
b. Do not say that for which you lack adequate evidence.

The maxim of relation (later called relevance): be relevant
The maxim of manner:

a. Avoid obscurity of expression
b. Avoid ambiguity
c. Be brief
d. Be orderly

There are several things a speaker can do with regard to the maxims. First of all, a speaker may simply observe them. Secondly, he or she can violate a maxim by lying, by trying to be sarcastic, ironic or funny and so on. Thirdly, a speaker can opt out of maxims. The use of hedges is a good case in point. Huang provides us with some useful examples for each maxim (Huang 2007, 26–27):

quality:

as far as I know,
I'm not sure if this is true, but …
I may be wrong, but …

3 The Pragmatic Dimension of Discourse as Articulation

quantity:

As you probably already know,
I can't say any more
I probably don't need to say this, but ...

relation:

Oh, by the way,
I'm not sure if this is relevant, but ...
I don't want to change the subject, but ...

manner:

I'm not sure if this is clear, but ...
I don't know if this makes sense, but ...
This may be a bit tedious but ...

There is evidence that speakers are aware of the maxims and generally orient to them. However, this does not mean that people will always talk sincerely, relevantly and clearly, even when they intend to be co-operative. Grice's point is that when talk does not proceed according to the maxims, the co-operative principle may still hold and that "the principles are nevertheless being adhered to at some deeper level" (Levinson 1983, 102). This happens when the co-operative principle and the maxims are strategically flouted or exploited in order to generate implicit meaning (Huang 2007, 27; Verschueren 1999, 31–36). Levinson exemplifies the way speakers may convey implicit messages as follows:

A (to passerby): I've just run out of petrol
B: Oh; there's a garage just around the corner

B does not tell A where to get petrol in any explicit way. Rather, he produces an utterance and relies on the idea that A will interpret his message according to the co-operative principle and the related maxims. As Levinson puts it: "if the speaker is observing the maxims in a fairly direct way, he may nevertheless rely on the addressee to amplify what he says by some straightforward inferences based on the assumption that the speaker is following the maxims". B's utterance may thus be taken to implicate that A may obtain petrol at the garage. B would certainly be less than co-operative if he knew the garage was closed or did not sell any petrol (Levinson 1983, 104).

When faced with conspicuous flouting of a maxim by a speaker, one may think that in addition to the maxims, the co-operative principle is being breached. In this case, the utterance is likely to be interpreted as a lie or as a deception. However, one may also assume that the speaker is still observing the co-operative principle. In this case, the interpretive process can be explicated in the following way: "If the speaker is still co-operative, and if he or she is exploiting a maxim in such a way that I should recognize the infringement, then he or she is doing so in order to convey some extra message, which is in keeping with the co-operative principle at some deeper level" (Huang 2007, 29). Huang provides us with a useful example. Consider the sentence 'Chomsky is a great sociolinguist'. If one knows that Chomsky is no sociolinguist at all, and if one still adheres to the co-operative principle, the addressee must assume that the speaker is trying to convey something different from what he or she has actually said. In this case, the utterance is likely to be interpreted as ironic (Huang 2007, 29–30).

In some language games, maxims are breached systematically. This frequently happens when norms of politeness or humour are involved. Verschueren points out that in both cases, the impossibility to be fully explicit can be exploited strategically in order to generate implicated meaning (Verschueren 1999, 35–36). It can be argued that inferences occur at every level of linguistic interpretation because there is no such thing as pure semantic content from a pragmatic perspective. Even the meanings of relatively straightforward words such as 'table' or 'opening' need to be worked out pragmatically if they are to make sense to interlocutors in concrete contexts (Kompa and Meggle 2011, 210–215).

The pragmatic interest in Grice's maxims has to be understood in relation to the component view of linguistics and the associated distinction between pragmatics and semantics. In this component view, the 'pragmatic' process of inference stands apart from 'semantic' types of implicit meaning such as implication, entailment and logical consequence. The latter types of implicitness supposedly hinge on semantic or logical contents. For instance, Levinson argues that "implicatures are not semantic inferences, but rather inferences based on both the content of what has been said and some specific assumptions about the co-operative nature of ordinary verbal interaction" (Levinson 1983, 103–104). However, if we consider pragmatics as a general perspective on language use, it becomes clear that "languages provide numerous conventionalised carriers of implicit meaning, tools for linking explicit content to relevant aspects of background information" (Verschueren 1999, 27). For instance, awareness of implicit meaning can be triggered by means of presuppositions, entailments or conventional implicatures (Bertucelli Papi 2009, 141; Verschueren 1999, 33–34).

Presuppositions are pragmatic inferences or assumptions that seem to be built into linguistic expressions and can be isolated by means of specific linguistic tests such as negation. They hold no matter if sentences are true or false (Levinson 1983, 167–168). Consider the sentence 'the year of prosperity and peace has ended'. Both the change-of-state verb 'end' and the definite description 'the year of prosperity and peace' presuppose that there has been a stretch of time that can legitimately be described in those terms (Verschueren 1999, 27–30). Presuppositions can be triggered by a range of linguistic forms including descriptions, implicative verbs, change-of-state verbs, verbs of judging, temporal clauses, cleft sentences, implicit clefts with stressed constituents, comparisons, contrasts and questions (Levinson 1983, 179–185).

Implicit meanings can also be triggered by means of logical implications, entailments or by what Grice called conversational implicatures. These terms refer to the type of meaning one arrives at by following a logical inferential process. For instance, A entails B if and only if B is true whenever A is true. Take an utterance such as 'this UN soldier is the local peace-keeper': 'the local peace-keeper' logically implies or entails that this United Nation soldier is *a* local peacekeeper. The former is true if and only if the latter is true. As with presuppositions, entailments can be generated in discourse in a multiplicity of ways. But in all cases, some background or contextual knowledge will come into play (Verschueren 1999, 30). As such, the focus on implicit meaning is a typically pragmatic point of interest.

Returning to the relevance of Grice to pragmatics, it is important to emphasise that his co-operative approach to conversation should not be mistaken for "a kind of cultural archetype of human interaction". It is important to keep in mind that these are merely principles for explaining a rational process of inference. Quite often, people will not act rationally and co-operatively. In this sense, Blommaert reminds us that "cooperativeness would better be seen as a variable than as a stable condition for communication". Language use is not always co-operative (Blommaert 2011, 125–126). But leaving this important caveat aside, the work of authors such as Grice, Searle and Austin contributed significantly to a pragmatic perspective in which language and the partial fixation of meaning are considered in terms of inter-subjective and performative language games.

3.7 Fixing Subjectivity Through Practices of Enunciation

The third approach that informs the perspective on discourse and language use outlined in this book is provided by French enunciative linguistics. Theories of enunciation offer a non-Cartesian and pragmatic understanding of language users as decentred, multifunctional and heterogeneous entities. At the same time, subjectivity is considered as an effect of language use itself. It draws our attention to language use as a reflexive process whereby we articulate and constitute our selves in relation to (inter-)textual, spatial, temporal and social dimensions of reality. Moreover, the enunciative perspective abolishes the old *langue–parole* distinction in favour of a notion of language grounded in articulatory practices marked by the principles of reflexivity and indexicality.

Originally, work on enunciation was carried out by linguists such as Charles Bally, Roman Jakobson and Emile Benveniste who focused on phenomena such as the usage of deixis, modality and reported speech. Foucault was neither the first nor the last author to use the concept. In fact, the notion of enunciation occupied a place of honour in the structuralist mode of discourse analysis developed by the Althusserian Marxist Michel Pêcheux (Hak and Helsloot 1995, Pêcheux 1994). Nevertheless, as French approaches to enunciation became increasingly pragmatic from the late seventies on (Angermuller 2011, 2993–2994; 2014b, 10–11, 24–25), parallels with poststructuralist notions of discourse and

3 The Pragmatic Dimension of Discourse as Articulation   145

subjectivity became more pronounced. In contrast to the project of automatic discourse analysis outlined by Pêcheux, Foucault's archaeological approach to discourse would benefit from this pragmatic turn in French linguistics (Maingueneau and Angermuller 2007).

Foucault devoted a lot of attention to the socio-historical practices that constitute subjects and emphasised the functional dimension of statements. But he did not develop a linguistic method or heuristic for analysing verbal or textual utterances. In contrast, French enunciative pragmatics can be interpreted as a linguistic variety, extension and/or radicalisation of the poststructuralist critique of the (unified and centred) subject (Angermuller 2011, 2994). From an enunciative point of view, subject positions should not be defined in terms of structurally defined places in a symbolic order (see Althusser 1970; Pêcheux 1994), but as practical achievements of interlocutors that need to deal with a multitude of voices and references in their attempts to determine who is speaking.

Both pragmatist and poststructuralist accounts of the self involve a problematisation of subjectivity on the basis of a study of (the functions and the usage of) pronouns and indexicality. The same goes for theories of enunciation developed by authors such as Emile Benveniste (Benveniste 1970), Oswald Ducrot (Ducrot 1984), Jacqueline Authier-Revuz (Authier-Revuz 1995a, b) or Catherine Kerbrat-Orecchioni (Kerbrat-Orecchioni 1980). A great deal of enunciative pragmatics deals with the question *how subjectivity is fixed* and articulated through indexical language use. This concern with indexicality can be traced back to Peirce who pointed out that signifiers and signifieds can be related to each other on the basis of a relationship of contiguity. This is the case when we point at things or people and when we interpret the presence of smoke as meaning fire. In the latter case, smoke indexes or means that something is burning (Chandler 2002, 36–37).

Enunciative pragmatics puts special emphasis on the opaque materiality of texts whose meaning cannot be accessed directly. The perspective breaks with the hermeneutic idea that the task of the qualitative researcher is to reconstruct meaningful experiences and subjective interpretations. It rather seeks to understand how texts provide instructions for interpretation in the form of formal linguistic markers. As such, there is a general tendency in enunciative pragmatics to opt for a non-essentialist understanding of discursive subjectivity. In many ways, this French variety of pragmatics is a decidedly poststructuralist enterprise that opposes three theoretical adversaries (Angermuller 2014b, 3–5):

> *the humanist, who believes in autonomous subjects as the source and origin of social and linguistic activity; the realist, who believes in objective realities that exist independently of discourse; and the hermeneuticist, who believes in a world of transparent and homogeneous meaning. It is critical of silencing the voice of the Other, of policing resistant practices and controlling disobedient knowledge, of homogeneizeing the social through representations of 'the' society, 'the' culture or 'the' discourse.* (Angermuller 2014b, 5)

The point here is that meaning does not 'reside' in texts or subjects. In fact, it does not have any 'location' at all. What language use offers is a series of instructions and pointers that allow us to orient ourselves towards each other and to link up with various dimensions of reality. Moreover, from an enunciative point of view, meaningful 'clarity' is something that has to be achieved. For an enunciative pragmatician such as Culioli (Culioli 2002), understanding is always "a special case of misunderstanding" or "a kind of optimization of flops of communication" whereby individuals manage to tune the production and recognition of an utterance (Culioli 2002 cited in Angermuller 2014b, 37). In order to understand this, it is important to take a look at the dynamics of enunciation as conceptualised in French pragmatics.

The enunciative tradition in pragmatics focuses on the way language users deploy the systematic features of language in order to generate discourse and subjectivity in concrete contexts (Angermuller et al. 2014d, 135–136). But the formal apparatus of language has no existence independent of concrete instances of use. In fact, Benveniste's challenge to the *langue/parole* distinction was grounded upon the idea that "nothing is in language that has not been before in discourse [in the sense of language use]" and that "before enunciation, language is nothing but the possibility of language" (Benveniste 1970, 14). In contrast to Foucault, his notion of enunciation is first and foremost of a linguistic nature. But like Foucault, Benveniste emphasised the relationship between enunciation and subjectivity. He did so by highlighting the fact that linguistic indexes constitute and mark—particular modes of—subjectivity.

The notion of enunciation refers to the act of speaking through which a locuteur (the speaker responsible for the utterance) appropriates the formal apparatus of language in order to position him- or herself with respect to real and/or imagined listeners. This means that every enunciation is inherently dialogical. All locutions are also allocutions directed at another "regardless of the degree of presence" we may attribute to this other. At the same time, enunciation is a process of inscription whereby the subject inscribes traces of his or her subjectivity in the utterance or *énoncé*. His or her subjectivity is constituted in this very process. We use language in order to articulate our relationships to past, ongoing and future speech. But we also use it in order to articulate ourselves to the entities that populate our (discursive) worlds (Benveniste 2014, 143; Johansson and Suomela-Salmi 2011, 82). Benveniste put it as follows:

Finally, in the enunciation, the language is used to express a certain relationship to the world. The very condition for this mobilisation and this appropriation of language is, for the speaker, the need to refer, via the discourse and for the other, to the possibility of co-referring identically, in a pragmatic consensus that makes every speaker a co-speaker. Reference is an integral part of the enunciation. (Benveniste 2014, 143)

It should be clear that both linguistic and non-linguistic varieties of enunciative theory refuse to consider discourse in terms of "the majestically unfolding manifestation of a subject who thinks, who knows, and who speaks". Instead, discourse is conceived of as "a set, in which the dispersion of the subject and his discontinuity with himself may be determined". Put differently, "it is neither by recourse to a transcendental subject nor by recourse to a psychological subjectivity that the regulation of its enunciation should be defined" (Foucault 1972, 55 cited in Angermuller et al. 2014d, 138). The parallels between Benveniste and Foucault emanate from their functional and relational understandings of subject constitution.

Consider Benveniste for whom people are able to constitute themselves as subjects in and through language by making use of markers of indexicality and inter-subjectivity. He described subjectivity as the capacity of a locutor (i.e. the discursive entity responsible for an utterance) to posit himself as a subject and stated that subjectivity is not so much "the feeling which everybody experiences of being himself" as "the psychic unity that transcends the totality of the actual experiences and that makes the permanence of consciousness" (Benveniste 1974, 259). Benveniste's unity of the subject is therefore not a pre-linguistic phenomenon but an indexical—and imaginary—effect of discourse that can be shown to operate with reference to shifters such as pronouns and other linguistic indexicals. As enunciative pragmatics took an increasingly pragmatic turn, researchers would turn to the complex ways in which the illusion of unity is maintained through language use. (see Angermuller 2014b, 21–24, 2011).

Pronouns and linguistic forms such as demonstratives, adverbs and adjectives organise the spatial and temporal relationships around which subjectivity emerges. The meaning of words such as 'here', 'there', 'now' or 'last year' can only become clear if we can link the utterance in which they occur with a context of enunciation and with an 'I' engaged in that enunciation (Benveniste 1974, 262). This insight would influence Jakobson's work on shifters (Jakobson 1971, 131–132) which would in turn impact on Anglo-American understandings of context and indexicality. The meaning of linguistic signs such as 'I', 'you', 'that' or 'there' shifts as we find (linguistic and non-linguistic) clues that allow us to articulate interpretive and functional relationships between utterances, identities and other aspects of potentially relevant context.

Shifters (Jakobson 1971) or *embrayeurs* (Maingueneau 1991) signal that contextualisation work is required for interpretation. Of course, the metaphor of a 'shifter' highlights the fact that the meaning of indexical symbols can never be fixed for once and for all. But one meaning is usually forgotten. The French word *embrayeur* (translated by Jakobson as shifter) is derived from the word *embrayage* that means *clutch, gear* or *engagement* (Angermuller 2014b). So, to use an *embrayeur of shifter* means that we use language in order to switch gears, tapping into and engaging with different layers of an ongoing contextual reality. An interpretive articulation of an utterance does not only require us to link signifiers to each other. It also requires us to link the 'empty' *shifters* with concrete spatial, temporal, social or intertextual co-ordinates. Articulation therefore always involves a form of pointing.

Shifters rely on pointing rather than on saying in the sense that they index and presuppose a context of enunciation in which one has to engage

3 The Pragmatic Dimension of Discourse as Articulation 149

oneself in order to understand an utterance. But this self is neither centred nor unified. If enunciative pragmatics is a non-Cartesian enterprise, it is so to the extent that inquirers avoid "falling into the trap of the rational subject directing signification via her/his rational intentions" (Williams 1999, 182–183). Benveniste pointed out that pseudo-dichotomies such as self/other or self/society are instilled in our usage of the language system itself. Consequently, subjectivity becomes a pragmatic effect of the communicative process (Benveniste 1974, 262).

Jacqueline Authier-Revuz made a useful distinction between constitutive and shown heterogeneity. The notion of constitutive heterogeneity captures the Lacanian idea that the subject is split and decentred by its very insertion into the symbolic realm of language. But it is the shown heterogeneity *that allows* linguists to investigate the way "certain types of linguistic forms encode the presence of otherness" (Johansson and Suomela-Salmi 2011, 90–91). Such forms include phenomena as diverse as negation, reported speech and intertextuality (Maingueneau 1991, 127–151) but always perform metalinguistic and indexical functions in the process of interpretation. Shown heterogeneity is the main theme of Oswald Ducrot's theory of enunciative polyphony (Johansson and Suomela-Salmi 2011). Ducrot drew on Bakhtin who rejected Saussure's idea that meaning is to be located in an abstract *langue* that could be opposed to *parole*. Instead, the latter developed an understanding of language, meaning, discourse, genre and literature in terms of a polyphonic dialogue between a multiplicity of voices that do not necessarily correspond with the voice claimed by the author of the discourse in question (Weir 1998, 1053; Roulet 2011, 209).

Bakthin's dialogism was a polysemic notion. It referred to the constant interplay of socio-ideological languages in society—a phenomenon that can also be described in terms of dialogic heteroglossia or interdiscursivity. Dialogism may also refer to the fact that all discourse is related to other discourse by means of multiple dialogical connections. In discourse studies, this phenomenon is frequently discussed in terms of intertextuality. Dialogism refers to the fact that every discourse functions with reference to preceding discourses while anticipating discourse to come. And last but not least, the concept implies that voices that do not belong to the author himself occupy important positions and perform many functions in his discourse (Roulet 2011, 209).

Ducrot's polyphonic theory of enunciation explores the implications of these dialogical principles for the way we articulate subjectivity at the level of concrete enunciations. For him, polyphony is the most fundamental principle of meaning, semantics, and textual structure in general. His subject is a split subject that emerges through the superposition of multiple voices in enunciation (Johansson and Suomela-Salmi 2011, 13; Anscombre 2009). At first sight, an enunciation may seem like the work of a single speaking subject, but this would be a mistake. It is more productive to understand the practice of enunciation in terms of a staged exchange, as a dialogue or even as a hierarchy of paroles (Ducrot 1984, 198–199). For this reason, Ducrot distinguished between a *sujet parlant*, a *locuteur* and an *enunciateur*.

The *sujet parlant* is the empirical or the physical agent of the utterance and must be distinguished from the *locuteur* who is the discursive entity taken to be responsible for the enunciation. The identities of the speaking subject and the locutor (*locuteur*) do not necessarily overlap. Moreover, enunciations are littered with *enunciateurs*, the discursive beings or voices corresponding to points of view that do not necessarily correspond to the point of view of either the *sujet parlant* or the *locuteur* (Ducrot 1984, 198–206; Anscombre 2009, 16–22; Roulet 2011). Enunciators or voices do not always 'talk' in the strict sense of the word. More often than not, they can't even be assigned concrete words or utterances (Maingueneau 1991, 128).

Nevertheless, the voices of enunciators perform important functions in the *mise en scène* of the polyphonic play that is discourse. Utterances function with various speakers (*énonciateurs*) that are kept at distance by their authors (*locuteurs*). For this reason, utterances can be understood as ensembles of nested voices chained together in the light of their argumentative value (Angermuller 2011, 2994). It is useful to recall Amane X. who staged a fictive but possible scenario in which my expectations as a majority member and her expectations as an Islamic minority member would clash about the way she would grow old in a dignified way. This complex operation can be described in terms of polyphony.

Amane articulated two antagonistic voices, attitudes, opinions or "expectations" that "are there but are not being articulated" in a *mise en scène* that indexed a wider ideological conflict in society. She did not fully

3 The Pragmatic Dimension of Discourse as Articulation 151

identify with either voice. Rather, the voices articulated in this (potentially) fictive scene were part of an argument about the structure of the Flemish integration debate. They did not necessarily correspond to the beliefs Amane held as a *locuteur*. She literally stated that it did "not matter" whether it was really the case that she wanted to grow old with a headscarf, thus establishing a distinction between the voices she claims responsibility for and those voices attributed to other socio-political actors that figure in this polyphonic interview situation as well as in society at large. Her point was that such agonistic (or perhaps even antagonistic) points of view stand in the way of a "true integration policy".

Polyphonic discursive scenes do not allow us to understand what is 'really meant' by a specific *sujet parlant* or a specific *locuteur*. But when readers or hearers examine such scenes, they can find clues in order to contextualise the auditory, textual or visual material in a meaningful way. Angermuller argues that language users work their way from the bottom up when faced with polyphonic utterances or texts. Confronted with a multiplicity of labelled and/or anonymous speakers, we seek to reduce discursive complexity by mapping voices onto a limited number of subject positions. And these positions are then interpretively linked with ideologically consolidated (discursive) knowledge about social and political actors. This way, interlocutors attempt "to reduce the complex organization of texts and spoken discourse to interpretive schemes which represent the relevant subject positions of discourse". (Angermuller 2011, 2998). At the same time, it is worth emphasising the following:

From an enunciative-pragmatic viewpoint, there are no given subject positions in the symbolic; the subject is not the property of a semiotic code; nor is it an effect of a textual play of differences. Rather, the discursive positions of subjects are creatively and dynamically constructed by readers cooperating with texts in context. As texts are contextually underspecified, they need a practical instance – the reader – whose interpretive capacities and contextual knowledge need to be mobilised in the production of meaning. (Angermüller 2014b, 140)

Such complicated interpretive procedures require a high degree of reflexive awareness. Throughout these processes, we make use of indexical markers in which the reflexive properties of language use and subjectivity crystalise in discourse. Metalinguistic and indexical forms allow us to mark and negotiate the multiplicity of physical, temporal, social and intertextual aspects of contextual reality with our interlocutors. As we link our discursive identities with other semiotic elements, this linkage shapes our sense of self as marked in discourse as well as the contexts in which we move. And this brings us back full circle to the issue of articulation as a partial fixation of contextual boundaries for interpretation.

3.8 Articulation as a Metapragmatic Negotiation of Interpretive Context

We already noticed that linguistic pragmatic and poststructuralist authors converge in their view that contextual boundaries are never simply 'out there' as objective structures that surround us and unilaterally determine every thought, utterance and action. They also converge in their refusal to explain context in terms of a matter of subject-based intentions. From a pragmatic point of view, context is an interactional and process-based achievement that requires interpretation and reflexivity. However, within linguistics, such reflexivity is more commonly dealt with in terms of metalinguistics, metapragmatics, metalanguage and/or metadiscourse.

Thus far, I have used such labels in order to describe how my interviewees marked a relatively high degree of awareness with respect to abstract political categories and values such as 'integration' as well as with respect to the particularities of the voices that populate their discursive worlds. The point to be made here is that every act of articulation and enunciation implies some degree of reflexivity that may or may not be marked in discourse. When marked, an analysis of markers of metapragmatic awareness allows us to follow the traces of subjectivity without taking recourse to a transparent and autonomous notion of the constituting subject. Moreover, it is through a rearticulation of the metapragmatic dimension of discourse that we can start to name the interpretive logics that structure our awareness of self, other and politics.

It may be impossible to delineate context in any ontological sense of the word (Butler and Laclau 2004, 335), but it is certainly possible to do so in a provisional and pragmatic manner. In fact, we do this all of the time. The main function of metapragmatic awareness can be described in terms of contextualisation. It is thanks to our (flawed and incomplete) awareness of the normative patterns concerning how to use (linguistic and non-linguistic) discursive elements in order to achieve particular interpretive and communicative effects that we are able to adapt and negotiate (ourselves to) the variable contexts through which we move. From a pragmatic point of view, choices have to be made at every level of communicative structure and this implies that "reflexive awareness ... is no less than the single most important prerequisite for communication as we know it" (Verschueren 2004, 53).

A pragmatic notion of articulation requires an understanding of the way reflexivity is marked metadiscursively. Within linguistics, there is no consensus with respect to the delineation of terms such as metalinguistics (Jaworski et al. 2004) or metapragmatics (Bublitz and Hübler 2007; Caffi 1998; Hübler 2011; Verschueren 2004). But there is much agreement on the fact that the topics studied under such headers tie in with questions of context, reflexivity and indexicality. Blommaert illustrates this point as follows:

> *every discourse simultaneously says something* in *itself (e.g. it describes a particular state of affairs 'out there') and* about *itself, about how that discourse should be interpreted, situated in relation to context, social relations, and so on. Such indexical levels can also be called 'metalinguistic' (i.e. about linguistic structure) or 'metapragmatic' (i.e. about forms of usage of language).* (Blommaert 2005, 253)

In the context of this book, I am concerned with metapragmatics in the sense of "the investigation of that area of the speaker's competence which reflects the judgments of appropriateness on one's own and other people's communicative behaviour" (Caffi 1993, 2461 cited in Hongladarom 2007, 32). The reason for this lies in the fact that political and critical discourses could not exist without such judgements. Caffi points out that "metapragmatics deals with the 'know-how' regarding the control and planning of, as well as feedback on, the ongoing interaction" (Caffi 1998, 581). The study of metapragmatics is therefore "concerned with linguistic traces of a speaker's awareness of the processes he or she is involved in" (Verschueren 2009, 22).

Metapragmatics may be described as "the systematic study of the meta-level, where indicators of reflexive awareness are to be found in the actual choice-making that constitutes language use, it is the proper domain of what is usually called metapragmatics" (Verschueren 1999, 188). It is a mental awareness of the way an aspect of discourse is (or should be) used. Like any other reflexive process related to language use, this awareness may or may not be marked explicitly in discourse. The (linguistic or non-linguistic) discursive items that mark mental awareness of the way an aspect of discourse is (or should be) used are called metapragmatic markers (Zienkowski 2011a, 432). They are empirically observable indicators of contextualisation strategies, discourse strategies, frames, repertoires, and/or large-scale interpretive logics deployed by language users. Such markers perform key functions with respect to the indication of one's awareness of self and other, one's awareness of the discursive processes one is involved in, as well as one's subjective stance towards a multiplicity of social and ideological phenomena articulated in discourse. Moreover, they are key tools for the articulation of the large-scale interpretive logics that constitute our political awareness of processes in the public realm.

Metapragmatic markers are functional entities that indicate traces of enunciative subjectivity. There is a metapragmatic dimension to all language use, but potential indicators include *embrayeurs*, "all of Jakobson's 'shifters'[2], Gumperz's 'contextualization cues' (such as instances of code switching), anything ever discussed under the labels 'discourse markers / particles' or 'pragmatic markers / particles' (such as anyway, actually, undoubtedly, I guess, you know, etc.), 'sentence adverbs' (such as frankly, regrettably), hedges (such as sort of, in a sense), instances of 'mention' vs 'use' (again as already suggested in Jakobson), as well as direct quotations, reported speech, and more implicitly embedded 'voices'", (Verschueren 2004, 446).

Metapragmatic awareness may be marked explicitly or may be left largely implicit in discourse (Hübler and Bublitz 2007). Nevertheless, it is impossible to achieve either full explicitness or full implicitness (Verschueren 1999, 26–36). Verschueren offers a useful overview of

---

[2] Jakobson's work on shifters is closely related to Emile Benveniste's work on pronouns. The meanings of words such as 'I' or 'you' constantly shift in interactions and texts. Their meaning can only be established with reference to indexicals that point at relevant co-ordinates for interpretation (Jakobson 1971; Fludernik 1991).

3 The Pragmatic Dimension of Discourse as Articulation

Table 3.1 Indicators of metapragmatic awareness (Verschueren 2004)

Explicit metalanguage	Implicit metalanguage
Metapragmatic descriptions (e.g. by means of metapragmatic lexical items such as speech act verbs or performative verbs) Self-referential expressions Discourse markers/particles or pragmatic markers/particles Sentence adverbs Hedges Explicit intertextual links Quoted and reported speech 'Mention' (vs. 'use') Some 'shifters' (e.g. some evidentials) Some 'contextualisation cues' (many of the above can be included in this category)	Most 'shifters': Deictic expressions (pronouns, tense, etc.) Aspect Mood and modality (Some) evidentials Many 'contextualisation cues' (e.g. prosodic patterns, code switching) Implicit 'voices' Proper names, that is, Jakobson's C/C, which may not be fully treatable on a par with the other metalinguistic phenomena

explicit and implicit markers of metapragmatic awareness (Verschueren 2004, 61) (Table 3.1):

We already saw that subjectivity may be marked with varying degrees of implicitness and explicitness in discourse. For instance, the meaning and function of the pronoun 'you' and the special qualifier 'this' in an utterance such as 'you simply can't do this' can only make sense if we are provided with some markers that indicate relevant aspects of reality we can take into account for purposes of interpretation. These aspects may be marked deictically in preceding or following discourse (words, topics, intonation, evidentials,[3] etc.), in non-verbal aspects of communication (e.g. gaze, pointing, etc.) or in any other aspect of communication that provides relevant indexical parameters.

Metapragmatic performances also serve as a means of commenting on and interfering with ongoing discourse or text (Hübler and Bublitz 2007, 6). As such, these performances are fundamental to the articulation of social and textual critique (Zienkowski 2013, 2014). Even though we have no

---

[3] Evidentials are linguistic markers that epistemologically indicate how one acquired specific information. In English, this happens lexically with reference to verbs such as 'to see', 'to hear', or 'to perceive' or with reference to adverbs such as 'allegedly' or 'apparently'. Other languages have specific particles, suffixes or other devices that grammatically encode the epistemological source of an utterance or statement (Papafragou et al. 2007, 255–256).

direct access to our own awareness or to the awareness of others, we do have access to a language that may indicate relevant aspects of our own awareness of the discursive processes we are involved in, as well as of one's subjective stance towards a multiplicity of social and discursive phenomena articulated in discourse. At the same time, metapragmatic markers allow us to (re-)articulate and (re-)structure our relationships with various dimensions of contextual reality.

In order to get this last point, it is useful to take a closer look at the way context has been conceptualised in pragmatically oriented discourse studies. In principle, all aspects of reality can function as contexts for interpretation. Five pre-theoretical but intuitively plausible notions of context include the linguistic co-text of an utterance; the non-linguistic sense-data in the surroundings of a linguistic activity; the situation in a physical sense of the word; features of the social situation of a text or utterance; and the channel or medium of communication. Considering the variety of contextual correlates of adaptability, it is therefore more useful to ask how something becomes an interpretive context for something else (Auer 2009, 91, 95).

All pragmatic perspectives on contexts share an outright refusal of container metaphors that explain (the meanings of) interactions and texts in relation to stable contextual environments. Such models assume "that interaction accommodates to fit the context rather as water does the bucket" (Heritage and Clayman 2010, 21). This implies that interactions cannot significantly impact on the form and shape of the environment. The problem is that when we think of interactions taking place 'in' specific spatial, temporal, social and/or historical contexts, we usually refer to interactions that follow normatively established patterns of communication. But as soon as people deviate from the normative patterns that mark a particular communicative event or genre, they start to impact and to redefine the very conditions of communication and—therefore—context.

One can find container notions of context in everyday language use (as in *you just have to put it in the right context* or as in *that's so out of context*), as well as in a great deal of social science. Van Dijk points out that the social sciences are littered with books that bear the notion of context in their titles but nevertheless deal with it "in a rather intuitive, pre-theoretical sense, namely as some kind of social, cultural or political environment for an

3 The Pragmatic Dimension of Discourse as Articulation

event or action – and more often as a condition than as a consequence of such an event" (Van Dijk 2007, 284). Even in the field of discourse studies, implicit or explicit container notions of context pop up with some regularity. This can be exemplified with reference to Fairclough's notion of discourse whereby texts are thought of as being embedded in larger discursive and social contexts (Fairclough 1992, 73).

One of the main difficulties of doing (critical) discourse analyses lies in determining how much and what sort of context one needs to take into account when accounting for a particular phenomenon. The way we deal with context impacts on the way we deal with critique. In fact, this issue has been at the centre of an important debate between critical discourse analysts (Billig 1999a, b; Wetherell 1998) and conversation analysts in the nineties (Schegloff 1998, 1997, 1999a, b). Van Dijk presents the tension between CA (Conversation Analysis) and CDA as follows:

Thus in CA, in principle, no contextual categories (such as power or gender) are postulated a priori in order to understand or explain ongoing talk unless these are (made) relevant, as such and in the interaction, by the participants themselves. In CDA, on the other hand, which does not have the same history of challenging the tenets of macro-sociology, the application of contextualization criteria is less strict. There is no hesitation in examining text and context separately, and once a feature of context has been observed, postulated or otherwise identified, CDA may be used to explore whether and how such a feature affects or is affected by, structures of text and talk. (Van Dijk 1999)

Conversation analysts take issue with the way abstract categories and social phenomena such as discrimination, inequality and power are imported as contextual determinants in CDA research. They prefer to view context as a road that unfolds before us as we converse and interact with each other. Orthodox CA considers relevant context to be a rather local phenomenon that is established through the realisation of conversational mechanisms and procedures. In the quote below, we can see how choice of context metaphor impacts on the way researchers deal with context:

Our alternative to the bucket theory is summed up by an unforgettable image associated with the Beatles' Yellow Submarine movie. In this image, the Beatles are walking along, and as they step forward a yellow brick road (like the one in

The Wizard of Oz) materializes and forms under their feet. Applying this image to interaction, the view we will take is that social context is never independent of actions (Duranti & Goodwin 1992). To the contrary, persons are continuously creating, maintaining, or altering the social circumstances in which they are placed – regardless of how massively, even oppressively, "predefined" those notions appear to be – and they do so in and through the actions they perform. (Heritage and Clayman 2010)

There is a clear pragmatic thrust to this conversation analytic conceptualisation of context. However, this notion of context is far from unproblematic for approaches in the field of critical discourse studies. It certainly makes sense to argue that discourse analysts need "observations – noticings – about people's conduct in the world and the practices by which they are engendered and understood" (Schegloff 1998, 414), but the idea that we can do so without making reference to theoretical constructs testifies to a certain blindness with respect to its own procedures. It also goes against the notion of (re-)articulation as a research practice (Glynos and Howarth 2007, 180–181). Even in CA, analysis implies (re-)contextualisation processes whereby researchers add (theoretically informed) metalinguistic qualifications to (traces) of existing speech and text in order to make sense of their data (Blommaert 2001, 19).

All forms of analysis thus involve an articulation of new contextual links. For instance, if one uses interview data in an academic paper, one is involved in lifting a particular type of discourse out of its context and linking it with another. In fact, every stage of the analysis, from data collection, over coding, transcription, preliminary analyses, writing and communication implies that subjects engage in more or less reflexive strategies of (re)articulation (Howarth 2000, 140–141, 2005). Those CA authors who believe that their analyses are grounded in data alone fail to recognise the metalinguistic dimension of their own practices (Verschueren 2001; Slembrouck 2001). So, even though the CA attitude with respect to social scientific categories such as ideology, hegemony or logic makes sense in relation to naïve container notions of context, it is not free from critique itself.

Notions such as discrimination, inequality and power can be useful categories of analysis on the condition that they are not dealt with as

3 The Pragmatic Dimension of Discourse as Articulation   159

a priori contextual co-ordinates (Blommaert 2001, 15). I therefore side with authors whose focus on empirical data and whose reflexive usage of social scientific categories informs a critique of both container and orthodox CA notions of context (Blommaert et al. 2001). While being sympathetic to the emancipatory goals of CDA, Blommaert warns us for ways in which implicit and explicit *a priori* statements such as 'power is bad', 'politicians are manipulators' and/or 'media are ideology reproducing machines' enter into analyses whereby references to 'power', 'institution', 'business' or 'the leading groups in society' are used in self-evident ways (Blommaert 2001, 14).

The point is that categories and 'structures' such as gender, class, age or institutional context do not influence the way people speak and write directly. They only become relevant for us to the extent that they impact on our variable, normalised and experience-based representations of ourselves and the contexts in which we move (Van Dijk 2007, 299). Blommaert's critique of *prima facie ethnographies* in CDA is informed by similar concerns. In order to make his point, he quotes a CDA study on doctor–patient interactions that includes explicit statements on status and gender:

> *For an understanding of the context, it is important to realize that the outpatients' ward has very low status and prestige in relation to the rest of the hospital. It is a type of outpost and ... serves as a training ground for young doctors, which results in inexperienced insiders working where experienced ones are arguably most necessary. Hierarchy, knowledge, experience and gender are interlinked in a strange and unique way in the outpatients' ward.* (Wodak 1997 cited in Blommaert 2001, 15)

The problem identified by Blommaert is that the author takes this ethnographic description for granted in the analysis without specifying where this crucial information comes from (Blommaert 2001, 15; Wodak 1997, 179). Within CDA, onsite observation and interviewing are often used in this manner. This implies that researchers run the risk of merely exemplifying *a priori* postulated empirical and theoretical claims, resulting in a high degree of predictability in research findings (Blommaert 2001, 15–16; Slembrouck 2001; Verschueren 2001). Fortunately, there is more to context than containers and yellow brick roads that unfold themselves as we walk them. Pragmatics offers several alternative ways of thinking which include context as figure and ground (Hanks 1992); context as an interpretive process of cuing and signalling relevant aspects of reality (Gumperz 1992a, b; Levinson 2003; Prevignano and di Luzio 2003); cognitive understandings of context (Van Dijk 2008, 2007); context as a process whereby we negotiate and carve out our interpretive and metadiscursive lines of vision onto the world and onto communication itself (Verschueren 1999, 76); and last but not least, context as critique.

The figure-ground distinction distinguishes between focal event and context in terms of the perceptual salience attached to specific aspects of communication: "the focal event is regarded as the official focus of the participants' attention, while features of the context are not highlighted in the this way, but instead treated as background phenomena" (Goodwin and Duranti 1992, 9). As such, the relation between focal event and context is basically a figure-ground relationship. However, what functions as background knowledge and what is foregrounded can shift in the course of communication and is dependent inter-subjective and intertextual processes of contextualisation (Bauman and Briggs 1990; Goodwin and Duranti 1992, 10–12). In neither case, however, contexts surrounds us as if it were a container.

Sometimes, context seems to be "brought along" and merely needs to be indexed in order to become relevant. But at other times, context seems to be "brought about exclusively" by the contextualisation work of the participants of a communicative event (Auer 1992, 26). In either case, context needs to be indexed or cued through the use of communicative markers that trigger processes of inference and interpretation. It is in this context that John Gumperz developed his notion of contextualisation cues. Such cues account for the way people indicate how utterances are to be interpreted in indirect and/or implicit ways. Contextualisation cues can be used in order to index and in order to guide (preferred) interpretations of specific utterances. We use them in order to mark, assess and attribute interactional intentions on which we base our responses (Gumperz 1982, 153–154). In a retrospective interview, Gumperz provides us with some useful definitions:

3 The Pragmatic Dimension of Discourse as Articulation 161

Contextualization cues are a class of what pragmaticians have called indexical signs, that serve to retrieve the contextual presuppositions conversationalists rely on in making sense of what they see and hear in interactive encounters. They are pure indexicals in that they have no propositional content. That is, in contrast to other indexicals like pronouns or discourse markers, they signal only relationally and cannot be assigned context-free lexical meanings. Yet they play a major role in transforming what linguists refer to as discursive structures into goal-oriented forms of action. (Prevignano and di Luzio 2003, 8)

Among the various types of contextualisation cues focused on by John Gumperz, we can find linguistic and paralinguistic phenomena related to prosody, code-switching, style-switching and formulaic expressions. He specifically asked himself how such phenomena interact with the way exchanges are ordered and how they make background knowledge relevant while constituting social actions (Prevignano and di Luzio 2003, 8). Contextualisation cues are subtle but observable signs marked on the surface of a message. They signal how speakers interpret what the communicative activity is and how the meaning of the message is to be understood in relation to what precedes and follows (Gumperz 1982, 131).

The work of John Gumperz has influenced many other linguists, ethnographers and anthropologists working on issues related to contextualisation and discourse. On the linguistic side, it is worth taking a look at the work of Jef Verschueren. He proposes a model of context whereby we shape and negotiate context through lines of vision we throw onto an infinitely complex reality. Verschueren provides us with the following scheme (Verschueren 1999, 76) (Fig. 3.2):

The lines of vision metaphor has to be understood in terms of the pragmatic concept of language use as marked by the principles of variability, adaptability and negotiability. In this model, utterers and interpreters make adaptable and negotiable choices in both the production and interpretation of utterances. The whole of discourse—not merely contextualisation cues—becomes a way of carving out contexts out of an infinitely complex mental, social and physical reality (Verschueren 1999, 2004, 2008). So, even though reality certainly exists, the process of discursive contextualisation allows us to deal with it pragmatically.

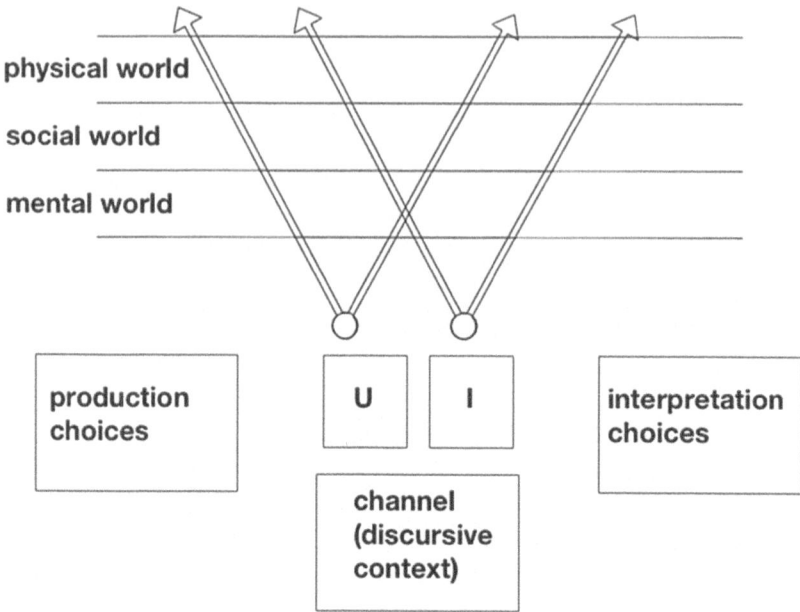

Fig. 3.2   Contextual correlates of adaptability (Verschueren 1999, 76)

Verschueren's metaphor implies that we articulate the *structural objects of adaptability* provided by the various layers of linguistic and communicative structure with *contextual correlates of adaptability*. Among the structural objects of adaptability, we find all the options we can make at the levels of phonemes, words, grammatical constructions, argumentation, narrative at any other level of reified linguistic 'structure'. In communication, these elements of discursive structure need to be related functionally with aspects of context that include the identities of the language users themselves, aspects of the physical, social and mental worlds, and last but not least, the communicative 'channel' or medium itself.

According to Verschueren, the catalyst for this process is Vigotsky's *mind in society*. As we saw before, this mind should not be mistaken for a unified and centred subject. The utterer and interpreter in the scheme above are functional entities and not necessarily real-world people. These entities can be described not only in terms of roles but also in terms of the categories defined in enunciative perspectives on discourse.

3 The Pragmatic Dimension of Discourse as Articulation

The lines of vision emanating from the utterer and interpreter in the scheme above always emanate from particular roles, voices or subject positions. By using language, we can mark aspects of reality we consider to be relevant for purposes of communication. But since communication is always part and parcel of the context in which it operates, interlocutors can use language to orient their gaze towards themselves, towards their communicative choices and towards the media through which they are realised.

The fact that context can never be grasped in its entirety does not entail that the notion becomes unworkable since communication serves to delimit, to generate and to construct contextual boundaries for interpretation. Through discourse, we make aspects of reality relevant. Language thus functions as a means to index contextual correlates of adaptability with varying degrees of salience. This is an inter-subjective process whereby we direct each other's lines of vision across various dimensions of contextual reality. However, our vistas never overlap completely because we never occupy the same exact positions in discursive space. Interestingly, this means that common ground is never really common, even though we may act as if it is. In this sense, context is always an act of discursive and cognitive imagination.

The establishment of 'common' ground is necessarily an interactive, imaginative and negotiable process. It is a reflexive process of articulatory performance because it involves processes of discursive co-ordination whereby we provide each other with flexible pointers that index what aspects of reality we want to use to fix the meaning of the context at hand. I will therefore define context as a (result of) discursive contextualisation processes that contribute to interactional clarity and/or to the establishment of an imagined common ground by taking resource to indexical communicative principles. However, before we close this chapter on the pragmatic approach to context and articulation, it is important to point out that the range of meaningful contextualisation practices is never completely random.

From a pragmatic perspective, there is always some room for discursive negotiation over the meaning of identities, discourses, narratives, events and any other contextual correlate of adaptability. However, it is also important to recognise that our interpretive orientations always take place in the presence of socio-political institutions that reduce the multiplicity of interpretive options by generating normative and hierarchical rankings of preferred interpretations. All ideological discourse therefore operates through what Silverstein (see: Silverstein 2003) and Blommaert call *orders of indexicality* (Blommaert 2005, 69, 73–75). When we use language, we do not only orient ourselves towards the potential effects of our discourse on our interlocutors but also towards the large-scale normative orders on the basis of which our communicative contributions are normatively valued. Indexical meanings are ordered in regimes that allow for judgments, inclusion, exclusion and sanctioning (Blommaert 2005, 73–75).

For instance, by using a particular sociological vocabulary, an interviewee may index his or her identity as a (particular type of) academic. But whereas this inscription into the order of academic and/or activist discourse may be valued positively in the context of academic research, jargon about 'imagined communities' or 'counter-hegemonic identity politics' is likely to be less popular among journalists looking for catch phrases or one-liners that might be described as 'clear', 'concise' or 'sexy'. Our metapragmatic interpretations of indexical constructs may be contingent, but they are far from arbitrary. The social, physical and mental worlds may seem rather undifferentiated in the scheme above, but in reality, our life-world is filled to the brim with institutions that centre our discursive value systems as well as the orders of indexicality we orient ourselves to while making sense of our selves and of the contexts through which we move.

All institutions are centring institutions. They function much like Benedict Anderson's imagined communities and include organisations as small as peer groups and the family, larger communities linked to churches or universities, as well as national, trans-national or global networks and organisations. For this reason, our social environment is as polycentric and stratified as our sense of self. Whenever we use discourse to articulate ourselves with the spatial, temporal, social and political contexts through which we move, we map linguistic forms and functions onto each other. The attribution of a particular social function or value to a particular utterance is largely dependent on the way we link utterances with institutional sources of authority. Of course, not everyone has the same degree of access to specific semiotic forms (e.g. jargon or slang) and to the institutional spaces of meaning ratification where form–function relationships can be (re-)articulated, valued and ascribed (Blommaert 2005, 75–76). For this reason, discursive contextualisation processes are inherently ideological phenomena marked by high degrees of heterogeneity.

We already saw that the poststructuralist notion of ideology developed in the Essex approach to discourse has nothing to do with the idea of ideology as false consciousness. Rather, ideology refers to those discursive processes that allow us to ensure that the contingent nature of our discursive structures remains in the background. It refers to those aspects of interpretive logic that infuse our world and our subjectivities with an affective drive through the articulation of narrative constructs in which ideals and obstacles for the realisation of ideals are constructed (Glynos 2008, 287; Glynos and Howarth 2007). Pragmatic accounts of ideology and discourse are also sceptical about ideology as false consciousness. Moreover, considering their overall approach to language, pragmatically oriented discourse analysts have developed notions of ideology that recognise both heterogeneity and reflexivity in ideological language use:

ideology as part of meaningfulness comprises conscious, planned, creative activity as well as unintentional reproduction of 'determined' meanings. It also comprises processes at various levels ranging from the individual to the world system, passing through different degrees of awareness, speed and capacity of development, and capacity to create innovative practices. In other words, it simultaneously comprises 'particular' as well as 'total', or 'established' as well as 'behavioural' ideologies, but they operate at different levels, offer different opportunities for people, and are of a different order in analysis. And hegemony may lie not so much in a single, unified set of ideological elements, but in connections between various sets. (Blommaert 2005, 74)

It is thanks to our metalinguistic awareness of the fact that the same signifiers can mean different things in different contexts that we are able to deal with the fact that ideologies are not fully coherent and integrated sets of ideas. This point has been most forcefully advanced in discursive psychology. In this context, Michael Billig developed the notion of ideological dilemmas (Billig et al. 1988) in order to challenge the Marxist view that "ideologies were integrated and coherent sets of ideas that served to represent the domination of the ruling sections of society as natural or inevitable" (Edley 2001, 202–203). Billig does not deny that integrated and coherent forms of ideology exist, but he emphasises that lived ideologies, in the sense of *common sense* ideologies, are quite often inconsistent, fragmented and contradictory (Verschueren 1999, 238).

Seemingly contradictory language use is actually quite common and functional in everyday reasoning. Contrary to many other commentators, Billig and his co-authors do not write off such ideological language use as faulty or unreliable but argue that "the indeterminacy of lived ideologies makes them wonderfully rich and flexible resources for social interaction and every-day sense-making" (see: Billig et al. 1988). In fact, the heterogeneous and often contradictory nature of ideologies is what makes them so suitable for everyday sense-making processes. In discourse, we can frequently observe the counter-positioning of contrary themes and rationalities. It is here that we can hear people struggling with the contrary themes of common sense and this is even more so when the topics are explicitly ideological. For instance, those making racist remarks often assert their own lack of prejudice, even as they make their racist utterances (Edley 2001, 202–203).

Since notions of indexicality and context are fundamentally intertwined, and since ideology is first and foremost a function of discourse *vis-à-vis* socio-political relationships, an investigation of the indexical function of language use allows for an empirical investigation of ideology and hegemony. The articulation of critical awareness in political discourse is also tied to indexical principles. As Chilton put it, "identity unfolds in discourse by positioning others on the axes of space, time and rightness, presuming the centrality and fixity of the self" (Edley 2001, 202-203). The articulation of a sense of self in the public realm can therefore not be analysed in isolation of the logics we deploy in order to delineate the boundaries of self, society and the public realm.

3.9 Articulating Political Awareness in the Public Realm

The time has come to return to the political dimension of articulatory practice. The fact that we are able to articulate and mark aspects of our metalinguistic or metadiscursive awareness in communication is a major condition for the emergence and articulation of political awareness in the public realm. Without an awareness of the distinctive ways in which communication can be used in order to (re-)articulate social and political relationships, it would be impossible to think and articulate alternative (relationships to alternative) worlds. Politics defined as a public (re-)articulation of social and relationships would cease to exist. For this reason, a public realm can only operate in and through the multiplicity of articulations through which social actors try to hegemonise their political agendas and subjectivities.

Whoever is able to articulate his or her preferred meaning of concepts such as integration or diversity as embodying the prevailing common sense has laid the groundwork for his or her political hegemony (Torfing 1999; Barret 1994; Mouffe 1979). Debates are dense intertextual structures in which actors articulate their identities in struggles over the signifiers that can fix the meanings and boundaries of selves and societies (Zienkowski 2014). Such signifiers can designate and construct norms, values, practices and entire policy domains. To debate means to rearticulate and to de-/re-/en-contextualise words, voices, sentences, narratives and other discursive elements. As such, the practice of contextualisation brings us to questions of ideology, power and control: "we may recognize differential access to texts, differential legitimacy in claims to and use of texts, differential competence in the use of texts, and differential values attaching to various types of texts" (Bauman and Briggs 1990, 73).

The link between metapragmatic (en-/de-/re-) contextualisation processes and ideology is of fundamental importance to the pragmatic notion of critique. If we consider critique as a label for those discursive practices directed at challenging (the presuppositions and conditions of) established power relationships in public settings, it is hard to imagine how we could articulate critique without the operation of (meta-)discursive functions such as validation, framing, argumentation, legitimation or identification (Bauman and Briggs 1990, 75–76). All of these processes are simultaneously cognitive, social, political and (meta-)discursive. They operate both at the level of reflexive subjectivity and at the level of the interpretive logics that structure our societies. Their social nature derives from the fact that such processes always require some degree of metalinguistic awareness of the discursive strategies we engage in while articulating ourselves publicly.

In liberal theory, debates are usually considered to be points of entrance for civil society into policy making. Nevertheless, this common and prototypical conceptualisation of debates curtails the fact that debates are never easily identified. What events, genres, participants and time frames constitute the boundaries of a debate? And how do such discursive coordinates relate to the outcome of decision-making procedures? Rather than considering debates in this liberal fashion, Jan Blommaert proposes to consider debates in terms of conflicts in which struggles over the texts and meta-texts are waged (Blommaert 2005, 185–186). Of course, it is not merely the interpretation of a particular text or discourse that is at stake, but rather the way we use discourse in order to structure our (relationships to our) selves and to the entities and practices that make up our public spheres. Consequently, an enormous amount of energy is put in *discourse about discourse*. Metalinguistic (re-)contextualisation strategies are such stuff society-wide debates are made of.

This brings us to the question what it means to articulate oneself in the public realm. From a pragmatic point of view, it makes no sense to think of public space as a clearly delineated location in time and space. Rather, we are dealing with a spatial metaphor that is meant to conceptualise communicative practices aimed at (re-)articulations of social and political relationships. The democratic qualification is based on the idea that such interactions contribute to a society in which citizens can exert maximum control over their living conditions. We frequently deploy spatial metaphors such as 'public realm' or 'public sphere' in order to conceptualise public and democratic practices that rearticulate social and political relationships in this way. But such metaphors are not without their limitations. This can be exemplified with reference to the notion of the public realm proposed by Jürgen Habermas:

> *By 'the public sphere' we mean first of all a realm of our social life in which something approaching public opinion can be formed. Access is guaranteed to all citizens. A portion of the public sphere comes into being in every conversation in which private individuals assemble to form a public body.* (Habermas 1989, 102)

In this classic formulation, Habermas writes about a 'realm', about 'access' and about a 'sphere' 'in which people assemble' to form a unified 'public body' in which a rather homogenous 'public opinion' can emerge. On the one hand, this concept of the public sphere refers to specific institutions, agencies and practices associated with churches, cultural associations, sport clubs, independent media, grass-roots initiatives, political parties and unions. On the other hand, it refers to a more general horizon of experience that integrates a multiplicity of relevant issues relevant to members of society (Habermas 1989, 102). The metaphorical character of this public 'sphere' becomes obvious if one considers that no one has ever *seen* such a thing. Even though we may think about newsrooms, about parliament buildings or city squares in terms of locations at which the public sphere is established, none of these spaces is necessarily public.

One of the implications of using spatial metaphors for public communication, discourse and socio-political organisation is a strong emphasis on politics as an attempt to achieve an ideal–typical common ground or consensus. According to Habermas, something resembling his ideal public sphere briefly existed in Germany, France and Britain in the late eighteenth and nineteenth centuries. However, this quickly changed because of developments such as the delegation of dialogue to parliaments and political parties, an increasingly blurred distinction between the state and society by interventionist welfare states and a commercialisation of the public sphere and the subjection of public debate by market forces (Goatly 1997, 66–77; Lakoff and Johnson 1980, 10–13; Koller and Wodak 2010).

Many critical students of discourse would agree with Habermas that today's notion of public opinion is all too often conflated with opinion polls rather than with the result of a power-free rational dialogue between citizens (Koller and Wodak 2010, 2; Wright 2010, 29–30; Briggs 2007). Other critiques dig deeper and take issue with the normative presuppositions of Habermas' ideal–typical public sphere. Authors have aimed their arrows at the distinction between the public and the private, at the rational basis for public debate and at the idea that the public sphere is ultimately oriented towards the achievement of rational and power-free consensus (Wright 2010, 30–33). One of the main problems of an idealised notion of publicness is that it reduces democratic participation to a matter of institutional access and to the following of procedures that supposedly guarantee neutrality and rationality in the consensual settlement of debates.

For Habermas, the goal of public and rational dialogue is the achievement of *Verständigung* through the creation of public opinion. In order to achieve this, no parties are to be excluded from public debate and all participants should be able to present a critique of the validity of the claims made by all others. Participants must be willing and able to empathise with each other's validity claims while neutralising power differences in such a way that they have no impact on the creation of consensus. Moreover, they are supposed to be transparent about their goals and intentions and seem to have access to an unlimited amount of time (Flyvbjerg 1998, 213).

Flyvbjerg argues that Habermas pays insufficient attention "to the preconditions of actual discourse, to substantive ethical values and to the problem of how communicative rationality gets a foothold in society in the face of massive non-communicative forces" (Flyvbjerg 1998, 111). From a pragmatic perspective, this is highly problematic. And from a poststructuralist point of view, one has to criticise the idea that power stands in opposition to discourse, reason and democracy. Foucault has shown us that it does not make sense to think of power-free dialogues. The question is rather what sort of power relationship is generated through specific discursive practices and techniques and what alternatives there are to the form of power known as domination. Power is just as much present in democratic, dialogical and participatory forms of interaction as in any other mode of communication (Grillo 2005, 31).

An all too strong focus on normativity easily leads one to gloss over the fact that public spheres do not precede interaction. They do not just exist 'out there' waiting for us to be accessed. In reality, the notion of a public reifies a heterogeneous set of speech events and language games that crosscut and overlap each other. Debates are held everywhere—from family tables to parliamentary buildings. But they do not function independently from each other. Both the heterogeneity and the coherence of the 'public realm' require the operation of logics through which citizens can imagine their relationships towards themselves as well as to the other(s) that populate their discursive realities. In this sense, public spheres are not unlike Benedict Anderson's imagined communities in which most members will never know most of their fellow members in spite of the fact that each one has access to an image of their communion (Anderson 1983).

3 The Pragmatic Dimension of Discourse as Articulation

If we take the imaginary and fantasmatic dimension of the public realm seriously, we can start to explore the relationship between our sense of self and our sense of politics. This may become more clear if we consider the public in terms of an audience. If we limit our understanding of the public sphere to mass media, it becomes very easy to conflate 'the public' with a relatively passive set of individuals that consume mediated products of various types. Clearly, a public can be more than this. Gal and Woolard argue that both the public realm and the creation of 'a public' require acts of imagination. To imagine oneself as a (member of) a public requires that one creates a sense of continuity and discontinuity with times, places and people who are not present in the context of the immediate interaction (Gal and Woolard 1995, 135). It requires a (re-)articulation of a complex network of identities, practices, institutions and other discursive elements.

The fact that a public is a discursive construct entails that it may be more useful to talk about a multiplicity of public spheres. Researchers focusing on minority groups and new social movements have proposed an alternative social topography in which people articulate their concerns across a variety of public spaces. Not all of these spaces are equally visible and accessible to all. For instance, in migration studies, authors have written about hidden or alternative public spheres (Fairclough and Chouliaraki 1999, 137). There are such things as interconnected diasporic public spaces in which people debate and celebrate the pleasures and predicaments of diaspora (see: Melucci 1989). Such a hidden public sphere "shares with that alternative sphere a sense of opening up a space for dissenting and emancipatory discourses, outside and beyond the official, national public sphere, of being the locus for the mobilisation in the social movements" (see: Fraser 1992; Calhoun 1992).

There are no *formal* differences between alternative and dominant public spaces. Both types of sphere are maintained by linguistic and non-linguistic practices and are characterised by imbalances of power. Moreover, neither type of sphere is accessible or transparent to everyone. The articulation of political awareness cannot be reduced to a matter of rational argument. It implies complex processes of linking concrete semiotic elements (texts, words, signs, gestures, images, sounds, etc.) to each other in empirically observable performances at various layers of discursive organisation (words, sentences, multimodal messages, arguments, narratives, genres, etc.). Being proficient in one public sphere does not guarantee proficiency in another one. Put differently, the types of capital valued in one public realm do not carry the same weight elsewhere. Universities, mosques and mass media may all have a public character but they are also centring institutions that regulate the way discourses and subjectivities are valued in a heterogeneous discursive field.

It is only because we imagine ourselves in relation to larger networks of discursive practices that we are able to articulate ourselves as being part and parcel of a public (sphere). Without this ability to discursively (re-)articulate and imagine a personal and collective relationship towards the social and political realities in which we find ourselves, it would be impossible to engage in any form of political engagement. The reason for this lies in the fact that political engagement requires acts of collective imagination. Political engagement is ultimately an umbrella term for the practices through which we collectively (re-)imagine, (re-)articulate and negotiate social and political relationships. Every articulation of political awareness necessarily implies an act of imagination in which we re-imagine our relationships with others. But the way we imagine and articulate our public relationships is not necessarily conflict free.

We already noticed that the Essex approach to radical democracy considers conflict not as an obstacle but as a key feature of democratic debate. Discourse theory proceeds on the idea that both an excessive lack of consensus on democratic values and a lack of agonistic tension among social actors constitute a threat to democracy (Mouffe 1993, 6). Democratic debate should therefore be based on a recognition and acceptance of dissent and on a deep respect for agonistic adversaries (Wright 2010, 32). From a radically democratic point of view, heterogeneity is to be welcomed in political debate as well as in the public realm. This heterogeneity becomes all the more important if we realise that a great deal of public debate is about the way we structure the public realm itself.

Like societies, subjectivities and discourses, public spheres have no objective boundaries. Consequently, a great deal of debate centres precisely on how such boundaries can and should be fixed. Public spheres thus become objects of critique themselves. This can be demonstrated with reference to debates about the relationship between privacy and security in the digital age. Such debates are never merely about laws and regulations. They structure the public realm itself by rearticulating relationships between public and private, citizen and state, law and police. Other examples of debates that restructure the public itself include debates about the role of religious symbols in public institutions or discussions about a green economy. The debates on integration that will be analysed in the next chapter constitute another case in point.

At the same time, debates can restructure our sense of self. In claiming hegemony, political projects have to be imagined collectively. Debates emerge as actors with different hegemonic projects clash and engage with each other. This implies articulatory processes that necessarily impact on the way we make sense of our own subjectivities. In this sense, debates are not only about issues such as welfare, crisis or immigration. Their complex social, political and fantasmatic logics impact on the way we articulate who and what we are as reflexive subjects. Once again, the case of European debates on integration provides us with a case in point. It is no coincidence that hegemonic incentives for migrants to integrate themselves are linked to debates about national identity. Neither is it a coincidence that minority critiques of dominant integration models go hand in hand with attempts to articulate alternative modes of citizenship and subjectivity.

4

Articulating the Problematic of Integration in a Minority Debate

Anyone doing research in the humanities has to come to grips with a simple question that colleagues, friends and family members frequently ask. Varieties of this question include "so tell me, what's your research about", "what do you do over there at the university" or "what is it you study again"? Relevant as such questions are, there is never just one way to answer them. My own strategy varied significantly depending on who was asking the question and on the context in which the question was asked. You don't give the same answer to a colleague on a conference as you might give to a friend, family member or stranger who supposedly has no background in discourse studies.

In general, it would be fair to say that I focused on the way intellectuals and activists articulated a preferred sense of self with a preferred mode of politics in interviews on political engagement. I sometimes mentioned that my research seeks to address a more abstract issue related to the way people interpretively use and value abstract categories in the discursive networks that constitute large-scale debates in the public sphere. And it is equally true that I wanted to shed some light on the way people shape themselves in relation to the actors, practices and discourses that populate the public realm. My usual answer was more concise though.

Most frequently, I told people that I investigated the world views of Flemish Moroccan intellectuals and activists in Flanders. Interestingly, this last answer usually prompted a response indicative of a strong hegemonic discourse centred on the notion of integration.

People frequently articulated a sense of recognition or an *aha-Erlebnis*. They came up with replies such as "so, it's about integration then". Others would conclude that my research was more specifically about "the integration of allochthons" or remarked that my research on "the integration of Muslims" was really relevant. Everyone seemed to have an opinion on this research on 'integration' even though I avoided using this term myself. Nevertheless, once people convinced themselves that my work focused on the 'problem of integration', they would ask me about a wide variety of issues including Islamic veiling practices on the work floor, criminal figures in migrant communities, gender-related inequalities among Muslim communities and Islam-inspired extremism or terrorism in Flanders, Belgium, Europe and/or the world. All sorts of moral panics related to Muslim minorities were lumped together in a big bag labelled 'integration'.

I often had a very hard time explaining that my research was *not* about integration. I had no intention of answering whether, how and/or to what extent the people I interviewed were 'integrated' in society. I merely wanted to understand the way people made sense of their political engagements in Flemish minority politics while shedding some light on minority-related issues from a minority perspective. Nevertheless, it became increasingly clear that the signifier of integration was even more important to the sense-making processes of citizens in Flanders than I expected it to be. There were two main reasons for this. First of all, in spite of progressive academic critiques on the usage of integration-related concepts in the minority debate, the concept keeps on circulating in academic, political and everyday discourses on diversity-related issues. The responses of people asking me what I did for a living are merely one indication of this fact. Secondly, the people I interviewed could not bypass the issue either.

The logics of integration that run through mainstream discourses on ethnic and cultural minorities in Flanders are so hegemonic that neither majority members nor minority members can ignore them. As I

4 Articulating the Problematic of Integration in a Minority Debate 177

mentioned before, I asked my interviewees a series of open-ended questions related to four key topics. None of these questions directly touched upon integration. Nevertheless, the notion popped up with a surprising degree of spontaneity and regularity. My questions centred on issues such as the political points of interest of my interviewees, the evolution of their political ideas and engagements as well as on their sources of inspiration. The goal was to empower my interviewees through active interviews in which they would be able to articulate their agendas and their concerns with a relatively high degree of freedom.

Almost all of my interviewees opposed dominant understandings of integration in the Flemish public sphere. The vast majority of them engaged in metalinguistic attempts to articulate an alternative logic for thinking minority-related issues. Doing so, some of them would come to reject the notion of integration altogether whereas others would redefine it in accordance with their preferred mode of politics and subjectivity. Frequently they combined both strategies, rejecting the notion in some instances while using it pragmatically in others. But even though most of my interviewees tried to move away from a debate that defines minority-related issues in terms of a problem of integration, most of them were unable to avoid the issue altogether. Neither could I.

Even though the main goal of my book is to provide an understanding of the way critical awareness functions in critical political discourse, this goal cannot be achieved without coming to grips with the key features of hegemonic discourse on Moroccan and Islamic minorities in Flanders. As we will see, there are strong homogenising and culturalist logics of integration that have marked Flemish debates on minority issues for decades. In order to understand how my interviewees articulated alternative logics for structuring society, we need to understand these hegemonic logics. For this reason, I will first explore the way the notion of integration has been used in mainstream academic, political and everyday discourses in Flanders. The barrier between academic and political discourse is extremely fuzzy in discussions about integration. The importance of integration-related concepts in both mainstream and minority discourse on diversity demonstrates that we are not dealing with a merely analytical concept. Notions such as integration perform key functions in the discursive value systems of both individuals and groups. In fact, they *are* values as well as empty signifiers: emotionally invested abstract categories that simultaneously shape our sense of self and our sense of society. Consequently, they play a key role in both the logics that structure the relationships between social actors and the interpretive logics that inform the reflexive and critical awareness articulated by individuals.

After a discussion of the usage of the notion of integration in academic and mainstream political discourses, I will present an interpretive and functional analysis of the way my interviewees rearticulated integration-related concepts. To say that my analysis will be interpretive and functional is to say that I will deploy a heuristic based on the multifunctional notion of articulation outlined in the foregoing chapters of this book. This implies an investigation of the various interpretive functions of integration-related notions. Put differently, I will focus on the pragmatically established relationships of categories such as integration *vis-à-vis* subject positions, topics and narratives that have been co-constructed in a series of active interviews.

My goal is not to 'reconstruct' a true meaning of integration. Neither is it to uncover any 'real' or 'authentic' intentions of my respondents. I rather seek to rearticulate the voices and utterances of my interviewees in a way that sheds new light on the Flemish integration debate. If my interviewees are able to challenge dominant understandings of integration-related concepts, this ability is grounded in their capacity for articulating a high degree of metalinguistic and political awareness. Put differently, their ability to articulate counter-logics of critical explanation is conditional upon their capacity to identify functional, indexical and interpretive relationships between the discursive entities and practices that populate their contextual realities. Nevertheless, it would be a grave mistake to focus too much on the notion of integration.

Important as the integration concept may be, almost all of my respondents tried to get away from the integration-related logics that structure mainstream approaches to migrants and their descent in Flanders. If my interviewees were able to come up with alternative world views, they did so by integrating alternative concepts, narratives, experiences and practices through interpretive logics that dislocate mainstream discourse. In spite of my focus on the signifier of integration, it is therefore important to emphasise that this book presents first and foremost an interpretive

4 Articulating the Problematic of Integration in a Minority Debate

and functional analysis of discourses on *political engagement*, the heterogeneous set of practices through which people re-imagine, rearticulate and negotiate their fantasy-infused and emotionally invested relationships towards each other and towards the practices and institutions that populate the public realm.

In the sections below, I will start with a discussion of the main characteristic of hegemonic understandings of integration-related concepts in Flanders. This includes a discussion of integration as a signifier at the crossroads of scientific and political discourses. We also need to discuss the debates surrounding the so-called failure of integration, as well as the rise and fall of a binary pair peculiar to Flanders and the Netherlands—allochthony versus autochthony. The discourse of the hegemonic voices in the Flemish debate on integration will then be named and explained in terms of logics. Once this scene has been set, I will move on to the way intellectuals and activists with a Moroccan background rearticulate the notion of integration in the context of interviews on political engagement.

4.1 Integration Between Science and Politics

Integration is a concept that finds itself at the crossroads of science and politics. Most of its meanings have been generated by actors and by centring institutions in the fields of politics and academia in attempts to fix, to define and to regulate nations, nation states, identities and their imaginary borders. The main reason for this shared point of interest between science and politics lies in the fact that integration is a category commonly used for describing the degree of cultural and social homogeneity and/or cohesion of whole societies. To say that there is a lack of social integration often amounts to saying that there is a lack of society. Integration is therefore a prime concern for both banal and non-banal forms of nationalism.

In a few decades, the concept of integration has become indispensable in debates about issues such as migration, racism, diversity and culture across Europe. The increase of migration flows due to processes of European integration and globalisation, as well as the increasing visibility of non-European and Muslim minorities in European public spheres have brought the notion to the centre of many public debates. This general development can be linked to a surge of nationalist, racist and ethnocentric feelings across the continent. This is not to say that there is no resistance to this type of discourse. But while "discourses on hybridity and multiple belongings circulate freely within intellectual settings, increasingly vociferous demands are made at the political level for undivided loyalty and affiliation to 'national cultures' for would-be denizens or citizens of European states" (Hogan-Brun et al. 2009, 6). As we will see, this also goes for a specific type of integration discourse we find in Flanders.

The notion of integration thrives in nationalist projects. Such projects are oriented towards the realisation of a mythical idea of society as a homogeneous entity whose members (should) share a uniform set of norms, values, rights and duties. Explicit academic and political definitions of integration usually stress that processes of integration imply respect for cultural and ethnic diversity and heterogeneity. But at the same time, many political, academic and everyday uses of the notion betray a deep concern and suspicion of such forms of diversity. In Europe, hegemonic notions of integration carry assimilatory overtones. The notion was meant to serve as an alternative for assimilation but in-depth analyses show that "over a period of ten years a shift can be observed from policies that acknowledge cultural pluralism to policies that emphasise assimilation into the host country". In such cases, "the word integration is not used in its reciprocal sense" since "its long-term aim is often assimilation" (Van Avermaet 2009, 17).

The concept of integration has become part of a shared vocabulary in political and academic discourses on migration-related issues. But a shared vocabulary does not imply a shared set of meanings. In European research on minority-related issues, definitions of integration frequently stress that the notion refers to a mode of migrant incorporation that acknowledges and accepts cultural diversity. Scientific and political definitions frequently stress that integration involves a process of adaptation on the part of migrants as well as on the part of the societies in which they find themselves. Assimilation is contrasted to integration as an undesirable mode of migrant incorporation. It involves the disappearance of migrant cultural traits and identities in a process of absorption (Hesters

4 Articulating the Problematic of Integration in a Minority Debate 181

2011, 54). Nevertheless, there are significant differences between explicit definitions of integration in academia and politics on the one hand, and mainstream understandings of the term on the other hand.

Integration-related questions lie at the heart of classic sociology. In fact, the idea of integration has been developed in sociology before it became a key topic in migration-related public debates. One might even say that the first sociologists invented society as an integrated object of investigation. They conceived society as an integrated whole of structures, functions, systems, subsystems by relying on organic metaphors of society. This involved a conceptualisation of society as a body whose order depends on an integrated functioning of its parts (Schinkel 2008, 111–112). From its earliest beginnings, sociology has been concerned with integration as a homogeneous and organic mode of cohesion (Schinkel 2008, 111–182; Van den Eede et al. 2009, 17–22). As such, it promoted an idea of society as a unified object with clear boundaries, an idea that is incompatible with both pragmatic and poststructuralist notions of society.

Progressive researchers, activists, politicians and intellectuals have repeatedly criticised homogenising notions of integration in Flanders and in the Netherlands (Alsulaiman 1998; Entzinger 1998; Foblets and Hubeau 1997; Talhaoui 1998). The interviewees presented in this chapter frequently follow this line of critique. However, in spite of the fact that there is a significant degree of political awareness concerning homogenising uses of integration-related concepts among progressive intellectuals and activists in Flanders, mainstream usage of the term continues to be marked by homogenising and culturist logics. Moreover, the organic legacy of early sociology is still present in a great deal of political and scientific discourse in the form of an implicit valuation of unity and stability of the societal whole in questions related to diversity and migration (Schinkel 2008, 111–113).

Academics have discussed integration as a debate, as a policy option and as an umbrella term for designating a variety of integration strategies. The objects to be integrated differ accordingly. Integration may refer to a process as well as to a goal such as the establishment of an integrated society or an integrated group. In all of these cases, social cohesion remains a central concern for researchers even when they highlight the diversity of integration trajectories. For instance, Van den Eede and his colleagues argue for a notion of integration and cohesion that values ethnic and cultural diversity or heterogeneity. They adopt a constructivist perspective that acknowledges the conflict-ridden and dialogical dimension of integration processes (Van den Eede et al. 2009, 5–6, 22–23). They view integration as a social, political and polity-related process entailing a wide range of ethnic and cultural diversification strategies aimed at the realisation of social cohesion. Integration thus operates at the level of policy as well as at the level of concrete individuals and ethnocultural groups (Van den Eede et al. 2009, 6, 18).

Nevertheless, in spite of the fact that these sociologists recognise the heterogeneous and conflict-ridden nature of integration processes and subscribe to a constructivist perspective, their concept of integration still carries an important characteristic of the organic logic that was the hallmark of early sociological approaches to social order. The authors argue that both too much and too little integration are dangerous for society. Writing from a systemic functionalist perspective, they argue that a balanced system should accommodate for conflict, diversity, autonomy and free choice. Nevertheless, they also claim that a lack of social cohesion could lead to a "disintegration of society" (Van den Eede et al. 2009). There is an interesting ideological structure underlying this idea that can be found in most integration research.

Those who question the orderliness of society nevertheless have to refer to society and attribute some kind of unity to it. Likewise, those who want to prove just how ordered society is have to posit a unity that can be questioned with respect to its order. Willem Schinkel points out that the ideal of an ordered society and the obsession with an orderly integration of its parts leads to a paradox in which "society is itself by not being itself" (Schinkel 2008, 123–125). Laclau wrote that in situations of radical social disorganisation, order becomes that which is absent. Signifiers such as 'order' and 'unity' can function as empty signifiers that political actors will try to fill or fix with their preferred meanings. 'Society' itself thus functions as an empty signifier marked by a constitutive impossibility (Laclau 1994c, 44). Interestingly, the same can be said about 'integration'.

Sociologically speaking, 'radical disorder' is hardly ever present in European nation states. The type of disorder Laclau had in mind resembled

4 Articulating the Problematic of Integration in a Minority Debate 183

Hobbes' state of nature (Laclau 1994c, 44). Without a doubt, a fully unintegrated society finds itself at the horrific side of the ideological fantasy that informs a great deal of integration discourse. But Schinkel argues that the discourses on integration—especially those of Flanders and the Netherlands—are symptoms of a society obsessed with its own health and integrity. This concern is fundamentally hypochondriac. Through its obsession with a paradoxical non- or disintegration, society becomes a hypochondriac fantasy whereby a complete integration of all individuals and groups related to a society is considered to be the ultimate ideal of health (Schinkel 2008, 136–138).

From a strictly sociological perspective, it is impossible *not* to be integrated into—some part of—society. Nevertheless, there are strong incentives and imperatives directed at specific groups to integrate themselves as if they are located outside of society's borders. In Flanders and in the Netherlands, calls for integration are first and foremost directed at lower-class, non-European and Islamic migrants as well as at their descendants. But the notion has also been used in order to problematise the integration of ex-convicts, criminals, psychiatric patients, women, homosexuals, the unemployed, the sick, the elderly or even the digitally illiterate. The fact that all of these groups are not considered to be—sufficiently—integrated shows us that the borders of society have become internal to the social system itself (Schinkel 2008, 136–138, 281–284). In integration discourse, society excludes parts of itself and then aims to reintegrate them. In spite of the fact that it is impossible to think of a 'disintegrated' person in the sociological sense of the word, the ideological structure of the minority debates allow us to do exactly this (Schinkel 2008, 154, 309–310).

The notion of integration does not only find itself at the crossroads of science and politics because it indicates an imaginary lack of cohesion that various political actors seek to fill. Another reason lies in the fact that it functions as a boundary concept. This becomes especially clear if we take a look at the discursive possibilities of the verb 'to integrate' and at the restricted pragmatic usage of this notion by members of a self-designated 'tolerant' majority. This majority consists of people who explicitly distance themselves from the far right and its racism but simultaneously refuse 'political correctness' and argue that 'the problems concerning integration' have to be dealt with. Put differently, we are dealing with the type of discourse in which people say that they are "not racist, but". Tolerant majority discourse is often marked by a rhetoric which stresses the "virtues of openness" while at the same time emphasising a need to manage, contain, restrict or discourage an excess of (particular types of) diversity, thus denying diversity as a simple fact of life (Blommaert and Verschueren 1998, 11–15). As such, "the tolerant majority only imagines its own tolerance". Consider its 'tolerant' notion of integration:

> *Central to the rhetoric of tolerance is the concept of integration. If homogeneity is the norm, the natural solution to problems caused by diversity is a policy of rehomogenization. While the extreme right proposes to rehomogenize society by removing all foreign elements, the tolerant majority envisages a rehomogenization based on 'integration' or the removal of disturbing differences This interpretation of integration is of course violently objected to by its adherents who, at the explicit level, claim full respect for diversity and profess a belief in absolute equality.* (Blommaert and Verschueren 1998, 120)

In order to understand this type of usage of the integration concept, we need to understand the pragmatic possibilities of the Dutch verb *integreren* (English: to integrate). A first thing to note is that it can be used as a transitive and as an intransitive verb. It is transitive when it is used with a subject that makes a patient undergo an action. In theory, one could say '*Jan integrates Mohamed*' or '*society has to integrate its minorities*' (Blommaert and Verschueren 1998, 112–115). However, such utterances hardly ever occur. In fact, statements such as '*Allochthons / Muslims / Migrants / Guest Workers have to integrate themselves*' are way more common. Moreover, the objects of integration are frequently pluralised and generalised categories of subjects (Blommaert and Verschueren 1998, 112).

The reason why Jan hardly ever integrates Mohamed and why tolerant majority members free themselves from their responsibility to integrate lies in the fact that the notion of integration is frequently framed as a matter of intentionality. In this sense, the problem is not merely that Muslims are not integrated. Rather, the problem is that '*they do not want to integrate themselves*' (Blommaert and Verschueren 1998, 112–115). The obstacle that stands in the way of the fantasy of a fully integrated society is thereby located in the lack of a will to integrate among minority members (Glynos and Howarth 2008, 287). At the same time, members of the self-designated tolerant majority and people who do not have a migration history and/or an Islamic background are supposed to be integrated by default. Their integration is turned into a non-issue.

It should also be noted that the verb '*to integrate*' is a process verb derived from the Latin word '*integer*', which literally means '*to complete*'. This meaning of integration as completion is activated whenever people are incited to integrate themselves *into* something. It is in this way that integration becomes a border concept whereby the objects of integration are placed outside of the imaginary boundary that constitutes society. This can be exemplified with reference to utterances such as '*they have to integrate themselves in our society / our culture / our nation*'. This restrictive usage can be explained with reference to three contexts. We see such usage of integration when people emphasise the conditionality of acceptance such as in '*if they only would integrate themselves*'; in reproaches such as '*they do not want to integrate themselves*'; or in the assignments of duties by using modal verbs such as in '*they have to integrate themselves*' (Blommaert and Verschueren 1998, 112–113).

Migrants and their descendants are usually supposed to integrate themselves into rather undifferentiated and reified entities such as societies, nations, cultures or civilisations. Of course, such expectations go radically against the grain of a poly-centred understanding of society and the public sphere. It also goes against the idea of a radically democratic society. Strictly speaking, it is impossible not to be integrated. On the contrary, our lives take place within and across a multiplicity of spatial, social and institutional settings in which we may be integrated to varying degrees. It is very much possible to be well integrated into one institution or social space and less in another. This can be exemplified with reference to cities that consist of various centres and centring institutions such as parks, shopping malls or schools that operate through very different activity types and normative forms of behaviour (see Maly et al. 2014).

If we are unable to learn the norms associated with specific public spaces, we do not only encounter identity-related problems but also problems of 'integration'. A night shop that advertises its products in a multiplicity of spoken languages within a super-diverse neighbourhood may be a better example of integration than the traditional bakery that advertises its traditional products in the hegemonic language alone (see Maly et al. 2014). Of course, such a poly-centred and dynamic notion of integration stands miles away from the hegemonic concept articulated by the tolerant majority in Flanders and in the Netherlands. But it can also be contrasted with sociological integration research that investigates indicators of the measure in which (groups of) people are integrated into the centring institutions of the hegemonic majority.

In sociological literature and research about migration, it has become common practice to investigate integration by focusing on a number of indicators such as language competences, religious affiliations, educational level, professional status, and so on (Schinkel 2008, 139–141). Nevertheless, this type of research frequently takes existing integration ideals derived from policy and politics as its point of departure. In combination with a lack of sociological reflexivity, this easily leads to the idea that migrants are the ones who lack in integration (Schinkel 2008, 165). Hegemonic discourse on integration in Flanders and in the Netherlands tends to hold individual minority members and communities responsible for their own integration. Especially people with Moroccan or Turkish backgrounds are expected to reduce their socio-cultural distance from the mainstream by speaking Dutch, by participating in mainstream civil society, and by subscribing to a usually under-specified set of practices, norms and values. According to public wisdom, such actions on the part of so-called allochthons would lead to a reduction of socio-political tensions between majority and minority groups. Nevertheless, this piece of public wisdom proved to be wrong.

Van Craen, Vancluysen and Ackaert compared a number of socio-cultural indicators of integration between three ethnic/cultural groups living in the former mining cities of Genk and Houthalen-Eekeren: Morocccan allochthons; Turkish allochthons; and Belgian autochthons. The authors acknowledged that the concept of integration is an "essentially contested concept" and explicitly state that they will not even attempt to come up with a definition. Nevertheless, they did adopt a distinction between socio-cultural integration and structural integration proposed by Penninx and Vermeuelen (Vermeulen and Penninx 1994; van Craen et al. 2007, 287).

4 Articulating the Problematic of Integration in a Minority Debate 187

Their notion of structural integration referred to the socio-economic position of ethnic and cultural minorities, whereas their notion of socio-cultural integration referred to "the measure in which minorities distinguish themselves from the society in which they live" (van Craen et al. 2007, 4). Indicators for measuring structural integration included work, income, housing, political rights and education. Likewise, indicators of socio-cultural integration included social capital, values, identifications and aspects of language use (Choenni 1992; Esser 2006; Veenman 1994). According to dominant ideas on integration, one would expect majority members to have more positive attitudes towards minority members that rank high on these indicators than to groups who rank lower on the scale of integration. However, Van Craen, Vancluysen en Ackaert countered this idea. Consider the following observations:

> *Turkish allochthons orient themselves more to their 'own' media, they have more friends in their own community, they are more often engaged in small talk with neighbours of their own community, and they often use their mother tongue (Turkish). Moroccan allochthons speak Dutch more often, they participate more in autochthon civil society, they have more positive image of autochthons, and consider themselves more Belgian.* (van Craen et al. 2007, 287)

Interestingly, autochthon respondents articulated more negative attitudes towards Moroccan than towards Turkish minority members. This negative perception was also mirrored in the fact that Moroccan Belgians report more personal experiences of discrimination than other groups. The authors formulated a number of hypotheses that might account for this integration paradox and concluded that neither differences with respect to education, socio-economic status, opinions, attitudes nor differences with respect to involvement in criminality provided a convincing explanation for this phenomenon (van Craen et al. 2007, 287–290). One dimension these authors did not look at were differences in terms of socio-political positioning in the public sphere. This is quite interesting considering the fact that the negative and hostile public image of this minority seems to stimulate action and mobilisation (Kanmaz 2007, 357).

Analysing the political opportunity structures for Moroccan or Maghrebian political mobilisation in Flemish contexts, Kanmaz explains the differential treatment and perception of Turkish and Moroccan minorities in Flanders with reference to the higher degree of political visibility of the latter (Kanmaz 2007, 357–358). During key events in the Flemish minority debate, Moroccan intellectuals, politicians, organisations and activists were comparatively more present in the public realm (Kanmaz 2007; Van den Broeck and Foblets 2002; Bousetta 2003). Nevertheless, Flemish or Belgian politicians tend to be very critical with respect to minority political engagements. This goes especially for identity political movements. For decades, political critiques with respect to hegemonic understandings of racism, citizenship and integration articulated by minorities have been met with scepticism and hostility by mainstream political parties of the left and right in Flanders (Fadil and Kanmaz 2009, 115–117). In this light, the integration paradox becomes less paradoxical.

In spite of the many problems with mainstream notions of integration, I do not consider sociological research on integration to be inherently dysfunctional. But the value-loaded connotations of integration in mainstream political discourse do not allow for an un-reflexive usage of the term. Especially notions of integration that implicitly or explicitly defer responsibility for social cohesion to those who supposedly find themselves 'outside' of a unified society are very problematic from a radically democratic point of view. Moreover, such understandings of integration are in blatant contradiction with polycentric notions of self, subjectivity, politics and society.

The function of integration as a border concept sustains an ideological fantasy of societies as static, homogenous and/or mono-centred entities and fuels antagonistic modes of politics. However, to simply get rid of the word or to disqualify the notion as essentially wrong is unlikely to yield major political results. It is more important to counter the interpretive logics that infuse the language games surrounding the notion of integration with undemocratic and ethnocentric values. In order to name and grasp the logics infusing hegemonic understandings of integration in Flanders, we have to take a closer look at the specifics of the debate in this part of the world.

4.2 On the 'Failure' of Integration and Integration Policy in Flanders

In Belgium, discourses and policies on integration were developed in response to the electoral success of the far right *Vlaams Blok*/Vlaams Belang (VB) on the *Black Sunday* of October, 9 in 1988. The resulting political shockwave was a direct incentive for the creation of a Royal Commissariat for Migration Policy (KCM) that was charged with an investigation of the 'migrant problem' and with a task to formulate policy recommendations in order to solve it. The KCM formulated an influential definition of integration and subdivided the group of people who had to be integrated into guest workers, migrants, minorities and—last but not least—allochthons. I will go into these categories in the next section. First, it is important to come to grips with the debate on the failure of integration.

The first report published by the KCM is arguably the most important document produced by this organisation (d'Hondt 1989). It is a three-volume oeuvre that served as a blueprint for the official Flemish approach to migration and integration. Its most crucial fragment is the definition of integration given below (Blommaert 2005; d'Hondt 1989, 38–39):

The proposals that will follow will be inspired by a concept of integration, which simultaneously

1. Starts from the notion of 'insertion', using the following criteria:

   (a) assimilation where the public order so demands
   (b) a consistent promotion of an optimal insertion according to the guiding social principles that are the basis of the culture of the host country and that revolve around 'modernity', 'emancipation' and 'full-fledged pluralism' in the sense given by a modern Western state.
   (c) unambiguous respect for cultural diversity-as-mutual-enrichment in the other domains;

2. And which is accompanied by a promotion of the structural involvement of minorities in the activities and the objectives of the authorities.

Blommaert points out that this formula has been adopted in the migration policies of governments since 1989. The above definition has never been officially revised or revoked. It was retained in the final report of the KCM in 1993. Moreover, its successor, the CGKR (Centre for Equal Opportunities and Racism) adopted this definition without criticism. Neither its practical usefulness nor its relevance with respect to combating racism was called into question by the CGKR (Blommaert 2005; d'Hondt 1989). The problematisation of this type of discourse was a task left for activists, minority members and critical academics. The publication of *Het Belgische migrantendebat* (Blommaert and Verschueren 1992)—the Dutch predecessor of *Debating Diversity* (Blommaert and Verschueren 1998)—was an important critical contribution to the debate.

The mediatised conclusion of this book "that the extreme right and the tolerant majority, represented in their purest forms by Vlaams Blok and KCM, 'think in the same way' (a simplified way of saying that diversity, which is completely rejected by the extreme right, is not fundamentally accepted by the tolerant majority either) caused a major controversy which then became an integral part of the debate". The farther one got from the centres of power within academia and politics, the more favourable this conclusion was received. The book was well received among migrant organisations, left-wing political movements and academics with openly critical attitudes towards society. From this angle, most critics argued that the analyses "stayed too close to the investigated discourse and did not go deeply into socio-economic determinants of minority-majority relationships" (Blommaert and Verschueren 1998, 141).

Many critics of the centre right and left opposed the idea that mainstream and far-right actors shared the same homogenising logic of integration. They usually categorised Blommaert and Verschueren on the far left and sometimes even on the far right. In the latter case, the approach to diversity advocated by the authors was misinterpreted as a plea for some kind of apartheid system. Critics also attacked the book on methodological grounds. The proposed linguistic pragmatic approach to implicitness and ideology was thereby considered to be an intellectually dishonest political strategy that exaggerated the homogenising thrust of Flemish integration discourse. Some even claimed that Blommaert and Verschueren did not differentiate between different varieties of

4 Articulating the Problematic of Integration in a Minority Debate 191

integration discourse. According to the authors, this reproach missed their point completely: "While using language, it is perfectly possible to talk about the migrant issue and even about 'problems' in a manner that reveals, at the level of implicit meaning and presuppositions, a fundamentally positive attitude towards diversity" (Blommaert and Verschueren 1998, 141–143). The problem is that such varied usage is hard to find in the mainstream discourse on integration-related issues.

The Dutch predecessor of *Debating diversity* is an example of a discourse analysis that had a significant impact on public interactions outside of the confines of the university. In fact, many of my interviewees referred to this book as a source of inspiration, more than 15 years after its publication. Moreover, Flemish progressive intellectuals and activists have come to challenge dominant understandings of integration in ways that parallel arguments made in this book. For instance, many people have challenged the vagueness of the term 'integration' by asking *what* one should integrate *into*. Generally speaking, opponents of integration policy and discourse find powerful allies in Blommaert and Verschueren (Van den Broeck 2002, 22). Nevertheless, the notion still figures prominently in debates on minority-related issues.

The far right accepts only the first part of the KCM definition—that is, assimilation to law and order. Other aspects are entirely left out of the equation. VB discourse does not allow for a reciprocal understanding of integration. Moreover, VB politicians such as Filip De Winter claim that the presence of people with Islamic headscarves in public administrations and in schools constitutes an admission of the fact that "integration is an illusion" (De Winter 1993 cited in Blommaert 2005, 200). In this sense, far-right usage of 'integration' is somewhat ironic. But, it is anything but funny. VB discourse systematically articulates a chain of equivalence in which Islamic practices such as the wearing of headscarves are equated with Islamic fundamentalism, with terrorism and with a stance against integration. Unfortunately, such views are not unique to the VB and can be found far beyond the confines of this far right party (Blommaert 2005, 200–201).

An important caveat needs to be made with respect to critiques about 'integration'. Debates about the 'failure' or 'bankruptcy' of integration are not simply about a presupposed failure on the part of migrants to integrate. The debate cannot be reduced to a simply choice *pro* or *contra* integration. As always, one has to ask how 'the failure of integration' is articulated and interpreted in particular contexts of enunciation. As such, it should not come as a surprise that proclamations of this failure are as polysemic as utterances about integration. Actors declaring the bankruptcy of integration often criticise interculturalism and multiculturalism as attainable and desirable goals for societies to reach (Van den Broeck 2002, 10). Others use the same notion in order to address problems in integration policy and the failure of policy to face up to the requirements of societies that are already marked by high degrees of diversity. This latter type of critique is directed first and foremost at integration policy.

The terms 'integration sector' or 'categorical sector' refer to a network of centres and services financed by the Flemish government that execute minority policies on the terrain (Verhoeven et al. 2003, 22). They do not refer to social, cultural and/or religious organisations organised by minorities themselves. The integration sector is not a grass-roots initiative but a collection of government-funded organisations that are meant to promote integration. At the time when I conducted my interviews, the Flemish integration sector was embodied by the Flemish Minority Centre (VMC). This organisation would later be transformed into the Crosspoint for Migration and Integration ([Crosspoint MI] Kruispunt Migratie en Integratie). The VMC and its successor were meant to stimulate, to support and to safeguard minority policies. It provided legal advice and support for policy-related questions and offered trainings for people involved in the integration sector. The VMC was meant to collect signals from the so-called ethnic or cultural minority sector in order to present the latter's concerns to the government (Kruipsunt M-I 2009; Verhoeven et al. 2003, 22–23).

The integration sector is also embodied in a series of provincial and municipal integration centres. Flanders and Brussels count eight of these institutions: one for each province, one for the Brussels *Gewest*, one for Ghent and another one for Antwerp. Their task is to stimulate, to support and to guard the execution of Flemish minority policies. In addition, there are 33 local or municipal integration centres that should not be confused with the communal integration services. The latter are tools of the municipal governments. In 2003, the Flemish government counted

4 Articulating the Problematic of Integration in a Minority Debate 193

25 integration services; in 2011, there were 34 cities containing such services. All of them are supported by the VMC/Crosspoint MI (Verhoeven et al. 2003, 24; Kruispunt M-I 2011). The debate about the 'failure of integration' frequently refers to an alleged failure of these institutions.

Migrant organisations—often designated as 'self-organisations'—are not part of what is meant by the 'integration sector'. Ethnic and cultural (read: non-religious) self-organisations started to receive funding after a 1993 decision by the Flemish government that allowed for their recognition. These organisations have to be supported principally by volunteers and have to testify to a democratic organisational structure in order to qualify for subsidies. Mosques and religious civil society organisations are not subsidised in this way (Martens 1997). After the establishment of subsidised integration centres and a great deal of hesitation, the Flemish government issued a decree that allowed for the recognition and support of socio-cultural—read non-religious—migrant self-organisations.

In 1996, a law was passed that allowed for structural subsidies for immigrant self-organisations. The most important condition for this funding was that such organisations had to organise themselves in federations active in at least two provinces. These umbrella organisations would then be responsible for distributing government funding to their member organisations (Bousetta 2001). In 2000, the Minority Forum (*Minderhedenforum*) was established. This Forum currently represents 13 federations of immigrant self-organisations. It also hosts other minority federations that count at least ten member organisations who can testify to at least one year of structural activity. The Forum also includes co-opted individuals whose participation guarantees the involvement of one or more subgroups of ethnic-cultural minorities in Flanders (Verhoeven et al. 2003).

When activist and philosopher Tarik Fraihi wrote his 2000 article on *The bankruptcy of the integration industry*, he articulated the outlines of a debate on the integration sector that would remain relevant until this day. He attacked the integration concept as well as the integration sector, defining this 'industry' as consisting of "all integration centres plus the Centre for Equal Opportunities (CGKR)" (Fraihi 2000). As we noticed before, the CGKR inherited the KCM's obligations to stimulate equal opportunities and to combat all forms of distinction, exclusion and limitation on the basis of criteria stipulated in the anti-racism law. The CGKR collects complaints about racism and discrimination and can file complaints against organisations that are suspected of breaching the anti-racism law (Vlierinck 2010, 104–108).

Fraihi's article challenged the integration industry with respect to its effectiveness as an emancipatory and participatory tool for minorities. He argued that—in spite of its good intentions—this sector frequently functions as a political buffer for demands made by minority members. The fact that Flemish social reality is marked by discrimination on the labour market and by a Eurocentric system of education does not help either. In a rather prophetic line for a country that currently has the highest percentage of Syria fighters among its citizens, Fraihi explicitly warned against the processes of radicalisation such a situation might trigger. Fraihi therefore called for a critical evaluation of the integration sector (Fraihi 2000). He concluded his article on the bankruptcy of the integration industry as follows:

> *The integration concept they* [politicians reacting to the electoral success of the VB] *conceived of in the past is nothing but a folkloristic model, based on a non-committal tolerance whereby integration is reduced to 'standing on good graces' with the autochthone population. The current integration concept has proved its bankruptcy. Its inventors, such as Johan Leman, should take the honourable way out and resign. A new concept needs to be developed whereby allochthons should be actively involved from the beginning, in a constructive way, with mutual respect and without any form of paternalism. To conclude with Gandhi: 'Whatever you do for me but without me, you do against me'.* (Fraihi 2000)

Fraihi's critique of the integration industry went hand in hand with an argument for the recognition and involvement of minority—'allochthon'—self-organisations in the drafting of migration-related policies. He also argued against a strict separation between minority organisations subsidised by culture-oriented policy domains and integration centres that derived their funding from the policy domain of welfare: "as if allochthons have nothing to do with the environment, with traffic, with media, with development policies" (Fraihi 2002, 104–105).

4 Articulating the Problematic of Integration in a Minority Debate 195

Another—even more influential—left-wing critic of the integration sector is former AEL chairman Dyab Abou Jahjah. He also declared the failure of the integration sector and articulated the AEL demands regarding this industry as follows:

> We demand that one deals firmly with racism and discrimination of all minorities. According to us, the integration sector can no longer function as such. It has to be given another function and another mission. Perhaps this sector could focus on new arrivals and refugees. Resources that have been put aside for the so-called 'stimulation of integration' belong to the self-organisations of migrants. They can use them more efficiently to promote the equal participation and emancipation of their own community. (Jahjah 2002, 119)

The bankruptcy of integration is just as polysemic a notion as the concept of integration itself. Debates on integration are never simply debates pro or against integration. To represent them as such is to misrecognise their complexity. Rather, one needs to ask oneself what usage of integration-related signifiers allows for democratic modes of empowerment and what usage tends to reproduce and/or legitimise relationships of domination. The question is what articulations are functional to the social, economic, cultural and political emancipation of citizens—no matter whether these are designated as allochthons, authochthons, minorities, majorities, migrants or guest workers. It is therefore important to realise that there is a difference between the critiques mentioned above and the neo-racist idea that integration has failed because cultural and religious minorities continue to perform their identities in the public realm.

In this context, it is also important to note that there is a tenacious and powerful discourse about the failure of multiculturalism circulating in Europe. Even though the debates about multiculturalism have their own particularities, they are marked by similar logics as the integration debate. This can be illustrated with reference to Angela Merkel who proclaimed the failure of multiculturalism in Germany, in October 2010. Other European leaders—including David Cameron, Nikolas Sarkozy as well as the Belgian Prime Minister Yves Leterme—responded by subscribing to her analysis (Hesters 2011, 22–23). In Flanders, a group of academics and activists responded to Merkel's anti-multiculturalism discourse by declaring the bankruptcy of the debate on multiculturalism rather than the bankruptcy of multicultural models of society. The authors link Merkel's statements on multiculturalism to the Flemish debate on (the failure of) integration:

> *Nowhere do we hear a self-critical voice, on the contrary, the discourse is still the same: 'migrants should adapt themselves culturally'. The presuppositions of this debate and the accompanying policy constitute the core of the bankruptcy of integration policies. It is about time to fully subscribe to a real acceptance of diversity, to construct a structural policy of anti-racism, and to develop a powerful socio-economic policy.* (Abicht et al. 2011)

The authors also warn against the "culturalisation of the other" that leads to the "abnormalisation of (children of) migrants", "racism" and "exclusion" (Abicht et al. 2011). Fraihi's call for an integration policy directed against existing social, economic and/or cultural inequalities remains relevant after more than 20 years of debating integration and its failure. It is therefore important to name and to explain the logics that characterise this debate. However, before we go into these logics, we need to take a closer look at the objects and subjects of integration.

4.3 The Rise and Fall of a Dutch Binary Pair: Allochthons versus Autochthons

Dutch debates on integration are characterised by a dichotomous terminology that is unique to Flanders and to the Netherlands. In spite of the many parallels between European debates on integration, every national context is marked by its own particularities. The centrality of the binary pair *'allochtoon – autochtoon'* (English: *allochthon–autochthon*) in Dutch scientific, party-political and everyday discourse is a case in point. The words 'allochthon' and 'autochthon' have become an integral part of hegemonic political discourse in Flanders and in the Netherlands. They are key signifiers that inform the self-understandings and political subjectivities that structure the Flemish minority debates.

4 Articulating the Problematic of Integration in a Minority Debate   197

Consider the following events. On September 20 of the year 2012, the Flemish quality newspaper *De Morgen* publicly announced an editorial decision to abandon the binary pair '*allochtoon – autochtoon*' in its articles. This decision triggered a cross-media debate that lasted for more than a week (Verschelden 2012). After five days, *De Morgen* stopped using these notions. No other newspapers followed. Nevertheless, most of them did spend a significant amount of time and space on the debate about this editorial decision. Interestingly, many politicians did welcome the new editorial line of *De Morgen*.

Belgian Prime Minister Elio Di Rupo welcomed this new editorial policy as a "beautiful and brave initiative", acknowledging "the power of words" in the battle against discrimination. The rhetoric of many other politicians in government was equally positive. However, no efforts to abandon the allochthon/autochthon terminology were made at the federal level of government (Windels 2012). Some local administrations did move beyond mere rhetoric. For instance, Amsterdam decided to abandon the allochthony–autochthony opposition in its public administration and to adopt a system of hyphenated identities instead (Moleman 2013). In March 2013, a progressive municipal coalition in Ghent (Belgium) decided to *bury* these notions in coffins in one of its central parks. The words 'allochthon' and 'autochthon' were printed out, put in coffins, paraded around the city and put to rest for once and for all. This burial was the climax of a festive 'funeral' organised by a civil society initiative called the Ghent Spring. After this ritual event, Ghent decided not to use these words in public policy and administration anymore (Van den Broeck 2013; Zienkowski 2014).

The symbolic burial of the binary pair *allochtoon / autochtoon* and the decisions to stop using these words in a Flemish newspaper and in a limited number of municipalities did not change the overall structure of the integration debates. The interpretive logics involved were too flexible and dynamic for this to happen. On the one hand, many politicians, journalists, activists and citizens simply continued to use this terminology because they believe these words describe an objective reality. Many of them refused to be censored by what they consider to be politically correct considerations. On the other hand, even those who did actively distance themselves from this binary pair were not always immune to the logics informing this discourse (see Zienkowski 2014, 293–295).

The intensity of the 2013 debate on the public usage of *allochtoon* and *autochtoon* is indicative of the centralising functions these signifiers perform in the logics people deploy when making sense of themselves and their societies. The rise and fall of this binary pair is part and parcel of the discourse on integration in Flanders. The following quote provides us with an insightful overview of the wider context in which allochthons and autochthons are named and problematised.

> *one is first a foreign guest worker, refugee, or asylum seeker; then one becomes a migrant: a migrant is a guest worker but is at the same time a 'whole person' (whatever that is supposed to mean) with a culture, a theology or a religion; then one becomes an allochthon who is described as a person with a different socio-cultural origin but who has also developed certain ties with the guest country; in the end these allochthons can disappear into the autochthon population or, if they fail to do so, constitute an 'ethnic minority', characterised by a socio-economically disadvantaged position.* (Talhaoui 1998, 75–76)

The quote above presents the different categories that have been used over several decades of debating migration, diversity and integration. It also sketches an ideal–typical migrant trajectory as conceptualised in Flanders and in the Netherlands. During the fifties and sixties, the debate centred around 'guest workers' who came from Morocco and Turkey in order to work in Dutch and Belgian industries. These workers were not expected to stay. As it became clear that many of them would not return to their countries of origin, the term 'migrant' would become more popular. This happened at a time of large-scale deindustrialisation during the seventies and eighties. During the late nineties, the main objects of integration were rebranded as 'allochthons'. Problems of integration were now reframed in cultural terms. The concept of allochthony objectifies first and foremost immigrants with an Islamic background. The notion does not only refer to immigrants but also to their children and grandchildren born in Belgium and in the Netherlands (Arnaut and Ceuppens 2009, 32–36; Blommaert and Verschueren 1998, 47–50; Jacobs and Rea 2006; Maly 2007d; Schinkel 2008, 143–151).

4 Articulating the Problematic of Integration in a Minority Debate 199

Etymologically speaking, the word 'allochthon' is derived from the Greek *allos* (other) and *chton* (country, land or earth). The noun was derived from geological usage of the term *allochthonous*, an adjective used for designating rocks, mineral deposits or other elements that did not stem from the location in which they are found (van der Haar and Yanow 2013, 237). Its large-scale usage in political and academic discourse on migration is a relatively recent phenomenon. Early uses can be found in administrative and academic reports of the fifties. Here, the concept was sometimes used in order to refer to groups migrating to culturally different areas within the same country. For instance, Van der Haar and Yanow refer to a 1959 province-level report that used the term allochthon primarily in reference to the migration of protestant groups from the North of the Netherlands to the rather catholic South of the country (van der Haar and Yanow 2013, 234).

In the Netherlands, the term allochthony entered into national policy discourse in 1971 through the work of sociologist Hilda Verwey-Jonker. In this context, the concept referred firstly to different types of groups crossing the national borders of the country and secondly to migrations from neighbouring countries (Belgium and Germany) and ex-colonies such as Indonesia, Suriname and the Antilles/Aruba. Interestingly, we are talking not only about migrants here but also about guest workers, refugees and foreign students (van der Haar and Yanow 2013, 234). In the eighties the notion started to appear more frequently in mediatised, political and mainstream discourses on migration and minority-related issues.

In 1989, the Scientific Council for Government Policy (*Wetenschappelijke Raad voor het Regeringsbeleid*) of the Netherlands formulated a recommendation to change the terminology for talking about 'non-native' Dutch people. Talk about (ethnic) minorities was to be replaced by a description in terms of allochthony. The Central Bureau for Statistics (CBS) would follow this recommendation and contribute to the development of an official definition of the term (van der Haar and Yanow 2013, 235):

At that time, the CBS used various definitions of allochtoon. One designated a person as allochtoon when s/he and *one parent were foreign-born (e.g. someone*

> *resident in the Netherlands who had been born in Indonesia to an Indonesian woman and a Netherlands-born serviceman) or when both parents were foreign-born (i.e., the Netherlands-born offspring of a guest worker and his spouse who arrived after family reunification [gezinshereniging] policies went into effect). The other definition designated a person as allochtoon when (s)he or at least one parent was foreign-born.* (van der Haar and Yanow 2013, 235)

The definitions of the CBS were streamlined in 1999. From that moment on, an allochthon became someone who was not born in the country *or* who has at least one parent of foreign origin. Note that one can perfectly have the Dutch nationality *and* be designated as an allochthon. In contrast, the category of autochthon is supposed to refer to ethnically Dutch citizens. Policy and official statistics in the Netherlands also distinguished between so-called Western and non-Western allochthons. However, these categories have nothing to do with the geographic West or East. Rather, this distinction is defined in socio-economic and cultural terms by the CBS. For instance, individuals born in Japan who have the Dutch nationality are considered to be Western allochthons whereas individuals with Turkish or Moroccan background are considered to be Eastern allochthons (van der Haar and Yanow 2013, 237–242). This distinction may seem arbitrary but is logically connected to hegemonic understandings of social, cultural and economic differences between ethnic and religious groups in the Netherlands.

The Dutch concept of allochthony was a welcome innovation for the policy makers who drafted the first integration policies in Flanders. The term entered Flemish policy discourse in the 1989 KCM report that also defined the notion of integration. Moreover, the Flemish 1998 *Minority decree* drew heavily on the definition of allochthony as developed by the CBS in the Netherlands. When the concept was imported into the Belgian context, some interesting changes were made. Firstly, the generational criterion for labelling people as allochthons was extended to the third generation. Secondly, the weaker socio-economic position that inspired the Dutch distinction between Western and non-Western allochthons became an official element of the Flemish official definition of allochthony (i.e. Japanese supposedly have a socio-economic lifestyle closer to 'ours'). And thirdly, the new definition was bestowed with a more explicit

4 Articulating the Problematic of Integration in a Minority Debate   201

socio-economic dimension as can be observed below (Jacobs and Rea 2006, 15–18, 21):

> *By allochthons we understand all persons who are legally residing in Belgium and simultaneously fulfil the following conditions, whether they posess the Belgian nationality or not: (a) have at least one parent or grand-parent which is born outside of Belgium, (b) find themselves in a disfavoured position because of their ethnic origin or their weak socio-economic position.*

It is not only interesting to note that people can find themselves in a weaker socio-economic position because of their ethnic origin but also that the KCM defined ethnic minorities as groups of allochthons that go back to one particular country of origin (Blommaert and Verschueren 1998, 105). Nevertheless, in contrast to the Netherlands, official figures on the number of 'allochthons' do not exist in Flanders because Belgian law does not allow the National Institute for Statistics (NIS) to collect data on race and ethnic origin. Some Flemish institutions try to be creative though. For instance, the Flemish unemployment agency VDAB has collected data on nationality and country of birth by using a system of voluntary registration and name recognition software program that could identify Turkish and Maghreb names. The goal was to identify ethnic groups and people that could be labelled as 'allochthon' (Jacobs and Rea 2006, 16–17).

In Flanders, the frantic search for a politically correct terminology to talk about migrants in a context marked by a far right party on the rise created an ideal context for adopting the neologies allochthony and autochthony on a large scale. From the eighties on, these concepts were widely adopted by a multiplicity of actors. It became the main way to designate 'problematic' groups of migrants. However, as is the case with 'integration', there are differences between official definitions and mainstream everyday uses of the term. With respect to allochthony, a process of semantic narrowing and associative widening occurred. The notion is usually reserved for migrants, Arabs and Muslims in general. Designations of migrants from England or the USA as allochthons are highly exceptional in mainstream Dutch discourses on integration.

The supposedly wider notion of allochthons inherited all of the negative connotations previously associated with migrants. In Flanders, both notions usually refer to people of Moroccan and Turkish decent: "the incorporation of other groups of foreigners into the category remains rare and only occurs for very specific rhetorical and argumentative purposes" (Blommaert and Verschueren 1998, 48–52). Little has changed since Blommaert and Verschueren made this observation. Merely mentioning that I interviewed people of Moroccan descent led people to conclude that my research was about the 'integration of allochthons'. The abolishment of the binary pair by some newspapers and municipal administrations as well as the symbolic burial of 'allochthon' and 'autochthon' in Ghent in recent years demonstrates that there is some degree of critical awareness with respect to the use of these notions. But neither the concepts nor the logics informing them have disappeared from the public debate.

Also, it should be noted that integration-related notions almost never occur in isolation from other abstract signifiers. The meanings of signifiers such as identity, allochthony, minority, community, nation, state, multiculturalism and/or (super-)diversity depend on the way they are articulated with each other in concrete instances of use. All of these notions have been articulated in the most diverse contexts and settings with the concept of integration. They are fuzzy, abstract and vague. Sometimes, such notions function as synonyms, at other times, they indicate conflicting modes of politics and subjectivity. For this reason, I choose not to deal with each of these notions in detail. Nevertheless, some brief remarks on diversity, participation and citizenship are needed in the light of the upcoming analyses.

Some authors have argued that the notion of *citizenship* has been replacing the notion of integration. Its introduction in the Flemish migration debate is a relatively recent innovation. Until the middle of the nineties, the notion of citizenship hardly ever popped up in this context. Talk about the citizen (*burger*) was mostly to be found in the political discourse of Flemish liberals. The most notable articulation of citizenship-related concepts can be found in Guy Verhofstadt's two *Citizen Manifestos* (Dutch: *Burgermanifesten*) (Verhofstadt 1991, 1992). These documents contain a rather assimilatory notion of *inburgering* based on the idea that new citizens should first and foremost adapt themselves to majority norms and values. From the nineties on, this concept would become increasingly

4 Articulating the Problematic of Integration in a Minority Debate 203

popular, leading to a specific policy of 'inburgering' (*inburgeringsbeleid*) (Foblets and Hubeau 1997, 21–22, 27–28). The relationship between political and sociological discourse on citizenship can be illustrated with reference to the following academic quote:

> *What notion of citizenship do we use when we talk about integration? What form of citizenship do we expect from newcomers and allochthons? What form of citizenship do we expect from autochthons? Do we allow for the possibility to participate and to create equal opportunities? Or do we opt for a clearly active notion of citizenship? To what extent may new arrivals and allochthons keep and develop their own loyalties? How can they express their loyalty towards the various autochthon networks and communities?* (Van den Eede et al. 2009, 29)

Note that the introduction and framing of migration-related issues in terms of citizenship does not displace or cancel out talk on integration. This can partly be explained with reference to the rather untranslatable idea of *inburgering*. This concept captures the idea of integrating into a status of citizenship (*burgerschap*). As is the case with discourse about migrants who have to integrate themselves into society, the concept of *inburgering* implies individualisation of societal responsibilities and a metaphorical movement from an imaginary outside to an imaginary inside. On a formal level, the status of citizenship is usually taken to imply that newcomers should accept a rather vague package of 'rights and duties'. Hubeau and Foblets therefore emphasise that one should not lose track of the material dimensions of citizenship, for this status implies concrete rights with respect to education, labour, housing and political participation (Foblets and Hubeau 1997).

According to Blommaert, the shift towards talk about *inburgering* and its right-and-duties discourse is indicative of a wider ideological shift from a welfare state approach to integration to a neoliberal understanding that defines integration as a personal responsibility. As the state gives way to neoliberal modes of government, the neoliberal citizen no longer automatically enjoys democratic rights and obligations. Rather, these have to be *earned*. Hence, there is always more emphasis on duties than on rights in this type of discourse. Moreover, within this logic, rights and obligations are increasingly made dependent on one's economic contributions to the nation state (Blommaert 2010a). Blommaert does not want to dispense with the notion of citizenship but prefers a more polycentric approach marked by a different logic of integration. Updating the discussions on integration to crisis-ridden times, he writes the following:

> *An anti-crisis policy that is going to cut into the welfare state generates all sorts of questions concerning integration: social, economic, and cultural integration, and integration as* a problem *for the entire society. How do I remain 'integrated' as someone who is entitled to a pension? As a single mother? As a long-term unemployed person? As a chronically ill individual? Whoever examines these questions critically, will note that they imply the same presuppositions as the citizenship related questions we ask about allochthons. The notion of 'citizen' is central to every model of society, it always constitutes its anthropological dimension, and it should therefore always be carefully analysed.* (Blommaert 2010a, 8)

Flemish discourse on integration includes talk about diversity. Van den Eede, Wets and Levrau conceptualise diversity policy as the whole of strategies and processes used in order to deal with ethnic and cultural diversity in a society, while simultaneously maintaining social order (Van den Eede et al. 2009). Diversity management was first developed in the context of multinational companies seeking to manage their multicultural and multinational workforce. In Flanders, the concept was initially adopted within the context of an equal opportunities policy within Flemish administration. Sarah Scheepers notes that the original arguments for adopting this set of management strategies were mainly economic. Nevertheless, there was also an ethical element involved: "a diverse workforce would make state bureaucracies more representative of the general population, and guarantee a more democratic service delivery" (Scheepers 2011, 27–28). Moreover, diversity policy is usually linked to a discourse on equal opportunities.

Scheepers notes that there are basically two models of equal opportunity in diversity discourse. On the one hand, there is a liberal variety that stresses the importance of fair procedures with respect to the selection and assessment of employees. These should be judged on the basis of their merits and competences. On the other hand, there is a more radical approach that emphasises the importance of affirmative action, positive discrimination and the redistribution of jobs and resources in favour of disadvantaged groups. According to this second view, the meritocratic liberal model functions as an ideology. In liberal organisation literature, diversity is often used in order to discuss the benefits of a varied set of workforce attributes such as skills, gender, race, ethnicity, sexual orientation, physical ability, age and educational level. The underlying idea is that an explicit valuation of people's differences enables them to work their full potential in a more effective way. The management focus on individual empowerment implies a shift away from policies directed at groups such as women, ethnic minorities or people with disabilities who are often the target of discriminatory practices (Scheepers 2011, 29–33).

Of course, there are many other categories that are commonly articulated in debates on integration. One may refer to notions such as participation, emancipation, empowerment, super-diversity and active pluralism. I will analyse the various ways in which my respondents use such notions, but the main focus of the upcoming chapter will be on integration. Nevertheless, when a notion such as emancipation proves to be relevant to the sense of self and politics of an interviewee, I will take its pragmatic significance into account. For now, however, the main point is to understand the hegemonic logics of the 'migrant problem'. An understanding of these logics provides a useful background for analysing the counter-discourses articulated by my interviewees.

4.4 Hegemonic Logics of the Migrant Problem

The large-scale patterns that structure hegemonic discourse(s) on minorities in Flanders can be described in terms of social, political and fantasmatic logics. As I argued before, it is important to identify these logics if we are to understand the sense of self and politics articulated by my interviewees.

Critical discourse involves the simultaneous (re-)articulation of hegemonic *and* alternative identities, arguments and discourse. As such, it involves both latent and manifest (re)articulations of dominant logics and counter-logics. Glynos pointed out that "counter-logics become visible in those moments when self-interpretations of subjects resist easy assimilation into an already existing mould" (Glynos 2011, 280). Subjects do not subscribe to and/or identify with both types of logic in the same way. Implicit and explicit (re-)articulations of dominant patterns or logics in the public realm involve a loosening of the fantasmatic grip of mainstream discourse. The reflexive features of metapragmatic awareness allow for ideological interpellation. But they also provide us with the means to grip discourse and to reflexively manipulate its functions in acts of critique (Zienkowski 2014, 289–290).

Since the sense of self and politics articulated by the intellectuals and activists I talked to was partly constructed in relation to mainstream understandings of integration and allochthony, it is useful to rearticulate the structure of this debate in terms of social, political and fantasmatic logics. Let us start with the social logics of critical explanation. Based on the literature discussed above, one can name a *logic of homogenisation*, a *logic of culturalisation* and a *logic of assimilation*. Together, these logics have structured mainstream understandings Flemish identity, Flanders, integration and autochthony. They also informed the institutional imperative to integrate oneself. An imperative articulated by autochthonous citizens, scientists, politicians and the various centring institutions of the integration industry.

In order to name the social logics of the integration debate, I will pass through the self-understandings articulated in *tolerant majority* discourse. Flemish hegemonic discourse on minority issues can be described in terms of a social logic of homogenisation that is based on the principle that the ideal society should be as uniform as possible. This is not to say that cultural diversity is abolished completely, but the 'problem' of integration is understood first and foremost as a problem of diversity with respect to a conflated amalgam of 'norms and values'. This logic informs a multiplicity of statements on issues as diverse as education, migration, multilingualism, racism and culture. It explains the large-scale usage of the binary pair allochthony/autochthony. Moreover, it plays a key role in nationalist self-understandings of Flemings *as* Flemings (Zienkowski 2014, 289–290).

The logic of homogenisation abnormalises the presence of (descendants of) foreigners who mark their different identities, cultures and religions publicly. Blommaert and Verschueren wrote about an ideology of homogeneism as a world view in which "a vague and largely imaginary feature cluster of descent, ethnicity, religion, language and territory, is seen as the

4 Articulating the Problematic of Integration in a Minority Debate 207

norm and as a condition for social harmony, yielding 'natural groups' with a self-evident right to self-determination" (Blommaert and Verschueren 1998, 109). As such, a homogenising logic that normalises negative reactions of autochthons to the 'abnormal' presence of 'allochthons' emerges.

The emergence of a bipolar discourse centred on notions of allochthony and autochthony can also be understood in terms of a *logic of culturalisation* that structures many Flemish problematisations of migration- and minority-related issues since the late eighties. In Flanders, as in most of continental Europe, the notion of race has been banned from academic and political vocabularies ever since the Nazi appropriation of the word (Hesters 2011, 55; van der Haar and Yanow 2013). The concept has been so intertwined with Nazi discursive practices that even the far right rarely uses the notion in public. Exclusionary discourse has taken other—more cultural—forms. The category of culture has become one of the main explanatory concepts for describing problems of integration in tolerant majority and right-wing discourse.

Etienne Balibar pointed at the emergence of a type of cultural or neo-racism in which culturalist and relativistic arguments developed by anthropologists such as Lévi-Strauss, Sapir, Whorf, hall, Mead and Benedict are being used against the advocates of multicultural and intercultural models of society. Neo-racism is based on a model of different cultures that are considered to be incompatible with each other: "whereas racism criticises the mixture of 'races', neo-racism directs its ciriticism at the mixing of cultures. Whereas racism is linked to the presupposed 'first nature' of man, new racism links up with his 'second nature' or 'culture'" (Schinkel 2008, 313; Balibar 1991). Such reified notions of culture flourish in the Flemish public sphere and inform a *logic of culturalisation* that runs through a multiplicity of minority-related debates.

The main feature of the *logic of culturalisation* is that it elevates the category of culture to an explanatory framework for social, economic and political inequalities. It operates in a political rhetoric that distracts from systematic analyses that take the socio-economic dimension of social problems, power and power relations into account (Maly 2007a, 183). After the fall of the Berlin wall, this logic gave rise to a bipolar political discourse whereby national and international conflicts came to be understood in terms of clashes between cultures and/or civilisations

(Maly 2007b, 243). Those who rearticulate this type of logic tend to posit cultures as reified and well-delineated objects that are able to clash and collide (Zienkowski and Maly 2007, 53; Verschueren 2011, 178; Hawkes 1996, 110). Cultural logics are inherent to many nationalist projects and were certainly present in a great deal of political discourse before 9/11. But they are by no means local phenomena. Similar logics can be found in books such as Huntington's *Clash of civilizations* (Huntington 1998; Maly 2007c).

After the fall of the Berlin wall, Islam came to occupy a place of honour as the ultimate other in polarising political discourse. This change involved a shift to a cultural logic whereby cultural, ethnic and religious features were seen to determine the actions and subjectivities of non-Western others in a top-down manner. As if Muslims were merely structural dopes without a will to integrate. Within this type of discourse, one's own 'Western' culture is obviously branded as hierarchically superior (Schinkel 2008, 317). At an international level, this type of logic can be exemplified with reference to the *War on Terror*. Military actions have often been justified in terms of democratic norms and values that had to be brought to those who supposedly lack them.

Logics of culturalisation take different forms in different countries but can be observed all across Europe in debates about the integration of (descendants of) migrants. Flanders is not the only European region where culture became a key concern for politics. For instance, in Germany the notion of *Leitkultur* has figured prominently in the debate (Manz 2013). In the Netherlands, the double nationality has been articulated as a matter of (potentially) conflicting feelings of loyalty on the part of 'allochthons'. In the UK, one can observe the emergence of a disunited kingdom in debates about Englishness versus Britishness. And in countries such as France and Austria, discord crystalised around issues of social and ethnic inclusion and exclusion of migrants (Omlo 2011, 18; Hogan-Brun et al. 2009). Also, all across Europe, one can observe rising concerns and moral panics with respect to the cultural implications of public Islamic symbols and practices in the hegemonic public sphere (Said 1981; Zemni 2009; Baker 2013).

Culturalism can also be observed in Flanders where socio-economic inequalities between 'allochthons' and 'autochthons' are frequently explained in terms of problematic features of allochthon culture(s). Those who highlight the importance of socio-economic contexts in explanations of migration- and integration-related problems are often accused of political correctness and a reluctance to 'see things as they really are'. From the nineties on, the idea that Islam threatened a supposedly homogenous set of Flemish/European/Western norms and values spread quickly. The explanations for this perceived lack of integration were of an increasingly cultural character. People did not integrate sufficiently *because* of *their* culture (Blommaert 2006, 209–210; Maly 2007b, 243–246; Zienkowski et al. 2007, 52–53). The third logic that works in tandem with the logics of culturalisation and homogenisation can be described in terms of assimilation. Even though the term assimilation is usually avoided and differentiated from integration in explicit and implicit definitions of the term, tolerant majority discourse is rarely marked by an explicit valuation of diversity.

The social logics of homogenisation, culturalisation and assimilation give rise to polarising politics and processes of identification. This polarisation involves an articulation of two chains of equivalence. On the one hand, there is a chain that is held together by the notion of allochthony. In spite of the rather broad academic definitions of this term, the concept of allochthon has become interchangeable with a limited number of identities such as Muslim, Moroccan, Berber, Arab or Turk. Other non-European and 'non-Western' minorities may also be included. Flemish autochthons, on the other hand, speak Dutch and have 'enlightened', 'democratic' and/or 'Judeo-Christian' norms and values that allochthons should develop and adapt to. The values that 'we' have and that Islamic 'others' supposedly lack include respect for women and gay people, a belief in democracy and gender equality, secularism and/or a belief in the separation of Church and state. Antagonism lurks around the corner.

On a fantasmatic level, these social logics inform a horrific fantasy whereby a mythical homogenous and integrated society is threatened by an increasing diversity and by a de-secularisation of the public realm. This is epitomised in the hysteria surrounding the Muslim headscarf. In the moral panics surrounding debates on integration and Islam, this cultural/religious symbol is frequently interpreted as a sign of religion-inspired sexist repression and/or as a threat to a supposedly 'neutral' public sphere. For this reason, several municipalities have issued policies of banning veils for administrative personnel coming in direct contact with citizens. This policy constitutes a clear attempt to realise the fantasy of a neutral and homogeneous public realm in which ethnic, cultural and religious aspects of identity are banned from sight. The horrific and beatific myths informing this policy allow actors to gloss over the contingent relationships between religious symbols and religious ideas, between Flemish and other identities, as well as between culture and politics. Reflexive and critical awareness on the part of Muslims who mark their religious identity publicly is denied altogether.

I do not claim that the social, political and fantasmatic logics described above inform *all* of Flemish politics. As the symbolic burial of the notions 'allochthon' and 'autochthon' in Ghent illustrates, this discourse is not taken for granted by everyone. But these logics do inform a large part of the mainstream discourse on integration. The fact that some cities and one newspaper explicitly distanced themselves from this binary pair and the associated politics is to be welcomed. But in themselves, these measures are mere cosmetic ideological operations. A critique of bipolar concepts is indispensible for many emancipatory political projects, but it is even more important to attack and to counter the logics that give rise to such dichotomies in the first place. If one does not criticise and rearticulate the logics informing such discourse, it is likely that the discursive functions of the old dichotomy will be taken over by a new one.

4.5 Integration in Counter-Discourse

The topic of integration popped up in all of my interviews. The hegemonic status of this concept did not allow my interviewees to bypass the issue altogether even though their politics usually involved attempts to move beyond this type of discourse. Most of my interviewees criticised the paradoxical and vague meanings of mainstream statements on the integration of migrants, minorities and/or (various classes of) so-called allochthons. They therefore occupied rather marginal positions in the debate. In order to understand how integration-related concepts

4 Articulating the Problematic of Integration in a Minority Debate 211

positively, negatively or partially defined their preferred modes of politics and subjectivity, I will look at the way they pragmatically and reflexively used integration-related signifiers.

The analyses below provide an overview of the various critiques articulated by Moroccan/Flemish/Belgian/European activists and intellectuals with respect to mainstream understandings of integration. By focusing on critical usage of this notion, I seek to rearticulate the structure of the integration debate through the self-understandings of people this discourse is supposedly about. The multidimensional concept of articulation as a reflexive and pragmatic performance through which socio-political actors imagine and reconfigure existing socio-political relationships informs the analyses below. Integration will be dealt with as a linguistic form, as a value and as an abstract category that can perform a multiplicity of argumentative and ideological functions. Its meanings have to be understood in relation to the preferred and disavowed modes of subjectivity and politics articulated by those who use it.

The data used for this analysis have been selected from 26 interviews conducted with 24 activists and intellectuals with a Moroccan background in Flanders. Almost all of these people are—or have been—engaged in governmental and/or (NGOs) or political parties. As I mentioned before, they cannot be said to be members of a unified community. Their common denominator lies mostly in their political activism and in their public articulation of stances with respect to the minority debate. They can be said to be active in the minority debate, defined broadly as a dense intertextual network in which actors articulate some degree of political and metapragmatic awareness in a discursive struggle over signifiers such as integration that fix the imaginary boundaries of self and society.

It should be noticed that representatives of organisations such as (associations related to) mosques who primarily deal with religious issues were absent from my corpus. My respondents were not selected on the basis of gender, age, generation or religion. Their Moroccan background (with the exception of a few prominent figures in the debate) and their socio-political engagement were the main selection criteria. The geographical area of my investigation was restricted to Flanders. Institutionally speaking, I talked to people engaged in various federations of migrant self-organisations (FMV, Project Allochthonous Youngsters [Dutch: *Project*

Allochtone Jongeren—PAJ]), socio-cultural organisations (Safina, Action Committee Muslim Women [AMV], Support Centre for Allochthon Girls and Women [SAMV], Global Socio-cultural Centre [Dutch: *Mondiaal Socio-cultureel Centrum*—MSC] Ahlan), student organisations (Student Focus, Association for Integration and Participation [Dutch: *Vereniging voor Integratie en Participatie*—VIP]), feminist organisations (Vrouwenstem Plus, BOEH!), political parties (Open Flemish Liberals and Democrats, [Dutch: *Open Vlaamse Liberalen en Democraten*— Open VLD] Spa, Spirit!, Muslim Democratic Party [Dutch: *Moslim Democratische Partij*—MDP]), integration services (DIA) and activist civil society organisations (Kif Kif, AEL, BOEH!).

All interviews were conducted and transcribed between 2006 and 2009. The data were transcribed and imported into a software program for computer-assisted qualitative data analysis (CAQDAS) called NVIVO8. In addition to these interviews, I inserted all newspaper articles in which my interviewees articulated an integration-related concept. These articles were found in the media database Mediargus by using the following Boolean search: "name respondent" AND (integratie* OR geïntegreerd* OR integreren). A similar search was conducted using Google. The importation of transcribed interview data and newspaper articles into NVIVO8 allowed for an automatic search in which I looked for a context of 100 words surrounding every occurrence of the Dutch lemma *integratie**, *geïntegreerd** and *integreren*. This random context of 100 words provided a first impression of the verbal and textual contexts in which these notions were articulated. Whenever necessary, I broadened or narrowed the discursive context required for my analyses.

The variety of results was impressive. Throughout our interviews, my respondents did not only talk about "integration". Integration-related signifiers also took the following forms: "to integrate oneself", "integration services", "integration centres", "the integration sector", "integration policy", "politics of integration", "degree of integration", "integration process", "integration project", "problematic of integration", "pattern of integration related expectations", "integration story", "Association for Integration and Participation" (Dutch: *Vereniging voor Integratie en Participatie*— VIP) and "Antwerp Service for Integration" (Dutch: *Dienst Integratie Antwerpen*—DIA). Moreover, issues related to the "bankruptcy of

4 Articulating the Problematic of Integration in a Minority Debate

integration" were raised as well. According to one of my respondents, there was "too much integration at this moment", whereas others put forward alternative interpretations of integration by describing mosques as "places for integration".[1]

The question to be answered at this point is what pragmatic and ideological functions usage of the the notion of integration performs in relation to the sense of self and politics articulated by my interviewees. Most of them criticised the paradoxical and vague meanings of integration-related concepts in mainstream discourse. As such, they tended to occupy rather marginal positions in the Flemish minority debates. This is all the more so, since their political engagements are not oriented towards the realisation of some process of 'integration'—at least not in the hegemonic sense of the term. The articulation of counter-logics requires one to move beyond the problematic of integration through complex and creative (re-)articulations of self, other and politics. It requires the articulation of new large-scale interpretive logics for imagining self and society.

The notion of articulation outlined above implies an interpretive and functional understanding of discursive practice. The analysis below can therefore be described as an interpretive and functional approach to discourse and politics. It is interpretive in the sense that it seeks to understand the discourse articulated by decentred subjects in terms of reflexive and metapragmatic acts. It is functional since it stresses the fact that any act of articulation involves the establishment of multiple linkages that impact on the meaning(s) of the elements articulated. Applied to the notion of integration, it is possible to explore a limited set of such linkages by asking the following interpretive and functional research questions:

- What function(s) does the articulation of integration-related signifiers such as "integration sector" or "integrated" perform in relation to the various voices (re-)articulated by my interviewee(s)?

---

[1] In Dutch, these integration-related lexical items read as follows: "integratie"; "zich integreren"; "integratiediensten"; "integratiecentra"; "integratiesector"; "integratiebeleid"; "integratiepolitiek"; "integratiegraad"; "integratieproces"; "integratieproject"; "integratieproblematiek"; "integratieverwachtingspatroon"; "integratieverhaal"; "integratiediscours"; "Vereniging voor Integratie en Participatie"; "Vlaams Centrum voor Integratie van Migranten"; "Dienst Integratie Antwerpen"; "integratie heft gefaald"; "failliet van de integratie"; "te veel integratie op dit ogenblik"; "integrerende plekken".

- What function(s) does the articulation of integration-related statements on the "bankruptcy of integration" or "integration story" perform in relation to the concept of politics (dis-)favoured by my interviewee(s)?
- What function(s) does the articulation of integration-related utterances such as "too much integration" or "politics of integration" perform in relation to other abstract categories that inform the sense of self and politics of my interviewee(s)?

These interpretive and functional questions require answers that do justice to the fact that any act of articulation involves an instantaneous establishment of linkages at multiple levels of discursive structure. When we talk about integration, we do not merely link sounds, words and sentences to each other in topical and narrative constellations. We also position ourselves in large-scale social and political debates whose imaginary structures can be called into question through public performances and uses of discourse. In the analyses below, I seek to describe these structures by (re-)articulating the discourse of my respondents with the pragmatic and poststructuralist frameworks and vocabularies outlined in the preceding chapters. Of course, there is no single 'correct' way to describe the multiple functions of discourse. However, I do hope to show that a metapragmatic understanding of the ways in which my interviewees rearticulated the concept of integration provides us with some insight into the way they reflexively establish a critical sense of self and politics.

4.5.1 Contradictory Logics of Integration Articulated by a Single Individual

In the first chapter of this book, we saw how former AEL activist Issam Z constructed an understanding of politics in terms of a struggle for "individuality". He articulated a complex discourse in which signifiers such as individuality (Dutch: *eigenheid*), culture and identity were linked to concrete political issues, personal experiences, stories and analyses with a high degree of metapragmatic awareness. Interestingly, Issam had a lot to say about integration as well. In fact, his distinction between preferred and disavowed modes of politics and activism went hand in hand with

4 Articulating the Problematic of Integration in a Minority Debate 215

an articulation of preferred and disavowed modes of integration (see also Zienkowski 2014).

The topic of integration was discussed at various points in this interview. We talked about "integration", "integration policy" and about something called an "integration trajectory". AEL activists have put a great deal of energy in rearticulating the boundaries of 'the debate'. For instance, in a contribution to a collective volume that analyses and criticises hegemonic understandings of Flemish identity, the Dutch AEL activist Abdou Bouzerda argued that integration should be abandoned as a policy goal. In a way that is typical for AEL activists, he reframed the notion of integration as follows:

> *The debate should be about equality, autonomy and citizenship. Summarised, it needs to be about emancipation. I argue against integration, because I am in favour of emancipation. This is more than a lame discussion about definitions, this touches upon the essence of building a new society upon the acceptance of diversity* (Bouzerda 2009, 132)

Bouzerda goes on and rejects the notion of allochthony as an unacceptable and inferior type of citizenship. This does not mean that identity is irrelevant to AEL activists and sympathisers. In fact, AEL discourse legitimises modes of citizenship that include strong articulations of culture, ethnicity and religion in the public sphere. This can also be demonstrated with reference to Issam's description of the "struggle of the AEL" as a struggle for a mode of "individuality" or "eigenheid" whereby ethnic, cultural and religious aspects of identity are marked publically. The AEL claimed the right not to assimilate and the right to be addressed as first-rate citizens who may publicly display and perform cultural and/or religious practices in any space of the public realm (Bouzerda 2009, 132; De Mul 2007).

Nevertheless, at the end of the nineties and at the beginning of the twenty-first century, Flemish political actors reacted with scepticism and hostility to AEL claims and practices. The organisation was labelled as an intolerant and polarising migrant equivalent of the far right VB. The moral panic surrounding the AEL and its chairman Dyab Abou Jahjah reached a peak on November 28, 2002, after riots broke out in response to an allegedly racist murder of an Antwerp teacher called Mohamed Achrak by one of his 'autochthon' neighbours. Politicians and media accused the AEL chairman Jahjah and his right hand of inciting these riots. In Parliament, Prime Minister Guy Verhofstadt labelled the AEL as a criminal organisation that merely intended "to chase the police from the streets, in order to be able to continue its criminal activities in certain neighbourhoods". Among other things, this statement was a reaction to civilian patrols organised by the AEL that were intended to counteract ethnic profiling by the Antwerp police (Jacobs 2005, 103–104).

Verhofstadt went as far as to accuse the organisation of using the "migration problem in order to terrorise a number of neighbourhoods" and denied that the AEL spoke on behalf of "those who already integrated themselves or abided by the rule of law". The Minister of Interior Affairs Antoine Duquesne even said that "if the legal apparatus in order to act against the AEL did not suffice", measures would be taken "to adapt this apparatus" (Belga 2002). On the evening of November 28, 2002, Jahjah was arrested. In the debate that followed, Jahjah acquired a martyr-like status among important sections of the immigrant population. A number of publicists and academics condemned the exaggerated statements by politicians such as Verhofstadt and the accompanying breach of powers. Moreover, these incidents gave an unprecedented amount of media attention for immigrant views on migrant incorporation (De Wit 2008; Jacobs 2005, 103–104). Jahjah would be released from custody a couple of days later. Nevertheless, he and his right hand Ahmed Azzuz were officially accused of inciting the 2002 riots in Antwerp.

Both Azzuz and Jahjah were convicted for one year of imprisonment and a fine of more than 5000 Euro in 2007. However, after being declared innocent of all charges in 2008 after an appeal to a higher court, some degree of public rehabilitation took place (De Wit 2008). For instance, in a letter published in *De Standaard* under the title '*We belong to the AEL generation*', several academics, journalists and intellectuals acknowledged to be influenced by this organisation (Fadil 2008b). Upon his return to Belgium in 2013, Jahjah became a columnist for *De Standaard* and appeared as a commentator in national media. The AEL has played a big role in the move away from the usage of integration-related notions. It influenced the development of a discourse that deals with diversity as

4 Articulating the Problematic of Integration in a Minority Debate   217

a central value for emancipatory modes of citizenship in Flanders. But as we noticed before, talk on allochthony and integration is still widely dispersed in the Dutch-speaking public spheres of Flanders and the Netherlands.

Based on the critical attitude of the AEL with respect to Flemish integration policy, one might expect that Issam would reject the notion of integration in a straightforward way. But things are not that simple. The way he values this concept is highly dependent on the logics within which this notion is embedded. Two diametrically opposed social logics can be identified in my interview with Issam Z: an *activist logic of integration* and an antagonist *assimilationist* counterpart. Articulated political awareness amounts to more than a mere questioning of isolated words and statements. It involves an ability to recognise, to identify and to (re-)articulate complex discursive patterns that can be described in terms of logics. Moreover, the ability to contradict and to counteract the hegemonic logics that inform particular statements and practices requires the development and availability of a discourse marked by equally complex counter-logics. This can be illustrated with reference to the way Issam Z uses the notion of integration.

Let us start by naming and (re-)articulating Issam's *activist logic of integration*. We already saw that Issam defined the struggle of the AEL as a struggle for the right to publicly articulate one's "cultural heritage" as a part of one's self. It was a struggle for "a society where people simply take you as you are". In order to understand this mythical image of society and the associated mode of subjectivity or "individuality", we have to home in on Issam's understanding of the link between activism and integration. I will do so through an interpretive and functional analysis of the polyphonic play of voices (re-)articulated by this interviewee. Consider the way Issam distinguishes between the voices of the AEL and another critical civil society organisation called Kif Kif.

While we were discussing the importance of the AEL in raising political awareness among people with a Moroccan background in Flanders, Issam told me that he had the "impression ... that activism among Moroccans here in Flanders really started with the AEL". In response to my question whether he could think of any other organisations that contributed to the development of a political awareness among Flemish Moroccans, he also mentioned Kif Kif. Personally, I have been involved in this organisation by organising workshops in discourse analysis and media training for its volunteers. At the time of my interview with Issam, I was already familiar with Kif Kif, but Issam did not know this. He described Kif Kif as "a praiseworthy website" but added that I should "take a look at one of their activities", some of which he considers to be rather "elitist". And even though he did not intend this as "a reproach", he did criticise the politics and the practices of interpellation of this organisation on the basis of the type of "activism" practised by this organisation (Zienkowski 2014).

Kif Kif explicitly presents itself as a democratic, anti-racist, leftist, progressive, pluralist, intercultural, anti-essentialist and critical organisation. Its baseline is '*Open your world before racism closes it*'. Kif Kif enjoys a high profile in the Flemish minority, integration, and/or diversity debates. But it is not merely an intellectual platform. The organisation has organised job fairs and socio-cultural talent fairs for so-called allochthons, trainings for aspiring journalists, and media-watch workshops based on CDA. Kif Kif activists regularly organise and participate in socio-political debates on citizenship, inter- or multicultural society, poverty, culture and identity. Nevertheless, Issam articulated "considerable doubts about the activism of Kif Kif". The problem being that Kif Kif either functions as an organisation for "progressive Flemings who are like 'I want to broaden my ... my worldview' " or for "allochthons who have made it between quotation marks". Note that Issam uses reported speech in order to characterise the discourse of progressive Flemings. This reported speech is marked by subtle changes in tempo and intonation. He also hedges his own usage of the category of "allochthons who made it" by putting this category verbally between "quotation marks" (Zienkowski 2014).

> IZ: a musical evening for instance you should go and see what sort of people participate in that. It is a very elitist happening. This is not a reproach but I merely observe that the people who come to that sort of thing are either progressive Flemings who are like "I want to broaden my ... my world view" or allochthons who made it between quotation marks eh
> JZ: yes
> IZ: to us having made it means when you have a job you made it eh ... that sort of people who only have a weak personal link with ...

4 Articulating the Problematic of Integration in a Minority Debate 219

JZ: I can't say I see any street boys there so yes
JZ: yes *voilà* ... but ... if we talk about problems of allochthons, problems of integration, problems of connecting to society, then it is not about that one per cent not even that who has a nice job, it is about the street boys. That is why I have considerable doubts about the activism of Kif Kif. To me it seems rather like ... the reward for some kind of integration trajectory. But I don't see any real activism in Flanders today eh ... BOEH! is the most activist thing I see.
excerpt 17 – 03/09/2007

Hedges, indicators of reported speech and metalinguistic comments are among the most important markers of metapragmatic and reflexive awareness in political discourse. They allow Issam to differentiate his voice from those of other actors in the debate. Moreover, they permit him to distinguish between different logics of activism and integration. In an earlier part of the interview, Issam described how the AEL was able to count on '*street boys*' enabling the organisation to mobilise a significant number of people for protests "in the street". As a response to Issam's remark that Kif Kif basically addresses progressive autochthon and allochthon elites, I acknowledged that I did not meet any "street boys" at Kif Kif. Issam replied that activism in the context of Kif Kif seems to function as a "reward for some kind of integration trajectory" (Zienkowski 2014).

The concept of an '*integration trajectory*' thus functions as a spatial metaphor in order to describe a process of integration whereby one moves away from a practice of interpellating street boy-related subject positions towards a practice of interpellation that appeals to elite sensitivities of progressive autochthons and "allochthons who made it between quotation marks". Having "made it" is defined socio-economically: "when you have a job you made it eh". Issam thus articulates activism with integration. An "integration trajectory" gains legitimacy when it involves activist practices aimed at the interpellation of so-called street boys who haven't "made it" in terms of having a job and climbing the socio-economic ladder.

A more positive evaluation of the notion of integration occurs during a discussion of Issam's positioning with respect to the political left and right in Flanders. According to him, "the Left ... is at least as much to blame for this, how shall I put it, for the bankruptcy of this situation". He points out that "the Left" "has never wanted to talk about" issues such as "exclusion", either "because of some desire to do good" or "because of some will to be progressive". On the other hand, Issam states that the Left has been less active in the problematisation of Moroccan and other Islamic groups in Flanders. In the excerpt below, Issam goes on to clarify his point of view (Zienkowski 2014).

> IZ: ... one has to credit the right for the fact that they want a debate about it. But Flanders simply hasn't held the debate yet ... Flanders has, how shall I put it, nipped it all off in the bud.
> JZ: The debate about its own integration policy or that sort of stuff?
> IZ: Yes ... yes ... very quickly the edge was taken off ... whereas in the Netherlands ... today still eh it it's incredible ... That is really a proof of integration that one has people ... Muslims Moroccans who can give their opinion and who can be assertive and who appear on television ... who can express their individuality without needing the help of someone else.
> **excerpt 18 – 03/09/2007**

According to Issam, "Flanders simply hasn't held the debate" on integration policy yet. To him, "proof of integration" involves a series of discursive practices whereby Islamic and ethnic markers are explicitly acknowledged: giving ones "opinion"; being "assertive" in public media such as television; expressing one's "individuality without needing the help someone else". This mode of integration is something he aspires to. Issam thus distinguishes metalinguistically between two modes of integration. In contrast to the assimilatory logic of integration, he considers to be dominant in Flanders, he dreams of an alternative type of voice as articulated by assertive minority members who give "their opinion" in an "assertive" manner as exemplified by minority members publicly expressing their "individuality" on "television" in the Netherlands (Zienkowski 2014).

Issam's preferred mode of integration can be explained as being informed by an *emancipatory logic of integration*. This logic is antagonistically opposed to the assimilatory mode of integration that shapes the non-activist subjectivities of many Moroccan Muslims in Flanders as well as mainstream ideas on integration. At some point, I suggested that it was possible to identify a shift within policy discourse from talk about integration towards talk about diversity in Antwerp. Issam Z acknowledged this but went on to argue that mainstream usage of the term diversity

4 Articulating the Problematic of Integration in a Minority Debate   221

functions as "a cover term" for the same kind of politics. As a case in point, he referred to the 2006 ban on religious symbols for public servants who interact directly with citizens. This ban is known as the headscarf ban in Flanders and was instituted under the administration of the social democrat mayor Patrick Janssens (SPa) (Zienkowski 2014).

IZ: Yes, but it diversity policy is a cover for the same politics. Diversity as far as I have understood it, implies that there is some room for a certain variety. The only thing I have seen from the SPa thus far is a ban on headscarves that discourages diversity. Of course, I understand what Patrick Janssens is doing. He says like "there are a lot of Antwerp people who are offended by that, so if you want to make yourself acceptable as a Moroccan, take that headscarf of". I think this is a very dangerous reasoning. I don't think this is the right way. I rather think that you have to help the Flemish to get used [to it]. Try [to involve] more people with a headscarf who are assertive, who master Dutch well. Try to involve people like that because they are going to disrupt that image of backwardness or of not being honest or of whatever. Try to involve Arabic as a language in education. I don't say that … education should be Arabic but incorporate it as a positive element, as a lever.
excerpt 19 – 02/09/2007

Issam points out that "this ban on headscarves discourages diversity". He rearticulates the voice of Patrick Janssens and disqualifies his "reasoning" as "dangerous". In accordance with his preferred mode of integration, Issam thinks that one "rather" has "to help the Flemish get used" to diversity. According to him, this could be done by involving people that can "disrupt that image of backwardness" and of so-called allochthons as not being "honest". Other strategies include "involving Arabic as a language in education" as a "lever" for social change and integration in the positive sense of the word (Zienkowski 2014).

To Issam, "assimilation" boils down to a non-desirable form of "integration". The excerpt below show how his distinction between legitimate and illegitimate modes of integration is linked to his concepts of activism and individuality. Issam explains that assimilation occurs when groups become so marginalised that they do not engage in any form of "political struggle". In turn, this lack of "political struggle" leads people to turn away from their Islamic and Arabic practices and norms. Issam thus establishes a mutually constitutive relationship between political activism and a mode of subjectivity in which individuals are able to articulate cultural and religious aspects of their individuality. This happens when he discusses the relationship between "parents" and youngsters in the Moroccan community on the one hand, and public institutions such as schools on the other hand. According to him, assimilated—that is, non-activist—religious parents and children run the risk of becoming "trapped in a net" that brings them "into conflict with themselves" (Zienkowski 2014).

> IZ: ... They get trapped in a net. They don't wage a political struggle. For instance, they are going to ... their own daughters can't wear a headscarf in school any more. You can't explain to me how someone who has been educated with a headscarf at home and who goes to school and experiences a hostile environment over there, or at least hostile in so far as the headscarf is concerned, ... that is someone who will definitely wind up in some sort of inner struggle. Puberty is already hard enough and that comes on top of it. To what extent someone gets out of that unharmed ... I have my reservations about that. A lot of parents mistakenly believe, and this is understandable somehow, one does not have a lot of skills, like "if I only raise them according to Islamic norms everything will turn out fine" ... that is bullshit of course. You are more outside than at home. And also, the impact of outside ... that's way bigger eh ... . Education has an enormous impact on the way you think. So a lot of people will get into conflict with themselves by noting that their children are taking a different turn and will not be as Muslim-friendly as they would like to think.
> **excerpt 20 – 03/09/2007**

Issam continues in the excerpt below and argues that keeping "aloof from society" impacts upon one's (sense of) self. It is in this context that the topic of the AEL is introduced once again. To Issam, the struggle of the AEL was as much as struggle for a preferred mode of integration whereby one can publicly claim one's individuality and place in the public sphere, as it was a struggle for a particular mode of subjectivity (Zienkowski 2014).

> IZ: I feel like, when you keep aloof from society, what are you doing to yourself? What do you learn in order to play a certain role in society. That is also something one has never understood with respect to the AEL. The

AEL ... there is no other organisation that has tried as hard [as the AEL] to involve Moroccans in the social debate. Exactly in order to play a meaningful role in that society. And I consider assimilation to be a kind of languishment in the margin, uhm, that first generation, perhaps that second generation manages to keep on doing that, but the third won't and will simply dissolve into the majority. Nobody wants marginalisation eh.
JZ: so marginalisation is linked to assimilation so to say
IZ: Well... firstly, my parents and perhaps my generation is still marginalised, but if in the end, there does not emerge a political consciousness, a social activism whereby your role in society ...
JZ: a socio-economic role?
IZ: that's right, whereby you start to play a role in society, guarding your individuality, if you don't do that, in the long run.
excerpt 21 – 03/09/2007

The fact that the AEL addressed street boys more directly and the fact that it tried "to involve Moroccans in the social debate" in order to "play a meaningful role in that society" implied a political strategy that targeted the assimilatory logic of integration that we identified as being key to hegemonic problematisations of minorities in Flanders. Issam fears above all that this lack of "political consciousness" and "activism" oriented towards an improvement of one's socio-economic situation will lead to a loss of "individuality" or "eigenheid". In activist discourse, preferred and disavowed modes of activism are constructed in tandem with a set of preferred and disavowed modes of selfhood. If politics becomes a way of life, it impacts upon the ethics of public practice as well on the ethics of self-construction (Zienkowski 2014).

4.5.2 Logics of Integration and the Imagination of Social Ontology

Interpretive logics are never completely individualised constructs but they are not all-determining structures either. Since the articulation of discourse requires language users to make a multiplicity of choices with varying degrees of awareness, there is always some degree of creativity and reflexivity involved. Discourse allows us to imagine our relationships with ourselves, with others and with the various institutions that centre our values. The logics that structure discourse and subjectivity do not merely structure what is already there. They allow us to imagine the ontological structure of interpretive reality and provide interpretive rules for shaping and interpreting its constituents.

The operation of hegemonic logics can only be understood through an interpretive and functional understanding of the way discourse operates at a more pragmatic level. One has to show how they operate through concrete articulations of discursive elements such as subject positions (e.g. allochthon/migrant/autochthon), abstract categories (e.g. diversity/assimilation), narratives (e.g. on the failure of integration), practices (e.g. to integrate/learning Dutch) and institutions (e.g. the state/integration centres/civil society organisations). The development of a counter-hegemonic logic therefore requires more than a critique of mainstream utterances and statements on integration. It may even require an alternative imagination of the dominant social ontology.

Different logics do not only imply the existence of different identities, subject positions and/or voices. They may also imply different conceptualisations of the way such discursive elements are generated. In order to illustrate this point, I will turn to interviews I conducted with Hicham el Mzairh and Najib Chakouh. Both interviewees are critical of mainstream discourses on integration. But their critiques are based on different imaginations of social structure. A comparison of the way Najib and Hicham indicate and articulate their understanding of social ontology allows us to see how they based their critique of integration-related concepts on different ontological grounds. The way we imagine social reality impacts on the way we deploy abstract categories and values such as integration.

Let us start with the interview conducted with Hicham el Mzairh. At the time of our interview, Hicham was a politician for the Flemish liberal party called Open VLD. In the period following our interview, he would change his party political affiliation to the social democratic SPa. Upon showing him my analysis of the interview conducted during his Open VLD period, he asked me to re-contextualise some of the statements he made. As such, he was careful not to discredit the Open VLD as a whole. He explained to me that even though there were many Open VLD members who were sensitive to his concerns about diversity, he felt that his personal impact could be bigger within the SPa. The analysis below does

4 Articulating the Problematic of Integration in a Minority Debate   225

not only clarify his views on integration but also provides insight into the flexible logics that justified Hicham's move from a liberal to a social democratic party.

Hicham told me how "shocked" he was by the "attitudes concerning religion" within certain Moroccan "circles" in Antwerp upon his migration to Belgium in 1999. While "Morocco has evolved" and "modernised" significantly since the sixties and seventies, he felt that a certain "Islamic conception" combined with "certain traditions" and a socio-political reality in which (descendants of) migrants "are being confronted with an other that wants to assimilate them" have led to a "defensive reaction" and a counter-productive preoccupation with practices considered to be *haram* by Moroccan minority members in Flanders. All of this runs counter to the "freedom of the individual" that is central to Hicham's preferred mode of politics and subjectivity. It also runs counter to the type of integration he advocates.

Interestingly, neither the "other" nor the Moroccan migrants who came to Flanders in the sixties and seventies "make a distinction between integration and assimilation" according to Hicham. Faced with the others' will that migrants and their descendants should assimilate, allochthons "withdraw themselves" and stop being "open to change". Instead, "they are stuck with that mentality or that culture and they remain stuck with the culture their fathers brought along from their country of origin". Note the density of spatial metaphors indicating openness and closed-ness in these utterances. For Hicham, "withdrawal" is antithetic to the freedom of the individual he advocates. His critique is not exclusively oriented at cultural and religious confinement. Rather, "that confinement ... I notice that one only occupies oneself with one's work with one's family ... that one uses one's uhm language and one's environment ... they don't know anything about uhm what is going on in the countries wherein they reside". Hicham's spatial imagination of subjectivity does not only inform his idea of freedom. It also impacts on his preferred and disavowed modes of integration.

Like all of my interviewees, Hicham el Mzairh is opposed to a concept of integration that is reduced to assimilation. In the excerpt below, he identifies and (re-)articulates two antagonistic voices whose discourses stand in the way of the full realisation of freedom through integration. One voice belongs to the Flemish other who articulate a desire for assimilation.

The other voice belongs to those who react to this call for assimilation by withdrawing themselves to their communities, cultures and identities. To Hicham, the question of integration boils down to the question how one can "cherish ... positive things in other cultures" while making use of the "freedom to choose for yourself" how to "take that heritage from the culture you brought along" into account without getting "stuck in some sort of community". Put differently, Hicham is trying to articulate a mode of integration that avoids both assimilation and socio-cultural apartheid in which everyone merely waves "that flag like 'we are right' ".

> HEM: When you want to integrate them ... When do you cherish ... uhm positive things in other cultures? ... That freedom to choose for yourself how you deal with that and ... and getting that heritage from the culture you brought along ... so that you don't get stuck in some sort of uhm community ... and close yourself off and live with your own culture and only wave that flag like "we are right" .... And that other who says like "we are right and you should change everything ... we have seen the light and follow us ... you should integrate yourselves" so ... that really is a vicious circle of uhm ... division on the one hand and on the other hand superiority I would say of one group and ... and with the other group there is a feeling of inferiority and the wish to defend ... and they do defend that's also ... just so uhm ... I think I just uhm ... experienced some things and that's my personal conclusion ... it's like ... the more that ... that freedom is realised ... the more ... those uhm those youngsters in schools uhm can be armed with certain instruments to ... make their own choices in life ... the more free they will be ... the more free they become from those currents that one calls community ... and the more contact you will have between individuals of various descent.
> **excerpt 22 – 20/05/2008**

Hicham describes the debate about integration as a "vicious circle" between two sets of voices that claim to be right. The feelings of "superiority" articulated by those who demand that (descendants of) migrants should integrate themselves are matched by feelings of "inferiority" on the part of migrant communities. In this way, both sets of actors are deemed responsible for the lack of freedom that characterises Belgian society according to Hicham. There is a powerful fantasmatic structure

4 Articulating the Problematic of Integration in a Minority Debate 227

underlying this argument. Hicham's political engagement constitutes a reflexive attempt to fill this lack of freedom. His discourse allows him to imagine a mythical future beyond the here and now and to transgress the vicious circle of the integration debate. Interestingly, he argues that both majority and minority members lack this (sense of) liberal freedom in Flanders. And he does so with a remarkable degree of reflexivity by characterising "liberalism ... as an ideology". In the excerpt below, freedom is articulated as an object of desire that can be attained through liberal politics. Hicham counters the *assimilationist logic of integration* with a *liberal logic of integration* that has an individualising effect.

> HEM: Not the liberalism of uhm ... of the companies not the liberalism of the rich ... or the liberalism that that the Fleming is confronted with here ... by the Flemish progressives uhm ... ex-patriots who are actually nationalists ... with certain far-right inclinations on the one hand ... and on the other hand there are the parties that I am sort of belonging to, where there is a big lobby of uhm companies and where there is uhm uhm a big lobby of uhm entrepreneurs. ... That party has also uhm ... in the beginning and well ... for many years ... waved the flag of the defender of the ... of the ... of the interests of entrepreneurs and the rich ... . And in between there is the ... liberalism as uhm ... as an ideology ... that rather ... defends ... the freedom of the individual ... that introduces the individual to its own freedom ... to its own ... to the power that is within a single individual ... that liberalism is lost in Belgium.
> **excerpt 23 – 20/05/2008**

Hicham is not arguing for the economically oriented liberalism associated with "the companies" or the "rich". His object of desire is "liberalism ... as an ideology" that "defends the freedom of the individual", "introduces the individual to its own freedom" and "to the power that is within a single individual". It is this latter type of liberalism that has disappeared in Belgium. The excerpt above illustrates how an empty signifier such as freedom can simultaneously centre a particular mode of subjectivity (e.g. the individual has to be introduced to the freedom (s)he already possesses) and be placed beyond its immediate reach within ideological discourse (freedom is lacking). It also shows that individuals may be quite aware of the fact that they act within ideology with respect to some dimensions of social ontology (e.g. community, culture) while leaving the ontological status of other discursive elements (e.g. freedom, the individual) in the background. As we can see below, all of this translates in a preference for a particular mode of political engagement, namely activism within the context of political parties.

> HEM: You have to associate yourself in order to favour available choices ... and the best way to do this in democracies ... in order not to take advantage of another group ... is to associate oneself with a [political] party. Why not? ... Or found a party if that is possible within a democratic framework ... Why not? ... And then try to uhm defend your standpoints.
> **excerpt 24 – 20/05/2008**

Critiques on integration can be based on very different social ontologies. As a point of contrast, it is useful to take a look at the interview I conducted with Najib Chakouh. Like Hicham, Najib articulated a critical understanding of integration that was closely related to ideas on social structure. At the time of our interview, Najib was chairman of the Left-wing intercultural organisation Kif Kif. Contrary to Hicham, Najib was born and raised in Flanders. He has been active in one of the first minority student organisations called "Talaba", in the "integration sector" and in various civil society organisations. As we will see, Najib is critical of the integration sector but believes that "integration happens anyway", irrespective of policy. At best, policy can facilitate the process.

In order to understand Najib Chakouh's reasoning, it is useful to take a closer look at the way he articulated his ideas on the nature of society. Even though he does consider himself to be "liberal" in a non-party political sense of the word, the individual occupies a less central place than in Hicham's discourse. Najib believes that individuals can contribute to minor changes in the "clockwork of society" but believes that "one's position in society" cannot be ignored either. In fact, Najib's metaphorical view of society as a "blob" makes him extremely sceptical with respect to social categories and borders. He explicitly uses a series of metaphors that stress the shapeless and uncontrollable nature of social identities and society in general. His opposition to dominant logics of integration is to a large extent informed by a rejection of rigid boundaries and

4 Articulating the Problematic of Integration in a Minority Debate

categories. This sceptical attitude does not only have implications for his critique of integration policy and the integration sector but also for his critique on the way social scientists deal with society. He reproaches "the sciences" and the type of statistics that "started with Quetelet" putting "people" "into boxes".

> NC: Quetelet QUETELET [spells it out]… to put people into boxes … and then you have the world as a filing cabinet … . "You are talking about" "ah" … "should we" … "ow" … "Greeks" open the locker … "migrant" open the locker … there seems to be a locker for everything even though this isn't so … . For me it's more like I explained it back then eh … like a blob.
> **excerpt 25 – 03/06/2008**

The problem with categories, boxes and boundaries lies in the fact that these do not correspond to social structure as Najib imagines it. As we can see, the excerpt below does not contain any integration-related signifiers. Nevertheless, the excerpt below does explain why he positions himself carefully with respect to integration-related labels and subject positions in other parts of the interview. Najib's use of the notion of integration will be discussed later. For now, it suffices to note that he frequently uses hedging strategies in order to distance himself from what he considers to be hegemonic understandings of key concepts in the Flemish minority debate. A viscous model of society and subjectivity informs his critical attitude regarding notions such as integration and allochthony.

> NC: It's like, well, during my lessons in critical criminology I said like "do I have to" like … I said "you are like holding it [the blob] and it is something an object so society is like that but … everything changes with the smallest movement and suddenly that blob does a thing of its own … it seems like chaos". I say "if you are very simple-minded it may seem like chaos but I say there is order to it" … . Why? "Because that blob has a certain cohesion and everything is well like connected" … I say and that's why from the moment you push here it affects all sorts of things eh… and that's how I see the world as well eh that's why I said back then [the world is like] "a wheelwork" that's also the case according to me yes … this is something solid eh but a blob that's well … you know such a
> JZ: yes yes it's more like

NC: yes it's a rather elastic kind of thing or a kind of blubber like status
JZ: I haven't seen the movie yet but uhm (laughs)
NC: (laughs) I haven't seen the movie yet either but it has nothing to do with the movie (laughs) yes shit uhm ... yeah but you know what I mean don't you
JZ: yes I can see ...
NC: Children also have that kind of
JZ: plasticine
NC: yes like plasticine but even looser
JZ: slime
NC: yeah that slimy stuff and that's actually that's society well that's how I look at society eh ... . And as you give a little push here or if you try to do that (uses his finger to prod into a fictive object in his hands) ... then everything pops out of it everywhere on all sides and you can see that happening in all things ... you can try to suppress and push push push ... but at a certain moment ... kaboom
excerpt 26 – 03/06/2008

If one imagines society as being characterised by a vicious structure whose constituents can never be contained, described and/or categorised by scientific and political categories, one's political engagement will be marked by attempts to transgress the discursive boundaries of the integration debate. Najib's reluctance to use labels is most clearly expressed in his talk about the main objects and goals of integration policies. Hicham's reluctance is marked by the way he puts hedges around notions such as "allochthony" or "integration" in verbal and/or non-verbal ways. However, like Hicham, Najib does not throw the concept of integration overboard. For if society is like a blob, it is always already integrated. What is to be problematised are particular policies of integration. We will go into his critique of the "integraton sector" in one of the upcoming sections.

4.5.3 Integration and Imaginations of the Public Realm

The way one understands integration is also related to the way one imagines the public debate. Mediatised voices of politicians, citizens and activists can play a role here. But the images that inform our practical definitions of what integration and society mean are also informed by everyday public interactions in other areas of the public life. We are not only confronted with the public in our interaction with media and public institutions. Our relation to the public is shaped by the interactions we experience and observe in the street, at public lectures and/or at events organised by civil society organisations.

It is important to recall that public spheres have no objective boundaries. They are imaginary constructs through which we imagine and negotiate social relations through concrete interactions. What we understand by the public is a reification of numerous overlapping speech events and language games that do not function independently of each other. As I argued before, both the heterogeneity and the coherence of the public realm require the operation of large-scale logics through which citizens can imagine their relationships towards themselves and towards the others that populate their discursive realities. It should therefore not come as a surprise that critical talk about integration frequently involves a critique of dominant (ideas on) public interaction. It is for this reason that questions about integration and the (imagination of) the public realm are always intertwined.

This last principle has already been demonstrated with reference to the case of Amane X who argued that "a true integration policy" should take the principle of the "transferability of dreams from older generations to younger generations into account". As we saw before, Amane rearticulated the basic structure of the debate in terms of conflicting and misguided expectations that minority and majority members may have about the way they will grow old. More specifically, she sketched a fictive scenario and problematised the interview setting by pointing at a potential mismatch between my expectations as a majority member on the one hand and her personal dreams on the other hand. Interpretive logics structuring the wider socio-political debate on integration were thus made relevant within the local context of the interview. The analysis I presented before thus serves as an adequate example of the way our imaginations of public interaction impact on our understandings of integration. Nevertheless, different respondents point at different aspects of the public debate in order to problematise integration-related concepts and practices.

The public realm cannot be reduced to a space populated by mass media and public institutions alone. However, such centring institutions do play an important role in our ideological orientations and in the distribution of discursive statements. It should therefore not come as a surprise that every single one of my respondents problematised (aspects of) the way minorities have been represented and imagined in mainstream media and in the public sphere in general. Below, I will discuss the interviews conducted with Karima Adouiri, Nadia Fadil and Abdelatif Akhandaf. Karima analysed issues related to the representation of minority stances on integration in mainstream media. Nadia Fadil tried to reconfigure the contextual boundaries in which integration is being discussed, whereas Abdelatif Akhandaf's words draw our attention to the link between representation and subjectivity.

At the time of our interview, Karima Adouiri worked as a public servant in the Flemish city of Lier. My principal reason for contacting her was her past engagement for a civil society organisation called AMV (Dutch: Actiecomité Moslim Vrouwen). She also used to be active in the context of the Association of Mosques and Islamic Associations of Antwerp (Dutch: Unie der Moskeeën en Islamitische Verenigingen van Antwerpen [UMIVA]). Prior to our meeting, I read several posts that were published on the AMV website. A great deal of this online AMV discourse focussed on issues related to the headscarf debate in Flanders. Nevertheless, Karima was keen on stressing that the AMV did not "focus exclusively on the headscarf" and argued that there were more important issues to be addressed.

The AMV shared some concerns with other feminist organisations but also raised issues of its own. According to Karima, mainstream—white—feminist organisations are typically concerned with issues such as the continuing inequality of wages for men and women. She recognised the relevance of such struggles but also claimed that her organisation had "a different list of priorities". AMV priorities touched upon issues such as the "discrimination on the labour market", "the socio-economic deprivation of the communities" and problems related to "education and schooling" that are more specific to Islamic minorities in Flanders. Karima went on and explained that politicians and journalists "always came back to the headscarf" by saying things like "yes, but that headscarf stands in the

4 Articulating the Problematic of Integration in a Minority Debate 233

way". It was the experience of AMV activists that any attempt to address issues relevant to their emancipatory agenda was made conditional upon taking off the headscarf. Consider the following excerpt:

> KA: from the Minister, from the media it always boomerangs like, yes ... and always questions about that headscarf. Very often one did not know us ... until something happened with respect to the headscarf and then all of a sudden one puts a microphone under our noses and then we were important enough to hear uhm what we do and who we are. But as long as we shouted like "let us work on the real issues, the socio-economic deprivation of the communities, the fact that the unemployment figures are so high, the fact that the flow to higher education is so dire, all of these problems have to do with the position of women as well. Emancipation, integration, has to do with work and schooling and education and development" but ... that was not picked up by anyone ... and then one keeps on [saying] like "yes but if you would take off that headscarf then you would find a job" yes ... and then you are back at go.
> **excerpt 27 – 28/08/2007**

Talk about the headscarf thus functions as a condition as well as a facilitator for getting access to mainstream media. Nevertheless, in the excerpt above, Karima claims that the more important "integration"- and "emancipation"-related issues were "not picked up by anyone". The circularity of the debate and the journalistic focus on the Muslim headscarf forced AMV activists to ask themselves whether going along with this focus would undermine or promote their cause:

> KA: Because the longer we are discussing this, the longer we get stuck with that headscarf, but on the other side ... we can't let it go because things are happening which are not acceptable and because we are like "if we remain silent about this it seems like we agree".
> **excerpt 28 – 28/08/2007**

Karima thus articulated a preferred logic integration. She considers education, labour and discrimination as the most important tools for emancipation. The headscarf has no place in this list and should not be an issue at all. But this emancipatory logic of integration proves to be incompatible with the culturalist logics that lead people to conceptualise the headscarf as one of the major obstacles to integration. The case of Karima shows how minority and mainstream imaginations of integration frequently conflict and clash with each other.

Abdellatif Akhandaf is another interviewee who explicitly articulated issues of integration with issues of representation. But he did so in a very different manner. Like Amane X, Abdellatif worked for the Antwerp Integration Service DIA. His engagement for DIA and for civil society initiatives such as *Borgerhout Beter Bekeken*[2] (English: Borgerhout Looked at More Closely) was based on a concern with representation and integration. Abdellatif framed his socio-political engagement as an attempt to normalise diversity. Contrary to interviewees such as Najib Chakouh, he disqualified the idea that "integration will happen automatically" if people just stay here "long enough". He clarified this statement as follows:

> AA: Actually that does not make sense. The bigger a group becomes the more social control you get uhm the more … uhm … there is uhm negative representation uhm. That is why the bigger a group becomes the more events there will be and this is normal uhm on a statistical level uhm … we also notice that media pick up on that. Positive issues are not are not ….
> JZ: interesting?
> AA: they are not interesting enough uhm, so they will not even be read. People are not asking for that either.
> **excerpt 29 – 18/06/2008**

Abdellatif sketched an image of the public realm in which the size of the group can explain the amount of negative media coverage this group will get. At the same time, he argued that the size of the group impacts on the amount of social control. But Abdellatif did not problematise the media alone. He also draws our attention to the impact of "images" we see in the

---

[2] *Borgerhout Beter Bekeken* was an initiative of people living in Borgerhout—an Antwerp district that acquired the nickname Bogerokko (a conflation of Borgerhout and Marokko). Especially during the eighties and nineties, Borgerokko was often associated with criminality and with migration-related problems. The initiative *Borgerhout Beter Bekeken* aimed to express a more positive image of Borgerhout. Abdellatif frames this initiative as an initiative aimed at "consultation" between "alloochthons" who "were called guest workers" at the time on the one hand and "autochthongs" on the other. The initiative was meant to foster a more positive image of Borgerhout.

4 Articulating the Problematic of Integration in a Minority Debate 235

street. He pointed at the heightened visibility and presence of "allochthons" in Flemish urban environments. The combination of these everyday images with a lack of "contact" between "people" belonging to different "communities" leads to "feelings of insecurity" that trigger a process of "negative identity development" marked by closure and a lack of flexibility. His preferred mode of identity or subjectivity implies a process whereby one develops one's identity on the basis of "self-confidence". In turn, this confidence can provide a basis for more interaction and consequently, "integration".

> JZ: So you really see like a connection between that insecurity and identity development
> AA: yes ... yes ... it is intertwined. Why? If you are self-confident in a society, in a society where you feel safe, you will also uhm broaden your identity, you will relish, you will take a taste from the other.
> JZ: mmh
> AA: and because of that you will also become more flexible uhm in the development of your own identity, and later on, you will be open to innovation
> JZ : mmh
> AA: uhm ... [if you] close yourself off or if you are slowed down by your own community
> JZ: mmh
> AA: social control and supervision and so on yes then you will close yourself off and everything becomes threatening ... all innovation
> JZ: mmh
> AA: of the other communities of the other culture will be blocked and will be perceived as being negative as threatening and uhm ... strong identities will be created within the particularity of that group or of that community
> JZ: mmh
> AA: and in the long run that is well ... uhm it leads to a confront a confronta uhm ... while twenty thirty years ago one always presupposed like if people only reside here long enough integration will happen automatically and uhm ... that's not true.
> **excerpt 30 – 18/06/2008**

According to Abdellatif Akhandaf, the process of integration is hindered by a lack of knowledge in combination with an increasing visibility of minorities in the public realm. In order to overcome the negative effects this may have, an identity marked by self-confidence is needed. At first sight, one might compare these statements with some of the statements made by liberal politician Hicham el Mzairh. Both are sceptical about closed communities that withdraw onto themselves. Abdellatif does so by sketching a horrific image in which "social control and supervision" create a situation in which everything external "becomes threatening". But Abdellatif is more community oriented than Hicham and this becomes clear when the former starts to discuss the topics of religion and Islam. One does not merely need recognition of one's individuality. One also needs recognition as a community member. According to Abdellatif, Islam is "purposefully not supported" by the government. This leads to a situation in which there is "no recognition" of one's (sense of) self as an individual and as a community member.

> AA: there is no full recognition of your individuality as a person, as a community, as an individual, ... with all your cultural and your religious uhm heritage. So, that influences the uhm character ... also with respect to communication. If we say like "integration will happen automatically", no, it will not happen automatically because certain messages certain reflections will be passed on from parents to children. If parents do not feel involved and feel unappreciated and unrecognised with respect to a particular part of their being, well you will reflect and transfer this to your child.
> **excerpt 31 – 18/06/2008**

In a way that is strongly reminiscent of the way Abdellatif's colleague Amane X talked about the "transferability of dreams" between generations, Abdellatif argues that "certain messages" and "reflections will be passed on from parents to children". These messages include general feelings of insecurity, lack of appreciation and recognition. Moreover, like Amane, he thinks that this is a crucial point where "we DIA sometimes miss the point".

A third example of the way our imaginations of socio-political relations in the public realm impact on our understanding of integration can be found in an interview conducted with sociologist Nadia Fadil. At the time of our interview, Nadia recently defended her Foucault inspired PhD on the religious and secular trajectories of second-generation Muslim

4 Articulating the Problematic of Integration in a Minority Debate 237

women with a Maghrebian background in Belgium (Fadil 2008a). Nadia was—and still is—active as a public intellectual who engaged herself in a variety of civil society organisations such as Kif Kif, the AEL, and the SAMV that was later renamed as Ella. She currently works as a professor within the Department of Anthropology at the Catholic University of Leuven.

In the context of an overview of the development of her political awareness, she explained to me how she experienced a "religious trip" when she was about 16 years old. This religious discovery caused some tension within a family that found itself on the "margin" of the "imagined" Islamic "community". Consider the excerpt below:

> NF: So uhm we have been sent to the mosque and stuff like that but … our daddy does not pray so that means that as a family you already are … living at the margin of the community because uhm you don't visit one of the most important integrating places and that's the mosque … you basically spend your holidays uhm at home and it's not as if you really have a strong connection with the rest of the imagined community and uhm … so for me becoming religious constituted a kind of resistance and rebellion a kind of legitimate rebellion uhm I remember that at a certain moment he told me "if you start to wear a headscarf then" uhm (laughs) "I won't appear in public with you anymore" and (laughs).
> **excerpt 32 – 22/08/2008**

The excerpt above provides us with a clear case of sociological usage of the notion of integration. Nadia's description of the mosque as "one of the most important integrating places" of "the imagined community" is unique in my collection of interviews. Nadia attributes some kind of integrating agency to the space of the mosque. As such, she highlights its function as a centring institution for a particular—Islamic—imagined community. She did so by constructing a statement in which the deictic centre of the verb to integrate is no longer occupied by a hegemonic actor, by a government, by a dominant social group or by a sovereign liberal subject. Rather, the entity responsible for this integration is posited as a public space where community members practice cultural and religious performances such as prayer and the likes.

Nadia rebelled against her parents by seeking a stronger connection with the imagined community that the mosque calls into being as a centring institution. Nevertheless, as we will see in more detail later on, Nadia's subjectivity and political engagements have undergone significant changes since this early age. What is important to remember at this point is that Nadia Fadil's rather unique usage of the concept of integration is part of a wider attempt to redefine the contextual boundaries within which the integration of minorities is discussed. Nadia focuses her political engagement on efforts that can make "the presence" of minorities more "visible" in the public realm. Her engagement is an attempt at "imagining" and "writing" a new "collective history" that shows the "diversity in stories and trajectories".

> NF: ... actually when I was with Kif Kif ... I was there first and foremost in order to create a kind of alternative forum where the minority question could be explored in a different way ... or where the debate could be held ... But I absolutely believe that we need this. Not only Kif Kif, but also different forums in order to ... counter fora well not contra fora but, well, alternative fora ... Alternative fora where you can uhm ... hold these debates in a different way. Also, more sensitive themes that are immediately hi-jacked in the public debate by this actor or that actor, they can be put to the fore as well ... but also by doing on collective history writing ... the collective ... the presence the ... well ... to write our history but writing not only literally writing but also imagining uhm ... cultural productions uhm ... really ... making the presence ... visible in all sorts of ways ... through images through texts ... musically on all ... and by making that diversity in stories and trajectories visible so that it does not ... But at the same time, ... to me it is very important that if I do this that it is not without engagement.
> **excerpt 33 – 22/08/2008**

As the excerpt above shows, Nadia's engagement involves an attempt to create alternative fora where the "minority question can be explored" in alternative ways. She wants to contribute in the construction of safe havens where minorities can think and talk about sensitive themes before they get "hi-jacked in the public debate" by some other "actor". But as we will see later on, this is not enough. Her engagement is also a

4 Articulating the Problematic of Integration in a Minority Debate

contribution to the imagination of a new Flanders, Belgium and Europe that grants a place to minority members and their stories. Nadia emphasised the importance of performances and texts that inscribe the presence of minorities in Europe should go hand in hand with a mode of "engagement". As we will see later on, this implies that such inscriptions should involve an "anti-racist" "class discourse" that allows for a "class analysis". Later on, I will provide a full analysis of the interview conducted with Nadia Fadil. But right now, it suffices to remember that one's integration into particular institutions and sections of the public sphere always involves an articulation with some imagined community. The discourses of Nadia, Karima, Amane and Abdellatif show us that the way we imagine the public sphere and its constituents always impacts on the way one conceptualises abstract categories such as integration.

4.5.4 Integration as a Natural Phenomenon and Integration as a Political Process

The meanings of integration are fixed in numerous ways. They are not merely generated in relation to the voices, practices and institutions that populate the public realm and in relation to one's ontological presuppositions. Part of its meaning is constructed in relation to the status we accord to this process. It makes a huge difference whether we articulate integration as a natural phenomenon or as a political and institutional process. Put differently, the fantasmatic and/or mythical status attributed to practices and processes of integration impacts on the way we fix its meaning. If integration—however we define it—functions as a lacking value in our discursively articulated sense of society, it acquires the status of a mythical goal. This means that the realisation of integration becomes a form of self-realisation. The fact that integration-related practices and discourses function as self-techniques explains why debates on integration turn emotional so quickly.

In order to explore this issue more thoroughly, it is useful to return to Abdellatif Akhandaf (DIA) and Najib Chakouh (Kif Kif). Whereas Najib claimed that "integration happens anyway", Abdellatif argued that this is simply "not true". Najib's stance can be explained in relation to his viscous world view. Abdellatif's point of view has to be related to his ideas on the representation and imagination of minorities in the public realm. One might say that the concept of integration performs a fantasmatic or mythical function in Abdellatif's discourse. He opposes modes of integration characterised by the assimilationist, culturalist and homogenising logics discussed above. But this does not make his discourse any less ideological. For Najib, integration does not perform this centralising function and integration does not function as a value or as a mythical goal. His imagination of social structure as a slimy mass, as a "blob" that defies easy categorisations, implies that integration is the natural state of social order.

Abdellatif Akhandaf does not consider integration in terms of a natural process: "integration" does not happen "automatically". For him, integration is something that needs to be stimulated actively by governmental institutions as well as by individuals who engage themselves in such a project. We already saw that Abdellatif's preferred mode of integration is based on a subjectivity marked by a self-confidence that allows for interaction with others and for public articulations of one's individuality, culture and religion. The realisation of integration depends on the way we evaluate the diversity we see in the public realm and on the self-techniques that allow us to develop the necessary self-confidence for integration. As long as identity formation is based on "feelings of insecurity" and on a lack of social "contacts", "integration" will remain nothing but an intangible mirage.

At this point in time, "we are not open to integration" according to Abdellatif. All too often, he sees defensive reactions in the way people from different communities deal with each other. Abdellatif's own engagement for DIA—the integration service of Antwerp—constitutes an attempt to change this. More specifically, he wants to contribute to integration and feelings of self-confidence by creating the right conditions for dialogue and interaction. According to him, the government has to put things "in motion" in order to make interaction and integration possible, even though "there are some things you can't do as a government from the top down". As an example, he refers to a policy whereby the government subsidies for (initiatives of) minority civil society organisations are made conditional upon the organisation of cross-cultural moments for

4 Articulating the Problematic of Integration in a Minority Debate 241

dialogue and interaction. The reason why governmental institutions are so important for process of integration is articulated in the excerpt below:

> AA: ... the uhm the migration from uhm ... from uhm well ... uhm Latin America and so on ... there the integration process will take less time. Why? Simply because the difference are ... smaller ... uhm. The differences are smaller uhm ... . The resistance to integrate oneself is smaller because there are a lot of similarities uhm ... . So growing towards one another intertwining with one another, will be accomplished within decades uhm within one decade. But where the differences are big with respect to skin
> JZ: with respect to what?
> AA: with respect to skin or with respect to values and norms or religion and religious differences ... those differences are too big and the integration process and the process of acceptance, the migration process is really about an experiential process uhm an experiential process of both groups uhm ... There it will take longer.
> **excerpt 34 – 18/06/2008**

According to Abdellatif, integration is hindered by a lack of interaction. And the main reason for this lack of interaction is framed in term of racial, cultural, religious and normative "differences". According to him, the more commonalities one perceives, the less "resistance to integrate oneself" there will be. Integration—defined as an "experiential" process of mutually "intertwining" "groups"—is framed as a slow process that takes at least a decade. The success of government policies is therefore made dependent on the extent to which governments recognise differences in terms of "values", "norms" and "religion". Abdellatif argues that the Flemish government does not sufficiently recognise the role of religious difference in its dealings with civil society organisations. He argues that the misrecognition of organisations of people who associate themselves on the basis of religion implies misrecognition of an "important" part of one's "being":

> AA: We can talk about emancipation we can talk about culture but we cannot talk about religion ... even though religion is part of their of their being. So it was always taboo especially ... we do support culture we do support

cultural activities we support uhm and we finance uhm culture. But one has to remain silent about religion ... and this led to a damper on the and it lead to reluctance with respect to integration uhm within the integration ...
JZ: In civil society?
AA: In civil society yes ... uhm one also looked with uhm ... one looked with distrust at a great deal of allochthon associations and also at the umbrellas [the federations of migrant self-organisations] like "no disrespect you can do your thing specifically about culture and uhm euhm about getting to know one another and about dialogue and so on" but uhm what is really important.
excerpt 35 – 18/06/2008

Implicitly, Abdellatif Akhandaf argues that governmental institutions are misinterpreting what "integration" and the "integration process" ought to mean. Abdellatif's preferred definition of integration includes a mode of subjectivity marked by self-confidence with respect to all aspects of identity—including religion. He argues that a misrecognition of the importance of religious identities by the government and by other actors and institutions can lead to the feelings of "insecurity" and to the "negative" processes of identity formation discussed in the previous section. It can also lead to a more general "reluctance with respect to integration" in general. This is why Abdellatif does not believe that integration happens automatically and requires a governmental policy that stimulates it.

Najib Chakouh—chairman of Kif Kif at the time of our interview—preferred to think of integration in terms of a natural process. This leads him to downplay the role of governmental integration policies and institutions. His rather fluid conceptualisation of society and his sceptical attitude with respect to social, political and scientific categories implies that integration is to some extent a non-issue. It is always already taking place. As such, he is careful to distinguish between Fraihi's "bankruptcy of integration" and (the failure of) integration as a social process. We already saw that Fraihi declared the bankruptcy of the integration sector or industry (Fraihi 2000). In this context, it is useful to note that Kif Kif started out as Tarik Fraihi's personal website for critique on the minority debate. The fact that Najib sympathises with Tarik Fraihi's ideas is not coincidental. At the same time, his viscous and fluid ontology of society implies that social actors are always already integrated to some extent. It is for this reason that Najib believes that "integration happens anyway".

NC: we are tired of the fact that way too much is [done] 'for us' .. but not 'by us' ... and if we are talking about uhm ... about uhm Tarik uhm well I don't know if I quote him literally but uhm 'the bankruptcy of integration politics' yes ... then ... that piece yes ... but that does not mean that integration does not happen ... integration happens anyway
JZ: mmh
NC: So I mean I uhm I once said something and that made people very silent especially people in the field of the social sector ... I said "what we are doing right now, from a historical perspective, this is lost time ... because in the long run ... it will solve itself ..."
JZ: mmh
NC: You can see that with respect to all sort of things ... even with respect to those who are most oppressed ... in the long run there will be a light [at the end of the tunnel] ... of course there will always remain some points of struggle uhm or some issues that need help but I mean ...
JZ: Why are you occupying yourself with it anyway then?
NC: In order to make sure that everything keeps on going in that direction.
excerpt 36 – 03/06/2008

According to Najib, the bankruptcy of integration is related to the fact that *"too much is* done *'for' us but not 'by us'"*. His critique is directed at a policy that does not sufficiently support emancipatory modes of citizenship. This is not a critique directed at 'normal' processes of social integration. Najib prefers a policy that facilitates a more emancipatory form of integration. This last point will be explored more thoroughly in the next section. In contrast to Abdellatif, he does not think of integration as something that is lacking in Flanders. Consequently, the signifier 'integration' does not carry the same fantasmatic weight in the value systems of these two interviewees.

4.5.5 The Failure of Integration Processes and the Failure of the Integration Industry

All of my interviewees engaged in implicit and/or explicit attempts to rearticulate the polyphony of voices that structure the Flemish minority debate. This has already been illustrated with reference to the interview conducted with Issam Z who categorised organisations such as the AEL,

Kif Kif and BOEH! with respect to their degree of "activism". Activism clearly operated as a value and as a key ingredient for his preferred mode of integration and politics. But actors map civil society in different ways. Considering the hegemonic status of the concept of integration, it should not come as a surprise that some of my interviewees mapped the voices in the debate on the basis of their stances towards the bankruptcy of integration.

In the last excerpt of the previous section, we saw that Najib Chakouh agreed to Tarik Fraihi's analysis with respect to the bankruptcy of the integration industry. To say that the integration industry has failed does not imply that integration has failed as a social process. Below, Najib positions some key actors in the minority debate on an axis that ranks from 'meek' to 'radical' depending on the way they criticise hegemonic ideas about integration policy. According to Najib, Kif Kif is anything but "meek". As an illustration, he rearticulates a dialogue in which he "shocked" the co-ordinator and board of directors of *Samenlevingsopbouw*[3] by asking what their integration-related activities amount to after "fifteen years" of work.

> NC: We, Kif Kif, are not meek eh we are no tree-huggers as they put it … so uhm well if we say 'bankruptcy of integration' … it's like that eh … I am [involved] in Samenlevingsopbouw … the board of directors … . Well the first thing I, well in different words, I said to the team co-ordinator of Borgerhout, I said like "sorry but uhm you have been at it for fifteen years and I don't see any difference" … "oh that that's not true and we uhm" … I say "some Moroccan women who are knitting somewhere upstairs in a group on an attic … I don't see what you are stimulating that way. Of course, they might like that, but those groups will probably have changed a lot by now, from the beginning until now" … I say with respect to social work well … . A face like that [Najib puts on a shocked facial expression] of course but still, I said it and I don't care.
> **excerpt 37 – 03/06/2008**

---

[3] There are several ways to translate the noun 'samenlevingsopbouw': society construction; society building; (the) construction of society; or (the) building of society. The organisation called 'Samenlevingsopbouw' aims to organise socially vulnerable groups. It aims to improve the quality of living together in villages, cities and neighbourhoods by collaborating with interest groups, with volunteers, with social workers and with policy makers.

4 Articulating the Problematic of Integration in a Minority Debate 245

Najib maps Kif Kif, the AEL, the FMV on the basis of the various ways in which they criticise the integration industry. He explicitly recognises the "merits" of everyone involved and refers specifically to the AEL whose discourse corresponds for "eighty percent" with the ideas circulating within Kif Kif. He argues that the voice of the AEL is "still needed" even if it was merely to benefit Kif Kif. Interestingly, he frames the relationship between Kif Kif and the AEL as a "strategical" game whereby both actors basically articulate the same critique with respect to the integration sector while positioning themselves differently on the axis of meekness and radicalism.

> NC: And that's why I say that everyone has his merits eh ... uhm ... this may seem as if I don't want to articulate an opinion on this but I see positive and negative things in any action eh ... I mean even take for instance something that many people in the field, to put it bluntly, approached negatively. When we are talking about the AEL ... as well ... because I mean like eighty percent did correspond. He [Dyab Abou Jahjah] used to be an old pall eh but for instance ... I think it was very positive what happened and even now I think they are still needed. To put it bluntly, purely selfish, for the benefit of Kif Kif ... but that's a purely selfish perspective. Why? Because they allow us to step into the spotlight. "That can be played like this", "then it can be played like that", "then it can be played like this". You can play it like this: one is radical and that one is less radical ...
> JZ: mmh
> NC: But yeah all of these are ... techniques you can ... play with on a strategical level eh. (this excerpt continues in the excerpt below)
> **excerpt 38 – 03/06/2008**

When I asked Najib what he meant by "radicalism", he responded by metapragmatically categorising the discourses of the AEL, Kif Kif, the Federation of Moroccan Associations of Mohamed Chakkar, the integration sector and the liberal policy of *inburgering* of Minister Keulen. The "demands and performances" of the AEL are described as being "less diplomatic" than those of Kif Kif. Kif Kif itself is "not exactly weak" but "reasonably [radical]". It is more "diplomatic" than the AEL and dears to "say" more than the FMV. Less radical than the public interventions of Kif Kif and the AEL is the FMV chaired by Mohamed Chakkar. Moreover, the integration sector itself is described as having "its tail between its legs", as "tree-hugging" and as "sweating in the heat" while "not daring to say anything" critical. The "policy" of Marino Keulen, a liberal Minister responsible for the Flemish policy of *inburgering,* is not even worth the label of a "policy" according to Najib.

> JZ: (this excerpt is a continuation of the excerpt above) And with respect to what do you consider it to be more radical for instance ...
> NC: their ... their demands and performances eh I mean uhm he does this and he does that ... a lot of very, a lot less diplomatic ... . And Kif Kif is not exactly weak eh, I mean it's also reasonably [radical] but not until that level. And for instance Chakkar is even less [radical] then Kif Kif I think ... well on that level at least.
> JZ: yes yes
> NC: While the integration sector well it's meek eh, it's like with its tail between its legs, tree-hugging and sweating in the heat ... and not daring to say anything ...
> JZ: mmh ...
> NC: The policy of Keulen [liberal Minister of Inburgering] for instance ... I don't call that a policy eh.
> **excerpt 39 – 03/06/2008**

Najib' metapragmatic characterisation of Flemish civil society organisations involved in the minority debate involves an evaluation of the bold and assertive ways in which these actors critique existing integration policies. At the same time, it is important to emphasise that Najib is well aware of the fact that both "integration" and "the bankruptcy of integration" can be interpreted in various ways. Consider the following excerpt:

> NC: I think that, at any rate, there are different interpretations concerning the bankruptcy of integration eh but ... . I think I think I think that this might be one of the reasons why Keulen is like this. Because he thinks "well yes, look, that [the bankruptcy of integration] has been put to the fore and I kind of like that, and you know, if it suits my purposes" ... . But people forget that 'my purposes' are put between quotation marks ... . And his purposes consist in eliminating everything so to say ... the individual is important.
> **excerpt 40 – 03/06/2008**

4 Articulating the Problematic of Integration in a Minority Debate 247

In the excerpt above, Najib points out that the notion of the "bankruptcy of integration" can be operationalised in very different political projects. His point is that liberal politicians such as Flemish Minister for *Inburgering* Keulen interpret this concept in a way that allow them to "eliminate everything" related to the integration sector and to articulate a policy centred on "individuals". Such a policy runs into conflict with Najib's view of man and society where communities do play a role in social integration, on condition that this policy is based on flexible, liquid or viscous notions of identity and community. Najib recognises that there is a "liberal" element in his position with respect to the emancipation of minorities. But this liberalism is rather philosophical than "political" in the party-political sense of the word. This means that individuals possess the power to obstruct the "wheelwork of society". One way to exercise this power of resistance is to criticise the integration sector in a "radical" way.

In order to illustrate a different interpretation of the "bankruptcy of integration", we can take a look at my interview with Ahmed Zizaoui. At the time, Ahmed worked for Atlas, the successor of the Antwerp Integration Service called DIA. In 2008, DIA changed its name to *Atlas: house for diversity and inburgering*. Interestingly, Ahmed associates the "bankruptcy of integration" first and foremost with right-wing voices in the public debate. In order to understand this, we need to take a closer look at the way he positions himself with respect to left-wing and right-wing subject positions. His position with respect to the statement that integration has failed should be understood in relation to this political topography.

Ahmed explains that he was "initially oriented to the Left" and made a "turn to the right". He now occupies a "centred" and more "objective" or "realist" position that should not be confused with "racism". Ahmed thinks that "a lot of allochthons" and a lot of his colleagues at Atlas "are too far in that leftist corner". And even though he does "not want them to sit in the rightist corner either", he would prefer a situation in which these people would adopt a more "objective" perspective with respect to "existing problems" such as homophobia and racism among minorities themselves. He explicitly rejected the idea that this form of "objective" criticism constitutes a form of "racist" discourse. In order to get a more thorough grasp on the way he conceptualises right-wing discourse, it is useful to take a look at the excerpt below.

AZ: if you go somewhere where a lot of people are really really oriented towards the right eh, like "the stuff that has happened thus far is not enough" ... "integration has failed" and so on, "it is about time that they all start to speak Dutch" and so on. Yesterday there was a screening of eh I told you about *My Story* [Dutch: *Mijn Verhaal*]. Very good very interesting and at the very end someone says like "yes I think we really don't uhm, I think it is really not an option that we have to make sure that the personnel of ... our institutions eh institutions for old people ... knows the language of those people. ... Because if I go abroad I have to speak that language as well" and so on ... well
excerpt 41 – 15/05/2008

The statement that "integration has failed" is put on a par with right-wing complaints such as the demand that "it is about time that they all start to speak Dutch" and that "the stuff" that has been done thus far did not go "far enough". Ahmed goes on and describes an incident that occurred during a debate organised after a screening of Mohamed Ihkan's *Mijn Verhaal*, a documentary on the life stories of two first-generation migrants from Morocco who arrived in Belgium during the sixties. The ensuing debate touched upon the issue of care facilities for elderly migrants who never learned Dutch. At the end of the debate, an audience member said that "it is really not an option" that one would "make sure that the personnel of our institutions for old people knows the language of these people", the reason being that "if I go abroad I have to speak that language as well". For Ahmed, this remark can be put on a par with right-wing statements on the failure of integration.

AZ: if you have that mentality in spite of the fact that, if you, ... look at the context well, how should you consider things in their context eh. People have come to here and did not receive, did not get the opportunity to follow Dutch classes and who are now too old and have never done anything but work work work. And now they are retired and growing old and you can't expect those people to actually study Dutch. ... Especially not if we are dealing with illiterates eh so uhm ... . In part I think that people who have such ah well such a vision or such a mentality and who make such remarks ... well they are really already too far in that rightist corner ... they are like ... "so many things go wrong and there is

so much going wrong and it is about time that" ... and so on. So yeah really they they... they put the limit rather close. At the same time, you might say that from a leftist perspective, one is almost entirely without limits eh like "those allochthons they can ... do nothing wrong", from their point of view.
excerpt 42 – 15/05/2008

Ahmed Zizaoui argues that one has to put things "in their context": elderly Moroccans who migrated to Belgium in the sixties were frequently illiterate; they were not offered the "opportunity to follow Dutch classes" and did nothing but "work, work, work". This type of contextualisation is part and parcel of the centrist position preferred by Ahmed. His "objective" position in the political spectrum between "left" and "right" implies a discursive strategy of analysing social phenomena and conflicts between various groups and individuals by putting them in the 'right' socio-historical context.

Of course, practices of contextualisation are never neutral, but in this particular case, Ahmed's socio-historical categorisations halted his "turn to the right" and made him critical about claims about the "failure of integration". They also kept him from claiming the "leftist" position that "those allochthons" can do "nothing wrong". This interpretation of what it means to occupy a "central" position in the debate explains why Ahmed is positive about left-wing people like Tarik Fraihi who make a "good analysis" with respect to "society", as well as with respect to the migrant "communities". The point to be made here is that both the 'failure of integration' and the 'failure of the integration industry' can function as empty signifiers over which political debates and struggles take place.

4.5.6 Integration as an Accomplishment and Integration as an Unfinished Process

The concept of integration can function as a mythical goal. It can also be considered as a key ontological feature of social structure. Whether we consider integration as an already accomplished fact or as an unfinished process depends in part on such conceptualisations. But it also depends on our (meta-)pragmatic definitions of integration and on the concrete criteria we use as touchstones for evaluating whether or not a person or a community can be evaluated as being integrated. It only becomes possible to qualify or disqualify the validity of the integration concept if one can semantically and/or pragmatically narrow down its definition. Many of my interviewees challenged dominant integration discourse by providing concrete definitions that could be used in order to challenge the validity of the rather vague imperative to integrate. The relevance and the futility of such imperatives can only be assessed on the basis of concrete criteria. Likewise, judgements over the status of the integration process are dependent on the way one defines this term.

My interviewees frequently articulated conflicting notions of integration. This can be illustrated with reference to an article written by Mohamed Chakkar, the chairman of the FMV. In a 2005 article, he commented on the "populist" idea that "allochthon organisations" are too much oriented towards their own "communities". In response, he attacked the idea that minority members should integrate themselves and labelled "integration" as an "outdated" concept, "integration policy" being one of the most "harmful" policies imaginable. Moreover, the notion of integration itself "has led to confusion in a thousand heads". In the excerpt below, Mohamed Chakkar rearticulates the rather common reproach that majority notions of integration boil down to assimilation. He also claims that the imperative to integrate oneself keeps non-autochthons in an ambiguous position, "at the front door" of society.

> *We are no migrants any more. Whether autochthons like it or not, we are part of this society. Integration policy constitutes the most harmful policy that has ever been conducted. It is mainly a political concept. It has created confusion in a thousand heads. To most Flemish people integration equals assimilation. They say: "become like us". That implies that they neither say whether you can stay or leave. No, you keep on standing at the front door. In the mean time we have a fourth generation of youngsters with Moroccan roots. So, can one still talk about integration? I prefer to talk about societal integration. Everybody should get a real opportunity in society. People of another origin or with another sexual orientation should be accepted as they are. Contemporary society happens to be diverse. This stands in contrast to assimilation, because the latter means pure discrimination.* (Concentra 2007)

Mohamed Chakkar considers integration to be a responsibility of society as a whole. He asks himself the rhetorical question whether one can "still talk about integration" in discussions about the "fourth generation of youngsters with Moroccan roots". Nevertheless, contrary to what one may expect, Mohammed does not do away with the concept. Instead, he proposes to talk about "societal integration", shifting the responsibility for integration to society as a whole, defining integration in terms of equal opportunities for all. Depending on one's perspective and position, integration signifies an accomplishment and/or an unfinished process. If one defines integration in the assimilatory sense, the concept is to be disqualified. If one defines it as being "part of society", the concept becomes obsolete. And if one defines integration in terms of emancipation and equal opportunities, a lot remains to be done.

Chakkar dismisses the idea that Moroccan organisations fall back too much onto their own communities. He considers this reproach to be an instance of classic integration discourse and argues that it is not the role of minority organisations to create the equal opportunities required to achieve integration. Instead, he argues that these organisations have an agenda-setting function. They try to identify "the needs of the community and try to put them on the political agenda". The responsibility for issues related to "the high degree of unemployment among allochthons, for the educational gap, and for racism in real-estate" is put on the shoulders of mainstream politics. At the same time, Mohamed Chakkar urges the people involved in minority organisations to "take up their responsibility", both in private and in public contexts. Chakkar's preferred mode of integration thus implies emancipatory politics on the part of minority members and the provision of equal opportunities with respect to labour, housing and schooling on the part of society in general.

> *"The associations* of minority associations *do not have the solution for the high degree of unemployment among allochthons, for the educational gap, and for racism in real-estate",* says Chakkar. *"They do constitute the emancipatory engine of the community. You discover the needs of the community and try to put them on the political agenda. It is also a struggle for independence. We inform, sensitise, and attribute responsibility to people. We point out that they should take up their responsibility. Not only at home, but also outside, in their street and in their neighbourhood."* (Concentra 2007)

Integration can also be defined in other ways. For instance, Mohamed Bouziani, involved in *Imane* (Initiative Moroccan Networks), clearly posits that integration has been accomplished already. Like other respondents, he is able to do so by semantically narrowing the definition of integration. He does this within the context of a discussion about minority voting rights. In Belgium, non-European migrants without the Belgian nationality can register in order to vote for local elections. But in contrast to Belgians, they have to register in order to do so. Mohamed pointed out that an "embarrassingly" low number of Moroccans made use of this right to vote. He goes on and deplores the fact that non-European migrants need to sign a "declaration" in which they promise to abide by Belgian law in order to register for the municipal elections.

> MB: ... it was a way of ... of saying like "well, you need to sign and it is a sort of declaration in which you declare that you are actually integrating yourself and [that you] respect the law, Belgian law", blabla, and so on.
> **excerpt 43 – 14/09/2007**

Even though Mohamed accepts the idea that integration involves adherence to Belgian law, he is critical of this implicit criminalisation of migrants in this declaration. At the same time, his narrow legalistic interpretation of integration as adherence to the law allows him to criticise mainstream notions of integration. For Mohamed, integration is an accomplished fact and he illustrates this with reference to a description of his father as someone who is meticulously trying to be in order with his taxes. Consider the following excerpt:

> MB: So most of the Moroccans here are people who really follow the law very well. I notice this with my father. Whenever he gets a letter in his mailbox, he will be the first to go to the postal office, to pick it up, because you never know. Traffic taxes are always payed. In other words, he gives up on his other budgets in order to pay for government business, in order to be in order.
> **excerpt 44 – 14/09/2007**

The fact that his father tries to be "in order" with his "taxes" and follows the law is sufficient ground for Mohamed to label his father as

4 Articulating the Problematic of Integration in a Minority Debate 253

someone who is integrated. Interestingly, Mohamed goes on and argues that "autochthons of Moroccan descent" generally "take care of being in order as much as possible". He even suggests that it would be interesting to "investigate" this compliance with the law and with tax-related administration. Mohamed is sure that the research results would lead to a conclusion that recognises the integrated status of many migrants.

Other fixations of integration-related signifiers have similar effects. For instance, Bilal Benyaich of the intercultural platform Kif Kif defines integration in economic terms. To him, integration is a process that starts with one's integration in the labour market. He is sceptical about explanatory models in which the non-integration of migrants into the labour market is framed as a cultural phenomenon. Put differently, he attacks culturalist logics of integration on the basis of a rather economic definition of the integration process.

Integration only starts if one has a job. Culture becomes twice as important if you are not doing well economically, and in turn, that culture will be used by others as an explanation for economical deprivation. This is an upside-down argument. First things first: first the socio-economical, then ethics. (Benyaich cited in: Henneman and Bervoet 2008)[4]

But even when integration is considered an accomplished fact, it can function as a basis for critique. As a case in point, we can refer to Amane X, the DIA civil servant who argued that a true integration policy should take the dreams and expectations of migrants into account. According to Amane, "allochthons" are disappointed in the "discourse and in the pattern of expectations with respect to integration". They are disappointed in the slow way in which institutions adapted themselves to their needs. At the same time, Amane points at "the equally just disappointment of institutions with regard to" the slow integration of "allochthons". Interestingly, this second aspect of the problem is being framed in terms of the speed in which the "human mind" can adapt itself.

---

[4] De integratie begint pas bij het hebben van werk. Cultuur wordt dubbel zo belangrijk als je het economisch niet goed hebt, waarna die cultuur dan weer door anderen als reden wordt aangegrepen voor economische achterstand. Dat is de omgekeerde redenering. First thing's first: eerst het sociaal-economische, dan de ethiek. (Benyaich cited in Henneman and Bervoet 2008)

AX: The disappointment ... the disappointment in the integration discourse and in the pattern of expectations with respect to integration ... among themselves not in policy ... perhaps also in policy but also with respect to their own expectations ... the disappointment of their parents the disappointment of the speed in which institutions adapted themselves. As much as the equally righteous disappointment of institutions with respect to allochthons like "come on that goes really slowly" ... but if anything evolves slowly, it is human mentality, the human mind of the homo sapiens.
excerpt 45 – 04/10/2007

According to Amane, feelings of disappointment about the integration process stimulate allochthon Flemish to fall back onto certain "patterns of values" and "forms of engagement". This does not mean that one separates oneself from Flemish people and Flemish institutions, but it does imply that people start to look for their "own warm nest". Interestingly, Amane blames the "integration process" itself for this type of retreat. She considers it to be a reaction to an excess of integration and to a fear for the loss of selfhood. It is the excessive focus on "the other" and "other cultures" that triggers a desire for this cultural practice of nesting. This does not mean that all of this implies radical forms of social exclusion. Rather, the search for "one's own warm nest" functions as a metaphor that explains why people enjoy community events such as the Ramadan and the Iftar together.

AX: Oh but of course. Everybody likes to do that, absolutely ... . Falling back, I am not even talking about falling back to one's own community and not having any contact with Flemish any more ... Quite the contrary. They are Flemish eh ... but falling back to ...
JZ: a pattern of values
AX: to a certain pattern of values for instance yes, to certain forms of engagement yes, to certain niches of engagement. Not so much integrative, but perhaps the common experience of a common culture, of a common link and not so much that bridge any more ... you see? They are Flemish eh, don't forget that eh, contacts with health insurance providers, contacts with the school, the neighbours .... All of that developed positively and that has a lot to do with going to school and [the fact that the knowledge of] Dutch has increased ... absolutely ... of course. But falling back 'to' means to discover your own warm nest and in all openness that you are

displaying every day ... [the practice of] falling back 'to' is triggered because of the integration process. Like okay, I don't want to lose myself, I want to retain a piece and enjoy that ... . Perhaps there has been an evolution of always being focused on the other, on other cultures, and so on and. And too little on.
excerpt 46 – 04/10/2007

Amane X implicitly defines integration as an everyday interactional process. The fact that majority and minority members are both disappointed in the (speed of the) integration process does not imply that the process does not take place. On the contrary, Amane provides us with an analysis in which the integration process itself becomes the main explanatory factor for the fact that people look for places in which they can find "a common experience of culture". It is in this context, that we have to understand the statement that both the excess of integration and the response in the form of a search for spaces in which one can experience a "common culture" and a "common link" are "all right" and "okay".

AX: Perhaps there is too much integration at this moment, and that's all right, and so one looks for warm nests, and that's okay too eh ... those two ... seem to exist.
excerpt 47 – 04/10/2007

To sum up, whether one conceptualises integration as an ongoing process or as an accomplished fact is co-dependent on the way one implicitly or explicitly fixes the meaning of the term. Definitions that provide concrete criteria for judging the integration-related status of individuals and groups are generally used in order to challenge under-specified concepts of integration marked by assimilatory, culturalising and homogenising logics. Without such concrete definitions, counter-hegemonic discourses run the risk of becoming as vague as the discourses they oppose.

4.5.7 Indexing the Location of Integration

In order to understand what integration means, we also have to ask ourselves what people, groups or communities are supposed to integrate *into*.

The usage of integration relation concepts varies according to the locus of integration. In the majority of the cases above, integration is a process that takes place in Dutch-speaking Flemish contexts. But there are other aspects of socio-political discourse that may be indexed in talk about integration. Some of my interviewees succeeded in articulating a critique of mainstream notions of integration through a re-contextualisation of the framework in which integration takes place. One case in point was provided by Nadia Fadil who talked about the mosque as one of the most important "integrating places" for the imagined Islamic community in Flanders. But the mosque is not the only integrating institution in the public realm.

From a sociological point of view, one might say that every centring institution is an integrating institution. Consequently, we are always integrated or integrating into a variety of contexts. Sociologist Nadia Fadil articulated clear opinions on this issue. She described her political engagement as a search for "alternative fora" in which "the integration debate" could be held and in which "the minority question could be asked". In this context, she broadens the general framework of the minority debate in a rather interesting way. She asks herself what the "imaginary community of Europe" is and how "we can make sure that migrants are going to be a part of this" so that they will "not be considered as allochthons or as outsiders any more". At the same time, she seeks to go "beyond Eurocentric activism" and to take a more "transnational" perspective.

> NF: And uhm I haven't made up my mind about that because it's not as if I am against Europe eh I am also part of Europe, but it's uhm , and at the same time ... yeah well I haven't made my mind up about how I can succeed in being simultaneously active in Europe and in positioning my place as a minority in Europe, in the uhm representation, in the identity formation of Europe, in order to ... inscribe the minority question there, in a manifest way. Because I think that is what constitutes the struggle .... In addition to exclusion and discrimination and all of that, the struggle is fundamentally about ... what is the imagined community of Europe and how do we make sure that those migrants will become a part of this and not be considered as allochthons or as outsiders any more. ... So, that is one thing but on the other hand, there is also uhm a continuous responsibility we have in Europe towards other parts of the world as being people

4 Articulating the Problematic of Integration in a Minority Debate 257

who are also partly coming from the non-Western [region] to uhm … yeah I don't know, to criticise the hypocrisy.
excerpt 48 – 22/08/2008

Nadia frames the "minority question"—which includes issues of integration—as a trans-national issue. It is about articulation in its performative and connective senses, about giving a discursive and institutional space to minorities in Europe and in the world. The establishment of an "imagined community" requires the shaping of "integrating places" or institutions. It is this type of space that Nadia seeks to create through her political engagement, an endeavour that clearly runs counter to the hegemonic logics of integration discussed in the previous chapter. The nationalist and/or ethnocentric features of culturalist, assimilationist and homogenising logics of integration can be undermined without explicitly mentioning integration. This can also be exemplified with reference to an interview I conducted with Karim Hassoun who succeeded Dyab Abou Jahjah as the chairman of the AEL.

Karim Hassoun described the AEL as a project against "islamophobia", "assimilation" and "racism" while also mobilising around "the international context" of "Palestine", "Iraq" and the "Arab world" in general. As we saw before, mainstream integration discourse was one of the main objects of critique of this organisation. But even when the issue is not being addressed directly, it is possible to distinguish why nationalist notions of integration run into conflict with AEL ideology. This can be illustrated with reference to the excerpt below:

> KH: So that also concerns us and that has nothing to do with what one has always accused us of like we … "import conflicts that have nothing to do with Flanders or Belgium or Antwerp" or whatever. That is nonsense. First of all, every organisation or every person may uhm devote oneself to a theme or devote oneself to justness or justice wherever on this planet. If there is injustice in Uzbekistan, then I have the right to make an issue out of that over here. Palestine, I have the right to make an issue out of it. And on the other side, we are also children of the nation. I may have been born here, but my connection to the Arabic world is very close and a lot of Moroccans or Arabs have that connection as well, that bond with the home country, with Morocco and in extension with the Arabic world and with

the Palestinian struggle. One person out of an identitarian factor, culturally, eh like "I feel like an Arab, I feel connected with the people that is being oppressed over there", another out of an Islamic identity like "those are Muslims that are being butchered there. And no one talks about that, or if one does talk about that, one talks about it in terms of 'terrorists' or 'Osama bin Laden' and 'attacks' and 'danger' and whatever and" ... So that thematic concerns us as well, and our political mobilisation is dealing with that over here as well.
excerpt 49 – 26/02/2008

During the moral panic surrounding the emergence of the AEL at the turn of the century, the AEL was frequently accused of 'importing foreign problems' into Belgium. In opposition to the idea that political engagement around conflicts in the Arab World can be described in terms of import and export, Karim Hassoun articulates the international agenda of the AEL in terms of a struggle for universal values such as "justice". At the same time, he grants legitimacy to people who connect with particular causes on the basis of cultural and/or religious identifications. Doing so, he articulates these identifications in spatial terms and uses his own engagement as an example. He explains how he feels a "connection" and a "bond" with "Morocco", as well as with the Arab World and with Palestine "in extension". In different ways, Nadia Fadil and Karim Hassoun articulate a sense of subjectivity, politics and society that dislocates classic nationalist frameworks in which integration is commonly understood.

The locus of integration is not always primarily inter- or trans-national in critical discourse on integration. Even though she praised the AEL with respect to the way in which this organisation has put issues of integration on the agenda, activist student Samira Azabar resisted the way the AEL articulated international issues in its discourse. In this interview, Samira proves to be sceptical with respect to the way in which the AEL used certain violent "incidents" (e.g. someone being "beaten up by an autochthon") and issues related to "the stuff the Palestinians are doing" in order to "incite the allochthons" to mobilise politically. Samira does not disqualify these issues as being irrelevant but does argue that there are "are more important issues" that one can "address here in order to help or to support the allochthons and the Muslims here in Belgium".

4 Articulating the Problematic of Integration in a Minority Debate 259

SA: I said like well ... "there are some aspects I do consider to be positive with respect to the AEL" ... especially because of the fact that they have raised [the issue of] integration and raised ... a lot of important issues. But they were actually first and foremost a counterweight for the Vlaams Belang I think. ... They were the far left whereas Vlaams Belang basically was the far right ... . They also raised some issues like, for instance, those small incidents, when someone gets beaten up by an autochthon and, ... that way they kind of tried to incite the allochthons. And I did not consider it to be relevant to say like "this is important". I also said like "perhaps there are more important issues than say Hezbollah or the stuff the Palestinians are doing, that we could address here, in order to help or to support the allochthons and the Muslims here in Belgium" but ... One did not really listen to that so it was not that important to them ...
JZ: you mean the international [dimension]?
SA: Yes exactly. I basically thought that uhm you have to hold your own ground ... before you raise international issues.
excerpt 50 – 16/09/2007

At the time of our interview, Samira saw her political engagement as an Islam-inspired mode of integration. The locus of her preferred mode of integration was relatively local. Whether this was so because of principled or because of pragmatic reasons remains a bit unclear. But she did believe that "you have to hold your own ground ... before you raise international issues". Upon reading my analysis a few years after this interview was conducted, Samira asked me to add that her engagement should be understood as a struggle against injustice and for solidarity, waged at a local level. She did not consider international politics to be irrelevant, but did feel that local political struggles could have more impact on the everyday practices of minorities in Belgium.

SA: My faith pushes me to engage myself with respect to, actually it is kind of weird and ehm you might probably call that contradictory uhm because it does not correspond to faith but ... . But faith actually stimulates us to engage yourself and to integrate. And how do you do that most efficiently? By always going into discussion with those who are basically ... the government. And I consider this to be very important so that is why I choose to or why I am in favour of the idea that there is a certain organisation ... it does not matter whether it carries a religious label or not ... . But basically,

it is kind of important that there is an organisation that ... raises certain issues related to faith and that are quite important to us.
excerpt 51 – 16/09/2007

Elsewhere in the interview, Samira claimed that the average "sixteen year old allochthon" knows all sorts of stuff about "Palestine" and "Israel" from the "independence until today". At the same time, his or her knowledge of the political situation "over here" is way more limited. This distinction between "there" and "here" is relevant to Samira's understanding of integration. The issues that have to be dealt with over here include questions related to "the headscarf" and the subsidising of "mosques". It is also interesting to note that her orientation to local and/or national political issues over "here" partly emerges from her "faith". Samira is very much aware of the fact that people often think she is contradicting herself when she says that Islam "stimulates" her "to engage" and "to integrate" herself.

I met Samira Azabar during a lecture on Antwerp integration policies given by Bob Van den Broecke at the University of Antwerp. At this event, she questioned and criticised this public official about the local Antwerp political decision to ban religious symbols—and therefore women with headscarves—from public functions at the municipal level. In the interview we conducted afterwards, Samira told me that she did not really see "a positive evolution in the debates". She felt that discussions with "parties that can do something about it" did not translate into concrete actions. As such, she was very critical with respect to "the integration service" DIA that claimed to be "on the side of the Moroccans, the Turks and the other allochthon communities, so to say". Nevertheless, she did consider it to be important to enter into a dialogue with "those who are basically the government".

Samira's primary frame of reference is therefore relatively local. Her preferred mode of integration and political engagement entails a preoccupation with issues that are mostly articulated at the regional level of Flanders and at the local level of Antwerp. Also, at the time of our interview, Samira felt very positive about the Green political party called *Groen*. She lauded this party's attitude with respect to "diversity", "integration" and the "headscarf". At the same time, she is very sceptical about the commitment of other parties to the idea of a "community" wherein all "all communities can live peacefully with each other".

4 Articulating the Problematic of Integration in a Minority Debate

SA: Even though it [Groen] is an autochthon party with autochthon directors, ... a chairman, they do have a number of issues including the environment for which I could give myself one hundred percent, and they also say like "look, to us, the headscarf isn't an issue ... you are people like everyone else. Whether you wear a headscarf or not, to us, this does not pose any problem". So, I can imagine ... participating in a party like this, even actively ... . And who knows where they uhm, where they, how well they're going to do. To me, this would be welcomed. ... So, ... I think it's simply great, this is the image of a party ... that can foreground diversity, including integration, ... and that is able to basically say like "look, we're working together with other communities here, and we do can go for a ... peaceful, harmonious community as they put it here in Antwerp. But I think that, that in other parties, including the VLD and in the SPa, this isn't as likely ... . Because they [VLD and SPa] rather use allochthons as figureheads ... so they can harvest votes instead of them really ... believing in a community where the communities can live peacefully with each other.
excerpt 52 – 16/09/2007

The meaning of a category such as "integration" is established through various forms of deixis and radically shifts as other agents are held responsible for this process. Spatial indexes are important because they indicate what one may be integrating *into*. Indexical references may refer to specific physical places but we may also use indexicals, labels, metaphors and metonymies in order to articulate our imagined relations to social and political reality. Within the context of political discourse, indexicals often indicate subject positions and voices within a metaphorical public sphere. This public sphere is marked by a high degree of polycentricity. Consequently, notions of integration should reflect this reality.

4.6 Integration in a Politicised and Polyphonic Public Space

By focusing on the way my interviewees articulated integration-related signifiers in interviews on political engagement, I have tried to provide an overview of the ways in which intellectuals and activists with a Moroccan background challenge the hegemonic logics of the debates on integration in Flanders. The vocabulary of integration and allochthony is not merely a scientific and political discourse that can be found in scientific reports and in parliamentary debates. It has become so hegemonic that it influences the value systems of majority and minority members alike. Consequently, talk about integration fuels emotional debates in bars, at dinner tables and in other everyday contexts. Moreover, the concept of integration is so omnipresent that even those activists who look for alternative vocabularies cannot ignore the issue altogether. The same goes for the binary pair of allochthony/autochthony.

Nevertheless, important as the concept of integration may be, its meanings cannot be understood in isolation of the use of other abstract categories such as diversity, emancipation or activism. Integration-related utterances and statements never occur in isolation. Their meaning emerges through complex articulations of semiotic forms and pragmatic functions in concrete contexts. These articulations can be described at the local level of sounds, words and utterances but can also be analysed at the level of narratives, ideologies and/or large-scale interpretive logics. By using a multidimensional notion of articulation that integrates pragmatic and poststructuralist insights, we can think of concrete utterances and statements as tools that allow us to index our relationships to contexts of interpretation that are not necessarily part and parcel of the ongoing speech event. I devoted particular attention to the way we use langue as a mode of political engagement that allows us to politicise the polyphony of the public realm.

As we noticed before, political engagement can be described as a cover-term for those practices through which subjects aim to rearticulate the relationships between social and political voices, resources and practices through imagined forms of public collective action. The active interviews conducted in this research projects were public events. My interviewees proved to be very aware of the fact that their statements would become part and parcel of a public document. Moreover, their discourse is filled to the brim with metapragmatic markers and utterances that indicate their awareness of the value-laden character of their statements. In this sense, their participation in the interviews itself can be interpreted as a contribution to the public debate. The interview context should not be

4 Articulating the Problematic of Integration in a Minority Debate 263

mistaken for a neutral medium in which individuals can safely comment about things that happen *out there* in the public realm. On the contrary, the very participation of the activists and intellectuals in the interviews analysed in this book constituted an act of political—and therefore public—engagement.

At the end of the first chapter of this book, I concluded that a proper understanding of the relationship between subjectivity, discourse and political engagement requires a perspective that allows us to analyse debates, ideologies and subjectivities as non-unitary objects of investigation. I also argued that we need a mode of analysis that allows us to recognise contradicting and conflicting definitions of reality, both within and between discourses uttered. And on top of this, this mode of analysis should allow for an investigation of the way individuals personalise their relationships with respect to signifiers and practices they may or may not share with others through large-scale processes of interpretation. I have theorised and analysed these processes in terms of adaptable, negotiable and variable logics that allow subjects to structure their sense of self, politics and society with varying degrees of reflexivity. Thus far, I have focused more on discourse about integration than on the overall sense of sense and politics my respondents articulated by linking multiple topics, issues, experiences and analyses with each other.

Nevertheless, this book is first and foremost about selves and politics as articulated in discourse. My focus on integration in this chapter should therefore not obscure the fact that integration was *not* the main topic in most of my interviews. And even though the concept of integration had to be addressed, it is important to keep in mind that there are many interviewees who articulated logics that inform a sense of self and politics that dislocates integration as an ideological value and as a fantasmatic goal. My focus on integration-related signifiers was necessary in order to see how intellectuals and activists challenge hegemonic logics of integration. But this focus also has a distorting effect because it over-emphasises the centrality of this notion in the interviews under investigation. This will become clear in the upcoming chapter where I will discuss the way interpretive logics inform preferred modes of subjectivity and politics.

Nevertheless, in order to investigate how integration-related notions function in the counter-discourses of my respondents, I did ask myself a series of interpretive and functional research questions. These questions were informed by the concept of articulation outlined in the theoretical chapters of this book. I focused on the interpretive functions of (1) integration-related signifiers and voices; (2) integration-related statements and the preferred and disavowed modes of politics articulated by my interviewees; and (3) integration-related utterances and the modes of subjectivity expressed by my respondents. The functional dimension of the analyses resided in a focus on the pragmatic and relational ways in which my interviewees fixed the meanings of integration. The interpretive dimension entailed a research focus on the way they marked their reflexive, metapragmatic and political awareness in concrete utterances.

The analyses show that it does not suffice to attack hegemonic notions such as integration or allochthony directly. One has to engage oneself in a larger effort by conceptualising a radically different ontology of the social. Another strategy may consist in articulating an alternative imagination of the public realm and of the relations between the voices, practices and institutions we encounter in the society-wide debate on integration. Even the ways in which we posit integration as a natural phenomenon or as a mythical and fantasmatic goal can offer opportunities for challenging the logics of assimilation, culturalisation and homogenisation. And last but not least, the space in which we imagine integration processes to take place significantly impacts on our critical understandings of the success and/or failure of integration as a process and/or industry.

Almost ten years after these interviews have been conducted, integration-related discourse remains strong in Flanders. The recent terrorist attacks in Brussels and Paris have reinforced all of the logics informing this discourse. In response to the attacks and the so-called 'refugee crisis', the right-wing Belgian government proposed that all non-European Union people who seek to stay for more than three months on Belgian soil would have to sign an agreement in which they commit themselves to do everything possible 'to integrate' themselves and their family. Flemish nationalist Secretary of State Theo Francken explicitly stated that a refusal to sign this document and non-compliance with the statements made therein can result in a discontinuation of permission to stay on Belgian soil. The statements made by my interviewees ten years ago have only gained in political relevance.

4 Articulating the Problematic of Integration in a Minority Debate

By providing contrastive examples of the various ways in which integration-related signifiers have been used by intellectuals and activists with a Moroccan background in Flanders, I have tried to provide a discursive map of the contextual boundaries that partially and temporarily fix the meanings of integration. Now, the time has come to move beyond this rather narrow focus and to deal with the concepts of self and politics as articulated in their full complexity by my interviewees.

5

Self and Politics in Activist Discourse

The logics that structure our self-understandings and the logics that constitute and organise our societies are closely connected to each other. But they never overlap completely. There is always a minimal degree of distancing involved in the process of ideological interpellation. The very process whereby one identifies one's self with a norm, an identity, a practice, an institution or any other discursive element requires reflexivity. If we are able to loosen the ideological and affective hold ideological discourse has over us, this is so because of our ability to distinguish between preferred and disliked identities, labels, narratives, practices and institutions. Every ideological subject shares this reflexive ability, from the ironic hipster to the religious extremist.

Discursive processes of identification and interpellation operate on the basis of principles such as equivalence, difference and indexicality. But there is more to it. We may doubt and question our identities. We may feel ambivalent about the labels, norms and values—used by ourselves and by others—that supposedly define and/or describe our selves. Love, hate, insecurity, over-confidence, playfulness, doubt and fear are common affective modes that modulate our relations to subject positions, voices, labels and identities. We adopt, adapt, ignore or reject such discursive elements as we activate and switch pragmatically between contexts. In addition to straightforward positive or negative identifications with particular norms, values, narratives and/or institutions, we can engage in partial, temporary or ambiguous identifications that entail weak commitments and articulations, the links of which can wither away and be broken easily without much consequence. In other cases, our identifications may be as dear to us as our selves are.

We invest our selves emotionally in particular subject positions and projects because these positions and projects provide social value(s) as well as various forms of capital for the self. These positions and values are hierarchically organised in and through a multiplicity of centring institutions. Our voices, utterances and statements posit subject positions from which truths can be generated and authority over one's identities and those of others can be claimed. Since enunciative functions organise social space, there is always a link between our sense of self and our sense of politics. We can play with, challenge and transgress the limits of these positions thanks to our metapragmatic ability to modulate and reflexively articulate socio-discursive relationships. The reflexive properties of the human mind and the reflexive possibilities offered by symbolic systems provide us with the means to develop political awareness.

Our affective and discursive stances with respect to the subject positions and voices we may or may not positively, negatively or partially identify with allow us to articulate a sense of self that does not reduce itself to pre-framed categories of discourse. Human beings can be ideologically creative. Selves are never mere binary entities even though some ideological discourses suggest exactly this. We may be immersed in ideological fantasies that deny the contingency of who and what we are, but we can also use the adaptable, negotiable and variable features of symbolic systems in order to loosen ideology's hold on us, shaping our selves and our societies ethically and in self-critical ways. In the upcoming sections, I will demonstrate how my interviewees have articulated alternative self-understandings and modes of politics in the face of powerful discursive forces.

The first section of this chapter details the research questions and procedures that allowed me to address the intricate links between self and politics as articulated in activist discourse in a systematic way.

More specifically, I will formulate a series of interpretive and functional research questions compatible with the heuristic principles outlined in previous chapters. I will also illustrate and discuss key features of the use of Computer Assisted Qualitative Data Analysis programs for qualitative coding such as NVIVO8 in this research project.

I will present my research results with reference to a limited selection of case studies. As such, I will explore the complex ways in which identification processes can be mitigated by critique, doubt and ambivalence. I will then move on to discuss the ways in which respondents may externalise and criticise large-scale logics that structure the public realm. This will clear the ground for an analysis of the critical ways in which my respondents reflect upon and reacted to discursive processes of recognition and misrecognition. Some of the large-scale interpretive logics discussed in these sections will also pop up in the final two case studies. One case study focuses on the way Marxist politician Zohra Othman articulates a more or less coherent sense of self, the other case study explores the way activism functions as a technology of the self for activist scholar Nadia Fadil.

5.1 Research Questions and the Use of CAQDAS in Discourse Studies

In the upcoming sections, I will focus on a series of case studies that focus on the way activists and intellectuals with a Moroccan background link a preferred sense of self with a preferred mode of politics. This implies a (re-)articulation of the large-scale interpretive logics that structure their understandings of self and society, across a wide variety of topics and processes of identification. In order to explore the modes of politics my interviewees articulated, it is useful to investigate the discursive functions of a limited set of discursive forms. I made use of NVIVO8 in order to identify and code subject positions and discourse topics. Afterwards, I autocoded all instances in which my respondents explicitly used politics-related lexical items. This allowed me to address the following research questions:

1. How do politics-related signifiers function in relation to the discourse topics addressed by my interviewees?
2. How do politics-related signifiers function in relation to the subject positions my respondents positively, negatively or partially identify with?

I also looked for instances in which my interviewees talked about the public sphere. In order to understand the preferred mode of politics and subjectivity articulated by an interviewee, one also needs to understand what it is *not* and how such an interviewee positions his or her self in relation to other entities, practices and discourses in the public sphere. Some of my interviewees explicitly discussed what was going on in "the public sphere" or talked about the need for "more debate" about minority-related issues. But others did not refer debates, public spheres or public opinions in this explicit manner and left their definitions of such terms largely implicit. But even in the latter case, it was possible to analyse their understanding of the public sphere by investigating the constellation of voices they (re-)articulated in their discourse.

Even if my interviewees did not address the logics of the public sphere head-on, they did so in a more implicit way. All of them articulated a sense of politics through a polyphonic (re-)articulation of the various voices that struggle over the meaning of diversity-related norms, values, narratives, practices and institutions across a variety of topics. I therefore added the following questions to the list:

3. How do interviewees link particular discourse topics to each other in their talk about politics and the public sphere?
4. How do interviewees functionally relate the multiplicity of subject positions they imagine to operate in the public realm to each other?

And last but not least, there is the question of the self in relation to the self and in relation to the selves of others. How do respondents talk about their own histories and their own discourse? If the self can be understood as a reification of the processes through which we position our selves in relation to the spatial, temporal, social and (inter-)textual dimensions of discursive reality, the image of the self should be painted all across my

5 Self and Politics in Activist Discourse 271

interviews. It is striking to see how much discourse on political engagement involves fantasies about ideal and horrific modes of selfhood. My fifth and over-arching research question can therefore be formulated as follows:

5. How Do Interviewees Articulate Preferred and Disavowed Modes of Selfhood in Relation to Preferred and Disavowed Modes of Politics

In the upcoming discussions, I will exemplify and discuss the interpretive logics that structure the sense of self and politics as formulated in the activist discourses of my interviewees. Doing so, I will rely heavily on the insights and terminologies introduced in the previous chapters. Nevertheless, before going on, I would like to shed some light on the way I coded and organised my case studies.

There are many ways in which one can carry out an interpretive and functional discourse analysis. There is no such thing as a ready-made toolbox that can be applied to all cases. To engage interpretively and functionally with discourse implies that one takes the functional and reflexive dimensions of articulatory practices into account while investigating the relationships of discursive forms to each other, to the practices in which they are embedded and to the metapragmatic performances of the actors involved. The exact ways in which the process of fixing meaning is to be described depends on the way one articulates academic discourse with the discourses under investigation in the process of constructing a problematic.

In order to find answers to the research questions outlined above, I chose to make use of a CAQDAS tool called NVIVO8. This program allowed me to investigate articulations of self and politics in a systematic manner. Each interviewee whose discourse I will rearticulate in this chapter received a separate NVIVO8 project, a separate coding tree and his or her own discourse analysis. My main goal was to understand the way intellectuals and activists articulated preferred modes of subjectivity with preferred modes of politics in self-critical ways, articulating themselves to the large-scale logics they distinguish in the public realm. The decision to analyse the discourses of my interviewees as separate case studies was informed by my interest in the creative and reflexive ways in which they may or may not loosen the grip of ideology. I did not want to conflate the varied usage of similar and identical linguistic forms in a single coding tree.

Discourse studies do not require coding. Qualitative coding is a heuristic and a mode of analysis that is more commonly deployed in the contexts of content analysis and grounded theory. Discourse studies and grounded theory should not be confused with each other but some aspects of the grounded theory heuristic can be adopted and adapted for discourse studies, on condition that one engages in a critical process of (re-)articulation. The grounded theory approach to data can be described as "a qualitative research method that uses a systematic set of procedures to develop an inductively derived grounded theory about a phenomenon" (Strauss and Corbin 1990, 24). This inductive process starts with coding or codifying data, an analytical procedure whereby one can make use of software programs such as NVIVO8.

The name NVIVO is derived from a key concept of grounded theory: in vivo coding. This type of coding happens at a low level of abstraction. In vivo codes are basically analytical labels that make use of the actual language found in the data. They are (reformulations of) terms used by the research subjects themselves. They are meant to grasp "what is significant" to those whose discourses and practices we study (Saldaña 2013, 91). In this research project, I have applied in vivo codes for the subject positions and discourse topics articulated by my interviewees, sticking as closely as possible to their original formulations in order to determine the spatial, social, institutional and political co-ordinates to which they orient themselves.

Grounded theorists do not always agree about the way in vivo codes should be linked to each other and to the researcher's background knowledge, theories and literature. Glaser takes the more radically objectivist stance. He argues that researchers should approach data without *a priori* research problems and questions. All practical and theoretical background knowledge could be harmful since the researcher could superimpose his or her categories on the data. Strauss and Corbin take a different stance, recommending an intensive study of relevant literature before the empirical work begins. They also propose a multiphased coding process whereby researchers organise in vivo codes in hierarchic relations in a process of

5 Self and Politics in Activist Discourse

axial coding. These axial codes articulate relationships between codes at lower levels of abstraction. Here, the researcher clearly articulates his or her own concepts with the data under investigation (Titscher et al. 2000, 81–82).

Nevertheless, both types of grounded theory are marked by a rather objectivist bias that is rather incompatible with the idea of research as an articulatory practice. Classic grounded theory can be counted among the most positivist qualitative research methods. Postmodern approaches to social reality criticised grounded theorists for being epistemologically naïve and voyeuristic. However, most critics do not realise that many researchers revitalised the grounded theory approach by taking a radical constructivist turn. Even though grounded theory has been interpreted by many people as a constructionist approach from the very beginning, the methodological procedures articulated by Strauss and Corbin gave this heuristic an objectivist cast (Charmaz 2008, 400–401). Sensitising concepts derived from literature, written memo's that systematically reflect upon every aspect of the research process and the analytical practice of coding itself, supposedly constitute a 'basis' that 'grounds' inductive theories about the subject under investigation.

Critical students of discourse and grounded theorists commonly share a preference for 'open' styles of research and stress the importance of reflexivity at every stage of the research process. Pragmatist-based grounded theory and poststructuralist modes of discourse theory are also alike in their argument for a reconfiguration of the relationship between theory and practice. But there are differences as well. Whereas grounded theory tends to focus on the subject as an entry point in the analysis, this is rarely the case in poststructuralist discourse theory where the subject is deemed to be a (pragmatic) effect of the discursive processes that constitute the main focal points for analysis (Gasteiger and Schneider 2014a, 143–145). Moreover, discourse analysts tend to be more sensitive to the question what shifting form/function relationships in discourse may tell us about discursive reality.

Generally speaking, discourse theory is more radically constructivist than traditional grounded theory. Some discourse analysts are therefore very sceptical with respect to the added value of coding and the usage of CAQDAS programs. For instance, Macmillan argues that CAQDAS packages are useful for practical tasks such as holding, organising, coding, searching and retrieving (fragments of) texts. But she also argues that the use of CAQDAS can be time-consuming and that the associated procedures may restrict the scope of discourse analysis. She concludes that "using CAQDAS with DA can, at best, be more time consuming than useful, and at worst, can steer the analyst away from the task of analysis" (MacMillan 2005). However, I am inclined to side with authors who adopt a critical but welcoming stance and argue that the analytical techniques and technologies of grounded theory can be adapted for doing various types of discourse studies (Gasteiger and Schneider 2014b, 165).

Any articulation of grounded theory techniques within discourse studies requires a critical and reflexive attitude on the part of the researcher. CAQDAS based on grounded theory principles certainly has drawbacks (Gasteiger and Schneider 2014b). For instance, codes in NVIVO can only be organised hierarchically. This makes the program rather unsuited for tracing the structure of networked intertextual and interdiscursive relationships between discursive elements. It has not been developed as a tool to investigate discourse as a system of dispersion of statements (Gasteiger and Schneider 2014b, 176–171, 177). At the same time, it is possible to rearticulate the functions of such CAQDAS tools for the purpose of discourse-oriented research. The very process of coding can be conceptualised as a process of (re-)articulation (Howarth 2000, 140–141; Glynos and Howarth 2007, 180–181). NVIVO allows researchers to code (parts of) documents under labels called *nodes* (Gibbs 2007, 31–46). Consider the way Gibbs describes the function of these *nodes* or codes:

> *A node in NVIVO is a way of bringing together ideas, thoughts and definitions about your data, along with selected passages of text. Passages of text from one or more documents are connected to a node because they are examples of the idea or concept it represents. This process is called coding the text at a node. This brings together passages of text that are about the same thing or indicate similar ideas, concepts, actions, descriptions, and so on.* (Gibbs 2007, 31)

If every stage of the research process involves processes of (re-)articulation, CAQDAS tools such as codes and memos are techniques of

5 Self and Politics in Activist Discourse 275

articulatory practice. By coding a discursive element as a node, researchers perform an act of (re-)articulation. The coding process constitutes a strategy through which researchers can explore how actors fix meaning. At the same time, the very process of coding is a clear example of an attempt to arrest the flow of meanings generated in particular contexts of enunciation, on the part of researchers themselves. Researchers and research subjects are therefore engaged in a practice of co-articulation. This is a point that has also been made by constructivist grounded theorists who stress that neither data nor theories are discovered but co-constructed by researchers and research subjects, each of them bringing in their own perspectives, theories and data:

> *My constructionist approach makes the following assumptions: (1) reality is multiple, processual, and constructed – but constructed under particular conditions; (2) the research process emerges from interaction; (3) it takes into account the researcher's positionality, as well as that of the research participants; (4) the researchers and researched coconstruct the data – data are a product of the research process, not simply observed objects of it. Researchers are part of the research situation, and their positions, privileges, perspective and interactions affect it.* (Charmaz 2008, 402)

The idea that researchers should recognise their prior knowledge and theoretical preconceptions in dialogue with the data under investigation connects nicely with the idea of the active interview proposed by Gubrium and Holstein and with the idea of research as an articulatory practice (Gubrium and Holstein 2003c, Glynos and Howarth 2007). As Charmaz points out, "the constructionist version of grounded theory redirects the method from its objectivist, mid-20th century past and aligns it with 21st century epistemologies" (Charmaz 2008, 402). The process of coding should therefore not be considered in terms of a so-called objective practice of labelling whereby data speak for themselves. Rather, coding is an articulatory practice of contextualisation that impacts on the meanings of the labelled identities, voices, statements and/or practices.

In the context of this research project, I have chosen to code subject positions and discourse topics. It is therefore important to keep in mind that the coding process itself does not constitute a complete discourse analysis. Coding is neither a necessary nor a sufficient condition for carrying out discourse studies. Nevertheless, in order to understand the logics informing the preferred modes of politics and subjectivity articulated by my interviewees, it is useful to focus on a selection of discursive dimensions. One may choose to code frames, narratives and/or genre-based aspects of discursive organisation. I chose to code the topical development of my interviews. One can distinguish between local topics (of sentences, utterances, and short discourse segments) and discourse topics (of more extended stretches of discourse). Discourse topics may consist of multiple (levels of) subtopics. Key lexical items in discourse can be indicative of topics and subtopics (Watson Todd 2005, 94). Identifying discourse topics plays a crucial role in the establishment of interpretive coherence.

Since discourse topics are expressible as noun phrases, labelling them is basically a process of in vivo coding. I coded topics and subtopics. Topic-nodes refer to the over-arching issues I made sure to address in each interview: the development of political points of interest; the development of socio-political engagements; the development of political thought; sources of inspiration; and the specific ways in which the definition of the interview situation was established. The coding of these over-arching topics was a top-down process that can be contrasted with my in vivo coding of subtopics. Subtopics are always grounded in the text itself. For instance, when a stretch of discourse is coded under the topic '(evolving) social and political points of interest articulated by the participant(s)' and under the subtopic 'neoliberalism', this means that the notion of neoliberalism provides coherence for an extended piece of discourse in which an interviewee talks about the development of his or her political points of interest.

The goal of this coding procedure was to allow for an easy identification of big segments of text with high degrees of cohesion that allowed for an inter-subjective realisation of a sense of coherence. Of course, topics and subtopics frequently overlap each other. For instance, it is perfectly possible to discuss the evolution of one's political ideas as well as one's political engagements at the same time. The boundaries between discourse topics are often fuzzy and whether a particular piece of text is about 'integration' or about 'minorities' cannot always be determined in

5 Self and Politics in Activist Discourse

a clear-cut way. It is therefore important to keep in mind that all codes reduce the complexity of discourse and that the basic material for the analysis remains the transcription and the interview itself. My choice to code only one topic and one subtopic simultaneously should not obscure this fact.

An overview of discourse topics coded for a single individual provides a rough idea of the main topics discussed within the context of the interview. But more importantly, it allows for a systematic analysis of the way my interviewees articulated subject positions and politics-related lexical items *across* a variety of shifting topics. In turn, this allows for an identification of the large-scale interpretive logics that structure the subjectivities of my interviewees (Fig. 5.1).

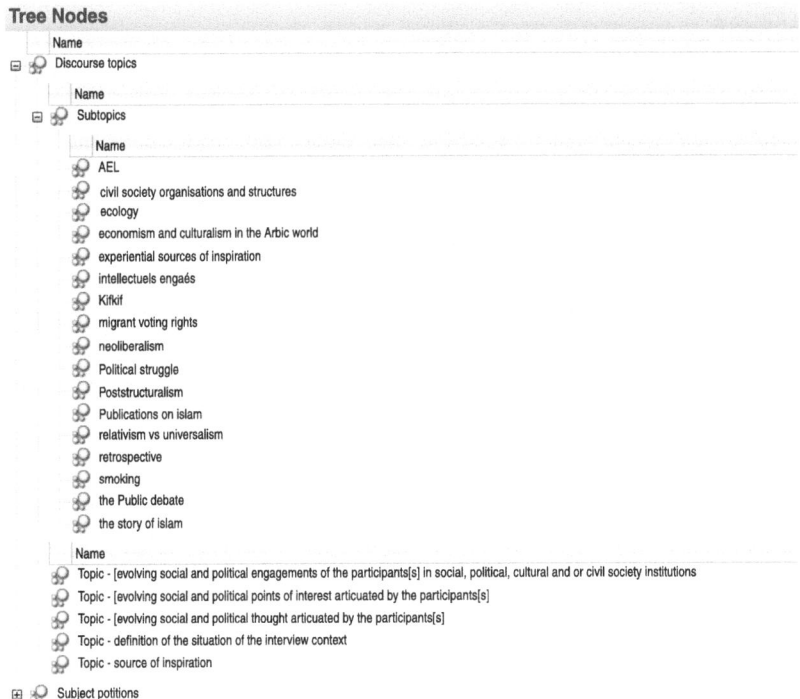

Fig. 5.1 Screenshot of coded topics and subtopics of the interview conducted with Sami Zemni

As interlocutors shift between topics, they activate and mark different aspects of their subjectivity in discourse. By coding the subject positions interviewees positively, negatively or partially identify with, it becomes possible to analyse the ways in which they articulate the network of voices and/or subject positions informing their imagined relationships to and with(in) the public sphere. Subject positions can be defined as enunciative functions that establish relatively fixed positions in public space. Language users relate themselves metapragmatically to such positions, to each other ('s discourses) and to themselves by means of spatial, temporal, social and/or (inter-)textual indexicals. The relationships between subject positions can be reconfigured through political engagements with public actors, practices and centring institutions. It is important to emphasise that subject positions do not code subjectivities, selves or interpretive logics. They operate at a lower level of abstraction and can be identified by means of a process of in vivo coding.

In vivo labels of subject positions stick as closely as possible to the utterances made in the interview itself. I frequently coded over 200 different subject positions in a single interview. This resulted in nodes as varied as: allochthon; atheist; autocrat; Christian; civil servant; communist; conservative; gender-girl; gender-mother; media worker; middle class; nationalist; poststructuralist; racist; Muslim; relativist; teacher; therapist; and worker. I also coded place-related subject positions because it is often unclear whether particular place names index spatial, social or political co-ordinates. The same interview therefore contains labels such as place—America; place—Middle East; and place—Third World. Party-political subject positions and positions related to civil society organisations were coded as well.

As I have emphasised before, individuals may modulate their relationships towards subject positions in rather complex ways. This can be illustrated with reference to the excerpt below. Professor Sami Zemni teaches at the University of Ghent where he co-ordinates MENARG (Middle East and North Africa Research Group). His area of expertise pertains to processes of democratisation and conflict in the Middle East and in Northern Africa. In Flanders, he is also known for his writings on migration, integration, racism and xenophobia. He has been involved in various civil society organisations and has positioned himself publicly in debates

5 Self and Politics in Activist Discourse 279

about minority-related issues. Many of my interviewees recommended me to talk to him in order to get a better insight into the Flemish minority debates. Nevertheless, it may be worth mentioning that in contrast to the other interviewees mentioned in this book, Sami Zemni does not have Moroccan roots but a Tunesian background.

SZ: I always had some scruples to formally join … organisations mmh institutions and so on formally
JZ: mmh
SZ: so I was active as a mmh student … as a volunteer or sometimes a bit more involved to put it like that with mmh … a while within the activity of Amnesty International of the University of Ghent because it had an important third world operation
JZ: yes … yes
SZ: but I never formally joined
JZ: mmh
SZ: the same with respect to all kinds of … political movements which situated themselves on the Left side both green and red.
excerpt 53

The excerpt above contains rather explicit utterances that index his relationship to institutional voices, practices and/or subject positions. These can be coded as 'student' or as 'volunteer'. His utterances also contain adjectives such as "left", "green" and "red" that index socialist and environmentalist subject positions or "movements". But subject positions can also be more implicit. For instance, interviewees make particular lexical choices and intertextual references that index their relations to particular positions.

A mere listing of subject positions does not guarantee insight into the way a subject's sense of self and politics operates. In order to arrive at such an understanding, one needs to investigate the complex metapragmatic patterns that structure the articulation of a particular sense of self in relation to the multiplicity of voices indexed in the discourse under investigation. Contextualisation cues and metapragmatic comments frequently modulate the ways in which interviewees position themselves in relation to other voices and positions active in the public debates in which they engage themselves. Self-talk is often marked by metapragmatic positioning strategies that go unnoticed but provide anchors we can use in order to establish a sense of coherence when interpreting complex discourses and subjectivities.Through subtle metapragmatic strategies, individuals rearticulate and problematise large-scale logics and practices of interpellation that negatively define a preferred mode of politics and political awareness. The associated sense of self cannot be reduced to a matter of positive or negative identifications with particular people, groups, discourses and/or institutions. It is not enough to enumerate the labels individuals accept and reject when talking about themselves and about others. It is at least as important to understand the particular ways in which they modulate these relationships in emotional and metapragmatic ways.In the excerpt above, Sami Zemni articulated an ambiguous attitude with respect to "formally"-joining "institutions", "organisations" and—as we will see—"structures". His "scruples" for doing so and the associated feelings of ambivalence are part and parcel of a subjectivity constructed at the crossroads of conflicting and overlapping academic and political discourses. We can find traces of this mode of subjectivity all across the interview with Sami Zemni. Since I am first and foremost interested in the way intellectuals and activists articulate a preferred sense of self and politics, not all subject positions and discourse topics need to be investigated in detail. I will restrict my attention to those subject positions and topics that prove to be relevant for the way my interviewees articulate large-scale interpretative logics on politics and the self.

5.2 Observations on Ambivalence in Political Discourse and Subjectivity

Sami Zemni's doubts, questions and uncertainties about organisational and narrative "structures" in the public realm paradoxically allow him to articulate a more or less coherent sense of self and politics. He does not understand politics as a realm "between the political and the private" but equates it with "the public sphere" as a whole. Politics is about "the art of the possible", about "making decisions" and about "dreaming" about "what society we want to become". At the same time, he argues that politics implies a "collision of particular interests" and involves "making

5 Self and Politics in Activist Discourse 281

a choice" between particular interests presented as "general interests". Moreover, he links politics to the question "how to conceptualise a community in the year 2009 ... which is not based on nationalism" or "on a particular conceptualisation of religion". According to him "politics" itself should provide an answer to this question. The conversation continues as follows:

> JZ: politics in the sense of ...
> SZ: What connects person a to person b, who happens to live in the same territory ... ? The N-VA[1] would say "language eh"
> JZ: mmh
> SZ: uhm and I don't know, the Vlaams Belang[2] [would say] "culture, our values" and so on and I don't know ..., and the liberals are kind of moving towards that as well eh "freedom, democracy" and so forth ... . But you don't solve anything with that, that's just ... that's just woolgathering. I think the problems that arise are also ... . How are you going to make sure ... that uhm people who live somewhere actually have something to say about the future of the place they live in eh ...?
> JZ: mmh
> SZ: uhm, as much democracy as possible. And then the question becomes "on what ... on what level does one deal with these issues in the best way?"
> JZ: yes
> SZ: And I think that one should be very flexible about this. There are certain uhm ... well, I think it may be necessary to decentralise in certain respects, ... to uhm, make cities and municipalities more important, and with respect to other issues, I think it is more important to strengthen Europe.
> **excerpt 54**

To Zemni, politics is a matter of articulation. It is a matter of asking oneself "what connects" people living "on the same territory". His preferred mode of politics implies that people have something "to say" over "the future of the place they live in". And even though he is certain that this control has to be exercised with "as much democracy as possible", he

---

[1] N-VA (New Flemish Alliance) (Dutch: Nieuw-Vlaamse Alliantie): a popular right wing, neoliberal and ethically conservative Flemish nationalist party chaired by Bart De Wever.
[2] Vlaams Belang (English: Flemish interest)—the successor of the far right VB (English: Flemish bloc) that was condemned for racism.

is still wondering at "what level" this democratic control over territory should be exercised. But whatever the adequate level of political organisation might be, Zemni disqualifies nationalist discourses that attempt to define the good political community in terms of a common "language", a common "culture" or a common set of "values". He also opposes liberal discourse on "freedom" and "democracy" as mere "wool-gathering".

Zemni is sceptical about religious, liberal and nationalist criteria for establishing a political community because of the homogenising logics such discourses tend to promote. According to him, future political communities should not be based on "language, culture, or any other homogeneous concept of being together". Instead, he sketches an ideal scenario in which "what binds us" is the mere fact "that we are entering the public debate together" while addressing "each other as equals". Nevertheless, even this beatific fantasy is not completely satisfactory to Zemni, for he is aware of the fact that such a situation in which "power is almost completely ... lacking" constitutes a big theoretical and practical problem.

SZ: Yes, ... yes, ... So I think that's the future, one cannot return to a political community based on language, culture, or any other homogeneous concept of being together, ...
JZ: mmh
SZ: But what binds us? The fact that we are entering the public debate together, ...
JZ: mmh
SZ: and address each other as equals.
JZ: yes
SZ: Of course, the problem is that one, ... because I don't believe in this, and this is the main problem of course, like, well, you write about that as well, you did so in ... . Habermas' concept of public communication is one without, ... where the, ... concept of power is almost completely uhm ... lacking eh,
JZ: mmh
SZ: and of course, that's a big problem.
excerpt 55 – 06/04/2009

Even though public debate constitutes the centre of Zemni's preferred mode of politics, he refuses a power-free Habermassian approach to discourse and politics. He does not believe in a mode of analysis and engagement that does not take "the concept of power" into account. Zemni's experience with coercive discourses and institutions in the public realm leave him with an ambivalent attitude towards social, political, intellectual and narrative "structures" as bases for political engagement. His feelings of ambivalence partly result from interpellations that conflict with his preferred mode of political subjectivity. But they also result from a tension between academic and political modes of subjectivity.

5.2.1 Being Dragged into the Stories and Debates on Islam

During his student years, Sami Zemni started to explore the question "how society works and how it could work better" in the context of organisations such as Amnesty International and to a lesser extent in the Ghent-based student organisation Politeia. In the nineties, he was approached by various political parties that were looking for "an allochthon who was … articulate (laughs) in Dutch". Such people were "spread thinly" at the university and "in the social sciences in general". After a stay in France, Zemni returned to Belgium in 1994 and started to work at the university of Ghent.

Upon his return to Ghent, Sami Zemni got involved in the debates on Islam. He got on the board of the inter-academic network AGI (Academics for Equal Treatment of Islam) and later became chairman of FOGI (Forum for Equal Treatment of Islam), an initiative that "wanted to bring together a group of secular and mostly rather atheistic humanist professors with Muslims". Zemni frames his engagements for AGI and FOGI as "a kind of opposition" against "the way in which the word integration was described" in the wake of "the first Black Sunday" and in the context of early anti-racist campaigns such as "Hand in Hand". Other people involved in these projects included intellectuals and activists such as "Herman de Ley" and "Jan Blommaert". FOGI was meant to "bring together" such progressive intellectuals with Muslims "who wanted to profile themselves" as such "in the public sphere".

SZ: and then I mean real Muslims not ... a bad word eh but allochthons uhm, they searched and they found [them], mostly in the Ghent region, ... with people who wanted to profile themselves as Muslim in the public sphere.

excerpt 56 – 06/04/2009

FOGI was also created in order to function as an interface for officials of the city of Ghent and Muslims who were prepared to position themselves publicly as such. Zemni claims that the organisation was eventually shut down as the city of Ghent started to bypass FOGI in order to communicate directly with Muslims on issues such as the organisation of Muslim-related religious activities. Nevertheless, in spite of this rather successful outcome, Zemni quickly "started to realise" that henceforward, he "would hardly ever become a member of organisations" and that his "engagement would be oriented toward the scientific, the academic, the intellectual". But even these academic engagements make him feel rather uncomfortable. Interestingly, it is this discomfort that provides a great deal of consistency with respect to the various issues Sami Zemni engages with in the context of this interview.

SZ: But even there in the academic world, I always experienced mixed feelings about it ... because I always felt a tension between uhm ... the positionings with respect to social standpoints, uhm political ideas, and uhm the rather analytical background ... .
JZ: mmh
SZ: I think there is a tension between those, and ... well sometimes uhm ... sometimes it ... sometimes it doesn't fit, I have to say, and because of that I don't like to be uhm captured by too many structures ... . And I slowly came to realise that, because, as far as I can be the judge of this ... and this may be a bit arrogant if I am going to put it this way, but this is how I experienced it back then, ... between say '95 and '96 and let's say uhm 2001, I felt isolated symbolically ... . Back then, I had no knowledge of other allochthons, except for Meryem Kanmaz who I met in '98 '99, because we had written a research proposal ... about those mosques, got the grant and announced vacancies, and she proved to be the best candidate.
JZ: mmh yes

SZ: Uhm so uhm she started to work at the university then. And as far as I knew, she was the only other allochthon, if I may use that word one more time, who was kind of, partly, dealing with similar issues, and with whom I could talk about that.
excerpt 57 – 06/04/2009

The excerpt above contains several tropes that are distributed all across the interview on Sami Zemni's political engagements. The "tension" and the lack of "fit" between "social standpoints", "political ideas" and academic or "analytical" subject positions make him feel rather uncomfortable. This discomfort is described in terms of a general dislike of being "captured by too many structures". As we will see, this attitude does not only inform Zemni's attitude with respect to civil society organisations and political movements. It also informs his attitudes with respect to the ideological narratives that inform the debate about Islam and the Left in Flanders. As he would become more aware of the "structure" of these debates, he would become more reluctant to engage himself in this way.

If we are to understand Zemni's preferred mode of subjectivity and politics, it is important to take a look at what he means by "the structure of the societal debate" and by his talk about being "sucked" or "dragged into the debate" on Islam. Zemni acknowledges that he has been less involved in the public debate on Islam in the last two years preceding the interview. He justified the fact that he took "less standpoints with respect to Islam in the last two years" with reference to the "structure of the societal debate" that does not allow one "the chance to do one's thing in the media". This "thing" involves an explanation of "the fact that Muslims fall back onto their own identity" in terms of a reaction to "racism" as an "ideological structure" and in terms of a failure of Flemish institutions dealing with "education, the unions and sports" to integrate Muslims successfully into their operation.

SZ: Because, the fact that Muslims fall back onto their own identity has to do with the fact that education, the unions, sports, and so on have largely failed. And that is a societal issue. Not … not so much an issue of people, because that is something that uhm … many people do not want to understand, like, I think that Jan Blommaert, when he says like "Flanders is racist", it's not because … x number of people are racist … . We are not dealing

with an ideological structure that is used to [legitimate] the behaviour of bad individuals .... So uhm, ... that has always been kind of the red thread throughout all of my engagement. But perhaps, because of that I uhm ... occupy less standpoints with respect to Islam in in the last two years, because I thought that uhm ... yes ... uhm .... Because of the structure of the societal debate at the moment you didn't have or one doesn't have the chance to do one's thing in the media in order to show that it [Muslims falling back onto their own identity] has to do with other issues [than Islam].
excerpt 58 – 06/04/2009

Zemni metapragmatically distinguishes between two "stories" that characterise the discursive structure of the debate on Islam in Flanders: "a story about Islam" and "a story about the Left". The combination of these stories in an increasingly problematic media context made it ever more difficult for him to tell his alternative story about Islam from the point of view of an "intellectuel engagé" in mainstream media. Even though his involvement in the debate on Islam was clearly a choice of his own during his AGI and FOGI years, he felt like he was increasingly being "dragged into the debate", being "sucked too much ... into that story about Islam" in the post-"9/11" era. The problem is that this debate—as it was being waged in mainstream discourse—forced him in a defensive position. Professor Zemni describes the "problem" of going along "with always taking up the defence of Islam" as follows:

> SZ: Uhm but of course, the problem is that when it is *bon ton* to ... to bash Islam and I don't know ... then you cannot deploy their discourse about Islam against them .... By the way, I always knew that the entire debate about "Islam this" and "Islam that", you can ... uhm .... With every religion you can legitimate uhm an inquisition as well as a liberation. So, you can do that with Islam as well. I therefore always considered it simplistic to say "Bin Laden has nothing to do with Islam", but I consider it even more simplistic to say that Bin Laden equals Islam ... uhm to put it in an over-simplified way .... But perhaps I went along with that ... for too long.
excerpt 59 – 06/04/2009

As we will see, Zemni considers his defensive position to be undesirable because the more one focuses on Islam as a problem, the less one can say about the more important social, economic and political issues he prefers to address in the context of the minority debates. Upon reading my analysis of our interview, Zemni emailed me and asked me to clarify this point as follows: "The obsession with Islam is not a psychological deviation, but rather a symptom of the gradual loss of politics and ideas on how to live together. To talk about Islam means to be silent about many other things. It usually acquits us from the responsibility to explain and contextualise the real causes of social problems". The problem with the dominant story about Islam is that it hardly provides space for voices that point at the fact that "every religion" can be used for purposes of "inquisition" as well as "repression". Zemni deplores having gone along too much "with always taking up the defence of Islam". The problem is that in the end, this leads to a reinforcement of the culturalist logic he seeks to criticise.

The second story Zemni cannot identify with is a "story about the Left" in which "the Left" is deemed incapable of "embodying the universal" because "it got ensnared in a cultural relativism where all cultures are equal". Zemni points out that people such as Wim van Rooy[3] and Benno Barnard[4]—traditionally associated with the Left and "who did not have

---

[3] Wim van Rooy and his son Sam van Rooy co-edited a book called *De Islam: kritische essays over een politiek religie* (English: *Islam: critical essays about a political religion*). Even though they describe their work as a critique of ideology, their book has been welcomed as "critical" by some and condemned as "islamophobia collected" by others (Carpentier 2011). I fully agree with professor Zemni that this book constitutes an illustrated guide of contemporary culturalist discourse on Islam in Flanders and in the Netherlands. It is worth noticing that Sam van Rooy got kicked out of Geert-Wilders' anti-Islamic Party of Freedom (PVV) after posting a YouTube clip of some Muslim women that walked past him in burkas in the Netherlands. This was the comment he posted alongside the clip: "Suddenly that scum passed by. So I decided to film them right away. Or should I consider it to be normal that my peace and quiet in Scheveningen is being spoiled by that type of imported backwardness out of the Islamic sandbox" (Carpentier 2011).

[4] On March 31, 2010, the writer Benno Barnard was invited by the non-confessional service of the University of Antwerp in order to give a lecture titled *Long live God. Away with Allah* (Dutch; Lang leve God. Weg met Allah). This lecture was interrupted by a group of Muslims who reportedly shouted "Allahoe Akbar" (English: God is Great). The extremist Muslim website of *Sharia4Belgium* called on Muslims to come to this lecture, and to respond to "this provocation" by Barnard. According to Benno Barnard, it was only due to the presence of his own bodyguards and of the police that he did not end up in a hospital after this lecture (GVA 2010). Barnard framed this incident as a breach of free speech and democratic principles. According to Jan Blommaert, Barnard's response is indicative of the way Muslims have been represented in Flanders throughout the last decades. In this sense, the men of *Sharia4Belgium* are depicted as so-called typical Muslims—that is, "guys who are either against free speech, who avoid or obstruct public debate,

anything to do with the Vlaams Belang"—now say "exactly the same things" as the far right. Zemni refuses the discourse of those who claim cultural superiority. He prefers to talk with those who "do not think that we are superior" but nevertheless argue that one "should still be able to take a universal standpoint and not get bogged down in ... a relativism that justifies no matter what". Sami Zemni does "not completely agree" with this idea either, but he does grant more legitimacy to this variety of the "story on the Left". Consider the following excerpt:

> SZ: and even though I do not completely agree with this type of criticism, there is some truth to it, in the sense that I too ... grew up in an academic world that was ... for a long time ... uhm well ... when I ... started to study and started to read and so on ... I think those were the heydays of ... of post-colonialism, of Derrida, of the rediscovery of Foucault ... of deconstruction ... new versions of poststructuralism and so on. I know you are dealing with that eh ...
> JZ: (laughs) mmh
> SZ: and somewhere I do think this uhm ... has gone too far somehow ... in the sense that ...
> JZ: mmh
> SZ: I still think there is a lot of interesting stuff in there. It's not like I am going to reject all of that all of a sudden, but it is a fact that I have been dissatisfied for a long time ... with respect to the translation of certain difficult writings into ... into uhm determinations of political standpoints in reality.
> **excerpt 60 – 06/04/2009**

The excerpt above is important because it shows how the tensions between academic and political discourses inform Zemni's discourse at an individual level. Zemni explains how he "grew up in an academic world" characterised by "post-colonialism", "deconstruction" and

---

and who rob someone of his democratic right to speak". According to Blommaert, little has changed since Edward Said published his critique of the way Muslims are represented in Western media in *Covering Islam* (Said 1981, Blommaert 2010b). The moderate Muslim is still considered to be an exception—if considered at all. Benno Barnard was also present at the presentation of *De Islam: kritische essays* by Wim and Sam van Rooy at Flanders' biggest book fair (*de boekenbeurs*) in 2010. Sharia4Belgium dissolved itself in 2012. In 2015, Fouad Belkacem was sentenced to 12 years of jail because of hate crimes and inciting violence with respect to non-Muslims. Several members of *Sharia4Belgium* have left Belgium to wage Jihad in Syria.

"poststructuralism". He does not reject these perspectives, but he does problematise the relationship between "certain difficult writings" and the practice of translating these writings into "political standpoints in reality". His acknowledgement that there is "some truth" to "the story about the left" being ensnared in "cultural relativism" refers first and foremost to this issue of translation or (re-)articulation. I will explore this issue further in the upcoming section. As we will see, Zemni's feelings of ambivalence with respect to his position(s) in the public realm are to a great extent mediated by the intellectual references that inform his thought.

Sami Zemni's attitude with respect to the narrative and organisational structures that organise Flemish debates on Islam is marked by a high degree of political awareness. He is particularly critical of those discourses that tend to entrap him in subject positions that incite him to articulate himself in a way that reinforces the culturalist logics informing right-wing discourse on Islam and Muslims in Flanders. He is also critical of those organisational structures that do not allow him to distinguish between his own voice and the organisation itself. The ambivalence Zemni experienced is a direct consequence of the overlap between academic and political discourses on Islam and culture-related issues. Taking this into account, it becomes clear why some modes of engagement appeal more to him than others.

SZ: (this turn is a continuation of an ongoing turn) Engagement in Kif Kif has always appealed to me, because over there uhm, I could distinguish between the organisation and myself eh. So uhm ... uhm, Kif Kif was not an organisation. It is rather like a network or something. It is rather a platform where all sorts of things were possible, within certain limits of course ... .
JZ: yes
SZ: And uhm that appealed to me because I knew that a multiplicity of standpoints was possible because I, well ... with those other organisations there was always the problem like ... "How long do you stay with an organisation where you think that this or that does not completely align with your own ideas?"
excerpt 61 – 06/04/2009

In spite of his general scepticism with respect to "organisations" and "structures", Sami Zemni admits that "engagement" in the context of Kif Kif "has always appealed" to him. In order to understand this, it is important to understand that he does not qualify Kif Kif as an "organisation" or "structure". He understands Kif Kif in terms of a "platform" or a "network" that allows for "a multiplicity of standpoints". The question of complete ideological alignment is less acute in such a context. For instance, opinion articles are generally signed with individual names and not with the name of the organisation itself. Consequently, Zemni feels less easily trapped or sucked into a particular ideological narrative or structure.

5.2.2 The Search for a Platform for Public Engagement

Sami Zemni's spatial metaphor of "a platform" as a good "basis" for political engagement does not merely apply to civil society networks such as Kif Kif. He also uses this metaphor in order to relate himself to his intellectual sources of inspiration. Zemni is looking for ways to counter dominant stories on Islam and the Left in Flanders and wonders to what extent postcolonial, poststructuralist and deconstructivist texts can "provide a solid basis for social action". He acknowledges that there is "a lot of interesting stuff" in the work of authors such as Derrida and Foucault but thinks that this type of writing constitutes "a very bad platform for social action". The writings of such authors are often too difficult to translate into "concrete standpoints". Nevertheless, Zemni continues his search for an intellectual "platform" from which dominant stories about Islam and the Left can be challenged.

Zemni agrees with activists such as Ico Maly who argue that "it is all about reclaiming hegemony" and about developing "another discourse". But the question is how one may do so in a way that allows one to "answer firmly and correctly to attacks coming from the right". Zemni admitted that he felt "unhappy" about a great deal of "literature". As a case in point, he referred to the work of acolytes of Edward Said. Their texts became so complicated that they did "not provide a solid basis for social action any more".[5] This does not mean that Zemni distances himself from Said's discursive perspective. He positions himself as a "fan" and does not consider Said to occupy the "relativist" position he associates with Said's acolytes. He also makes it clear that he refuses to move "to the right" in spite of this difficult intellectual and political situation.

> SZ: (this excerpt is a continuation of the excerpt above) For instance, I am a very big fan of [Edward] Said, but a lot of people categorise Said within poststructuralism and so on. And indeed, he is a linguist, he is a linguist, he occupied himself with language and you name it, that's true. But he did not belong at all to that group of … let us call them relativists for the time being, and I don't mean that in a simplistic sense like the rightists always use it today … . So, I remain a big fan of Said, but it is true that many of his … 'acolytes' …, according to me, wrote all sorts of … incredibly complicated pieces, that, according to me, do not provide a solid basis for social action any more … .
> JZ: yes
> SZ: uhm … and that is a difficult situation at the moment because you uhm … uhm … if you reach that conclusion, one quickly kind of moves towards the right, I think. But I don't do that.
> **excerpt 62 – 06/04/2009**

---

[5] The book *Orientalism* launched Edward Said's intellectual career. In this book, he explicitly acknowledges his debt to Michel Foucault. However, in contrast to Foucault, Saïd believes in the deciding influence that individual writers may exert on a discourse. Said describes orientalism as a discourse based on an ontologic and epistemological dichotomy between the *Orient* and the *Occident* (Said 2005, 27). His book is both a description and a critique of orientalist ideas, notions and practices that have survived until this day. As Zemni points out, Said may be labelled as a linguist in the sense that he was part and parcel of what we may call a linguistic or discursive turn in the social sciences. As such, he contributed to disciplines as diverse as literary theory, the history of ideas, music, the sociology of intellectuals and political analysis. Islam was a continuous point of interest to Said. But it should also be noted that Said's interest in this topic was closely connected to other issues such as the role of the intellectual in the public sphere. To Said, critical intellectuals should be involved in "the creation and the critique of borders – physical, national, cultural and spitritual" (Turner 2004, 173–174). Said was a prominent critic of Huntington's *Clash of Civilizations* (Meeks 2003, 137). He explicitly wrote that taking up the role of an intellectual implies going beyond the suffering of particular nations and cultures. Intellectuals should explore the universal aspects of human suffering and oppression in order "to universalize the crisis, to give greater scope to what a particular race or nation suffered, to associate that experience with the suffering of others" (Said 1994 cited in Turner 2004, 174).

Sami Zemni admires intellectuals such as Jean-Paul Sartre who were able to craft an intellectual "platform" on which they could base their "social activism".[6] He does not feel so much attracted by the latter's Marxist humanism as by his success in bringing his "social activism" and his "writing" "into a symbiosis". It is this symbiotic relationship that "has largely been undone" by "poststructuralism at large" and by the works of Lévi-Strauss, Foucault and Derrida specifically, according to Zemni. In order to clarify his point, he described a scene in which an "Iraqi refugee" he met in Jordan asked him to explain the title Jean Baudrillard's "*The Gulf War did not take place*.[7] Such encounters and conversations leave Zemni with a "sour feeling".

---

[6] Sartre emphasised the systematic nature of colonial practice(s) and discourse(s). His approach is closely related to the Marxism of the anti-colonial movements. As such, it articulated the universal principles of Marxism with the local conditions of (post-)colonial contexts. Interestingly, Sartre's emphasis on colonialism as a system went hand in hand with an affirmation of the significance of individual subjective experience (Young 2006, xix-xxi). Sartre acknowledges that Western humanism and human rights discourse in general "had worked by excluding a majority of the world's population from the category of the human". However, contrary to anti-humanists such as Althusser, Sartre refused to do away with the concept of humanism altogether. Quite the contrary, he attempted "to articulate a new anti-racist humanism, which would be inclusive rather than exclusive, and which would be the product of those who formed the majority of its new totality" (Young 2006, xvii). Young points out that even though Lévi-Strauss' and Althusser's critiques of Sartre "enabled the later postcolonial deconstruction of the ethnocentric premises of European philosophy, it was Sartre's work, particularly of the 1940's, that was most influential on postwar French anti-colonial intellectuals" such as Césaire, Fanon and Memmi (Young 2006, xviii). Interestingly, in his book on the debate about Islam, Sami Zemni argues for the figure of an intellectual engaged in a practice of humanist critique. This type of humanism is never finished. It involves a view of history that includes other perspectives than those of Western man. It involves a plea against types of universalism that consider forms of diversity to be deviations. It is a plea against unidimensional and homogenising thought. At the same time, Zemni describes this type of humanism as a plea against relativism. Consequently, Zemni's humanist critic is someone who builds intellectual bridges without shying away from potential conflict with majorities and/or minorities (Zemni 2009, 13–19).

[7] *The Gulf War did not take place* is a compilation of three essays written by Jean Baudrillard. These articles were originally published in the French newspaper *Libération* (Baudrillard 1995). Stephen Pfohl provides us with a book review that summarises some of the key themes addressed by Baudrillard. Baudrillard did not question the horror of the First Gulf War. But he did wonder whether 'war' was still a useful term to describe this event: "promotional, speculative, virtual: this war no longer corresponds to Clausewitz's formula of politics pursued by other means" (Baudrillard quoted in Pfohl 1997). In order to understand Baudrillard's statement, we have to link these articles to his criticism of hyperreality. According to him, we are becoming increasingly immersed in an endlessly mediated and symbolic deterrence of images and simulations. These make it ever more difficult to contact the real. Note the Lacanian overtones here. Pfohl paraphrases Baudrillard as follows: "No matter how deadly its violence, this campaign operated more to deter contact with the 'real' exigencies of history, than – as would be the case with a 'real war' – to open history to the

For Zemni, the issue has never been whether or not he should engage himself, but rather what platforms allow him to position himself in the public realm without getting trapped in the organisational and discursive structures that pin him down in subject positions he does not want to occupy. This attitude informs his stance towards many discourses circulating in civil society and in academia. At the same time, he does not want to idolise thinkers, keeping Mark Lilla's *The reckless mind* in mind. Lilla's book explores how "brilliant minds" such as Arendt, Schmitt, Benjamin, Foucault, Derrida recklessly made "wrong political choices" in favour of causes such as the Iranian revolution or Maoism. Zemni proves to be acutely aware of the fact that the development of an intellectual platform for political activism offers no inherent protection against making such choices. But he does continue his search.

My interview with Sami Zemni is filled to the brim with intertextual references to the work of intellectuals and academics. Together, these references constitute a discursive web, a network and a debate in which Zemni articulates public voices with each other and with a preferred mode of doing politics. The figure of the "intellectuel engagé" appeals strongly to him, but at the same time, Zemni cannot ignore the risk of choosing the wrong intellectual platform. Moreover, translating intellectual ideas into political action involves making things more "concrete" and less "poetical". In postmodern, poststructuralist and postcolonial literature, the "balance" between the concrete and the poetical is "sometimes lost" according to Zemni. This is why he grants Jean Bricmont and Alain Sokal "a point":

> SZ: yes yes Jean Bricmont, and actually, if I am not mistaken, the article was just Jean Bricmont … but the book intellectual impostors was written together with Sokal … . And that kind of did change some things for me

---

agonistic challenge of enemies pitted in general economic struggle with one another." Pfohl criticises Baudrillard for his rather "hyperbolic language and sweeping terms". As such, he makes a point quite similar to Zemni: "The situated complexities and contradictions of Western people's lived reactions to conflicts within the oil-rich Persian Gulf is not well served by such homogenizing language. Nor will Baudrillard's exhortation to oppose the simulated illusions of media 'realism' by becoming 'more virtual than the events themselves' be hailed by many critics as a meaningful strategy of activist resistance" (Pfohl 1997, 139–141).

.... Uhm, not that I agreed with everything, but still, I said like "damned, he has a point", and sometimes when I read, I think like that.
JZ: mmh
SZ: uhm ... an accumulation of issues that are being described like "it's all very beautiful, at times it's almost poetical sometimes"
JZ: mmh
SZ: I've never understood Derrida, I admit that but ... when you read him it all seems fine but let's just try to translate this to ... uhm, imagine a person in the street who says "Could you summarise that for me? What does he want to say with that exactly?"
JZ: yes
SZ: and I always had a problem with that, and according to me, that balance is sometimes lost. And in some pieces I read by Homi Bhaba for instance, about the post-colonial situation and intertextuality, then I think like, well, I almost don't dare to say it because ... of course I feel very humble with respect to such intelligent people as Homi Bhabha, but sometimes I also think like "am I not understanding this very well?" ... or maybe I kind of fail to link it to concrete issues.
excerpt 63 – 06/04/2009

The figure of the "intellectuel engagé" that Zemni seems to aspire is the very opposite of the intellectual impostor criticised by "Jean Bricmont" and "Alain Sokal" during the science wars. Bricmont and Sokal are famous for their critique of poststructuralist and postmodern jargon and for Sokal's famous hoax in the journal *Social Text*.[8] And it is this critique

---

[8] In 1996, the mathematical physicist Alain Sokal sent the bogus article *Transgressing the boundaries: towards a hermeneutics of quantum gravity* to the journal *Social Text* (Sokal 1996b). As soon as this parody of postmodern and poststructuralist discourse was published, Sokal revealed his hoax in the journal *Lingua Franca* in an article called *A physicist experiments with cultural studies*. In this second publication, Sokal asked himself the following question: "Would a leading North American journal of cultural studies – whose editorial collective includes such luminaries as Fredric Jameson and Andrew Ross – publish an article liberally salted with nonsense if (a) it sounded good and (b) it flattered the editors' ideological preconceptions?". He also explained the procedure he used in order to write this text. Sokal was motivated both by intellectual and by political reasons. Intellectually, his article constituted a charge against "a particular kind of nonsense and sloppy thinking: one that denies the existence of objective realities, or (when challenged) admits their existence but downplays their political relevance". Politically, Sokal points out that his anger is triggered by the fact that "most (though not all) of this silliness is emanating form the self-proclaimed left" he considers to turn towards "obscuritanism" in "one or another form of epistemic pluralism" (Sokal 1996a, 4). In collaboration with Jean Bricmont, Sokal would outline his critique in a more systematic way (Sokal and Bricmont 1997).

that sometimes comes to mind when Zemni reads the rather abstract works of authors such as Derrida or Bhabha.[9]

5.2.3 Intellectual Engagements with Culturalist and Neoliberal Logics

There are at least two logics that define professor Zemni's preferred mode of political engagement negatively. These can be named and described in terms of *neoliberal* and *culturalist* logics. According to Zemni, the Left-wing preoccupation with culture and identity has created a situation in which neoliberalism has been neglected for too long as an object of critique. He does not want to "throw away the child with the bathwater" by getting rid of poststructuralist or postmodern literature. According to Sami Zemni, *poststructuralism* allows us *to understand what happens* "elsewhere", in non-Western cultures. The idea that poststructuralism leads to a relativism in which "it's all the same" does not make sense to him. The real problem, is that many left-wing intellectuals fascinated by "culture" and "identity" have ignored issues related to "economics" and "neoliberalism" for too long.

> SZ: (this excerpt is a continuation of an ongoing turn) because I still believe that one should not throw out the baby with the bathwater ... Also, well, according to me, and also according to many others I think, Lévi-Strauss did not write his poststructuralism, his respect for other cultures, ...

---

[9] Homi Bhabha is a postcolonial writer who is probably most famous for his book *The location of culture*. Within this book, Bhabha challenges a multiplicity of aspects related to cultural boundaries. His writings are heavily laced with references to thinkers such as Jacques Lacan, Michel Foucault, Gayatri Spivak, Stuart Hall, Ernesto Laclau and Chantal Mouffe. His notion of intertextuality is borrowed from Bakhtin and Kristeva. In *The location of culture*, he writes that "Culture is heimlich, with its disciplinary generalizations, its mimetic narratives, its homologous empty time, its seriality, its progress, its customs and coherence. But cultural authority is also unheimlich, for to be distinctive, significatory, influential and identifiable, it has to be translated, disseminated, differentiated, interdisciplinary, intertextual, international, and inter-ratial" (Bhabha 1994, 195). He explains how "in the moment of liberatory struggle, the Algerian people destroy the continuities and constancies of the nationalist tradition which provided a safeguard against colonial cultural imposition. They are now free to negotiate and translate their cultural identities in a discontinuous intertextual temporality of cultural difference" (Bhabha 1994, 55). Differently put: "Cultural diversity is also the representation of a radical rhetoric of the separation of totalised cultures that live unsullied by the intertextuality of their historical locations, safe in the Utopian-ism of a mythic memory of a unique collective identity" (Bhabha 1994, 50).

going into other cultures in order to understand them better, in order to conclude like uhm "it's all the same" and so on. No, [he wrote it] in order to understand better what happened elsewhere … . But uhm … I do think that one of the consequences was, that because of that, a tendency was initiated … . And because of that, we have been insufficiently concerned with economics, with neoliberalism that impacted on basically everything from the eighties on, but with respect to Flanders perhaps mostly from the nineties on … . On media structures as well as on the public debate … . Yes, it is simply a farce.
excerpt 64 – 06/04/2009

The fact that postmodern or poststructuralist texts do not provide adequate grounds for criticising the underlying logics of the stories about Islam and the Left in Flanders does not mean that all of these texts become invalid. But since the dominant story about Islam is informed by culturalist logics, one cannot "use the same framework" as a tool "to oppose" the culturalisation of social issues related to Muslims. Zemni recognises that "the cultural", "the human" and "the identity related" aspects of human experience should have "a certain place" in left-wing political projects and academic explanations. But left-wing actors have gone "way too far" in emphasising these aspects of politics at the expense of a critique of the "neoliberal" logics that inform problems of poverty, inequality and "culturalisation".

SZ: I think that the struggle for people, for emancipation, lies elsewhere. Nevertheless … there is still that … the cultural, the human, the identitarian, should also be granted a certain place [in the analysis]. [...] So, I definitely don't want to return to the times of vulgar Marxism or anything like that, or I don't know, to economic determinism. [...] But I do think that it [the cultural, the human, the identitarian] is going way too far … . [...] That is basically the point … . And because of that, it is not always a good thing to, … suppose that well uhm … . The fact that uhm … that unemployment strikes Muslims much harder than others, the fact that poverty and so on is … is uhm … being culturalised, even though we really should be dealing with a socio-political question [...]. And it is difficult to oppose that, if you don't use the same framework in which this is being posited. [...] The culturalisation of these issues is really a deplorable fact.
excerpt 65 – 06/04/2009

5 Self and Politics in Activist Discourse 297

Zemni rejects "vulgar Marxism" and its "economic determinism". But he does argue that the Left-wing tendency to focus almost exclusively on identity and culture-related issues is counter-productive for the story he wants to tell. His point is that a critique of culturalist discourse should go hand in hand with a critique of neoliberalism. In all of this, it is important to keep in mind that Zemni prefers a mode of politics that is based not on homogenising nationalist or religious concepts of community but on a lively and conflict-ridden debate that addresses issues of power. According to him, both the emergence of "anti-Islamic" culturalist discourse and "the fact that many Muslims" turn to "fundamentalist", "conservative" or "reactionary versions" of "Islam" can be explained with reference to a "neoliberal" destabilisation of "social order". This can be illustrated with reference to the excerpt below.

> SZ: And does one have to say like "it's all the fault of neoliberalism"? No. Evidently, it's not as simple as that. In the end it is about your political, economic, social order ... and in America one has pushed the principles of the free market so far, that what remains, is an atomised individual that kind of floats around freely. One has only one possibility left and that is the community, and a community is very easily embedded in a religious tradition eh, and that is what you see with Muslims ... since 9/11 and because of the pressure coming from everywhere, also because of the economic order and so on ... . Because the fact that Muslims fall back onto themselves has to do with the fact that education, the unions, sports, and so on, have partly failed in that respect, ... and that [problem] lies with society ... and not so much with people.
> **excerpt 66**

In the excerpt above, Zemni explains how "neoliberal" or "free market" principles promote a societal model that consists of "atomised" and disconnected individuals. This image constitutes the horrific site of his political fantasy. This logic is directly opposed to Zemni's preferred mode of politics that "binds people to each other". In combination with the post-9/11 context whereby Muslims are increasingly addressed on the basis of their Islamic belonging, many turn to "religious tradition" in their search for "community". In a neoliberal context where "unions", "education" and even "sports" seem to fail in providing a sense of belonging for

Muslims, the latter "fall back onto themselves" and eventually reinforce the culturalist logics that guide contemporary forms of cultural racism and discrimination. Zemni's preferred mode of political engagement is thus opposed to the logics *of neoliberalism* and *culturalisation* that work in tandem within hegemonic stories on Islam and the Left.

5.2.4 Issues of a Young Intellectual 'Allochthon' in the Public Sphere

If Sami Zemni was sucked into the debate on Islam by voices whose discourses were structured according to culturalist logics, it is important to consider how and where this happened. Because if Zemni claims to have been symbolically isolated in the university during his early years as an intellectual, this does not mean that he was isolated from the media. He felt isolated from other so-called "allochthon" intellectuals. The media, in fact, were keen to contact him "as soon as something happened with Muslims". His ability to produce "one liners" got him media access, but at the same time, he felt that the "format" in which he was asked to articulate his ideas did not allow him "to occupy a position". After a while, Zemni felt "abused" by the media and looking back, he wishes he had "dealt with the media … in a completely different manner".

Generally speaking, the media functioned as a very bad platform for Zemni's preferred mode of political engagement. They neither provided the time nor the symbolic space in which he could challenge the logics structuring the debate on Islam. In the excerpt below, we can see how Zemni experienced the media from his position as "a young allochthon in the public sphere". He explains how changes in the Flemish media formats provided him with less and less time to formulate his "one liners" up to the point where he "did not want to be part" of it anymore and "started to figure a lot less in the media". In addition to the problems with televised media interviews and the increasingly limited amount of time he got in order to articulate his analyses as an engaged intellectual, Zemni points out that the nature of "the debate" itself changed significantly around 9/11.

The "tension" between his academic position and discourse on the one hand and his socio-political position as a so-called "allochthon" involved in public debate on the other hand changed after 9/11. The tone of the debate shifted along with the way he was interpellated by interlocutors in the public realm.

> SZ: the public debate was different, if, when you said something people did not like to hear …
> JZ: mmh
> SZ: then I might receive a letter of an uhm e-mail, even though this was not that common back then, … with a remark, a question … uhm and most of all
> JZ: you received those
> SZ: I yes, … because I …
> JZ: ah okay
> SZ: but most of the times it was along the lines of "yes mister Zemni, what you said over there, yes this and that and this". And I always used to, I am always open to that … . But at that moment, I was simply a doctoral student at the University of Ghent uhm … just like John Doe, and after 9/11 that was no longer the case.
> **excerpt 67 – 06/04/2009**

Before 9/11, Sami Zemni frequently got responses from people who reacted to his utterances in mainstream media. At the time, he felt "simply as a doctoral student at the university of Ghent" since he was being addressed on the basis of the arguments and statements made in the public realm. After Al Qaeda flew two planes into the Twin Towers, the nature of the debate changed. People stopped responding with a "remark" or with a "comment" but started to engage in an entirely different type of language games. Zemni describes the post-9/11 climate as a time in which he was being accused of being "a Moroccan Islamist" with "Tunesian roots" and as someone whose discourse was merely "a smokescreen" for his radical intentions. Within this context, "slander" and "character assassination" became "part and parcel of an 'honest' public discussion".

> SZ: I mean, there are open letters circulating on the internet about me where I am considered in terms of some kind of missionary … of Moroccan Islamists, even though I have Tunisian roots, apparently they know all about that. This sort of stuff whereby they are going to consider everything I say … to be a smokescreen behind which I supposedly hide my true intentions.

JZ: yes yes ... yes
SZ: Okay, if this would come from the Vlaams Belang, then you could still contextualise it and laugh with it but is uhm ... this really hits me hard ... it comes from environments of people who simply belong to that generation of people who think that uhm ... an opinion constitutes an argument and for whom every opinion is equally valid, and that you should just ... well uhm one, a character assassination, uhm ... should commit slander as part and parcel of an honest public discussion.
JZ: mmh
SZ: That really hurts me. Honestly speaking, I deplore this a lot, and on top of that, it is uhm well also a reflection of a disappointment ... . Perhaps I was a bit too naïve about that, but uhm ... well ... uhm, ... I am convinced that I am accused of things that my colleagues Carl De Vos and Rik Coolsaet will never be accused of.
excerpt 68 – 06/04/2009

These accusations hurt Zemni because they did not address him on the basis of his preferred intellectual or ideological positions. Instead, they addressed him on the basis of his pre-supposed ethnic, religious or cultural identities. Zemni points out that other academics at his university may be criticised by voices "from the right wing" but would never receive accusations of being "a traitor". This mismatch between Zemni's preferred mode of subjectivity—modelled on the idea of an intellectual engaging himself in a public debate where people struggle to exert maximum democratic control over their environment—and culturalist interpellations such as these, significantly impact on Zemni's sense of well-being.

SZ: And of course, we sometimes talk about that eh. Rik Coolsaet also gets attacked for this and for that, certainly from the right corner ... . But never in a way that ... in an identitarian way, so to say.
JZ: Yes
SZ: you see, one is never going to reproach him for being a traitor, for being badly integrated, ... that sort of stuff
JZ; yes yes
SZ: and of course, that is a severe disappointment, but I really don't feel up to it anymore.
JZ: mmh

SZ: to well , I mean, if I have to prove that I am integrated and all of that ... I have left that behind me a long time ago.
excerpt 69 – 06/04/2009

As was the case with many other people I interviewed, Zemni experienced a "severe disappointment" and felt discouraged by this repetitive confrontation with speech acts and discursive practices that addressed him on the basis of associations with Islam and a perceived allochthon identity according to a culturalist logic. Note that Zemni felt like he was expected to offer proof of his integration *because* and not *in spite* of his active engagement in the public realm. This sentiment is far from unique among my interviewees. Like many others, Zemni articulated an experience in which the public realm offers a narrow set of subject positions for those who seek to criticise mainstream discourses on integration, culture and Islam.

Zemni's preferred mode of subjectivity requires intellectual and organisational platforms in which one can distinguish between one's overall sense of self and the local subject positions one may occupy at a specific point in time. His preferred mode of politics is constructed in opposition to discourses, practices and subject positions that articulate homogenising logics of culturalisation and neoliberalism. But it is also positively informed by a tension between relativist and universalising logics that (re-)articulate his relations to the network of intellectuals, politicians and activists populating his imagination of the public realm. In the chapter on recognition and misrecognition, we will see that the emotional need for such interpretive logics is a direct consequence of the ideological language games that are being played in the public sphere.

5.3 Identifying Large-scale Logics in the Public Realm

In the sections below, I will succinctly discuss the interviews conducted with: Minority Forum director Naima Charkaoui; AEL activists Brahim Harshaoui and Karim Hassoun; and Federation of Moroccan and Global Democratic Organisations (Dutch: *Federatie van Marokkaanse en Mondiale Democratische Organisaties*—FMDO) chairman Youssef Souissi. The goal of this chapter is to exemplify how activists and intellectuals succeed in objectifying and externalising large-scale patterns in the discourses and practices of the societies they seek to change. As we will see, it is very difficult to distinguish between a person's self-interpretations and the social logics he or she observes in society. The logics we name, identify and externalise paradoxically inform our sense of self and politics.

Considering my focus on individual cases, it is important not to lose track of the fact that discourse is a social phenomenon and that our discursive patterns never exclusively belong to a single individual. Many of my interviewees refer implicitly and/or explicitly to each other's positions, discourses and/or organisations. It is even possible to identify similar interpretive logics in the discourses of many interviewees. For instance, Naima Charkaoui and Sami Zemni share a critical attitude with respect to the culturalist discourses that circulate in the public realm. And the interview with Brahim Harshaoui and Karim Hassoun contains elements that are shared with many sympathisers and (former) members of the AEL. For instance, many of my interviewees have problematised discursive practices marked by a *logic of assimilation* and admit to being influenced by AEL discourse.

Nevertheless, individualised use of discourse is always marked by the pragmatic principles of adaptability, negotiability and variability. No two discourses will ever by the same in form, function or meaning because contexts of enunciation are never repeatable. Ultimately, interpretive logics allow for a sense of coherence because logics are basically patterns in the way we articulate discursive elements with particular functions. Two stretches of text or speech may look nothing alike formally and still perform similar interpretive and ideological functions. It is quite likely that people engaged in similar political projects will use similar signifiers, arguments and narratives. But sometimes individuals objectify societal logics more creatively, as I seek to demonstrate with reference to the interview conducted with Youssef Souissi.

By focusing on this selection of people and the way in which they critically identify large-scale patterns or logics in the public realm, I seek to demonstrate the highly adaptable and negotiable ways in which we articulate ourselves to ourselves, to each other and to the societies we live in.

5.3.1 Countering Patronising Logics in the Political Game

The large-scale interpretive logics that inform the self-interpretations and the political engagements of my interviewees are social constructs. Individuals may become partially aware of large-scale interpretive patterns that inform the politics of their societies, but they cannot do so in isolation of the discourses of others. If there is no such thing as a private language, there can be no such thing as a private logic either. All individuals who engage in acts of public critique have to cast a discursive network over the Real. But these nets are too big to be woven by singular individuals. Even the most individualised of discourses can only make sense because its elements are fixed into particular form/function relationships through social convention and the exercise of power.

We already saw that we can think of large-scale societal debates in terms of an ever-shifting network in which agents (re-)articulate and (re-)imagine their relationships to each other, to themselves and to the discursive practices they are engaged in. This public realm is not a homogenous space. It can only be imagined as such. The fact of the matter is that the public only comes to us in a multiplicity of language games and speech events in which actors use discourse in order to cast a net that allows them to fix the meaning of particular identities, experiences and/or practices. At the same time, the casting of this net implies that we position ourselves in relation to others and their discourses. If there is no escape from the political, there is no escape from the social either.

To engage reflexively with discourse means that one can become aware of the way discursive networks ensnare individuals in restrictive patterns. But it also means that we can start to imagine alternative futures. We can (re-)articulate discourse in ways that are more amenable to the selves we want to be and to the societies we want to live in. Individualised as our interpretive experience of such ideological fantasies may be, the articulation of this experience requires us to inscribe and articulate our sense of self with the discourses of others. This can be illustrated with reference to each and every interview conducted in this research project. But as a case in point, I will focus on the interview conducted with Naima Charkaoui, who was director of the Minority Forum from 2001 to 2014.

Naima articulates a unique perspective on issues and concepts such as emancipation, democracy and politics but we can also observe how part of her discourse is informed by the discourses of others. Naima favours a mode of minority political engagement and discourse marked by an *emancipatory logic*. She considered it to be "logical" that the themes of the Minority Forum would appeal to her. The "thematic of minorities in society and the chances they may or may not get" constitutes the "red thread" running through her engagements in the public realm. She seeks to "participate in the debate" on the basis of the voices of "the people themselves" in order to counter the "patronising attitude" that interpellates people as allochthons.

> NC: uhm, so I think, I think that this is kind of the red thread one can distinguish, like yes, a theme that comes from my personal background, that I simply consider to be very important. And because of that, you're also like "yes, if I can work on that, and definitely …". Well, the Minority Forum also appealed to me because there's really this emancipatory aspect to it, you can really participate in the debate …
> JZ: mmh
> NC: from the bottom up, on the basis of the people themselves, and not … on the basis of an institution that works from the top down, with this patronising attitude.
> **excerpt 70 – 29/04/2009**

The *patronising logic* opposed by Naima Charkaoui structures everyday inter-subjective speech events and marks a great deal of mediatised political discourse. It also used to inform her own attitude towards "the South" before she commenced her academic studies in political science and started to work at the Minority Forum. It is a logic that is not so much marked by active acts and claims for domination, as by a "naïve" feeling of superiority with respect to people who supposedly belong to other cultures or who live in other parts in the world. People deploying this logic often "mean well" but nevertheless adopt *essentialist, culturalist* logics as they go.

Naima admits that her perspective on "North-South" relationships has changed over time. As a child, she always wanted to work in the development sector. But she increasingly realised that "the difference" she could make in the South would be "infinitely more small than the difference" she could make in a context she knew better. She did not consider her "competences" as a "political scientist" to provide her with the "expertise" required to be of value in the so-called South. For Naima, there is a patronising logic that runs through Flemish attitudes towards so-called "allochthons" and "the Third World" alike.

> NC: Well, I think that we often kind of like uhm ... take a superior attitude. Like, well, people who come over here have to *inburger* themselves for ten years so to speak, before they become entitled to, to, to, no matter what.
> JZ: mmh
> NC: But we are going to tell them over there how they should manage things, because we .. we don't need to know the language in advance, we can manage with English and French, and they should simply make an effort. We don't need to know how a society like that functions, what its values and norms are. We ... we don't have to know any of that. We can simply be dropped over there, and, and help them ... .
> JZ: mmh
> NC: and this, this logic, I really, also because of my job here [at the Minority Forum], I think,
> JZ: mmh
> NC: because you see how important it is to stick as closely as possible to ... reality. Something like that [Naima's childhood dream to help people in the South], well no, that was actually a naïve idea I had, ... ha, "as if they would be needing me over there", so to speak.
> **excerpt 71 – 29/04/2009**

In the excerpt above, Naima argues that "we" often take a "superior attitude" towards the South that shows in the way we deal with cultural difference. Whereas migrants coming to Belgium are forced to attend courses in *inburgering*[10] in order "to become entitled" to "no matter what", "we" don't hold ourselves to the same standards when we visit countries in the so-called South. Naima sarcastically remarks that "we can simply be dropped over there, and help them" without knowing the

---

[10] For more information on the Dutch notion of *inburgering*, see Sect. 4.3 on *The rise and fall of a Dutch binary pari: allothons vs. autochthons*.

"language", how the society in question functions and what its "values and norms" are. Her experience at the Minority Forum allows her to realise that it was "actually a naïve idea" that "they would be needing" her "over there". As we will see, her studies contributed significantly to this change in perspective.

Naima may be able to recognise the patronising logic informing her childhood desire to be of significance for the South, she also argues that this very logic still informs a great deal of discourse on minority related issues. People often "mean well" in a "patronising" way, but their desire to help people is often based on "naivety". As a case in point, she refers to the way applicants for jobs at the Minority Forum motivate their applications. In the excerpt below, she problematises two types of applicants: those who "still have a lot to learn" but nevertheless articulate a desire "to help people" and those who feel like they are "suitable for working at the forum" because "they have been in touch with strange cultures" around the globe.

> NC: You often see things like "I want to help people", ... "ok, great, you're coming to help us", like, like, with an aura of 'I'm going to help you' ... . Whereas you can see on a CV like "well, ok, you still have a lot to learn about this". There's also the other extreme like "yes I uhm ... I have travelled all around the world, I finished a training period over there, I wrote a paper about it over there, really in all the corners of the world so, ... I am suitable for working at the Forum" ... . Because what is the logic? They have been in touch with strange cultures, so ... they immediately know ...
> JZ: mmh
> NC: And then I think, "come on, that's such a wrong assessment of ... of what we are really", well actually, we don't work on culture ... .
> JZ: mmh
> NC: Perhaps, we will, we might do something about it. Culture is always interwoven with it, but, ... we don't work on strange cultures. We deal with real policy issues. It's the same thing as applying at a union.
> **excerpt 72 – 29/04/2009**

The director of the Minority Forum gets irritated by both attitudes because her Forum focuses less on culture than on so-called "allochthon themes" such as the position of minorities in the labour market, in the housing market and in mainstream media. This is why she says that the Minority Forum does not "work on strange cultures" but on "real policy issues", much like a union would do. The interaction above continues in the excerpt below. Naima emphasises that both types of statements are "patronising" because they push people into "that exotic role". She points out that this makes one feel like "an exotic object in society". In contrast, she prefers a mode of interpellation that addresses minorities as human beings and as citizens that aim to combat the "social exclusion" they experience and to "change something" with respect to so-called allochthon "themes".

> NC: Uhm, So, … and I consider that to be sort of patronising … . Then you really feel like being pushed into that exotic role again, …
> JZ: mmh
> NC: sort of an exotic object in society, like "ah, yes, we are going to help these strange … people, other cultures, and … and this", whereas you really want to be approached as … a human being, as a citizen who may [come] … from a group … that is dealing with social exclusion, who wants to change something about these themes … .
> JZ: mmh
> NC: But most of the time it really is pure naivety eh. And, and, … this does not always makes them uhm … potentially bad staff members, but you do have to give them this chance, and …
> JZ: yes yes
> NC: and then I think that by working here, they may develop another perspective, like "yeah, okay, not all of them are losers, what do you know …" (laughs).
> **excerpt 73 – 29/04/2009**

Naima's *logic of patronisation* may be grounded in ignorance and "naivety", it also works in tandem with a *culturalist logic* and an *essentialist logic* that many of my interviewees have come to criticise. Like many others, Naima felt that "something isn't right" in the way "themes" concerning "culture" and "the Other" were being "approached" within academia and within the media. But it is the identification of an academic "framework" that would allow her to describe the processes that made her feel excluded and misrecognised. She explicitly refers to the positive impact the lessons of "Sami Zemni" had on her subjectivity. Her intertextual reference to Zemni's academic discourse on relativism and essentialism illustrates the social, interdiscursive and networked character of large-scale self-interpretations and public debates. Naima describes the impact of Zemni's lessons on relativism and essentialism as follows:

> NC: Well, it was quite interesting to, things that you ... felt for so long, but couldn't get a hold of exactly, and where you start to think like "okay it's probably just me, I'm probably too subjective, or it might be to close to my heart", that you are taught such a framework,
> JZ: mmh
> NC: in order to look at something, but you can also use it to distance yourself from it, and think about it more ... rationally, instead of just saying like "mmh, I don't seem to feel good about this".
> **excerpt 74 – 29/04/2009**

Zemni's discourse on relativism and culture allowed Naima to move beyond mere feelings of misrecognition and discomfort about mainstream discourses on minority-related issues. As is the case with many intellectuals and activists I talked to, political discourse allows them to act reflexively upon their emotions and experiences. As Naima puts it, such frameworks allow you "to look at something", "to distance yourself" from those aspects of society that you feel bad about and to "think" about your relationship towards society in more "rational" or reflexive ways. In the excerpt below, this process is illustrated with reference to the way Zemni's "framework" impacted on her analysis of the role of "Islam" in "the Middle East".

When I asked what bothered her specifically, she pointed out that mediatised analyses of the "the Middle East" tend to highlight "Islam" as the principal "explanatory factor for everything [laughs] that happens over there". Naima argues that "Islam" is held accountable for all sorts of "social", "political" and "economical developments" that take place over there. In the excerpt below, she explains that "something is not right" in this discourse that "does not correspond" to her "experiences". The "friction" between mainstream academic discourse and her own experience made her receptive for Zemni's "framework". Zemni's lessons taught her to analyse media representations in the Middle East in terms of an interpretive logic in which "certain elements", "people" and "groups" are "basically being esentialised to the Islam".[11]

NC: and then you have a feeling like, "well, that's just weird, okay, I'm not a specialist, but I have been there, and I don't have the impression that this or that". Okay, Islam is important, ... you feel like, there, there, there is something not right, that does not correspond to my experiences, but yes, if the specialists say so, well, then you are kind of left with this friction ...
JZ: mmh
NC: and then you're taught this framework about well yes, how certain elements are effectively being represented, and ... and about how people and groups are basically being essentialised to *the* Islam eh, something that's hundreds of years old, and that is, ... placed on a pedestal, frozen, and "voila, this is it, this is it, Islam is like this, like this, and like this, and because of this, that, that, and that".
JZ: mmh
NC: and all elements that ... that basically prove the opposite, are kind of ...
JZ: mmh
NC: cast aside ... . But yes, I can't put this into words that well, it has been such a long time (laughs), I think (laughs).
excerpt 75 – 29/04/2009

Naima Charkaoui refuses to go along with this essentialist logic. But like Sami Zemni, she is also sceptical about relativism. To her, "cultural relativists" and "essentialists" represent two "extreme" positions in "discussions about the other". Moreover, like Zemni, she prefers a "critical" attitude that allows her not to lose herself "in big theories". The parallels between Zemni's discourse and the discourse of Naima Charkaoui should become increasingly clear. Naima does not merely identify processes of culturalisation in discussions and media representations of the Middle East. She argues that the same logics can be observed in discussions on topics such as "arranged marriages" and the "repression of women" in Islamic migrant families within Flanders. In this context, she argues that even people on

---

[11] In the original Dutch formulation of this statement, Naima stressed the determinate article in front of Islam: "de Islam" [English: "the Islam"]. By doing so, she ironically referred to Islam as a supposedly homogenous and singular entity. In English, inclusion of this article may seem strange, but considering its meaning, I have nevertheless chosen to incorporate it into the translation.

"the left" ask the Minority Forum "to break" these so-called "taboos". She deplores the fact that people who relativise the importance of these issues on the basis of their "knowledge" of these issues are very often accused of "relativism". All across the interview, we find echoes of Zemni's critique on mainstream stories about Islam and the left in Flanders.

> NC: And then you are kind of like pushed into this corner, like ... "you, you are relativists, you relativise everything, to you, everything should be possible because of 'culture' ". And that's why, well, I just want to say, let's be a little bit critical ... critical, or at least pragmatic, like that you're like "come on, ... let's just take a look at reality, and not be too pompous and lose ourselves in big theories".
> JZ: yes yes
> NC: you have to consider like "what are things like". And I basically feel like this is an attitude that lives among a great deal of allochthons. Like, "okay, what's the problem and what can we do about this problem" ... but don't forget that this problem is not the only aspect to our ... to our lives, just like ... alcoholism does not equate Flemish culture.
> JZ: yes
> NC: even though sometimes, it's an aspect, or an excess of it, but.
> **excerpt 76 – 29/04/2009**

Naima calls for a problem-based "critical" and "pragmatic" stance in response to culturalist accusations of relativism. Such a stance automatically implies an attitude that does not focus on culture in an *a priori* manner. Unfortunately, the *culturalist and patronising logics* remain observable in the "political game" played by politicians. This game is marked by a differential and selective application of social and political logics to different categories of citizens. According to Naima, the resulting inequality is most visible in the Flemish discourse on citizenship and *inburgering* whereby the duties of immigrants are emphasised at the expense of their rights. Even though she states that the Forum is "not fundamentally against" *inburgering*, she deplores the fact that new migrants are obliged to follow such courses.

According to Naima, it is unthinkable that one would "force" obligatory courses upon autochthon Flemings in the same manner. The political statement that "we are going to oblige these allochthons [to follow courses on] inburgering" thus testifies to the fact that "one does not deploy the same logic" for all citizens. The underlying logic of this "political game" is marked by a discourse that stresses obligations over rights. But it also links up with classic integration discourse in the form of an implicit imperative for migrants to prove that they are integrating themselves.

> NC: and yes, to us, that's sort of a political game, like … just showing one's muscles, and saying like "look, … allochthons don't get off easily anymore eh, … social housing code, we are going to oblige them … and perhaps, within the framework of legislation on nationality and residence, we should also, …". And after a while, you think like "How many times should an allochthon prove that he can speak Dutch, and that he … wants to integrate? And what do you do with people who, in spite of all these courses, … who, who simply started too late, in order to … . Come on, you, you are always thrown back to, … coming from somewhere else, and … having to prove that … . I think this is a detrimental evolution in society, I really think that you uhm … partly push allochthons back in their being allochthon.
> **excerpt 77 – 29/04/2009**

The "political game" criticised by Naima is thus marked by a discriminatory application of a discourse on rights and duties. This type of discourse consistently pushes "allochthons back" in their allochthon status and undermines the emancipatory politics Naima prefers to pursue with the Minority Forum. She metapragmatically comments that "the word 'allochthons' is always so sensitive", that "many people don't want to be labelled as allochthons" and certainly do not want "to engage themselves on this basis". She also laughed and pointed out that she did not want to "keep on labelling people as allochthon" herself. Even though she recognises that there is "no term that everyone agrees upon" as a good alternative, she prefers to talk about "minorities" for the following reason:

> NC: We also motivated this in our, well, … the first publication on which I collaborated, the report of the Forum in 2001. It included conclusions, and it contained in a nutshell, a vision, well, this is a big word, but two pages with kind of … 'what is integration', and so on. About education, youngster, and media, recommendations … . And back then, the motivation was … . Well, I was saying, … I proposed this, and they agreed

(laughs) uhm … like "look, minorities are within, within society eh, you are within uhm … you have society at large, and within, there are minorities, ethnic-cultural minorities, and other minorities as well … . Whereas, 'allochthon' … rather points to difference, to somewhere else, and then you get an image … ". Well, I often compare it like, you have a, a house and … those ethnic-cultural minorities are within this house.
JZ: mmh
NC: And allochthons, that's kind of an outhouse … they are not in there, they still have to join, so.
excerpt 78 – 29/04/2009

In the excerpt above, Naima Charkaoui uses spatial metaphors in order to highlight the processes of exclusion fostered by the discourse on allochthony. She prefers the notion of minorities as a more inclusive alternative. Whereas the notion of "allochthon" deictically points at a "somewhere else" outside of society, minorities are located within society. At the same time, Naima is not unaware of the drawbacks of minority-related discourse either. As such, she points out that the concept is sometimes associated with the less powerful in society even though "there are powerful minorities as well". Nevertheless, the greatest benefit of the term is that it allows for a more "inclusive vision" in which minorities can make emancipatory statements about their positions as citizens of the society they live in.

5.3.2 Staying True to Oneself in the Face of a Politics of Assimilation

All of my interviewees display a high degree of awareness with respect to the ways in which political discourse shapes the social relationships constitutive of entire societies. But they are also aware of the problematic ways in which political discourse may impact on the formation of self and subjectivity. This awareness is deeply political. Moreover, since all discourse—including talk about the self—is social, it should not come as a surprise that there are strong family resemblances among the ways in which activists and intellectuals talk about the way mainstream political discourse impacts on the self. As we saw before, meaning is never truly shared, but it can be imagined as such. The critical discourses of my respondents share many family resemblances because the development of critique is always—in part—a social project.

We saw how Issam Z interpreted the struggle of the AEL as a struggle for "individuality" (Dutch: *eigenheid*). He argued that those minorities who do not wage a "political struggle" against assimilationist practices will "get trapped in a net" and will ultimately get "into conflict with themselves"—a situation that leads to a loss of cultural and religious particularity and/or individuality. In contrast, Issam's preferred mode of political subjectivity is marked by an *emancipatory logic of integration*. This logic informs politico-discursive practices whereby minorities assertively voice their opinions in the public whereby they claim their right to articulate their cultural, ethnic and/or religious identities publicly. Both Issam's critique of assimilationist politics and his explicit call for activism, emancipation and political awareness are hallmarks of AEL discourse.

Issam Z's discourse contains creative and critical analyses of personal experiences and socio-political processes. But the family resemblance with the discourses of other AEL activist and sympathisers cannot be ignored. This becomes especially clear if we compare Issam's interview with the double interview I conducted with AEL chairman Karim Hassoun and AEL activist Brahim Harshaoui. Even though AEL discourse also addresses injustice in a more "international context", I will focus on talk about assimilation and the self in the excerpts below. Like Issam Z, Karim Hassoun and Brahim Harshaoui stress the importance of raising political awareness among minorities in Flanders. They challenge hegemonic homogenising, assimilationist and culturalist logics in their struggle for "individuality" and particularity or 'eigenheid'. For Karim Hassoun, the ultimate goal is to create a society where people can remain "true to themselves".

Irrespective of their personal opinions about the organisation, many of my interviewees recognised that the AEL played an important role in raising political awareness among so-called allochthon youngsters in Flanders and Brussels at the turn of the century. Karim Hassoun was not surprised when I told him this. He responded by telling me that the AEL has been a "sort of a catalyst for political awareness among minorities". He was careful not to claim all the glory but did point out that "the AEL has played an important role ... in Flanders and in the Netherlands with respect to ... the development of political awareness among minorities". According to him, this is all the more important because Flanders is evolving towards "a more right wing politics" which includes "a more repressive" and "islamophobic policy" towards "minorities".

As a case in point, Karim referred to xenophobic attitudes towards veiled Muslim women and bearded Muslim men. In the excerpt below, we can see how he directly attacks the "politics of assimilation" as a homogenising "frame" that fosters cultural "uniformity", a type of politics that crystallises around debates about "the headscarf". The AEL has tried "to highlight" and "to unmask" this assimilatory and homogenising logic for years.

> KH: These days, every municipal council wants a ban in order to follow this trend. It has become fashionable to include a ban of the headscarf at helpdesks in one's [municipal] regulations. And of course, this is not a stand-alone issue, its frame consists of a certain type of politics, and this is the type of politics that AEL has been trying to highlight, to unmask, for years. It is a politics that is meant to assimilate minorities into Flemish or into Belgian society, [and it is meant] to smooth over the differences that exist among different communities within the country, in order to arrive at a, well, apparently, a uniformity. They always claim that this isn't the case, but if you look at the policies, and at the rhetoric, and at the agenda, the points that are being put on the agenda with respect to minority policy, and so on, then you cannot do anything but conclude that one wants to conduct a politics of assimilation where Muslims should try not to show that they are Muslims, where Arabs should try not to show they are Arabs, not speaking the language publicly in schools.
> **excerpt 79 – 26/02/2008**

Considering the AEL involvement in debates about the headscarf, it is important to point out the "secular" character of this organisation. Karim Hassoun states that the AEL does not "speak on behalf of Muslims": "We merely say that freedom of religion is fundamental for Christians, for Jews, for Muslims as well as for non-believers". Brahim adds that the organisation defends the right to wear a headscarf "on the basis of a democratic principle and not on the basis of an Islamic principle". The AEL

5 Self and Politics in Activist Discourse

is explicitly described in terms of an organisation that offers room for a variety of democratic positions and subjectivities—including religious ones. Karim claims that the organisation includes people who "believe" in the Islamic veil as well as people who do not consider it to be a "priority". Brahim adds that the AEL houses "agnostics" as well as non-religious people, whereupon the AEL chairman sarcastically contrasts this "secular" self-description with mediatised accusations of AEL members being "fanatics" linked to "Al Qaeda" and "hate-Islam".

According to Karim Hassoun, the thing that politicians fear the most is "an allochthon with a political awareness who chooses consciously" during elections. And what "politics does not want" above all is a "minority that starts to claim its rights and becomes aware of oppression, of systematic exclusion, and that forces the government to take measures against this". Nevertheless, the stakes are high for minorities, according to Karim. In an argument that parallels the point made by Issam Z, he argues that "an apolitical community" is "the last thing you want in a society that represses you" because the question of political awareness is intimately linked to the question how to remain "true" to yourself. Demoralisation and identity-related "complexes" constitute the horrific alternative to Karim's utopian fantasy. Consider the following excerpt in which Karim outlines the beatific and horrific ideological fantasies that inform his political engagement.

> KH: Hopefully, I hope that within a couple of years, my son can grow up in a society where your children, as well as the children of others, can deal with one another without looking at each other with suspicion, standing in front of each other without complexes, so that my son will not have any complexes about his identity. Like, "should I out myself as an allochthon, should I out myself as an Arab, should I out myself as a Muslim, or should I keep that to myself". I want my son to become a good person, someone who feels well in the environment wherein he lives, … . and who can, … behave in a healthy way within that environment. Someone who is … balancing between different identities and who does not know whether he is fish or fowl … uhm … will ultimately …
> BH: have to deal with questions and …
> KH: never never uhm find satisfaction in uhm … in his life … . So he will always be left with questions and never dare to position himself in a

concrete way, but always leave political discussions, decisions to be taken by others in his name ... and we think that ... . Then we get people who think for themselves, stand up for themselves, and don't have any complexes about themselves, who do not want to be forced to renounce their uhm, their individuality in order to belong. On the contrary, take an attitude like "I belong in spite of the fact that I am different" .... . And uhm ... as long as I am able ... and motivated, can motivate myself, I will go for it.
excerpt 80 – 26/02/2008

Karim articulated a utopic image of a society where children with varying backgrounds "can deal with one another without looking at each other with suspicion". He wants his son to grow up without "complexes about his identity". He wants him to "feel well" and to "behave in a healthy way" in the environment in which he lives. He hopes that his son will develop a subjectivity that is not marked by doubts about whether he should or should not "out" himself "as an Arab" or "as a Muslim" in the Flemish public sphere. Karim does not believe that people who continually balance "between different identities" and who do not know whether they are "fish or fowl" can find satisfaction in life.

Like Issam Z, Karim Hassoun understands the political project of the AEL as a struggle for a particular type of subjectivity. He engages himself for a society in which people will not have "complexes about themselves" and will not "renounce their ... individuality in order to belong". As long as he can, Karim wants "to go for" a society in which people "take an attitude like 'I belong in spite of the fact that I am different' ". The horrific and utopian fantasies that push Karim in his political engagement for the AEL can be distinguished in terms of the self-interpretations they support. On the horrific side, there is the deplorable image of his son asking himself questions that make him doubt what aspects of his sense of self he should or should not perform publicly. On the utopian side, such questions do not enter the picture at all. In the ideal case, minorities can claim belonging as well as difference.

KH: ... but those who uhm ... remain true to themselves, they uhm ...
JZ: remain true to themselves?
KH: remain true to themselves and who say like "look, I am a citizen of Flanders, I may be uhm ... culturally a little bit Flemish, but I am uhm still

Arab, or Berber, or whatever as well, Moroccan, simply culturally, and I want to show that, I am also a Muslim and I want to show that", it's difficult for them to find a job in spite of the fact that they are schooled for it. And that has demoralising effect. But today, you see that in spite of the importance they attach to higher education ... the more ... politically conscious a community becomes, the more people belonging to that community will start to occupy themselves with education. And in the end, education translates into more opportunities in a society that you like. You have to arm yourself with the weapons available to you, at that moment. Walking around without a degree is a fiasco.
excerpt 81 – 26/02/2008

In order to realise the utopia sketched by Karim Hassoun, assimilatory logics of integration have to be overcome. In order for people "to remain true to themselves" by publicly performing "Flemish" identity on the one hand, and "Arab", "Berber", "Moroccan" or "Muslim" aspects of their culture and sense of self on the other hand, they need to become politically aware. According to Karim Hassoun, this requires education. Education provides people with "opportunities" and "weapons" to arm themselves against depoliticising and "demoralising" politics of assimilation. As we saw before, AEL discourse puts a lot of stress on a notion of citizenship that legitimises the performance of cultural, religious and/or ethnic aspects of subjectivity in the public realm. But Karim also stresses the importance of "education" as a weapon that helps people to arm themselves against the logic assimilation.

The family resemblance between the discourses of Karim Hassoun and Brahim Harshaoui on the one hand and Issam Z on the other hand are no coincidence. The AEL has successfully objectified some of the most problematic logics underlying key approaches in the Flemish minority debates. This objectification goes hand in hand with an alternative logic emphasising the importance of citizenship, emancipation as well as an active and assertive embrace of diversity in the public realm and in one's sense of self. The type of politics opposed by the AEL is characterised by a *logic of assimilation* that strives for "uniformity" or homogeneity on the basis of culturalist principles. AEL activists and sympathisers deem this logic to be detrimental to democracy as well as to any attempt to stay true to oneself.

5.3.3 Pragmatic and Humane Politics in an Open Dialectic of Dissent

Political subjects do not merely identify and rearticulate what is already there in the public sphere. Political engagement is also grounded upon a sense of *lack*. Those who engage themselves for an ideal aim to fill this lack through discursive practice. As a case in point, it is useful to take a look at the way Youssef Souissi imagines his engagement for a more "humane" society that is not governed by "individual interests". What is lacking into contemporary politics is a true "dialogue" marked by a logic that fundamentally accepts dissent. Souissi argues that we live in a society marked by a destructive type of "show politics" that celebrates superficial displays of diversity and thus inhibits a true exchange of standpoints between different communities and individuals.

Youssef Souissi is one of the names that popped up most frequently when I asked people who I should talk to if I were to understand the Flemish minority debates from a minority perspective. Note that Sami Zemni also mentioned him as one of the Muslims involved in FOGI, the initiative that brought together intellectuals and Muslims "who wanted to profile themselves" as such "in the public sphere". I interviewed Youssef Souissi twice. During these interviews, he was chairman of the non-profit organisation VOEM (Association for Development and Emancipation of Muslims).[12] He also used to chair VOEM's predecessor called VILV (Association for Islam Teachers in Flanders) and used to be active in the socialist teacher's union ACOD (General Central for Public Services; Dutch: *Algemene Centrale Openbare Diensten*) Onderwijs.

---

[12] Like the FMV chaired by Mohamed Chakkar, VOEM is an umbrella organisation. It grew out of the Organisation for Islamic Teachers in Flanders called VILV and has existed since 1996. VOEM associates sport clubs, women's associations and youth groups. It explicitly states that the common point of reference for these organisations is a "Muslim identity or the fact of having Muslims as a target group"—regardless of the "nationality" involved. Its goals include "building a colourful, open, free, liveable and tolerant society"; "contributing to a positive representation of Muslim communities"; "stimulating inter-religious dialogue"; and "helping Muslims to find their place in Belgian society". The organisation issues a yearly Emancipation Prize to persons or organisations that have made significant efforts in fostering the emancipation of Muslims. In addition, VOEM organises lectures, debates, workshops, visits to Museums, cooking classes and other activities in order to reach these goals (see VOEM).

5 Self and Politics in Activist Discourse 319

When I first approached him, Youssef Souissi refused to be interviewed and told me that if I wanted to talk "politics", I should contact Mohamed Chakkar of the FMV instead. Nevertheless, after being introduced personally by Kif Kif chairman Najib Chakouh, he agreed to the interview after all. Youssef framed his engagement as a fight against "injustice". He is very much aware of the utopic character of his vision for a more "humane society" without exploitation, abuse of power and a mode of politics governed by "individual interests", but he nevertheless attempts to reach this goal. According to Youssef, it is deplorable that the only actors who "work with a long-term perspective" are those who occupy positions in law and order on the one hand and the financial world on the other hand. Unfortunately, the political agenda of these actors is governed by private interest and leads to a "mechanic" society that loses touch with its humanity. Youssef deplores that "society removes itself from this utopia" of a more "humane society" whereas he would like to get "ever more close" to it.

> YS: Every politician will say to you like "Ah, but that is what we need in society, and the rest does not count, it is in the interest of society". That's right, but to me that's an artificial society … . That's a mechanic society and not a humane society. A humane society requires those two, banks and institutions that guarantee law and order such as police and the army, but, … one or two things can become superfluous, when it's no longer required to demonstrate one's power, when we are able to live with each other without money, … without exchange and so on, … . Why not? Why should I exploit you … and you exploit me? Then we will be standing with drawn [knives in front of each another] … . Of course, this is a utopia I am talking about, but ever more, society removes itself from this utopia, and I would like to get ever more close to this utopia.
> **excerpt 82 – 09/02/2009**

As is the case with all ideological fantasies, there are some obstacles to be overcome if Youssef Souissi's ideal society is to be realised. Youssef does not oppose "law and order" or private interests as such. His point is that "order and interests" are required for a society to function but that one also needs to take "an interest in each other" in order to guarantee "human life" and a "humane society". This process of taking an interest in each other requires a discursive politics that goes beyond superficial "performances" and mere "displays" of pluralism, diversity and humanity. Souissi's preferred mode of engagement is explicitly constructed in opposition to this type of "show politics" that merely gives lip service to human values and pluralism. Interestingly, his critique of "show politics" is directed at institutional actors linked not only to "police", the "army" and the "banks" but also to "politicians" and religious representatives of Jewish, Islamic and Christian religion.

> YS: Once in a while there's a performance by a bishop, there's a performance by an imam, there's a performance by a rabbi, there's a performance like "OK, we are going to visit a mosque", or "we are going to uhm organise a tea moment in order to show that we are still human" ... .
> JZ: but then that's ...
> YS: these are rituals, rituals that basically ... maintain these two other forces.
> **excerpt 83 – 09/02/2009**

The ritual character of such intercultural or inter-religious events all too often obscures a lack of genuine interest into each other according to Youssef Souissi. He relies on metaphors and metapragmatic qualifications that stress the superficial, ephemeral and manipulative character of this type of pseudo-pluralism. Even though he also criticises mosques and other organisations for whom opening up towards other communities is "still taboo", his main point is that communication between different communities should be normalised. According to Youssef, this is not the case in contemporary Antwerp politics. All too often, intercultural events such as visits to mosques are merely "fashionable" or "fancy" displays of "show politics" that basically mark "pluralism" as a remarkable and uncommon feature of society.

> YS: Now ... that's still the case in certain regions today and some want to ... put on a show that there is pluralism, that there is ... . It has become fashionable, whereas it should be fashion nor taboo ... it should simply be a normal thing to do.
> JZ: yes
> YS: So that's the case ... in Antwerp. Whenever one wants to do something fancy ...

5 Self and Politics in Activist Discourse

JZ: mmh
YS: "Let's visit a mosque, and then I will arrive as the alderman, or as the mayor, or as this, or as that", and so on ... and that is show politics ...
JZ: mmh
YS: ... it's a fashion ...
JZ: yes
YS: that does not change anything content-wise about the situation.
excerpt 84 – 09/02/2009

Youssef continues and stresses that you neither "have to put on a show" nor make this type of event "taboo". On the contrary, the type of event where people visit each other's houses of worship and each other's organisations should be "a plain and normal thing" to do. Souissi is not merely talking about mosques but also about the associations of migrant organisations, churches, temples and synagogues. He claims to be one of the first Islam teachers who invited holocaust survivor Regine Beer to his class in order to talk about her experiences to his students. In the excerpt below, all of the tropes that inform Souissi's plea against show politics and in favour of a more human society pop up again. His plea for a normalisation of intercultural encounters between communities crystallises throughout implicit and explicit articulations of a preferred mode of politics and interaction that is marked by a *logic of dialogism*.

YS: And back then, the reaction of the school was like ... "Why are you going to talk about concentration camps during a class about Islam?" ... . And now it has become fashionable, now it has almost become an obligation, whereas according to me, it should not be an obligation either ... . It shouldn't be fashionable, ... but it should not be forgotten either.
JZ: Mmh ... yes ... . Why did you consider it to be important to ...
YS: Because it's kind of part of the memory of Flemish culture eh ... . It's in there eh, ... in history eh ... . But without overemphasising it, and without forgetting it eh ... . It's a fact that should be stated ... . Whereas some people are making a fashion out of it ... eh ...
JZ: yes ...
YS: or an item that is ... going to return their virginity to them. Whereas it's...
JZ: Because then, one should not think about it anymore?
YS: ... (long silence) ... good make-up for a political policy that is unstable

JZ: This political policy then, what would you like to ... well, how would you like to see things differently?
YS: more humane.
excerpt 85 – 09/02/2009

Youssef's preferred mode of communication and politics is based on interaction, exchange and dialogue. But the dialogue he has in mind is not conflict free. It involves both internal and external conflicts and processes. Youssef embraces conflict because conflict presupposes that his utterances have been heard. He prefers honest and conflicting responses to his statements over the cynical indifference of politicians and other actors in the public sphere that engage in "show politics" in order to cover up their lack of humanity.

> YS; It's only when I am faced with someone who clashes with what I am telling him, that I'm sure that this person means well with me ... .
> JZ: yes ...
> YS: because that person has heard and reacted ... what I have said has penetrated ...
> JZ: yes, I can imagine that
> YS: you see what I mean?
> JZ: yes
> YS: it's only at that moment that I'm sure "that's someone who is honest" ... . Even if one does not accept my standpoints eh ..., does not agree, ... I may not like you and so on but OK ..., then I am sure that this is not someone who remains indifferent.
> **excerpt 86 – 09/02/2009**

It is important to realise that interaction in itself does not offer any guarantees for the "humane" mode of politics that Souissi argues for. In order to be truly counter-hegemonic, this type of interaction needs to include a discursive practice of looking oneself in "the mirror". Youssef argues that there is a "duality that has been evacuated from Flanders". According to him, many Flemish feel guilty about the "norms" and "values" they have given up. He polemically claims that this lack and the associated "guilt" fuel the "headscarf problematic". Youssef suggests that a guilt-driven jealousy informs most reproaches towards Muslims who

5 Self and Politics in Activist Discourse 323

organise their lives around traditional norms and values. For this reason, Youssef half-jokingly remarks that "every Fleming should go see a psychiatrist".

> YS: You see … ? So, that's the duality … that has been evacuated in Flanders … exactly … in order not to have to look at oneself in the mirror … and that is exactly what is happening right now with that headscarf problematic … those who reproach … not because they are racist … well, I am exaggerating eh …
> JZ: those who, the ban on the headscarf uhm ?
> YS: yes voila … but simply because some of those people consider themselves as … having no values … who say like … "I have … given up … my values, my norms".
> JZ: mmh
> YS: given up, … and they shouldn't give that up … .
> JZ: yes …
> YS: So, … they attach, they are going to be difficult in order to still,
> JZ: yes
> YS: You see … ? That's guilt … . Every Fleming should go see a psychiatrist, really.
> JZ: (smiles)
> YS: I am serious eh.
> **excerpt 87 – 09/02/2009**

The "duality" Souissi talks about refers to a mode of political communication whereby people become reflexively aware of their sense of self and their relationship towards others. By engaging with others, one can start to look oneself in the mirror. To look oneself in this "mirror" is a metapragmatic metaphor for a type of interaction whereby one becomes aware of the fact that one's sense of self is closely associated with one's sense of others. Souissi's statement that this "duality" has been evacuated in Flanders therefore ties in with his analysis that too many people "in Belgium", "in Flanders" and "in the world" opt for "a flight forward" when confronted with disturbing images of themselves: "cowardice" and "egoism" drive people away from "humane" modes of politics.

The refusal not to look oneself in the mirror and to accept the "dualism" of politics and selfhood explains why people ignore problems as diverse as the export of waste products to African countries, the "headscarf problematic" as well as the Flemish approach to "racism". At various points in the interview, Souissi stressed the importance of facing the darker sides of one's identity and history. This goes for the "holocaust" as well as for the way we think about "racism" in general. Below, Youssef argues that the Flemish "anti-racist" movement has "lost terrain" because of a "naïve" emphasis on the desire of people to be good. According to him, anti-racist discourse all too often reasons that "you have to be good, and because of that you shouldn't be a racist". This type of discourse denies the "duality" of man and does not require him or her to look oneself in the "mirror" and "to work" on one's "bad side".

> YS: That's basically the reason why the anti-racist movement has … to put it in French, in a *vaniteuse* way … eh
> JZ: *vaniteuse*
> YS: *vaniteuse* eh … a kind of naïve [moves his arms and hands as if he is trying to grab something]
> JZ intangible
> YS: yes … has lost terrain … . Because one departs from … the goodness of people … . You have to be good, and because of that you shouldn't be a racist … . No. Within you, there are things that are not good, within me as well, and I have to be aware of this, you have to fight these things.
> JZ: mmh
> YS: I don't have to show my good side, no, my good side is not what I need to show. People should observe this good side for themselves.
> JZ: yes
> YS: I don't have to show that … . I have to work on my bad side, not on my good side … . I don't have to adorn my good side in order to show it.
> **excerpt 88 – 09/02/2009**

Ethical work on the self and on society can only start if one looks oneself in the mirror and if one engages in modes of politics and interaction marked by a *dialectic logic of dissent*. To face oneself in the mirror and to truly see oneself implies that one moves beyond the "show politics" Souissi criticised so fiercely. The process of coming closer to Souissi's "humane society" is a public process. It requires pragmatic and dialectic discursive practices. In the excerpt below, Youssef Souissi highlights the pragmatic and dialectic character of his own engagement. He does so with reference to his involvement in the socialist teacher's union ACOD Onderwijs—"the syndical organisation in which God is basically non-existent". Within this context, he engaged himself for the "recognition" of people teaching Islam in Flemish schools on the basis of his subject position as a union member.

> YS: ... but there has been a dialectic, a pragmatism, a discussion, that started within a syndical organisation [slams his fist on the table], towards that recognition [by the government of people teaching Islam in Flemish schools] ...
> JZ: yes
> YS: a syndical organisation where God is basically non-existent ...
> JZ: yes ...
> YS: where I am free to take a standpoint in order to shut the door to Minister Van den Bossche ... with my syndical card eh ... to say like it's like this or nothing ... also, to negotiate with [Minister] Cools about the language problematic and so on, and also with regard to [Minister] Marleen Vanderpoorten, one of my best friends, uhm, to stand up for that, and to say like "this is what we want to achieve".
> **excerpt 89 – 09/02/2009**

In the excerpt above, we can clearly see how Youssef Souissi associates abstract signifiers with concrete interactions that are part and parcel of wider public debates. On the one hand, notions such as "pragmatism" and "discussion" refer to concrete interactions and negotiations he was involved in. On the other hand, they function as values that inform a preferred mode of politics and public interaction. They allow him to metapragmatically qualify specific types of interaction over others, thus providing him with the tools to identify and combat "injustice". The notion of "pragmatism" enables Youssef to establish a high degree of interpretive coherence between various practices, institutions and debates in which he engaged himself. It does so by allowing for a flexible stance towards the subject positions he occupies, the organisations he is involved in and the sources of inspiration he draws upon.

YS: I am not a philosopher, I am a pragmatician …. I say like "I take little bit of philosophy, a little bit of … politics, a little bit of religion, a little bit of [slams his fist on the table] reality, … and a bit of self-brewed ideas".
excerpt 90 – 09/02/2009

Souissi's pragmatic attitude also explains his general dislike of labels. During a debate organised by the intercultural platform called Kif Kif in Antwerp, he explicitly positioned himself as a Muslim. The debate focused on the topic of *Islam: a house with many chambers* and was advertised as follows: "In the debate 'Islam, a house with many chambers', we bring together various approaches and religious beliefs, in order to debate the schools, the perceptions, and issues within Islam. Because some persons are more strict in their interpretations than others. More specifically, the debate will be about the place of youngsters in contemporary Islam." Youssef Souissi debated with Marxist PvdA politician Zohra Othman, Mohamed el Omari of *Diverse and Active* (Divers en Actief) and Bilal Benyaich of Kif Kif. Sociologist Meryem Kanmaz acted as moderator. Listening to the debate, I was surprised to find out that Youssef Souissi systematically rejected most religious labels. In fact, the debate quickly moved away from the advertised topic towards issues such as racism, education, religious radicalism, discrimination and allochthony.

When I confronted him with these observations, Youssef Souissi acknowledged having avoided such "labelling" practices during the debate. Explaining himself, he resorted to a series of spatial metaphors in order to articulate his views on identity-related processes in the public sphere. As is the case in the discourse of many of my interviewees, it is possible to distinguish between spatial logics of closure and disclosure. Like many others, Youssef associates "labelling" with closure. People are "put in a parking box" that restricts their possibilities for movement, the "expansion" of "space" is stopped and one makes it difficult or impossible to "cross" the mental borders thus established. This *logic of closure* is to be opposed of course. The operation of the *dialectic logic of dissent* that marks Souissi's preferred sense of self and politics operates in tandem with a pragmatic *logic of disclosure*.

YS: yes yes yes … yes … if you practice labelling, then you stop, then you stop that space …

JZ: like between groups and so on …
YS: yes, then you stop this space. From the moment that you label it, you get a ghetto, a parking box, … you park people there en then you stop this space … that that that expansion stops …
JZ: yes
YS: because you cannot cross that border here [points to his head].
excerpt 91 – 09/02/2009

The same logics of closure and disclosure can also be identified in the scenarios that Youssef Souissi sketches for the Flemish public sphere. According to him, Flanders is faced with a bipolar "choice". Either the Flemish choose to live in a mental "ghetto" or they stop the "evacuation" of dialogue and choose for "an opening in the mind", so Flanders can start to "blossom".

YS: Flanders … has a choice … to live as a ghetto … and then it will be a desert country within fifteen years … . You go one way and I go
JZ: mmh
YS: another way. And then you will have old people who remain here against their will because they have nowhere else to go …
JZ: yes
YS: either it chooses an opening … in the mind, not in terms of borders eh, this [points at his head] has to open eh …
JZ: yes
YS: the minds, not narrow but … larger … . And then it can blossom incredibly, incredibly.
excerpt 92 – 09/02/2009

It may be useful to summarise. In Souissi's world view, "show politics" based on private interests gives rise to a fake pluralism that does not allow for true dialogue and interaction. Souissi's utopia requires that we overcome this situation by looking ourselves in the "mirror". This implies that all actors in civil society—citizens, civil society organisations, religious authorities and politicians—have to oppose the *logic of closure* and address the lack of dialectic discursive practices in Flanders. It also implies the development of a mode of subjectivity marked by a logic of *disclosure* and an active embrace of a *dialectic logic of dissent*, so a more "human society" may be realised.

5.4 Recognition and Misrecognition in Political Discourse

All of my interviewees pointed out that their political awareness and/or engagement started out as a reaction to the voices of actors who called them into subject positions they did not want to occupy. When peers and authoritative figures such as teachers, media workers or politicians systematically misrecognise who and what we are, feelings of misrecognition become an everyday experience. Such feelings result from a confrontation between conflicting ideological discourses and subjectivities. To recognise these feelings for discursive effects of political discourse requires a high degree of metapragmatic and political awareness. Misrecognition often occurs in situations where contextual frameworks clash and where interlocutors intentionally or unintentionally mistake what identities are relevant in a given context of enunciation.

One may speak as a Muslim while discussing the inaccuracies and distortions of mediatised representations of Islam. But the same person may not attribute any pragmatic relevance to this aspect of his or her self in a discussion about the Belgian tax system. Sometimes, misfiring interpellations may be rather innocent or funny. We mistake each other's professional and gendered identities all the time. But if these mistakes become systematic, it is likely that there are stereotypes involved. Repeated experiences of misfiring interpellations whereby one's preferred sense of self does not correspond to the subject positions one is called into frequently trigger strong emotional reactions.

In the context of the Flemish minority debates, feelings of misrecognition on the part of minority members are far from uncommon. In fact, my interviews are littered with accounts of situations in which interviewees did not recognise themselves in the way they were addressed, labelled and objectified by fellow citizens and by representatives of centring institutions. Some of the intellectuals and activists I talked to addressed the issue of recognition directly. But all of them testified to feelings of discomfort, ambivalence, anger and disappointment with respect to the way other actors attempt to fix their sense of self. The political engagements of my interviewees are productive and democratic attempts to counter these feelings and the discourses that give rise to them in the first place.

We already noticed how former AEL activist Issam Z felt like he had to give up his "individuality" and how he felt that "something was not right" about the way people talked about Islam and allochthony. It is this feeling that set him on a "search for individuality", "identity" and pride. Issam turned to literature on Islamic civilisation and would eventually engage himself for the AEL. The importance of emotions can also be illustrated with reference to Amane X who talked about feelings of "disappointment" with respect to the integration process. Even Sami Zemni testified to such a feeling when confronted with accusations of not being sufficiently integrated. These emotional responses should not be understood in mere individual terms. They occur because abstract categories such as "individuality", "identity", "integration" and "identity" function as discursive *values* that inform our images of self and society.

People value and order abstract notions such as "community", "freedom", "choice" and "neutrality", "democracy", "Islam" or "Europe" hierarchically. These empty signifiers inform our fantasies about who and what we want to be. They structure our relation to social norms and inform the force with which we pursue them (Glynos 2008, 289). The very vagueness of these categories allows us to evaluate particular identities, practices and experiences as matters of public interest and political struggle. But at the same time, our usage of such terms is always linked to concrete experiences. Our choice for a specific political discourse never seems completely arbitrary to us because our sense of self operates through the articulation of discursively articulated histories that infuse our emotionally experienced self-interpretations with a sense of fixation and stability.

Discourse allows people to articulate potentially empty signifiers in large-scale interpretive logics that provide meaning to individual and collective experiences. When the legitimacy of key signifiers is called into question, when one's basic interpretive categories are being challenged, this can easily be experienced as an attack on one's preferred sense of self and society. Such experiences explain why political debates can be counted among the most emotional of language games. Within these speech events, the legitimacy of our most cherished values can be called into question, leading to a dislocation of the logics that inform our very sense of self and society.

Some individuals reach the point where they can politicise the voices of those who objectify them. This requires that one can metapragmatically qualify one's emotional experience as a response to public discourse. Metapragmatic awareness proves to be a condition for political awareness once again. In themselves, emotions do not politicise anything, but they can set individuals on a search for explanatory frameworks that explain the injustices they face and that allow them to imagine different and better worlds. The discourses people encounter on their search for meaning may help them to name and to problematise the social, political and fantasmatic logics they seek to challenge. Negative emotional responses to public discourse can therefore provide powerful incentives for raising one's political awareness.

5.4.1 On the Desire for Recognition and the Pain of Exclusion

The director of the Minority Forum Naima Charkaoui addressed the issue of recognition directly. Her discourse provides us with a clear example of the high degree to which subjects can become aware of the processes of ideological recognition they are involved in. Her metapragmatic analyses and stories about interactions in which such processes misfire provide insights into the emotional and politicising effects of such experiences. Nevertheless, to have a more or less coherent sense of self and politics does not arm oneself against the disturbing effects of misrecognition and the associated pain of exclusion.

People with a relatively coherent understanding of who they are and what they want for themselves and for others in society can be shaken thoroughly when faced with conflicting discourses and interpellations. Abdellatif Akhandaf testifies to occupying an "unstable position" as a government representative who has to walk a "thin line" if he is not to be seen as "an adversary" by minority actors in civil society. The emotional impact of not being recognised for what he wants to do as a civil servant at the Antwerp Integration Service DIA caused his voice to break during the interview. The desire for recognition and the pain of exclusion are powerful factors for triggering political awareness and engagement.

At the time of our interview, Naima Charkaoui was director of the Minority Forum. This Forum represents a multiplicity of federations of minority civil society organisations in Flanders and in Brussels. It is useful to take a look at the way she talks about recognition. Like many other interviewees, Naima could recall how people in her childhood "environment" could make "stupid" and "denigrating" "statements about Moroccans". In order to illustrate how "allochthons" are pushed back into "being allochthon" and into "coming from somewhere else", she recalled an anecdote from her days as a Flemish high school student during the First Gulf War.

> NC: When I was in high school, the [first] Gulf War had broken out, uhm, against Saddam Hussein … . And there was this friend in my class, Ok well, … of course she was only fourteen or sixteen, … who said "well, are you [plural] on the side of Saddam Hussein, or on our side…". And to me, this was so, I was so struck by this, because I was like … "Come on, how come you even ask this question? Because you are … . Come on, Saddam Hussein was a real dictator, and all of that, and human rights?". And it was so weird that she even asked this questions, like … well, I thought this was kind of alienating, because you have this feeling … . I, I was almost the only, I was the only allochthon, I think, in my entire school, and definitely in my class … . … Yes, you, you usually don't think about this, but there are moments when you are faced with a mirror, like, "to us you are still this".
> **excerpt 93 – 29/04/2009**

Naima's classmate asked her what "side" she was on: "our side" or "the side of Sadam Hussein". "Struck" as she was by this question, she experienced this interaction as a fundamentally "alienating" experience. Even as a high school student, Naima was interested in issues of "human rights" and it was therefore obvious to her that Saddam was a dictator to be opposed. The question whether she would support "a dictator" shocked her to the core and made her aware of the fact that she was put into a category of people who did not automatically belong to the collective 'us' her classmate refers to in her question. The question posed by her friend thus functioned as a distorting "mirror", presenting her with an image of herself as an "allochthon".

Naima's feelings of "frustration" about the discourse on allochthony would not lessen over the years. Her preferred mode of political engagement involves a mode of activism that creates opportunities for minorities "to speak for themselves". In the "current affairs" programs of mainstream media, minority members do not get sufficient opportunities to articulate themselves according to Naima. An additional problem is the media practice of selecting random persons as minority representatives. The "frustrating thing" about this is that "you don't recognise yourself" in the discourse of these so-called representatives. By engaging herself for the Minority Forum, Naima set herself the goal to change this.

> NC: uhm .. and also, yes what really appealed to me in the Forum, I think I would have not have applied that quickly for another organisation in this, in this sector. The fact that uhm ... yes, as I said before eh, really 'from the minorities themselves'.
> JZ: mmh
> NC: and that was like 'wow, wow'. So, ... also because if you followed current affairs, it was always so frustrating that all of the time, everyone talked about allochthons, and you are like "Yes but ... let people uhm ... speak for themselves, and do not present the nearest person as a representative,
> JZ: yes
> NC: whereas you don't recognise yourself in it [in the discourse of such people] ... . Rather, real people, who have a mandate from the group, ... uhm, like from the bottom up, from the associations, that really appealed to me uhm ... . And also, they [the associations represented in the Minority Forum] are also focused on policy, well, I, I actually studied political sciences, and how does it feel to ... . Well, I think that pure fieldwork ... would be something that I would find quite difficult, or that I would be unable to do for a long time.
> **excerpt 94 – 29/04/2009**

Naima Charkaoui's engagement for the Minority Forum constituted an attempt to create a space where "minorities" could express themselves with a voice of their own. By working at the Forum, she attempted to counter the very discourse that triggers the "alienation" she experienced herself. By offering minority members the opportunity to articulate their voices in the public sphere, the potential for experiencing feelings of recognition could be increased. Issues of recognition lie at the centre of Naima's engagements. In the excerpt below, she explains that growing up in an almost exclusively "autochthon environment", she frequently felt "alone" because she did not have any "soul mates" with whom she could exchange ideas.

At several points in the interview, Naima testified to the powerful attraction people such as Tarik Faihi, Sami Zemni, Mohamed Chakkar, Nadia Fadil and Meyrem Kanmaz exerted on her. She admires these "key figures" in the Flemish minority debates for different reasons: for their "ability to speak up"; for their "experience" in the world of minority civil society; and for their "intelligence". But above all, the discourse of these people offers the possibility of an ideological feeling of "recognition". In the excerpt below, Naima is rather explicit about this:

> NC: yes ... I think that it is mostly a feeling of recognition that attracts me to these people ... whereas for a long time ... I had the feeling that I was alone with a number of ideas, because I never really, ... I didn't have like, you know, I ... I grew up in, in an ... almost completely autochthon environment ...
> JZ: mmh
> NC: and I didn't have any soul mates in that respect ... . You, you look at things and you have a number of ideas about this, but in the end, you have nobody to check these [ideas] ...
> JZ: mmh
> NC: and then, in my job, I did, but ... uhm ... . But these are people about whom you think like ... "they can put it so nicely into words", so you feel like "wow, this is what I always kind of meant" ...
> JZ: mmh
> NC: But it's not as if you ... really get new ideas here ...
> JZ: yes
> NC: Sometimes, there are things that make you think like "ah, yes" ... that's certainly true with respect to Nadia [Fadil], but she, she looks at things from a very ... theoretical perspective, and then that's new to me ... and then I am like "yes, I hadn't looked at it this way" ... . But it's not so much the ideas that I remember, but rather like "wow, wow, that's how I would like to put it myself". It is ... well, that feeling of recognition is really quite important, so you don't feel like you're on your own.
> **excerpt 95 – 29/04/2009**

The "feeling of recognition" that Naima experiences is not merely a matter of agreeing to the truth of certain "ideas" articulated by others. It is an emotional experience that allows her to move beyond her sense of isolation and the experience of being pushed into the position of an excluded allochthon. Naima's "feeling of recognition" is an articulatory experience whereby she connects her sense of self to specific subjectivities and analyses. If some classmates pushed Naima into the subject position of an isolated allochthon, it is the discourse of people such as Nadia Fadil and Sami Zemni that makes her feel like she is not on her own anymore. This is especially true for people whose discourse helps her to counter the *patronising logic* that structures the discourse on allochthony and culture in Flanders.

The emotional impact of not being recognised in one's preferred sense of self was probably expressed most clearly in my interview with civil servant Abdellatif Akhandaf. It is useful to recall that Abdellatif considered integration in terms of a process that should be stimulated by the government. We also saw that his engagement for DIA—the integration service of Antwerp—is constructed as an attempt to normalise the visible presence of the so-called allochthon population in the public realm. According to Abdellatif, the "government" has to put things into motion in order to stimulate openness towards "diversity" and "integration" among majority and minority members alike.

In order for integration to happen, people have to feel appreciated and recognised with respect to their "individuality". And this requires a "full recognition" of one's "community" and "all your cultural and your religious heritage". Abdellatif does not believe that integration happens automatically in a situation where minorities "feel unappreciated and unrecognised with respect to a particular part of their being". He considers his engagement for DIA and for the process of integration in terms of a struggle for a society-wide recognition and acceptance of diversity. It is also an attempt to overcome feelings of "insecurity" among minority members and a contribution to a general sense of openness between communities. Experiences of not being recognised for these efforts at times of high political tension create the ideal conditions for an intense emotional experience.

Abdellatif was already working as a civil servant at DIA when Hans van Themsche went on a racist killing spree in the city centre of Antwerp. Van Themsche shot and killed the two-year-old Flemish girl Luna Drowart and her pregnant Melanesian nanny Oulematu Niangadou in 2006. He also wounded the Turkish woman Songül Köç before being shot in the belly by a police officer himself. Both Köç and Van Themsche survived and the latter was sentenced to life for this racist attack. In the excerpt below, Abdellatif describes his role as a representative of the government and the integration service:

> AA: ... So, by the evening, you know what has happened. You have to keep ahead of the facts, to summon a number of partners, the umbrella's, ... Okay, what are we going to do? Uhm, well, the umbrellas, the associations, will evidently want to take it to the streets, and then it will be like "we against", well, "we are the victims, the allochthons are the victims". Whereas, as a government service, as an integration service, you continually look for a, for a, ... try to consider society, the whole, uhm you try to ... uhm create something positive, a surplus value, out of something which is negative uhm ... . So, to us, from the beginning, it was very important ... that ... it was clear that everyone would be a victim, and not just the allochthons ... . Not only the African, not only the Turkish, but also the Flemish, so it has to ... . If something will happen in the streets, it has to be clear that it is supported by everyone. So, from the beginning, we had to make sure that civil society went along ... and that was not easy.
> **excerpt 96 – 08/07/2008**

Abdellatif points out that "as a government service, as an integration service, you continually ... try to consider society, the whole". For this reason, it was important to him that "everyone", "and not just the allochthons" would claim the status of "victim". Anticipating the desire to organise an anti-racist demonstration, DIA set out to bring together allochthon "associations" and autochthon civil society together. Abdellatif and his colleagues at DIA wanted to make sure that "autochthon civil society" would be present from the beginning and that society as a whole would position itself as a victim of Van Themsche's racist murders. He wanted to avoid that there would be more than "a minimal presence of Flemish" at this event. Moreover, not only the people marching in the demonstration but also the "security" of the event should be diverse and be "a reflection of everyone" in society.

> AA: Uhm, also, something that I considered to be important, was that with respect to uhm, to security, uhm ... that it would be a reflection of everyone, and I have organised this, ...
> JZ: yes

AA: uhm, uhm, ... so that ... like ... the image in the front is a reflection of the image on the back ... I always get a lump in my throat (smiles)
JZ: a lump
AA: a lump in my throat when I uhm talk about ...
JZ: Really?
AA: Yes, it's a ... well, it remains an emotional ...
JZ: and ... where does this, where does this ...
AA: Emotions.
JZ: and because of the uhm, the events?
excerpt 97 – 08/07/2008

Explaining the need for "everyone" to be involved, Abdellatif's voice broke. His eyes went moist and he admitted to feeling "a lump in his throat" every time when he recalls his role in these events. However, this emotional response is not merely a reaction to the murders themselves. Rather, it is a reaction to the fact that some of the people he wanted to bring together pushed him into the position of an "adversary", a mode of subjectivity that misrecognises his preferred mode of subjectivity as a representative of a holistically oriented government service.

AA: Especially as a government, you're not uhm, ... one sees you as ... one sees you as a government, especially when there are demonstrations, one basically sees you as the adversary, uhm, you are the one who uhm ...
JZ: has allowed it to escalate
AA: Yes. The one who has let it come this far. So you're always in a very unstable position, and at the same time you want to, ... move something, you want to offer uhm ... opportunities, you want to trigger evolutions and processes, that's ... uhm
JZ: is it because you get reproaches addressed to you or uhm
AA: Yes. Yes yes, of course, so uhm, we really walk a thin line. Uhm, very subtly, in the backstage, you work the different ... interest groups ... . The African umbrella, the Turkish umbrella, the Moroccan umbrella, uhm, ... the youngsters, and then also the social service, the city, in order to join them, in order to allow for a number of facilities.
excerpt 98 – 08/07/2008

Abdellatif has to "walk a thin line" in order not to be excluded from the collective 'us' articulated by minority groups. And this implies a careful balancing act between allochthon and autochthon subject positions, concerns and discourses. It also requires a careful articulation of governmental and public concerns on the one hand and the concerns of specific groups in civil society on the other hand. Interpellations on the part of minority members that do not recognise his efforts to achieve such a balance trigger feelings of misunderstanding and loneliness. When I asked him what made the days following the racist murders by Van Themsche so intense, Abdellatif answered as follows:

> AA: you're caught in between, because you uhm … . You want to do good for everyone, uhm, and it is not always … perceived like that. From the perspective of the allochthons you're seen like uhm, well, you're the government, you belong to the other party, uhm from the government, you're not always considered to be … ' part of us' uhm, well, … . Apparently that's typically human … . So, … one cannot always understand you uhm, and … that's not easy. And because of that, you always walk a thin line, and, … you don't have a scenario, uhm, so, you're, you're lonely at that moment … and the result is very uhm … uhm … . It's either on or off, it's uhm, … it's quite demanding.
> **excerpt 99 – 08/07/2008**

The processes of recognition and misrecognition are everywhere. They are not the sole prerogative of majority or minority groups and can be triggered by any type of discourse that makes identity and value-related claims. Processes of misrecognition can be extremely challenging on an emotional and psychological level. But thanks to our reflexive capacities and our ability to recognise such patterns metapragmatically, it becomes possible to weaken the hold such discourses have on us. The question to be addressed at this point is how to counter misfiring identity claims with alternative logics of self-interpretation.

5.4.2 Building Bridges and Crossroads in Response to Misfiring Interpellations

The metapragmatic ability to make a distinction between the discourses one prefers and the discursive practices one rejects lies at the basis of political awareness. It is this ability that allows processes of recognition and misrecognition to occur in the first place. To experience a feeling of misrecognition and to name it as such is to evaluate a particular form of address. As we move through different contexts and cast our limited lines of vision upon an ever-changing and multidimensional discursive reality, different aspects of our sense of self become relevant to us. Others may therefore not always recognise us for who we are and for who or what we want to be.

Human beings put a lot of work in the construction and maintenance of a more or less coherent sense of self and society. In some cases, this work involves a salient political dimension. For instance, many of my interviewees noticed that the performance and recognition of their preferred sense of self required them to challenge established discursive norms observable in the discursive practices of fellow citizens and in the discourses of (representatives of) centring institutions. To reach this critical level of awareness is an impressive but everyday accomplishment. It requires emotional, political and metapragmatic (re-)articulations of discursive events that shape one's sense of self and society. It also requires the construction of a complex discursive network that can be analysed in terms of its arguments, narratives, frames and logics.

Nadia Babazia's account of her engagement for the non-profit organisation SAMV and the other "worlds" and "environments" she moved in allows us to illustrate the complex articulations of activism, selfhood and the way we metapragmatically distinguish between normative forms of address by intellectuals and activists involved in Flemish minority politics. At the time of our interview, Nadia worked for the SAMV. This organisation was created as a project of the Intercultural Centre for Migrants and became a non-profit organisation in 2000. On its tenth birthday in 2010, SAMV would change its name to *Ella: knowledge centre for gender and ethnicity* (see also Zienkowski 2013). This name change was partly based on ideological considerations concerning the notion of allochthony.

On a practical level, SAMV organised workshops, protest actions and debates about the involvement of mostly Moroccan and Turkish women in civil society. The organisation aimed to inform women of their rights and possibilities. It also worked with allochthon youngsters—including boys—from 2004 on. SAMV developed educational games about sexuality, role patterns and relationships. Another interesting project was a play based on women's stories about sexuality, forced marriages, divorce, virginity and Islam. The general goal was to stimulate the so-called "internal debate" within the 'allochthon' communities. This "debate" involved a discussion of sensitive topics such as partner choice, marital migration, inter-religious relationships and homosexuality. The name change to *Ella: knowledge centre for gender and ethnicity* was informed by a critique of the notion of allochthony as well as by the following considerations:

> *Whereas during the first five years, SAMV focused mostly on individual empowerment of allochthon women by means of various methods and courses, from 2006 on, SAMV developed a new track. Because, with respect to sensitive gender issues, 'taboo themes', and traditions that obstruct or hinder individual emancipation, the individual and communal levels are fundamentally intertwined. It is difficult to break certain taboos on your own, if there is no support within the community. We therefore never suggest only one solution or model. Rather, we want to stimulate people to think independently, to be critical with respect to common opinions / convictions within one's own community, and to make their own choices.* (Bouzarmat 2010)

For Nadia Babazia, her job at SAMV signified way more than a pay cheque at the end of the month. She discussed this "job" in terms of an "engagement" with the themes mentioned above. SAMV constituted one of three "worlds" through which she used to travel. These worlds include SAMV; a "Flemish", "Belgian" or "white" "environment"; and an "environment" provided by her "family". The point to be made here is that Nadia distinguishes metapragmatically between these three spaces. She does so with reference to the different forms of address, language games and approaches to emancipation prevailing in these contexts. These differences can be described in terms of interpretive logics that impact on the type of subjectivity projected on Nadia's engagements.

Because of her job at SAMV, Nadia and her colleagues are used to being interviewed by social scientists and journalists. Nevertheless, she found my interviewing style rather atypical. At the very end of our interview, Nadia remarked that she found our talk "kind of interesting" and that she did not know "what to expect" when we made our appointment. I merely told her that the interview would be about her social engagements, her political ideas and her sources of inspiration. Nadia's response to my question what she found so atypical about this interview sheds an interesting light on the dynamics of ideological interpellation. In the excerpt below, Nadia explains that she gets "tired of always explaining" the "basics" of "identity" to journalists and researchers. As we will see, such questions systematically misrecognise her preferred mode of subjectivity.

> NB: sometimes it's rather … well yes … sometimes, sometimes you do get tired of always explaining this. And I liked it like right now, that it wasn't just about this aspect. Well, it went a step further, like well, "Why do you engage yourself?", so you don't have to talk that much, well, you do have to talk about yourself of course, but not … well, I don't know, the basics, the basic identity …
> JZ: What do you consider to be basic?
> NB: well, … I don't know, like "Do you feel Moroccan or Belgian?", and "How about you being a Muslim", you know … . And you can really get quite exhausted after such a conversation. It's like "shit, yes, uhm how does this work again", and you think like "shit, that's not what I am working on at all", or "this is what I am working on", and that's so, … well, sometimes, very exhausting, and then you're like … "should I still do this sort of thing?".
> **excerpt 100 – 11/06/2008**

What bothers Nadia specifically are the "questions" that force her to make choices between different religious, national and/or ethnic identities. She explains how "exhausting" questions such as "Do you feel Moroccan or Belgian" can be. What made our interview special to her was the fact that I let these issues operate in the background and that I focused on her ideas and engagements rather than on "basic" identity-related questions. In order to understand why these questions are so "tiring" to her, it is useful to take a closer look at the interpretive logics that structure Nadia's political subjectivity and engagements for SAMV.

Nadia's preferred mode of subjectivity is marked by a *spatial logic of rapprochement* or *connection*. This logic allows her to switch between the different "worlds" or "environments"—SAMV, her family and the "Flemish" or "white" public sphere—while maintaining a high degree of interpretive coherence. Nadia's discourse is littered with spatial metaphors that help her to categorise the ideological language games she prefers and dislikes. She explains how she would like to be a "bridge for others", connecting the interactional settings that make up her social reality. She also emphasises the difficulty of drawing "a line" between her self and her job. Moreover, she looks for a "road" between a "Moroccan" and a "Belgian" way of being. This trope of connection lies at the core of Nadia's political engagement and preferred sense of self. Moreover, it is this sense of self that is undermined by classic "identity"-related questions.

Nadia characterises the three "worlds" or environments in which she moves with reference to three types of language games and with reference to conflicting definitions "emancipation"—a key concept constitutive of her preferred mode of political engagement. First of all, there is the SAMV environment. Nadia explained to me that she grew up in a provincial Flemish town described in terms of "a very Belgian environment". Hers was one of the only Moroccan families in her village. It was only when she started to go out at the age of 15 or 16 that she started to notice normative "differences" in the way "boys" and "girls" were being treated in her family. In order to come up with "arguments" for the "conversations" she had with her "father", she started reading authors such as "Fatima Mernissi", a well-known Islamic feminist sociologist.[13] In the excerpt below, she shows how these gender-related issues are still relevant to her work at SAMV.

> NB: […] And I still feel this today, in my job, that you … you're very much involved, also because it's about yourself … . Well, we work with allochthon women, and it's about emancipation and that sort of stuff, but … . Well, partly it's also about ourselves, and sometimes it's rather difficult to draw the line like "this is just my job" … . It's very close to uhm … one another. But that's also what's so nice about it, I don't want something that's simply …, well without engagement, or about a theme that does not really uhm …
> JZ: touch you
> NB: No, […]
> **excerpt 101 – 11/06/2008**

---

[13] Fatima Mernissi is a Moroccan sociologist. She is also a well-known Islamic feminist who argues that the Koran does not justify an unequal treatment of men and women.

At the time of our interview, Nadia found it "rather difficult to draw the line" between her job and her sense of self. On the one hand, the organisation seeks to stimulate the organisation of "allochthon women" but she admits that the concern with "emancipation and that sort of stuff" is also relevant to her and her colleagues at a more personal level. Her "engagement" for SAMV is a project that is closely related to her sense of self. The themes that are being dealt with within SAMV are "close" to her skin and Nadia points out that her "job" and her self are "very close" "to one another". This is why the border between her sense of self and the activities she is involved in is hard to draw.

The second world Nadia moves in is the "white environment". This is the space in which Nadia is faced with exhausting identity-related questions. As an example of one setting in which this happens, she referred to her apprenticeship in the production team of the Flemish soap opera *Thuis* (English: Home), broadcasted by the Flemish public broadcasting company (VRT). In the excerpt below, we can see how Nadia was "once again confronted with all these questions" that do not correspond to her preferred sense of self and engagement. The main difference with the SAMV environment is that conversations in SAMV have "passed this stage". SAMV focuses on emancipation. Sometimes, questions about "girls", "the headscarf" and the "Ramadan" do not pop up "for days".

Another problem with the Flemish or white environment of the VRT was that a job within this context "implied a lot less engagement" with the feminist gender and ethnicity themes Nadia wants to address. Her "themes"—the SAMV issues related to the "internal debate"—required more attention. In combination with the type of misrecognition she had to deal with in the VRT context, this consideration informed her decision to keep on working for SAMV.

> NB: […] I was at Thuis, … the soap, and yes, that was a lot of fun, but still, within this white environment, you are once again confronted with all these questions (sighs), "Well, what about this Ramadan?", and "Girls?", and "Did you ever have to wear a headscarf?". So you get all these questions once again. And well, within the Support Center, we have really passed this stage. Well, we simply do our jobs, I don't get this sort of questions for days and yes, … . It implied a lot less engagement with respect to content, it was kind of, I did like it, … but that personal engagement was not deep enough

in order to … . I was offered a full-time, but (sighs), I was like, "I am not ready at the Support Center yet, I still want to … work about these themes". And I still would like to work in the media, but yes, … on my themes, not merely.
excerpt 102 – 11/06/2008

The third "environment" Nadia Babazia mentioned in the course of our interview is her "family". Interestingly, the "little world" of "the Support Center" sometimes "clashes" with the realities of her "community" and family contexts. Note that at SAMV, there is agreement on the importance of "emancipation". Nevertheless, the "clash" with other contexts, forced Nadia to ask her self "how to give meaning to" her "emancipation" "on a personal level". As we will see, different ideas concerning the meaning of "emancipation" are among the most distinguishing features between these environments that "sometimes" "clash" metaphorically.

NB: At the Support Center we are like "yes, we have to stimulate the internal debate about role patterns, we have to stimulate it, men and women, and", well, you know the theoretical ideas about that … . But in the evening you go home, and, and, I have a husband at home [laughs], and, and it's not … well, it clashes at times. Sometimes you can, well, you are within your own little world, and then you are confronted sometimes, often, with well, "what is it really like in the community" … . You know what I mean? Sometimes we can go on a weekend with the entire general assembly of the Support Center, and then we are all like "we want this and that, and this and that", after that, everyone comes home, … and, and you too, have to manage, how to give meaning to your emancipation.
JZ: On a personal level?
NB: On a personal level, yes, … . And sometimes, … well, sometimes, this is how I, with respect to my environment eh, how I deal with it … . I don't know if this is a complete answer to
JZ: yes yes, but
NB: yeah, sometimes it can kind of clash.
excerpt 103 – 11/06/2008

Nadia's preferred sense of self is frequently articulated by means of spatial metaphors. This can be exemplified with reference to the excerpt below. She explains that she wants to be "a bridge to others". She does not want "to separate" herself from her "community" even though her social "trajectory" went reasonably well". She values the "connection" she can make between the different "worlds" in which she moves. The operation of a spatial logic of rapprochement should be clear at this point. It informs Nadia's preferred mode of engagement as well as her preferred mode of subjectivity.

> NB: [...] it's fun to work on ... on such themes uhm ... . Because I feel like it's not because I ... my trajectory went reasonably well, that I don't want to be ... a bridge to others or, I don't know. Well, somehow, I consider this to be my responsibility ...
> JZ: And where do you think this comes from?
> NB: Well, I don't know, it's, it's, well, ... it's a feeling, I don't know, It's a feeling I have, like ... "it is sort of my community ... I don't want to separate from it", or something. I do want to be able to do my own thing. And, ... probably, ... I don't know what the Moroccan community, ... well, some will agree with some things and others won't, but I , ... I do think it's important to ... have a connection with it, and if possible, to bring a positive energy, ...
> JZ: in it
> NB into it [laughs], yes, and especially with regard to youngsters.
> **excerpt 104 – 11/06/2008**

A closer analysis of the SAMV "environment", the family "environment" that is partially located in the "internal debate" and the "white", "Flemish" and "Belgian" "environment" shows that these "worlds" are characterised by different *enunciative logics* according to which the notion of "emancipation" gathers very different meanings. One might claim that all the logics identified in this paper involve an enunciative dimension. Nevertheless, I will use the notion of enunciative logic in order to highlight how an individual may link various modes of speech and/or writing to each other by means of (meta-)linguistic categorisations and metaphors.

> NB: [...] But I do think that uhm, ... because I have been raised in a very Flemish environment ... and uhm ... well for instance, my physician can really say to me like, ... because I still go to my physician in Wuustwezel, ... like uhm "well, I really think it's nice what you're doing, you can play a very important role within your community", but ... in such a paternalistic,

5 Self and Politics in Activist Discourse 345

mothering way .... Whereas I don't want to, well, I do want to play a role for my community, but not in the way she means it .... She has like this image of women like "those women are being repressed", and yes, ... you know, as if you ... as if you are liberating them or something, whereas I .... Well, I do not consider this to be my role. I do not want to deal with my community in this way, ... They give another meaning to it ....
JZ: Yes
NB: I think they may all be quite enthusiastic about uhm, about what I'm doing eh, but I think they give it another meaning.
excerpt 105 – 11/06/2008

The excerpt above indicates that people in Nadia Babazia's "Flemish environment" tend to give another meaning to her engagement in SAMV than the one she prefers. Even though people such as her physician in Wuustwezel may be "enthusiastic" about the "role" she plays with respect to her "community", Nadia suspects they interpret this "role" in a rather "paternalistic" or "mothering" way. Her physician may mean well but clearly misrecognises her preferred mode of engagement. Nadia Babazia does not consider it to be her "role" to liberate "women" in this particular way. Her preferred mode of engagement and emancipation is informed by an ethical refusal to define such notions for others. She even wonders "how to give meaning" to her "emancipation" within her own family context. It is therefore quite understandable that she refuses to do so for others.

Nadia's response to the problem of misrecognition lies in a mode of engagement that is marked by a polysemic understanding of what it means to emancipate oneself. One might say that a *polysemic logic of enunciation* structures her preferred mode of "engagement". Nadia refuses to define "emancipation" and "participation" on behalf of others. The same logic can also be found in the way SAMV/*Ella* prefers to deal with the "taboos" of the internal debate within the so-called community.

It is difficult to break certain taboos on your own, if there is no support within the community. We therefore never suggest only one solution or model. Rather, we want to stimulate people to think independently, to be critical with respect to common opinions/convictions within one's own community, and to make their own choices. (Bouzarmat 2010)

The logic informing Nadia Babazia's approach to minority- and gender-related themes is quite different from the logic informing the discourse of her physician and her co-workers at the VRT. Both her physician's "paternalistic" and "mothering" comments and the "questions" asked by her colleagues at the VRT involve rather narrow definitions of concepts such as "engagement", "emancipation" and "participation" and aim to fix the trajectories of emancipation minorities are supposed to go through. The definitions of emancipation and the questions regarding identity Nadia is faced with in her "white" and "Flemish" environments can therefore be named in terms of a *monosemic logic of enunciation* that does not allow for sufficient reflexivity and choice-making on the part of minorities themselves.

We can conclude this section by noticing that the enunciative logics that inform dominant modes of discourse in particular contexts also inform the prevailing interpellations and forms of address. An individual's ability to identify large-scale enunciative strategies by means of metapragmatic language use correlates with his or her awareness of a preferred mode of interaction, politics and self. Nadia Babazia is quite aware of the fact that the political tensions between individuals and organisations in the public sphere are to a large extent informed by different interpretations of the categories that give meaning to her preferred mode of engagement and subjectivity. By metapragmatically classifying different types of voices, questions and definitions of emancipation, she managed to construct a sense of self as someone who bridges and connects different worlds through her socio-political engagement (see Zienkowski 2015).

5.4.3 Common Logics for Dealing with Feelings of Misrecognition

Feelings of misrecognition and injustice lie at the basis of many political engagements. In order to deal with these feelings, my interviewees gathered and mobilised a great deal of symbolic and cultural capital in function of their social and political engagements. They moved from a relatively passive experience of feelings of misrecognition to a subjectivity marked by a high degree of political awareness and engagement. They learned to objectify and to (re-)articulate their affective reactions to misfiring interpellations in the context of wider social and political dynamics. People may rely on very different theories, ideologies and frameworks in order to give meaning to their world. Nevertheless, the family resemblances in the way my interviewees counter feelings of misrecognition can be described in terms of a recurring set of logics that may be named as follows: *visual* and *tactile logics of embodiment*; *spatial logics*; and *logics of enunciation*.

Such logics allow my interviewees to deal metapragmatically with misfiring forms of address. Let us start with the *visual* and *tactile logics of embodiment*. Many interviewees objectified their emotional experiences in terms of visual and tactile metaphors. Raising one's political awareness involves a process whereby one uses abstract signifiers such as citizenship, discrimination or emancipation in the construction of interpretive logics that allow one to grasp or fix otherwise diffuse and confusing emotional responses to problematic ideological interpellations. Subjects often prove to be aware of the emotional functions of discourse and mark this awareness through the use of spatial and/or visual metaphors. The use of these metaphors helps them to indicate how particular discursive frameworks helped them to get 'a hold' of their emotions and 'to see' what was going on in the public sphere.

In order to cope with feelings of misrecognition, many (future) activists and intellectuals relied on large-scale *visual* and *tactile logics of embodiment*. These logics enabled them to reflexively articulate a more powerful and coherent sense of self. The interview with Naima Charkaoui provides us with a case in point. Before Naima started her studies and became director of the Minority Forum, she felt that "something" was not "right" even though she "couldn't get a hold" of what bothered her exactly in the way mainstream media dealt with minority-related topics and voices. Naima reported a sense of "friction" between her own experiences on the one hand and the discourses on minorities she observed in the public sphere on the other hand. In order to name and to explain her feelings of misrecognition, she would have to learn how to articulate her subjective experience and sense of self with and within a critical explanatory logic.

Naima Charkaoui found such an explanatory discourse in the lessons of Sami Zemni on culturalist, essentialist and relativist ideologies. His lessons provided an intellectual discourse that allowed her to adopt a "pragmatic" and reflexive stance of her own. A *tactile interpretive logic* runs through the way she describes her early feelings. The inability to objectify or to "get a hold" of her feelings and the discursive processes that give rise to them could only be overcome by adopting a "framework" that would allow her to "look at" the issues that had been troubling her for years in a more "rational" way. By relating her own discourse to frameworks such as those articulated by Zemni and other people she looked up to, she was finally able to move beyond expressions such as "mmh, I don't seem to feel good about this". The attainment of this deeper mode of reflexive and political awareness is often articulated in visual terms.

The visual logic of embodiment that structures the way Naima Charkaoui talks about her emerging political awareness is closely intertwined with her acquired capacity "to distance" herself from the themes that lie "close" to her "heart" and to deal with them in a more "rational way". Naima explained how she suddenly could "get a hold" of the mechanisms and processes of interpellation she was involved in. It is only after the acquisition of this analytical gaze that she gained more control over her feelings and over the way she could position herself in the public realm. Nevertheless, even though she described her preferred mode of subjectivity as being marked by a "critical" and "pragmatic" attitude that allows her to "look at reality", she does not want to lose herself in "big theories" either.

Visual and tactile logics of embodiment work in tandem in Naima's political sense of self. Even though "insight" is important to her, feelings continue to drive her in her public engagements with the minority debate. Even though she considers herself to be "on the sensitive side" of the emotional spectrum, she claims to have become "increasingly sensitive" to the "increasing complexity" of issues related to minority politics. Moreover, she explicitly stated that "feeling" and experiencing "injustice" and "inequality" is more important than "rationally" seeing what is going on, if one is to understand what drives her political engagement. Similar patterns of self-interpretation can be found in many other interviews. This will be exemplified later with reference to the "eye openers" discussed by activist scholar Nadia Fadil and with reference to some of the visual metaphors politician Zohra Othman used when describing the development of her political awareness.

Another common set of logics that structures a great deal of political discourse on political engagement relies heavily on spatial metaphors. Spatial logics can be named and (re)articulated in different ways. For instance, it is possible to identify *spatial logics of closure* and *disclosure* in the interview conducted with Youssef Souissi. We also identified a *logic of rapprochement* or *connection* that performed key functions in Nadia Babazia's preferred mode of subjectivity. Language users frequently make use of spatial metaphors in order to categorise different types of interaction. For instance, Youssef Souissi identified a lack of "dialogue" in Flanders. The problematic "evacuation" of "duality" and dialectics in Flanders prompted him to "make room" for a politics of dissent.

Youssef relied heavily on metapragmatic metaphors of closure in order to categorise practices of "labelling". His preference for a *logic of disclosure* is manifestly present in the "choice" he presents Flanders with: one either opts for "an opening" of "the mind" or one continues the current "show politics" that will result in a situation where everyone lives in his or her own mental "ghetto". Youssef is not alone in his use of spatial metaphors. We saw how Nadia Babazia attempted to be a "bridge" across the various "environments" and "worlds" she lives in. Articulating a preferred mode of politics marked by a *logic of connection* or *rapprochement*, she stated that she is looking for a "road" between "Moroccan" and "Belgian" ways of being.

Likewise, liberal politician Hicham el Mzairh argued that assimilation politics leads to a situation in which people start "withdrawing themselves" and creates a situation in which "they are not open to change". Instead, people "remain stuck" within traditions, mentalities and cultures that hinder "the freedom of the individual". Moreover, Amane X argued that "allochthons" may be "falling back" onto their own "nest" in response to an excess of "integration". Spatial metaphors and logics can be found in every single interview I conducted. They allow language users to acquire and articulate a sense of coherence across the multiplicity of interactions we are faced with in the public realm. They allow us to anchor or to index our sense of self in relation to the shifting contexts through which we move.

The last common set of logics I would like to discuss here is of an enunciative nature. In a general sense, all logics are of an enunciative type since they all involve an articulation of voices and statements in and through discursive practice. However, there are systematic patterns in the way people organise these voices in relation to each other and in relation to the practices that constitute the public sphere. I will reserve the notion of *enunciative logic* for identifying specific ways in which people establish such patterns.

For instance, we saw how Nadia Babazia distinguished between three sets of language games, environments and "worlds". Each of these contexts was marked by different forms or address and by different definitions of "emancipation". Nadia clearly preferred a *polysemic enunciative logic* that allows minorities to fix the meanings of such signifiers on their own terms. The ability to identify large-scale enunciative strategies deployed by others by means of metapragmatic language use correlates with one's awareness of preferred modes of interaction, politics and selfhood. Nadia Babazia opposed the *patronising logic* that informs many "white" or "Flemish" environments and the *monosemic* understanding of emancipation that goes along with this. She demonstrated a high degree of awareness of the fact that political tensions between individuals and organisations are to a large extent informed by different interpretations of abstract categories. Different discursive spaces often imply different language games whose rules may "clash" with each other (see Zienkowski 2015). Awareness of the normative patterns that structure contexts of enunciation and interpellation is a key aspect of the human capacity for political awareness. The way in which this awareness is articulated can be described in terms of enunciative logics.

5.5 Establishing a Coherent Sense of Self: The Case of Zohra Othman

The experience of feelings of misrecognition implies some degree of reflexive awareness with respect to a preferred mode of subjectivity. This does not mean that we always have a very clear concept of who and what we are as persons or as human beings. Neither does it imply the existence of a stable core of selfhood that can be uncovered by investigating a subject's discursive practice. Subjectivity remains an opaque phenomenon. However, the experience of having to deal with mismatching self-interpretations does intensify the need for reflexive strategies for self-affirmation and constitution. In order to maintain a manageable degree of coherence in one's sense of self, human beings engage in a perpetual balancing act whereby they incessantly rearticulate their indexical relations to themselves, to each other and to discursive reality in general.

The self is anything but a stable entity and all accounts of the self can be described in terms of "working frameworks and divisions we use in practice to derive a sense of the varied truths and authenticities we are" (Holstein and Gubrium 2000, 71). If we stick to William James' interpretation of the pragmatic maxim, we can consider the self as an idea we ride. Those who seek to understand the constitution of the empirical self will therefore have to investigate the practical consequences of this idea as it is articulated in specific discursive contexts. However, the ideas we ride—including our ideas about our selves—are instable as well. James once used the image of the self as a long succession of different herdsmen who rapidly come into possession of flocks of ideas and experiences they try to keep together. Selves can therefore be analysed as interpretive functions of the way we articulate experiences with each other and the way we infuse these discursive elements with emotions and affects.

To say that the self is an idea we ride is to say that its constitution requires an act of discursive imagination that configures the way we act upon ourselves, upon others and upon the world. Ultimately, the very concept of the self is a reification of processes that allow individual bodies to reflexively position themselves as more or less coherent entities in relation to spatial, temporal, social and (inter-)textual aspects of contextual reality. As I mentioned before, the self can be thought of in terms of an assembly that is just as stable as the self-techniques and practices we engage in while we fix our sense of self into a temporary semblance of substance we act upon. In the subsections below, I will present an analysis of the metapragmatic processes that allow Marxist politician Zohra Othman to realise this ethical feat. This implies a focus on the way she establishes relevant contexts for self-interpretation.

Zohra Othman is a politician involved in the Marxist–Leninist party PvdA (Worker's Party of Belgium). At the time of our interview, she also worked as a lawyer for *Progress Lawyers Network*, a network of progressive law firms in the Belgian cities Antwerp, Ghent and Brussels. This latter organisation devotes special attention to human rights, racism, equal opportunities, migrants, refugees and union-related issues. The organisation explicitly seeks to guarantee "the best possible defence for the victims of contemporary society and for those who strive for change" in a society where "more and more people are becoming victims of a system where profit is paramount". In 2003, Zohra Othman participated in local elections as a candidate for the alliance between the AEL and the PvdA named *Resist*. However, she did not get elected until 2012 when she received the highest number of votes in the Antwerp district called Borgerhout. In 2013, she became the first district alderman of the PvdA ever.

I met Zohra Othman at the debate on *Islam: a house with many chambers* discussed in my interview with Youssef Souissi. However, I asked her for an interview at a fundraiser for the Al Awda hospital in Gaza. Zohra is interested in a wide variety of local, national and international issues. Our interview touches upon issues as diverse as her participation in Resist; her experiences with racism; the systemic inequalities triggered by capitalism; the election of Obama; the wars in Iraq and Palestine; and her involvement within the debate on Islam in Flanders. In the subsections below, I will focus on the metapragmatic strategies and logics that allowed Zohra to articulate a relatively coherent sense of self throughout her discussion of these topics.

As is the case with many other activists and intellectuals, her political awareness was triggered by "a gut feeling" or with "a feeling of injustice" and a "spontaneous indignation" that set her on "a search for answers" to questions about the way "the system functions". The very articulation of this 'systemic' question is already indicative of an active Marxist subjectivity. As we will see, Zohra would gradually learn to name and articulate a *systemic logic* that negatively defines her preferred mode of subjectivity and politics. Nevertheless, her gut feeling of injustice "did not originate in a Marxist education" but in a dislocation of the religious "values" her parents passed on to her. Zohra is therefore critical about people who create a "false opposition" between Marxism and the type of religious subjectivity that drives people to "change things in the world". She ironically remarks that she does not consider this type of opposition to be "dialectic".

5 Self and Politics in Activist Discourse   353

ZO: Well, I uhm … I have become a Marxist, but I was actually uhm … raised … in uhm … in a Muslim family, and I consider this to be an important part of me. Because, … when I, uhm … this, well, this spontaneous indignation, or this feeling of injustice I have, did not originate in a Marxist education, but in uhm … my education at home, and uhm … these are basically values that were passed along by my parents, through their religion, and these are things I carry along. And to say like "I am going to renounce faith, because it does not amount to anything good" … well … in my particular case, I don't consider this, I don't consider this to be dialectic
JZ: [laughs]
ZO: [laughs] well, to say it with a Marxist term … . It does not make any sense either, it's uhm … . I think, … if you look around you, there are many people who uhm … . Their engagement, my engagement, has become more strong due to Marxism, but my engagement did not originate … in a Marxist education. And I think this is important, because there are many people who are driven by their education, by their faith, … to do things, and [who] want to change things in the world. And uhm, … that's why sometimes, I consider this to be … a false opposition.
excerpt 106 – 04/02/2009

Zohra Othman embraces both Islamic and Marxist discursive elements as part of her preferred sense of self. Nevertheless, the religiously inspired values of her upbringing did not provide her with an explanation of the injustices she observed in the world and in her own family context. Put differently, even though she embraces the religiously inspired values of her parents, religion did not provide her with the answers she was looking for. Marxism did. The Marxist theoretical framework allowed her to articulate distinct confrontations with injustice into a coherent analytical framework. More specifically, Marxism enabled her to articulate issues of racism, the economy and the international dimension of injustice with each other in a systematic way. These three points of interest correspond to three phases in the development of her political awareness: "it really was like first racism, then the economic situation of workers, and then the international". Zohra pinpointed the start of her engagement in the context of her work for *Objectief* (English: Objective), a movement promoting equal social and political rights for all Belgian residents.

Objectief was created as a response to the breakthrough of the far right on the Black Sunday of 1991. Its initial goal was to collect just as much signatures for equal rights for migrants and for an automatic recognition of the Belgian nationality as the number of votes that went to the far right VB: 479 971. Today, *Objectief* helps people who seek to apply for the Belgian nationality. The campaign *Objectief 479 971* collected more than a million signatures by 1995. These signatures were handed over to the Prime Minister but the political impact of this petition remained limited due to the association with the radically left-wing party PvdA (Stouthuysen 1995, 87–88; Van Puymbroeck 2014). According to Zohra Othman, these signatures "ended up in a drawer of some desk" because of electoral considerations. This experience rocked her "faith in the bourgeois parties" and after the petition, Zohra decided to engage herself for the PvdA. In the sections below, I will discuss the development of Zohra Othman's political awareness and engagement in more detail.

5.5.1 Opening One's Eyes to the Film of One's Life

The first phase of Zohra Othman's political awareness is marked by a preoccupation with the topic of racism and by her engagement for *Objectief*. As a student, she focused on migrant voting rights, but it was not until she started to work as a lawyer that her "eyes really opened". There is a clear visual logic of embodiment that runs through Zohra Othman's account of her developing political awareness and engagement. In spite of her feelings of injustice, Zohra admitted that she grew up in a "protected environment". Due to her subject position as a lawyer, she was faced with racism in a way that made her reconsider events and stories that took place in her family during her childhood.

During the second year of her apprenticeship, a Moroccan couple consulted Zohra's firm. Their five-year-old kid was not allowed to re-enlist in the third year of kindergarten with the argument that the toddler needed special education.[14] According to Zohra and her colleague, this did not

---

[14] In Flanders, the notion of *special education* (Dutch: buitengewoon onderwijs) is used in order to refer to educational facilities for people who are unable to participate in the regular educational circuit because of learning difficulties, behavioural problems and/or physical, mental or sensory disabilities.

have anything to do with the cognitive capacities of this toddler but everything with the emerging phenomenon of so-called concentration schools. In Flanders, the notion of concentration school is used in order to designate schools with high 'concentrations' of students with migrant backgrounds. The school in question noticed that many of the "white parents" moved to other neighbourhoods and schools. It tried to counter this situation by referring kids that did not fit its "pedagogical project" to special education. Zohra and her colleague lost this case, but the kids did not go to "special education".

The point to be made here is that Zohra's confrontation with the story of this family triggered a strong feeling of recognition on her part. She engaged in a process of association that allowed her to link the story of her clients to the story of her own sister and to the wider issue of racism in society. In the excerpt below, Zohra uses the visual metaphor of a film that started to play in front of her eyes when confronted with the story of the toddler's parents. Doing so, she throws contextual lines of vision onto the situation of her sister who followed an educational track that did not conform to her intellectual capacities either. Moreover, throughout this association, Zohra started "to see how the system works" with respect to "poor people" and with respect to racism. A few lines further down the interview, she remarked that "as a lawyer" she has to deal with racism-related issues all the time. It is in this sense that her job is very "confrontational".

> ZO: You can't imagine how you feel then, …. These parents come to you, and yes, you feel related to them, because, well … these are Moroccan parents, these are families, … . Well yes, it's as if this is … a family in which you grew up yourself, and then you think like "come on, … this, this cannot be", and then uhm, the film starts to play … . When we were little, my eldest sister, fortunately she escaped this because she is very intelligent, … she was also simply referred to professional education, because one thought, well, she was fit for tailoring, and for nothing else. She was, she simply did not fit in tailoring, she was simply … very intelligent. And so, that film starts to play, and then you think like, yes, … even though you always felt protected yourself, … you do start to see how the system works with respect to sort of, poor people … . And then we instituted legal proceedings, uhm, against that school, uhm, for refusing these children.

excerpt 107 – 04/02/2009

The second phase in the development of Zohra Othman's political awareness is marked by an increasing focus on the economic dimension of the system. The same visual logic of self-interpretation pops up here as well. Even as a kid, Zohra realised that she did not want the life her parents had. Her father did "hard and dirty" work. He was "always tired" and in need of "peace of quiet". Her mother was therefore "saddled with all the care for the family". When Zohra commenced her studies, many doors opened for her and she rolled almost "automatically" into "the life of an intellectual". Because of this, the "reality" of people who "have to do such work" faded "into the background" and it was not until she got into contact with "unions and syndicates" in the context of her engagement as a PvdA politician that she could "open" her "eyes" to this economic aspect of reality once again.

> ZO: And then, little by little, … I rolled into it politics. And then I went along … to a number of uhm factories, and talked to workers, and their delegations, … yes, … . And then, well, the working conditions of these people, then you think like [sighs] … and then, everything comes …
> JZ: mmh … and then you see your father again
> ZO: everything comes back yes … and then you make this link with racism of old, with this discrimination of that school that you, through your practice as a lawyer… . And then, by going back to the factories, … there is a part of reality that you lose sight of, from the position of an intellectual … .
> JZ: mmh
> ZO: that comes back to you, and then, … then I thought like … "it's not only with respect to racism, but also with respect to … the economic side that there's a lot that isn't right" eh … and then, … little by little, more and more [laughs], I engaged myself … and then, … well, the international aspect was added to it.
> **excerpt 108 – 04/02/2009**

In the excerpt above, Zohra explained how everything came back to her as a consequence of the conversations and talks she had with "workers and their delegations" and as a consequence of her confrontation with "the working conditions of these people". Moreover, she explained that "you lose sight" of this "part of reality" while occupying "the position of an intellectual". Nevertheless, her awareness of the economic aspect of discursive reality was clearly reactivated in the context of her political practices for the PvdA. As everything came back to her and as she saw her father again in the film playing before her eyes, the thought came to her that "it's not only with respect to racism, but also with respect to the economic side that there's a lot that isn't all right".

As Zohra opened up her "eyes", as the "film" of her life started to play in response to experiences with others whose lives are not that different from the lives of her family members, Zohra started to contextualise isolated events and stories as instances of a more general problematic linked to racism and socio-economic inequality within an over-arching system. Visual tropes play an important role in the establishment of these articulatory links. They articulate specific experiences with large-scale social, economic and political processes in the public realm. As such, Zohra's metapragmatic contextualisation strategies allowed her to critically articulate her own subject positions (e.g. lawyer, daughter, PvdA politician) with those of others (father, mother, sister, worker, Muslim). But in order to understand the particularities of the way in which she configured her relation to these positions, we need to take a look at what she meant by "the system" and its "logic".

5.5.2 Objectifying the Systemic Logic of Capitalism

Zohra Othman did not find the "answers" she was looking for at the university. There was no one there who explained the workings of "the system" and its "excesses" to her. Zohra would develop her Marxist framework almost completely outside of the academic context. She learned about Marx and about political economy through "self study" because her professors dealt with Marx "in two sentences" and only treated the "political economy" of Keynes. Based on recommendations of people she met outside of the academic context, she started to read Marx himself. She also studied Lenin's writings on the role of the state, on the revolution and on the history of the Soviet Union. But what is more relevant for our current discussion is to see how "Marxism" provided her with the "answers" that allowed her to "see" the way the system functions with respect to racism, with respect to the economy and with respect to injustice at the international level.

ZO: so, in the, I, well, to me, ... Marxism, it gives me, uhm ... answers about, about many things that ... that go ...
JZ: mmh
ZO: uhm wrong. Uhm, yes, for instance, [about] imperialism and [about] how imperialism basically used racism in order to uhm ... eh, [about] how the, well, the West to put it like this, started to colonise other continents, informed by ...
JZ: yes
ZO: by an idea like "they are uncivilised, and we,
JZ: superior
ZO: are going to [laughs] bring civilisation". In order to introduce the image of uncivilised cultures ... so yes, ... you probably know about this eh ...
JZ: yes [laughs].
excerpt 109 – 04/02/2009

In the excerpt above, Zohra Othman explicitly stated that "Marxism" provided her with the answers she was looking for. As an example, she referred to the way she started to understand "how imperialism basically used racism" in order to "colonise other continents" on the basis of an "image of uncivilised cultures". Zohra remarked that I probably knew about this because she was aware of the fact that I contributed to some articles in a book that explicitly criticised this type of culturalist politics (Zienkowski et al. 2007; Zienkowski and Maly 2007). The point to be made here is that Zohra's statements on the logic of the system are marked by a trope of reification. Zohra Othman heavily relied on abstract terms that explained the workings of "the system" to her. However, it should also be noted that she illustrated its operation with reference to concrete events and narratives.

In order to illustrate her point about the relationship between imperialism and racism, Zohra told me about the first black pilots of the US army. She read in a Flemish newspaper how these men were "filled with emotion" at the inauguration dinner of Obama's first term as the President of the USA. The article explained that initially, "black people" were prohibited to partake in pilot exams because their brains were supposedly "not able to resist the G-forces" at play. Zohra read this story to her seven-year-old son who reacted by accusing those who hold such ideas of not having any brains themselves. Zohra smiled while she recalled her son's critique of this racist idea, but she also pointed out that these are the very "theories and ideas" that "Imperialism or the West has been using in order to install racism for a period of two hundred years or longer". Moreover, she stated that this way of thinking continues to resonate in Belgium.

> ZO: But more concretely, … in Belgium, I think that it's also uhm … well, a politics of pitting people against … each other, in order to prevent, … for instance, with respect to labour, …
> JZ: mmh
> ZO: uhm … one basically … says to employees like, "well", the idea like "well, there are migrants who make you lose your job, and who create poor working conditions", and so on. Whereas that poor migrant probably makes even less money, and has probably even less work. So you see it's the economy that pits people against each other exactly … in order to prevent that they … become a strong group that stands up for common interests, and … well, … I don't know if, … you know what I mean, don't you?
> JZ: yes, yes
> ZO: So, it has basically given me an answer, like, … "why does racism appears … in Belgium", and then you sort of see the, … the broad outlines.
> **excerpt 110 – 04/02/2009**

In the excerpt above, Zohra elaborated on the way racism operates in Belgium and in the world in general. She believes that "racism" appears in response to an economic politics that pits people against each other in order to prevent the articulation of common interests. People are being made afraid of migrants causing them to lose their jobs and their beneficial working conditions. To Zohra, it is the workings of the "economy" that explain why racism appears in Belgium. When I asked her whether she considered this to be a conscious politics, we get to the core about Zohra Othman's ideas on the *systemic logic of capitalism*. To Zohra, the question whether the workings of the system are consciously planned proves to be irrelevant.

ZO: Well, conscious or unconscious? I think it doesn't really matter whether it's conscious or unconscious. It's rather a … a … well, a logical consequence of the … the uhm … the model wherein we live. So, this, … this economic system wherein we live, which is established in order to uhm … to make maximal profits. And this maximal profit has to be achieved at the expense of people, at the expense of working conditions, … . And uhm, well, … if you see that it's the same companies that uhm, well, in India, or in uhm, in Africa, produce, … well, [that] let people work for minimal wages, [who] say over here like "yes, it's those people who take your work away" … . Nothing impedes them from offering these people (laughs) the same

JZ: no, (laughs)

ZO: working conditions, or work environment, so that no one has steal jobs from, well, you know, …

JZ: yes yes,

ZO: they are the ones who, well, it's the economy that organises things in such a way that one population group … is pitted against … another. And well, you can sort of see this in the crisis as well … . This protectionism, and uhm, … . Well you see it in the …

JZ: the uhm … nationalistic protectionism?

ZO: it, it, it, yes, in Belgium, it is played, … well, with GM against Germany and, … and then you think like, "something isn't right here", well … .

JZ: no

ZO: well, it's not uhm … . So, uhm, … Marxism gives me answers uhm … uhm, to this. And on the international level it's obvious that uhm, … that it's always about strategic interests, eh.

excerpt 111 – 04/02/2009

To Zohra, the emergence of racism and socio-economic injustice is a "logical consequence" of "the model we live in". The system is designed to make maximal profits at the expense of people, working conditions and the environment. Zohra argues that it is "the economy" itself that pits population groups against each other. The *logic of the system* is thus marked by a self-serving systemic instrumentality. It is a logic marked by "strategic interests", something that is noticeable not only in the local struggles against injustice but also at "the international level". Zohra is very clear about the fact that it is a Marxist framework that allows her to answer the question

5 Self and Politics in Activist Discourse 361

how the system works. By objectifying and externalising this systemic logic, she is able to engage in discursive acts of resistance. At the same time, her description of this logic colours her discourse with a lot of reified terms and generalisations. According to Zohra, racism has become increasingly normalised in Flanders since open displays of racism are ever more common. She explains this rise in racism with reference to a systemic crisis:

> ZO: The way I see it, … the more a system gets into a crisis … the more it resorts to … well … to weap, well, to weapons such as racism in order to divide people more and more, and [in order to] pit people against each other … uhm … so that the ones who are really responsible for the crisis, … or, or, in order to avoid that people realise that the crisis is actually caused by the system itself, and not because, … not because one person is black, and the other one is yellow. This, this this simply does not cause the crisis … . The crisis simply lies in the organisation of the economic system. So, I think, yes. It has gotten worse.
> **excerpt 112 – 04/02/2009**

The system described by Zohra has an agency of its own. It resorts to "weapons such as racism in order to divide people" in order to divert attention from those "who are really responsible for the crisis" and the fact that the crisis is actually caused by "the organisation of the economic system" itself. Nevertheless, in spite of the fact that things have gotten increasingly worse—a situation aggravated by post-9/11 "islamophobia"—Zohra does "feel like … we are at a turning point". In spite of this rather bleak analysis, Zohra Othman is not a pessimist. Her objectification of the *systemic logic of capitalism* allowed her to distinguish between the way the system works and the preferred mode of politics and selfhood she pursues in her political engagement.

5.5.3 Lightening Up the Dark Space in One's Inner Centre

Zohra used a series of spatial metaphors in order to articulate her relationship between the public realm, her sense of self and the narrative structure of our interview. Thus far, we discussed the way she developed her political awareness about "racism" and the "economic" aspects of inequality at a relatively local level. The third component of her political awareness was triggered by a series of confrontations with injustice at a more "international" level. In 1999, Zohra Othman had the opportunity to travel to Iraq where she was faced with the way "ordinary people" and "children" suffered under the UN-imposed embargo. This confrontation with "the international" brought her "full circle" on a narrative level.

Zohra recalled how this embargo impeded doctors to treat people suffering from cancers that were probably caused by contamination by depleted uranium used in the First Gulf War. One of the doctors working in a hospital she visited told her that he could not even administer morphine to his patients. Instead, he had to resort to sugar for "psychological" effect. Zohra also talked about a visit to a bomb shelter for Iraqi civilians "scorched black" on the inside after a bomb hit the structure. She recalls the "handprints" and the "shadows" left by people burned alive. Such experiences in the international domain "impact" just as much on her "engagement" as injustices at the local level of Antwerp and/or Belgium.

In the excerpt below, Zohra Othman explains why these confrontations made it impossible for her to "to stay at home" in spite of the fact that she sometimes feels "powerless in the face of so much injustice". She explains that she cannot do "nothing", "knowing that all of this is going on" because of an intricate connection between her sense of self and the structure of the outside world. She used the metaphor of a "dark" "little room" in her "inner centre". This metaphor informs mode of self-interpretation marked by a permeable inside/outside distinction. The room in Zohra's inner centre has a "door" that sometimes opens. Through this door, "emotions" and "light" can enter. By doing things that make the world a better place, one's inner centre can become a "more bearable" and "comfortable" space.

> ZO: Yes ... . Yes, I also think, well, it's (sighs) being able to do something ... gives me ... it's like ... an ointment on the wound, it's really uhm, ... I was thinking about it this morning because of what happens in Gaza and in Iraq today, I think, ... Well, you can't (sighs) think about it all the time, but still, ... There's a little room in ... in your inner centre ... and its door ... opens occasionally. And then you sort of allow for ... these emotions. But sometimes, I also have to keep this door, well, shut, and then ... . But it's still

there, this little room is always there, and .... Well, I just think, ... you want to do something in order to make that room ... more comfortable. It's sort of a dark ... well, a dark ...
JZ: sort of a dark little hole (smiles)
ZO: Yes. But you want to make it more comfortable, you want to, you want to, ... Well, you want to do something. Yesterday, I talked to someone who said like "if we can do something, we all gave money, but ...", and I said like "yes, sometimes giving money, ... is the only thing you can do". But well, if there's something ... you can [do] ... well, it makes everything more bearable. Not that I want to have the pretence like ... "I am going to change everything", but nevertheless, you ... can contribute, and take little steps, ... changing the situation, and uhm.
excerpt 113 – 04/02/2009

One might say that Zohra Othman's preferred mode of subjectivity is characterised by a *logic of disclosure* that allows her to link her sense of self with people, events and injustices in the outside world. It is also important to note that Zohra believes that "dark times" are always followed by "better times" because of "the power of people who organise themselves ... and do things for others". Here, we see a first glimpse of her preferred mode of politics. It is a mode of politics marked by "hope" and perseverance. She believes that as long as we "don't shy away in our little corners", something is bound to change. As a case in point, she refers to "all of those people who have been silent under Bush" and who "started to organise themselves" in order to make "Obama" possible. Zohra continues in the excerpt below.

ZO: Yes, I just wanted to say that, ... yes, of course you feel small, and, ... and insignificant, ... as if you're alone ... against ... everyone else. But, ... I have learned myself to ... not to think this (laughs)
JZ: (laughs) that's another little room uhm
ZO: No. Because, this simply isn't true .... There are many people who, ... each of them in their own domain, ... go on, ... every day. And yes, this isn't always visible .... But there are moments where you can see this, and then I think, well, ... "they're there", and yes, ... and something like this can't happen every day .... But it is possible because there are people ... who keep on ... picking up their engagement very quietly. And then, all of a sudden, there is a moment when, ... when it's being outed.
JZ: when it's being expressed

ZO: Yes. And then, and then, … this makes you persevere as well eh, "come on", … this is what I think about instead of thinking about … . Of course, often, it's often a futile fight, but there's always a moment when uhm …
JZ: that isn't the case
ZO: no, when you can [fight] against uhm … and when things change nevertheless … so.
excerpt 114 – 04/02/2009

Zohra's preferred mode of politics involves a collective political practice of people uniting themselves through the articulation of "common interests" undermined by the *systemic logic of capitalism*. And even though one may feel "small" and "insignificant" in the face of the "system", one has to realise that the image of people shying away in their "little corners" is simply incorrect because there are always "many people" engaging themselves in ways that frequently go unnoticed. It is because so many people pick up "their engagement" under the radar that change can come about quickly. For this reason, she believes it is important to "persevere" and to resist the idea that one is engaging in a "futile fight". These transformational moments do not only make the world a better place, they also shed light upon one's "inner centre".

5.5.4 Towards a Preferred Mode of PvdA Politics After Resist

Zohra Othman's preferred mode of political engagement and selfhood crystallises clearly in her discourse on the PvdA and the electoral failure of its alliance with the AEL under the banner of *Resist* in the Belgian federal elections of 2003. In the excerpts below, Zohra reflects on the "lessons" she learned and on the "memories and feelings" of this temporary collaboration with the AEL. According to her, the main reason for the electoral failure of this project should be located in "the obstinacy of racist thought within" the traditional PvdA "constituency" of "workers". Like many other interviewees, Zohra explicitly lauded the AEL for triggering "an enormous dynamic" and a "political awakening" among migrant youth who started to make "political demands" in order to make "the situation for migrants in Belgium more liveable".

ZO: But this Resist [project] didn't really uhm … take flight … . Uhm, a great deal of our constituency, of the Worker's Party of Belgium has uhm, … pulled out because of this … . This basically confronted us with uhm … the uhm obstinacy of racist thought … within our own constituency, workers, … uhm, … . This was the other side of the coin. It was very sobering, and uhm, … . Well, I really had some difficulties with this, uhm … . The notion of young migrants who are claiming their rights, sort of after the example of, … the American civil rights movement, … uhm, … was met with so much resistance. This was really, uhm, … a very hard, a bitter pill to swallow.
excerpt 115 – 04/02/2009

Taking into account Zohra Othman's overall analysis of the way capitalism capitalises on racism in order to block the articulation of common interest, it should be clear why the failure of *Resist* was "a bitter pill to swallow". However, this "difficult" but "sobering" experience forced the PvdA to rethink the way this party interpellated its constituency. Ultimately, she reached the conclusion that the party made the mistake of forcing its constituency to be anti-racist in a top-down manner. The experience with *Resist* made her realise that the PvdA strategy of forcing its constituency to be "anti-racist" and "to advocate equal rights" did not work.

Zohra recalled a conversation with an anonymous "Moroccan" interlocutor who told her that the party should profile itself less with respect to migration-related issues. Her interlocutor suggested that the PvdA should position itself more clearly "as a labour party". The point is not to ignore migrant issues but to focus on "economic demands" so that migration issues can be dealt with in the context of a broader "battle for equal rights". In the excerpts below, we can see Zohra's account of the "lesson" learned by the PvdA after its disappointing experience with the list *Resist*.

ZO: … The lesson to be learned is uhm … there has been a long discussion, but because of this, there has been … a renewal … uhm … of the party, in the sense that there have been several congresses and uhm, … the party decided to uhm, … to re-establish the link with the workers and with the labour movements. This is the … the primary task … of our party. Well, this is a priority. Whereas with Resist, the first [priority was], well, … the international aspect eh, the, … against war, against imperialism.

We basically started to, how shall I put this, uhm, to consider migrants, or migrant organisations as uhm, ... the driving force for change ... and uhm, ... well, after long discussions, we simply returned to uhm, to, to Marx who says like "the driving force for ... for change, is the working class, no matter whether they happen to be migrants or Belgians, it's the working class". And so, well, ... you have to, well, we had to return to our basis, to the core of uhm, ... well, of our existence, of our reason for existence.
excerpt 116 – 04/02/2009

According to Zohra Othman, the "renewal" of the PvdA was predicated upon a discursive strategy in which economic issues, relationships with "workers" and with the "labour movements" were prioritised over "the international" aspects of injustice. This does not mean that "war", "imperialism" and other international problems became less relevant to her political awareness and engagement. Her point is rather that racism and inequality can be dealt with implicitly by focusing first and foremost on economic inequalities and by addressing people on the basis of their "working class" identities. This "return to Marx" and the associated class-based rearticulation of the PvdA project is framed as a "return" to the "basis" and the very "reason for existence" of this political party. As long as the PvdA takes worker's interests at heart, there is no need to address migrant workers separately.

The *Resist* experience also led to a new strategy whereby the party moved away from merely "shouting slogans" to the development of "making demands" and "proposing alternatives" that could be supported by large groups of people. As a case in point, Zohra referred to the so-called *Kiwi Model* for public healthcare whereby social security reimburses the cheapest generic variety of any particular drug. This New Zealand model has been introduced in Belgium upon the publication of PvdA politician and doctor Dirk van Duppen's book on the excessive pricing strategies of the pharmaceutical industry. In 2005, a slimmed-down version of the New Zealand model was adopted in the Belgian healthcare system for a limited number of drugs. To Zohra, this success is a nice example of what "a small party" such as the PvdA can achieve.

For Zohra Othman, the successful introduction of the Kiwi Model was indicative of a shift in the PvdA discursive strategy. According to her, the party no longer advocates mere "demands" that people may consider "utopian" and/or unachievable. Rather, the point is to make demands with respect to "very concrete issues" that can have an impact on "the daily lives" of people. Whereas the pre-*Resist* discursive strategy mainly involved "shouting slogans" about "how unjust the system is", the post-*Resist* PvdA tries to articulate concrete "alternatives". The Kiwi Model is such an alternative. Moreover, in this renewed PvdA discursive strategy, people are asked "to draw their own conclusions" whereas the old-style PvdA "tried to force" its voters into seeing that "you have to be anti racist and you have to advocate equal rights".

> ZO: So uhm, … he, … accuses the big pharma-industry which makes a great deal of uhm … a great deal of profit at the expense of people's health … . It's not merely [a matter of] uhm accusing like "the pharma-industry makes so much profit, and it's simply normal that they contribute too", but [it's also a matter of] exposing the system behind it, … so people can draw their own conclusions like "yes, … actually, it is sort of outrageous". But not merely up to the point where people consider this to be outrageous, but also proposing an alternative they can support themselves …. This is something that, before Resist, we would never have done anything like this. Because we basically, well, … to put it in a disrespectful way, [we] were shouting slogans like "look how unjust this system is". "Well, … OK, the system is unjust, so what eh" … … and this is uhm … well, something which has changed.
> **excerpt 117 – 04/02/2009**

The renewed PvdA identity is characterised by the same mode of politics Zohra Othman argued for in other parts of this interview. It is marked by a socio-economic analysis of "the system". It is also characterised by a mode of engagement that addresses people on the basis of their feelings of injustice and on a class-based identity with reference to concrete issues. Zohra's preferred mode of engagement is marked by a mode of subjectivity that allows people to decide for themselves whether they should collectively advocate their interests. As such, it moves beyond the mere articulation of "slogans" about the systemic injustice of the system by enabling collective action at critical moments in space and time. According to Zohra Othman, this strategy will allow the party to break through its isolation.

ZO: We are no longer that isolated, exactly because we don't make these ... demands, where people say like "that's utopian", or "we don't like this", or "that isn't feasible", anymore. But [rather], very concrete issues that can mean ... a great deal for people in their daily lives ... . And uhm ... . Whereas we used to say things like "well, the only solution is socialism" (laughs), these days we will say like "no, well, ... there are things that you can realise even though we are a small party, ... on a daily basis, for people" ... .
JZ: yes
ZO: So, this is basically, well, the result of Resist, so uhm, ...
JZ: yes
ZO: As a party we were forced to face the, well, ... we really walked into a door ... . And I think we have become stronger because of this.
excerpt 118 – 04/02/2009

5.6 Activism as a Self-Technique: The Case of Nadia Fadil

Political engagement can operate as a technology through which people shape an ethical and political sense of self. It involves a series of discursive practices through which one attempts to rearticulate social relationships with and within the public sphere through forms of imagined collective action in the image of fantasy-infused ideals. But activism is not merely a matter of changing things in the outside world. As we throw our lines of vision onto the various contexts through which we move, we alter our self-awareness and the shape of our sense of self. The multidimensional concept of articulation outlined in this book clarifies this phenomenon. The discursive practices that allow us to establish interpretive and functional relationships with particular identities, concepts, practices and institutions have a pragmatic component that impacts on self-awareness as marked in discourse.

In order to maintain a more or less coherent sense of self and society, human beings engage in a continuous process of contextualisation whereby the indexical relationships between signifiers, identities and practices to particular meanings are temporarily and partially fixed. We already saw how subjects articulate reflexive stances with respect to particular signifiers, identities and enunciations. We assemble ourselves through the establishment of interpretive and functional links with discursive elements in concrete contexts. Discourse allows us to position ourselves with respect to identities and practices we may or may not identify with. But metapragmatic awareness also allows for a deeper mode of reflexivity that is oriented towards entire constellations and dynamics of sense-making. Language users can become highly aware of the discursive patterns that inform their political subjectivities when reflecting upon the authenticities they are, have been and want to become.

In order to demonstrate how political activism may function as a self-technique, I would like to focus on the interview I conducted Nadia Fadil. It is useful to recall that Nadia is an activist academic who currently teaches as a professor at the Department of Anthropology of the Catholic University of Leuven. We saw that she distinguished between various modes of politics and that she opposes dominant discourses on integration by engaging with a problematic that she labels as "the minority question". Nadia articulated this question as follows: "what is the imaginary community of Europe" and "how do we make sure that migrants are going to be part of this". Interestingly, she notes how her engagement with this double question provides her with a "framework" or "structure" she draws "personal meaning from" and that gives her a sense of direction for the way she wants to lead her "life".

> NF: Well, the minority question has been entertaining me for quite some time. So, I think that this is sort of the big umbrella term under which I act … . Uhm, yes, during the last years, I have been less active. So, it's also like, I am currently in a kind of … break, a phase of contemplation like "OK, in what way do I uhm, … want to be active?". Because being active really is the red thread throughout the last five to six years, … and I want to keep it this way because it sort of gives you an important uhm … an important framework for life, and, and a structure to life like 'where you're headed'. So, it's more than merely contributing. It's also something you get personal meaning from … . But yes, I would say that the minority question sort of remains the most important … the most important framework.
> **excerpt 119 – 22/08/2008**

Note that "being active" is the "red thread" that provides an important structure for her life—and as we will see—for her sense of self. The self may be an "idea we ride" but it is also an object and an experience to act upon within very concrete social and historical contexts.

5.6.1 Shaping the Self at the Crossroads of Class, Ethnicity and Religion

Nadia Fadil's engagement with the minority question is both a personal and a socio-political project aimed at a legitimatisation of the "different worlds that shape us". We already noticed that Nadia is supportive of the construction of "alternative fora" and spaces where sensitive minority themes can be dealt with. But she also believes that efforts have to be put into the public "writing of a new collective history". Minorities need safe havens in civil society, but their "presence" also needs to be made "visible" through different types of "cultural productions" in the wider public sphere. There are strong enunciative and visual logics at play here that are common among the discourses of the intellectuals and activists I talked to.

However, in order to understand Nadia's engagement with the public sphere as articulated in our interview, it is useful to pay attention to the spatial metaphors she uses. She does not only talk about different "worlds" that feed us or about "trajectories" of minority members, she also frames her activism as a struggle for "some breathing space" that allows people to combine elements from these different contexts, as they engage in public interaction. Her argument for more breathing space is an argument for more articulatory freedom.

> NF: ... these different worlds that shape us ... . I think it's, I think it's important to [develop] a legitimate discourse about this, also in order to, ... in order to grant legitimacy to the fact that there are different worlds shaping you ... and this doesn't mean you're assimilated. It doesn't mean you're segregated either, but it simply ... it grants you some breathing space in order to make your own combinations out of this, and uhm.
> **excerpt 120 – 22/08/2008**

Nadia Fadil argues that the process of inscribing (the stories of) minorities into the collective histories of Flanders, Belgium and Europe should involve a mode of "engagement" that includes a "class analysis" as well

5 Self and Politics in Activist Discourse 371

as an "anti-racist discourse". In the excerpt below, we can see how she positions herself at the "crossroads" of three overlapping problematics: "the global anti-colonial, anti-capitalist struggle", the "internal issues" of the minorities in Flanders and the "anti-racist" issues that fall under the header of the "minority question". Note that Nadia allows herself a high degree of pragmatic adaptability. Her ongoing concerns are not fixed for once and for all: "depending on the moment", any of these issues may "gain priority over another". The question is what logic underlies these prioritisation strategies.

> NF: So, well, ... the minority question, in the sense of anti-racism, making minority issues visible, and writing about them, by picking up one's voice, uhm, ... The global anti-colonial, anti-capitalist struggle, uhm, and then, ... and then, well, the internal ... issues, these are basically the different crossroads where I find myself and which I consider to be important, and which once in a while, depending on the moment, gain priority over each other.
> **excerpt 121 – 22/08/2008**

Nadia Fadil's preferred mode of political engagement involves a critique of the processes that limit the space minority members have to freely articulate their identities and worlds with each other. In the excerpt below, she engages in a highly reflexive piece of discourse by articulating a need for a "voice", a "story" or a "framework" that allows her to bring the various trajectories, crossroads and identities of her generation together. She explicitly states that "all people" find themselves on the crossroads of different contexts, but that her generation had to face a geopolitical shift that has led to an objectification and to a problematisation of Islam-related subject positions and identities. Nadia identifies herself with a generation of migrants who find themselves "on the same crossroads" while being faced with the question how to articulate "different identities" with each other into a "coherent narrative".

> NF: And I think I'm currently in a phase where I do want to do ... sort of want to be able to do my own thing, picking up my own voice, and my own story, ... And why do I say that I don't think that we're exceptions? I think we're all sort of on these crossroads ... . This is what is specific to our generation, to all people by the way eh, but, ... in our case, and here I'm

talking about second generation migrants who experienced a particular period wherein … a kind of geopolitical shift has occurred in the nineties, establishing itself, and crystallising itself at the beginning of 2000, wherein Islam became an object of discussion, and because of this, your own position and your own identity as well. And because of this, we're all sort of on the same crossroads, without knowing how we have to bring all of this together, … in a narrative, … all these different identities we carry along as a woman, as a migrant, as a Maghrebian, as a daughter, or even uhm, as uhm, as well, yes, as an Arab, as a post-colonial, as uhm, … all of these things.
excerpt 122 – 22/08/2008

According to Nadia Fadil, most people of her generation opt for an "Islamic framework" in order to quilt their identities together into a more or less coherent sense of self. For many people, Islam functions as "an umbrella term that allows you to capture all the different things you're concerned with". But as we noticed before, Nadia's current "umbrella term" is the minority question rather than Islam. This does not mean that she rejects the Islamic framework and its self-techniques, but she does believe that "other frameworks" need to be developed "in order to imagine" the variety of "experiences" and in order to legitimate the different "worlds that shape us". Interestingly, Nadia described Islam as "the first identity framework" in which she has been politicised. Nevertheless, her relationship towards the Islamic aspect of her identity has changed significantly over time and other frameworks would become just as—if not more—important to her politicised sense of self.

> NF: And, and, well, … you might think like "I'm the only one who's concerned about this", but I don't think this is het case. I think everybody, … in one way or another, is concerned with this. But it's never put like this because there is no framework in order to … . And this is why you, … why everyone has to be able to do this on his own, … which isn't necessarily a bad thing. Because you do get … differences. But I feel like, in the end, most people decide upon … make a choice, either a choice for an Islamic framework, or a choice for another framework … . Because it, well, gives you sort of an umbrella term that allows you to … capture … all the different things you're concerned with. But, … I think it's important that we, …

in addition to this framework, offer other frameworks as well. Exactly in order to imagine, … these various experiences, … these different worlds that shape us … . I don't think I'm an exception, I think uhm, and also this class dynamic, because this is also an important dynamic that concerns me ever more.
excerpt 123 – 22/08/2008

We already saw that Nadia went on a "religious trip" as an act of "resistance" and "legitimate rebellion" against her parents who were living "at the margin of the [Islamic] community" because they did not frequent the mosque regularly. Today, Nadia still considers Islam to be a legitimate framework for emancipation that may allow for the development of a "counter-discourse on the basis of your own references". However, her own "way of experiencing Islam" has become rather unorthodox. She clarifies her current stance towards this framework by distinguishing between an orthodox experience of the Islamic "identity framework" on the one hand and an "ethnic" or cultural mode of engagement with the world on the other hand:

> NF: And [I feel] that my framework is not merely Muslim, but is first and foremost an ethnic framework, rather Maghreb, Arabic. These are things that have come to the foreground … . So, the identity framework, Islam as an identity framework is definitely still, … . But not in the same way … . It's definitely there, in the geopolitical struggle. So, … when Islam is being attacked, I will position myself as a Muslim … . Uhm, I am a Muslim, uhm, … in uhm, when it's about, well, Islamophobic issues, and so on … . Uhm, … . But personally, I would dare to say that at this moment, it plays a less central … role. It's rather the ethnic, and ethnic in the broad sense, like, not merely Maghreb, but rather Arabic, Arabic as a geopolitical area, as a cultural area of reference that is very complex and very diverse … . As a really pro-Palestinian, like a classical Arabic, well, not a classical Arabic nationalism, but sort of a post-Arabic nationalism (laughs), an Arabic post-nationalism.

excerpt 124 – 22/08/2008

In a way that parallels the discourses of many other AEL sympathisers, Nadia distinguishes between religion-, ethnicity- or culture-based understandings of being a Muslim on the one hand and religious understanding on the other hand, while granting legitimacy to both. Her framework has become increasingly cultural and identity based. She identifies herself positively as a Muslim in the excerpts above but highlights the fact that this subject position has come to play a "less central" place in her sense of self. Other types of identity are just as—if not more—important to Nadia in most contexts. Ethnicity rather than religion has become the framework she uses in order to articulate her sense of self to a broad and rather vague "cultural area of reference" in which different minority-related identities and political ideologies such as "Arabic post-nationalism" and "pro-Palestinian" stances can be articulated into complex discursive networks.

Nevertheless, important as the "ethnic" or "cultural" framework might be for Nadia Fadil, it does not provide her with all the tools she needs in order to deal with the minority question in a satisfactory manner. She and her generation do not only find themselves at the intersection of different cultural, ethnic and religious worlds. They are also located at the intersection of different social classes. In the excerpts below, Nadia discusses the problems she and some of her friends experience in the process of acquiring a middle-class status. The different worlds Nadia talks about do not only pertain to ethnicity or religion but also to a class-related "habitus". Using the generic "you", she identifies with others who find themselves in a process of upward "social mobility" and experience feelings of uncertainty when confronted with white middle-class codes in Flanders.

> NF: So, social mobility, the fact that one increasingly starts to belong to a middle class. And that one, this middle class basically, well, you're very much aware of … of the consequences of your social mobility. Like, … you're in, … you end up pretty quickly in a white environment … . For instance, the entire cultural sector. If you do something leisure wise, like occupying yourself with art, this is very intimidating to me, going to the theatre or something … . There, you meet people for whom, well, for whom this is home, but to me, this isn't the case at all … . I usually don't know anything about it, so you feel, … or, or, well, a type of general knowledge where you, you feel like "well, it's because you're … coming from a working class that you're, … not equipped with all of these things, that you're not as well read, and that you're definitely not, … not", well, all these things, they're not self-evident, … and you're not equipped with

uhm, the type of cultural background ... . And uhm, you're very much aware of, well, a certain, ... ease, with which certain people move in certain circles, ... be it in the academic, or in ... . To me, this still isn't self-evident.
excerpt 125 – 22/08/2008

Nadia explains how the process of upward social mobility is a process that leads one "pretty quickly" to "a white environment" that has proved to be quite "intimidating" to her as well as to many of her friends. She finds the "type of knowledge" that is required in order to participate in the cultural life associated with this environment anything but "self-evident". Nadia does not claim that it is impossible for people with a "working class" background to acquire this type of knowledge. She even points at people who "get absorbed" completely and adopt the overall "habitus" of this "bourgeois" environment. This is not the type of social mobility she opts for herself.[15] Even though she recognises that "some interesting stuff is going on" in the "upper middle class", she does not want to be "absorbed" by it. This makes sense considering the type of engagement she advocates throughout the entire interview.

So, these are rather small things, ... but it has to do with social mobility, and there is, well, ... a kind of uncertainty with respect to this, and, ... Well, in the white story, it happens frequently that people get absorbed by this social mobility ... . A friend of mine, her father comes from a poor

---

[15] Nadia relies on her social scientific background and uses the framework of Pierre Bourdieu in order to understand the feelings of uncertainty people from the second generation of Moroccan migrants experience when climbing the socio-economic ladder. She makes uses of notions such as habitus, capital and distinction. Pierre Bourdieu distinguished between cultural, social, economic and symbolic capital. Together, these forms of capital determine the place an individual may occupy in a specific social field. It also determines his or her habitus. Cultural capital pertains to sets attitudes with respect to learning, to cultural products (e.g. books and films) and to its institutional variants (e.g. degrees). Social capital is a notion that designates the whole of potential resources available to an individual located in a network of relationships of mutual recognition and support. It pertains to the benefits of group membership. Economic capital is capital that can be turned into money at any given point. In specific contexts, these forms of capital can be exchanged with each other. Symbolic capital is important as well. It pertains to the capacity of people to exert an influence on their world by influencing the representation of their reality. It provides individuals and groups with the symbolic power to determine what sort of habitus should function as the norm in a particular social field. For instance, Bourdieu argued that within the education system, middle-class norms supporting a middle-class habitus tend to prevail (Bourdieu 1986).

background, and if you see him now, ... you wouldn't think so. He comes from a poor family, ... His habitus, his way of talking is so upper middle class, ... Well, by now, in my case, that's probably the case as well eh, but ... he distances himself completely from uhm, you know, La Distinction, really ... really hard, doing anything to locate himself in this bourgeois ... context. Reading the right books, going to the right performances, to, ... Whereas I have refused to do so for a very long time. Because, I was like "I am not going to be absorbed by ... this upper middle class". But I notice that I have sort of become like "well, there is some interesting stuff going on over there, and I can, ... It's not because I am going to a performance, that I'll suddenly be absorbed by this upper middle class".
excerpt 126 – 22/08/2008

Nadia does not feel like the only one with feelings of insecurity with respect to environments in which white middle-class codes dominate. She claims that a lot of her friends experience similar uncertainties as she does. In contrast to the generation that preceded her, Nadia could share the experience of her own "social mobility" because she experienced a "collective dynamic". When Nadia went to college, she resolved not to have any contact with other "Moroccans" but failed to do so. She explained how she soon met Nadia Babazia who soon became one of her best friends and conquered a "little Moroccan corner" close to the university restaurant where she and other second-generation "Moroccans" frequently met. Within this context, she and her "Moroccan friends" could share stories about feelings of "uneasiness" experienced when engaging in "social contacts" in middle-class environments.

> NF: Well, we were able to sort of experience this, this social mobility .... You know, this is something I really share with many of my Moroccan friends, like, I'm, ... You know, it touches you, like, a friend of mine who is uhm, ... sales manager in an international firm, she has dinners with her clients, and so on, and these are also, uhm, well, people from uhm, from the world of sports, ships, ... and so on. And there's always a kind of uneasiness that you have to confront, a sort of ease that is not self evident, and you notice that you can share this with each other, ... a kind of uncertainty in these social contacts ....
> JZ: A class bound uncertainty.

NF: Yes, indeed, ... a social insecurity, I analyse this in terms of class eh, not ethnically, because, I know that this simply is about class.
excerpt 127 – 22/08/2008

Nadia is very much aware of the fact that her explanation of this "uneasiness" in terms of class says more about her subjectivity than about the subjectivities of her friends. She acknowledges that many of her friends would interpret these shared experiences in ethnic rather than in class-related terms. Nevertheless, she maintains that many people of her generation find themselves at "the crossroads" of both dimensions of social reality. Crossing over from one socio/ethnic framework to another implies a shift in "habitus", a different valorisation of social and symbolic capital, as well as an articulation of a different list of "priorities" in the process of shaping one's life.

NF: but, ... Whereas my friends might interpret this in rather ethnic terms, ... but to me, it's a crossroads. It really isn't uhm, ... And uhm, you can share this with each other, and I'm glad that I can do this, this social mobility, ... little, subtle psychological uncertainties, mechanisms, ... that you can somehow bear this with ... other people. You know? Whereas the priorities, whereas other people are concerned with building [a house] and all of that (laugh) what the fuck (laughs).
excerpt 128 – 22/08/2008

Whereas many white middle-class people may be concerned with bourgeois concerns such as investments in real estate, Nadia and her friends are looking for ways to deal with the uncertainties and mechanisms of social mobility and crossing the crossroads of ethnicity and class. The minority question can therefore not be answered with reference to ethnicity-, religion- and/or identity-related frameworks and signifiers alone. In order to make sure that migrants become part of the imaginary communities of Europe, the issue of class needs to be addressed as well.

Nadia's preference for a mode of politics that takes class and structural inequalities seriously reflects in her attitude towards an emerging Maghrebian middle class in Antwerp. According to her, this group is being politicised in a rather "bourgeois" way. Its politics are marked by "soft"- and "charity"-like forms of "political mobilisation". Nadia notices how "they are not making a class analysis at all" while being "completely unaware of their own bourgeois position". Interestingly, it is not the rising socio-economic status of this group that bothers her, but its "liberal discourse", its concern with "reputation" and its distancing from the type of politics associated with the AEL. This latter point is not only informed by Nadia's sympathy for this organisation. The dissociation enacted by this upcoming middle class also goes against the idea of the writing of a collective historiography that recognises the efforts made by all minority actors.

NF: They are very much aware of these problematics [racism and community building], about the headscarf for instance, ... uhm, about reinforcing the community, and all of this ... . But they are not making a class analysis at all, and [they] are completely unaware of their own bourgeois position. So, for instance, you can notice this by the fact that they are going to ... distance themselves with respect to the youngsters on the streets. They're sort of like ... . For instance, with respect to the AEL story, I sometimes noticed these bourgeois reflexes and, and reactions as well ... these really bothered me. Like "well, they [youngsters associated with the AEL] are [dragging down] our reputation" ... . And also, well, a kind of self-celebrating discourse like "we have to make it for our community", but [they] don't make any class analysis at all, and [they] are also buying uhm, stocks, uhm, you know (laughs), becoming really rich, something I'm not opposed to, uhm, I don't consider this to be bad at all, uhm bad at all, because we *need* money (laughs), but ... . But, well, it is really goes with this liberal discourse eh. And well, this really bothers me (laughs).
excerpt 129 – 22/08/2008

5.6.2 Eye-Openers and Shifting Subjectivities

Nadia Fadil developed her preferred mode of subjectivity in response to a series of "eye openers". The basic characteristics of her preferred mode of politics include an engagement with the minority issue from a minority perspective; a discursive practice aimed at the writing of a collective historiography; the establishment of alternative spaces where the minority issues can be discussed; a structural analysis of class and power relationships; and a perspective whereby one does not lose sight of the humanity of things. The "eye openers" in question stimulated a reflexive stance towards her own subjectivity and towards the processes that shape the public realm. They refer to critical moments in which Nadia became aware of aspects of social reality and subjectivity she was previously unaware of. Put differently, these eye openers describe processes, experience and discourses that allowed her to reorient her lines of vision towards different dimensions of context and to rearticuate her sense of self and society accordingly.

Nadia Fadil's first "eye opener" allowed her to look at her own story and at the minority question in "a different way". Even though she did go on an "Islamic trip" as a teenager and read authors such as Fatima Mernissi and Tariq Ramadan during her time at high school, she admitted that by the time she went to the university, she had acquired a "rather white", "racist" and "mainstream" attitude with respect to "the minority question and the problematic of integration". Nadia told me that she did not have that many friends during high school and that her relation towards her Moroccan and Flemish friends was not always that positive. Nevertheless, this started to change at university. Her studies in sociology provided her with a first "eye opener" that allowed her "to look at the minority question from the point of view of a socio-economic narrative" and "to make more structural analyses". Moreover, she would become increasingly aware of the fact that her story differed significantly from the stories of other "Moroccan girls" as she started to interview them in the context of her Master's thesis.

> NF: And how did this start to change? Actually, it started to change with my thesis ... my Master's thesis, well, my education in sociology was basically quite important. Because, well, unavoidably, ... you start to look at this minority question from the point of view of a socio-economic narrative, so basically, you can use this paradigm in order to make more structural analyses ... . So, this has been a first important ... eye opener to me. And then, secondly, there's my thesis, because of which I started to interview Moroccan girls, ... contacting them, not just from a conflict situation, ... but also, ... By interviewing them, ... you discover, well, these are different stories eh, ... you start to realise that they basically grew up in a very different environment.
> **excerpt 130 – 22/08/2008**

Before conducting these interviews, Nadia was rather unaware of the "racist" and "white" characteristics of her environment. In order to illustrate just how "mainstream" her perspective had become, she recalls an interaction with a secretary at her high school. When Nadia told her that some of her neighbourhood friends would enlist at her school as well, her secretary commented that this was just fine as long as the school would not end up with "too many Moroccans". At the time, Nadia found this completely normal and did not "frame" this stance as being "racist". All the less, because her parents actually tried to avoid that she would end up in a "concentration school" where she might encounter more difficulties on her educational trajectory.

> NF: You grew up like, … rather protected, well, rather, rather white, racist as well, … but at that moment you don't frame it like this. I remember, when I was about fourteen or sixteen, … one of the secretaries, when I told her that some friends of mine were going to come over, I was one of the few Moroccan girls at school, … the Saint Jozef Institute, … . When I told this secretary that some friends of mine, from my neighbourhood were coming over, she told me like "okay, but preferably not too many, uhm, Moroccans, because otherwise we might get too many Moroccans over here". And well, at that moment, you're thinking like "okay, sure". You actually understand this (laughs). You don't rebel eh, because you know, you think like, "well, my parents have … enrolled me in a school where there weren't too many Moroccans.
> **excerpt 131 – 22/08/2008**

Sociology provided Nadia Fadil with a framework with which she could approach these issues differently, but it was a particular experience that made her dig more deeply into issues of racism, discrimination and identity construction. For her Master's thesis, she wanted to conduct a series of interviews with veiled girls. When a sister of a friend of hers refused to be interviewed, Nadia felt "affronted". The girl in question found Nadia rather "arrogant" and when Nadia found out, this threw her "out of balance". This critical judgement by her would-be interviewee made Nadia question her position as a social scientist who made self-evident claims over the voices of others.

5 Self and Politics in Activist Discourse 381

NF: But you go along with, like I said, I was really in a mainstream framework. And at a certain moment, I started to uhm, conduct an interview. I recall this very clearly, I wanted to interview a girl that didn't want to be interviewed at all. And I didn't understand … . I was like "come on, I am Moroccan, and uhm, I am going to write a thesis about us, and uhm, …". And, and, I told her this, actually, I was sort of affronted, and she was basically, well, very pissed off because of me being affronted, rightly so … . She thought I was very arrogant, and uhm, … she told this to her brother. And I was basically, well, I was put out of balance because of this.
excerpt 132 – 22/08/2008

In the excerpt below, Nadia clarifies how she started "to question" her "own position" when confronted with "stories about racism" and discrimination. She "started to look at these girls in a different way" as she realised the "powerful position" she occupied as an academic. These interview experiences were "significant eye openers" for Nadia. And as she opened her eyes to issues of power, identity and discrimination, things would evolve quickly. Nadia started to immerse herself in an intertextual network of "literature about identity construction within cultural studies" and mentions the work of Blommaert and Verschueren on the Belgian migration debate as one of her "ideological eye openers". She is very much aware of the impact these eye-openers have had on her sense of self.

NF: I started to look at these girls in a different way. Perhaps, I also started to realise, to realise what powerful position you have, … by basically taking interviews, by [making] a sort of self-evident, a self-evident claim. And then you start to question your own position as well, these different stories, stories about racism, discrimination, uhm, … . At that point I really started to dig into literature about identity construction within cultural studies. So, these have all been significant eye openers to me. Uhm, Blommaert and Verschueren, to me, this was really … Het [Belgische] migrantendebat[16] was really one of my ideological eye openers … . And uhm, well, you start to look at your own story in a different way, and to realise from what position you're speaking, and that there are many things you simply didn't

---

[16] *Het Belgische migrantendebat* been reworked and translated into English as *Debating diversity* (Blommaert and Verschueren 1998).

experience, so you don't necessarily have to presuppose you have the right to speak .... And I'm really glad I experienced this. This really shaped me in a fundamental way.
excerpt 133 – 22/08/2008

The first series of eye-openers that Nadia experienced made her aware of the power-infused subject position she occupies when speaking as an academic and when making self-evident claims over the stories and voices of others in interview contexts. Her newly acquired sociological perspective allowed her to hear stories and to see processes of discrimination and racism she was previously unaware of while throwing her discursive lines of vision onto structural issues pertaining to inequalities in the social world. But Nadia also threw these lines of vision inwardly, realising that these different eye-openers "shaped" her "in a fundamental way". Other eye-openers would have an equally profound impact on her sense of self.

A second major "eye opener" made Nadia aware of "the power of the media". After sociology, Nadia studied anthropology and spent two months in Morocco doing interviews with women active in secular and Islamist women's movements. Her original idea was to write on secular left-wing women's movements and their relation to Moroccan family law.[17] Initially, the Islamist women's movements were to be considered as "adversaries" in her mind. However, as she started to delve into Moroccan newspaper articles about the debates surrounding the Mudawana, she noticed the voice of Nadia Yassine, a feminist figurehead of a big Islamist faction in Morocco. Nadia Fadil found a great deal of Yassine's discourse rather interesting: "it was all about antiglobalisation and anticapitalism and stuff I basically considered to be very recognisable". Eventually, she got Yassine's contact details and met with her on a number of occasions, meetings that constituted a new "eye opener" in the development of Nadia Fadil's political awareness.

---

[17] The new Moroccan family code is commonly referred to as the Mudawana. The adoption of a new family code in 2004 was hailed as a significant step towards equal rights for men and women who have the Moroccan nationality. The Mudawana governs matters such as marriage, divorce, child custody and inheritance. The 2004 reforms have sparked a public dialogue on gender equality in Moroccan families (Zoglin 2009, 964–965). Both the new and the old family codes are grounded in Islamic principles. For a detailed overview of the legal aspects regarding this reform, see Foblets (2008). For an analysis of the events leading to the 2004 reform along with a preliminary analysis of its impact upon the Moroccan population, see Zoglin (2009).

NF: And to me, this was another eye opener, because it makes you realise uhm, that we don't consider the extent your view on things is influenced by a particular representation, by … . You basically start to realise, the power of the media, basically. This was the first time, I felt and saw the power of the media and of a particular representation, … .
JZ: You mean the representation of Islamism?
NF: The gap that existed, yes, between what I read and what I heard at the spot, and, and the people I talked to, and the image that you were … presented with. And I remember coming back, and my supervisor at the time, … I was completely impressed by Nadia Yassine, and she [Nadia Fadil's supervisor] asked me like, "Yes, but wouldn't she [Nadia Yassine] perform a two-sided discourse?", and then you're like come on, why? … . Well, then you realise how, … how, how, how powerful the power of discourse is, and that counter discourse, counter discourse, it basically, … . Well, certain subaltern voices, uhm, don't get any credit, no legitimacy … . And even if they do get some forum, they are not taken seriously.
excerpt 134 – 22/08/2008

The excerpt above is littered with social scientific concepts and analyses. The discrepancy between the mediatised discourse about the Moroccan feminist Islamists and her conversations with Nadia Yassine made Nadia Fadil realise how her "view" had been "influenced by a certain representation". Nadia Fadil "felt and saw the power of the media" and observed the effect of a certain "discourse" operating on a number of "subaltern voices" that did not get any "credit" or "legitimacy". Upon her return to Belgium, the realisation that mediatised discourses impact on even "the smallest of conversations" deepened her sense of "a moral consensus" that was being constructed with respect to certain movements and people. Throughout the interview, Nadia's confrontation with large-scale processes of distorted representation, racism and discrimination was always mediated through stories about interactions and voices at a more interactional level.

NF: [You start to realise] to what extent the Eurocentric, how hegemonic, and how normative things have become, and even in the smallest of conversations eh, people don't believe you if you tell them things, and tell them a different story, a different story. [You start to realise] there's a kind of moral consensus with respect to certain people, with respect to certain movements, … . And to me, this was, …

JZ: How do you mean? For instance,
NF: moral consensus. So, for instance, Nadia Yassine, when I mentioned her name with other people, there was always a rejection, always negative, and I didn't understand. And after a while, you start to think like "Well, am I the one who is allowing herself to be manipulated?", you know …? Because, this is the image, the impression you're presented with, as if you're this naïve, ignorant brat, and uhm, and uhm, as if they must be [right].
excerpt 135 – 22/08/2008

Nadia Fadil was disturbed by the reactions of people when she mentioned Nadia Yassine's name. The common "rejection" of her interpretation of Yassine's voice and the suggestion that she let herself be manipulated by this Islamist politician caused her to doubt herself as being a "naive" and "ignorant brat". Nadia proved to be very much aware of the fact that the ideological functions of discourse are not restricted to the domain of mass media alone but that ideological processes operate in everyday interactions as well. Still, up to this point, she had not engaged herself politically. It was only after experiencing a profound sense of *déjà vue* when confronted with the way the AEL was being treated by the Flemish media that she would perform her first act of "activism". After having spent a brief holiday in Morocco in the summer of 2002, Nadia was overwhelmed by the escalating media circus on the AEL and the figure of AEL chairman Dyab Abou Jahjah in Belgium.

After a controversial interview with Abou Jahjah in which he suggested the possibility of introducing Arabic as a fourth national language in Belgium, "things continued to go crescendo" in 2002. Upon her return from Morocco, Nadia was so overwhelmed that she collected all articles that had been published on the AEL in order to understand what was happening. She soon experienced a strong feeling of recognition when comparing the representation of the AEL in Flanders with media representations of Islamists in Morocco. Nadia felt that "the same thing" was "happening all over again". The same process of "associative widening" whereby people and organisations are articulated with notions such as "terrorism" and "Al Qaeda" occurred and a "powerful discourse" was "being generated" in politics and in the media. As we will see, this discourse would be so powerful that it impacted on some of Nadia's personal relationships.

NF: I was like, "what the fuck", and I had this feeling of déjà vu with respect to the Islamists, … I was like "shit, the same thing is happening all over again" …. . And also, because, well, you know what's going on, all these associations that are being made eh, Al Qaeda is being mentioned, terrorism is being mentioned, … . As soon as this happens, you basically know, … I realised like okay, … "a particular discourse, which is powerful, with respect to certain persons is being generated". And also, I read Blommaert and Verschueren, associative expansion, all these chains of associations, …. . So, well, yes, I was like "what the fuck is going on", and then, … uhm, there was the arrest of Dyab, …. . And shortly after this, I still remember I came home in the evening, and I put on the late night news cast, … and what I heard back then was beyond my imagination.
excerpt 136 – 22/08/2008

When Dyab Abou Jahjhah was arrested for his alleged role of inciting the riots in Antwerp that took place in response to the murder of Mohamed Achrak in November 2002, Nadia would perform her first act of activism in the form of an open letter directed at "all policy makers". This letter was a direct response to the parliamentary discussion of November 28, where the AEL was accused of trying to terrorise Antwerp and to gain control over certain neighbourhoods by hindering the work of the police so it could carry out its "criminal activities". The letter condemned the riots but also called for "structural solutions" for "societal problems such as poverty and discrimination". The article argued that "the debate should not be simply about Abou Jahjah and the AEL, who are merely catalysts for an increasing resentment". Instead, "the debate should be about a future society where autochthons and allochthons, young and old, men and women, are given a fully fledged place that allows them to take their responsibility" as "citizens" (Fadil et al. 2002).

NF: And, and then we [Nadia Fadil and Danny Neudt] wrote an open letter, in hindsight, this was my first act of activism, uhm, … . Back then, we thought like, "We'll quickly put this on a mailing list, well, send it around", and all of a sudden we got, well, I don't know exactly how many, hundreds of signatures of academics across various Flemish universities, and also, it … it made the headlines eh. De Morgen used it as an exclusive, and uhm, well, back then, I think, … . I think, to me, this was basically the trigger.

This was my trigger, AEL was the trigger, because there were many things that had been piling up … . So, my thesis, 9/11, the framework, … and basically the fact that Islam was increasingly being subject to discussion, … going to Morocco, getting in touch with the Islamists, … the representation, the gap between the representation in Western media and the reality on the ground, … and then, coming back.
excerpt 137 – 22/08/2008

The excerpt above includes a summary of the various eye-openers that prompted Nadia to perform her first act of activism. As such, the mediatised establishment of moral consensus surrounding the AEL and its chairman was merely the final push for her to become active. From that moment on, the "minority framework" would come to occupy an increasingly central place in her political subjectivity. It would become the "dominant perspective" in her world view in terms of a "politicised" and "structural framework" that she never lets go of when dealing with the minority question. Nevertheless, her sense of politics would continue to evolve.

5.6.3 Shifting Modes of Politics and Self-Awareness

As Nadia opened her eyes to the dynamics of power and discourse in relation to minority politics, her political subjectivity started to change as well. We already saw how interviewees may articulate awareness of the fact that they partially, positively or negatively identify themselves and their politics with subject positions, practices and/or institutions. In the excerpts above, we could see how Nadia Fadil gradually articulated new elements with her sense of self and society. However, interviewees may also mark their critical awareness of the different modes that identification processes may take. This becomes especially clear if we take a look at a piece of interview data in which Nadia Fadil discusses the impact political discourse can have on "personal relationships" as well as on one's relationships towards the institutions of the "establishment". In the excerpt below, Nadia reflects on the lessons she learned from the way the AEL was dealt with by mainstream social and political actors.

NF: … it shows, it made me realise that, that certain discourses are more powerful than, than personal relationships. Well, … if [personal] bonds are very strong this may not necessarily be the case, but you, … . Well, [it showed me] that the personal is really political, that the political can really become personal, that discourse can even corrupt personal relationships … . It uhm, … [showed me] how they [discourses] can influence thoughts, how they [can influence] the positionings of people, … people who are all supposedly critical and independent, and no one is exempted from this [principle]. And uhm, well, I'm not easily impressed by people who claim they are critical intellectuals or anything like that anymore. You know … ? I don't really believe this story any more. Myself included … . I really realise that we are very much shaped by what we see, and by our context, and by what we read, and no one stands apart in this … . And uhm, and well, it's really, [at the AEL] you could see this from the front row, so I am very glad I was able to experience something like this … . It's really an education, a very important education.
excerpt 138 – 22/08/2008

The way "politics", "the media" and even "the legal system" reacted to the AEL destabilised Nadia's trust in the institutions of the establishment. But the dislocation she was faced with went deeper. Her belief in the ability to be "critical and independent" with respect to "discourse" and power was deeply shaken and she would become deeply sceptical with respect to people claiming to be "critical intellectuals". After seeing what happened to the AEL, she did not "believe this story any more" and started to realise "that we are very much shaped by what we see", by "our context" and by "what we read". Nadia's "déjà vue" with respect to the AEL did not only make her aware of the fact that "discourse can even corrupt personal relationships". It also forced her to engage in a different mode of relationship with respect to herself and with respect to the actors and institutions that populate the public realm (e.g. "critical intellectuals", the "media", "politics" and the "legal system").

Witnessing how the AEL was dealt with by representatives of these institutions was particularly "shocking" to Nadia because these events disrupted her previously held belief in a "story" that frames Western Europe as "a democracy" and as "a haven of well-being" where politicians are primarily concerned with "well-being of the people". Nadia did not only start to reconsider the position of minorities in Flanders and in Europe. She also started to rearticulate the stories and dichotomies (e.g. "first world" vs. "third world") she grew up with in order to rethink Europe's position in the world. Between her twenty-two and twenty-six years of age, Nadia Fadil would "start to question" all the "paradigms" she grew up with.

> NF: To me, it was like, well, it was really shocking, it really was. I was distressed by it all. Because, well, you grow up with this story, … "you are in Western Europe, in a democracy, … in a haven of, of, of well-being" … . But basically, it isn't that different, and you realise ever more that it is isn't really that different with respect to other non-European countries … . the only difference is that the West is prosperous, … they have money and because of that they can pay for their facilities … . But merely looking at, at, at, thought on uhm power, or about the well-being of the population, and things like this, … it isn't any more developed than other countries. It is evident that you would have more facilities in Morocco if people were able to afford them, and of course, the doctor would like to treat everyone, treat everyone free of charge , … but unfortunately you're in a system where the doctor can hardly afford for drugs himself. So, if you don't by your own medicine, he cannot treat you, it's as simple as that … . That's really tough, but that's the way it is. But fundamentally, there's no difference … . This is basically the insight that makes you re-think, … this entire story about … 'first world', 'third world', 'white', 'underdeveloped countries' and 'developed', … you start to question all of these paradigms you grew up with, … and this is basically what happened between my … twenty-two and twenty-five, perhaps twenty-six years of age. I started to question all these paradigms I grew up with. (laughs)
> **excerpt 139 – 22/08/2008**

In the excerpt below, Nadia is even more explicit about "what the AEL meant" to her. The entire AEL experience allowed her to "see the so-called border-zone of the democracy" in which she found herself. Moreover, she explained how "power" became "visible in a naked way", a process whereby Nadia started to realise that the institutions and practices associated with the establishment are more interested in maintaining the status quo than in a mode of power that functions in the interest of the "well-being of everyone". The AEL pushed her to rearticulate her personal and

5 Self and Politics in Activist Discourse 389

institutional relationships in terms of "a story about power". Within this story, Nadia modulated her relationship towards the centring institutions of Flanders with an "anti-attitude" and with a strong feeling of "distrust".

> NF: what the AEL meant to me is that even with respect to one's own institutions over here, ... that you basically see the so-called border-zone of the democracy wherein you find yourself for the first time ... that power becomes visible in a naked way, and that it's not about the well-being of everyone, but really strictly about the conservation [of power] .... And uhm, ... And yes, it's a kind of fundamental crisis [of trust] ... in everything associated with the establishment ... I think it basically boils down to that ... . [A crisis of trust] in the media, in politics, as well as in the legal system ... . You start to question these things fundamentally, and you realise that in the end, everything's a story about power relationships. And, and, ... this does not mean that it is [about individual] *people*. So, I think this is when I realised this ... . In the years after that, this insight really translated itself into a kind of anti-attitude on my part, like, like uhm ... distrust, a real distrust.
> JZ: With respect to?
> NF: With respect to the establishment, with respect to everything ... . Whereas today, I wouldn't say I am in a better phase yet, but I ... still have this distrust, I still don't trust it, but I do make a distinction between people.
> **excerpt 140 – 22/08/2008**

At the time of our interview, Nadia had been "less active" for a couple of years and found herself in a "phase of contemplation" in which she tried to determine how to be active in the future. In the excerpt below, we can already catch a glimpse of this newly evolving mode of subjectivity. Whereas her previous mode of subjectivity was dominated by feelings of distrust and by a mode of analysis that stressed the "mechanic", "automatic" and "abstract" workings of "interests" in society and discourse, she now starts to see "the humanity" in things and the "anti-attitude" is somewhat mitigated.

> NF: but, but, you start to, the humanity, in the end it's like this, you simply start to see the humanity of things ... . It's not all mechanic, and automatic, and abstract any more ... . In the last instance, it also has to do with interests and with, this also plays a big role, ... [but] now I am able to frame all of this, whereas five years ago, I wasn't able to frame this at all.
> **excerpt 141 – 22/08/2008**

The humanity of things that Nadia talks about takes the form of personal stories about experiences related to migration. These include stories about financial problems, about suffering and discrimination. But these stories are also about the history of movements and migrant organisations that should be written into the "collective historiography" that should shape the imagined community of Flanders, Belgium and Europe. Nadia wants to contribute to the emerging visibility of minorities while taking the "position" she occupies as an academic into account. The articulatory possibilities of this position interest her. Nadia does not consider herself as someone who founds civil society organisations herself. Instead, she considers it her role to facilitate the establishments of links between people and organisations. She considers it to be her role to facilitate contacts between civil society actors and to create more spaces in which they can move and articulate themselves in order to leave "a mark in the public forum".

NF: well, there is a kind of visibility related to minorities that is starting to emerge. It's important that we, well, I want to help to uhm, ... establish this visibility. It only happens if you do something eh. So, I want to help to shape this visibility, and uhm, that's basically the thing ... I focused on. And I'm also increasingly taking into account who I am, what position I occupy ... . And the thing I can do best, what I do best, is writing and talking (laughs)
JZ: (laughs)
NF: and eating (laughs), and especially writing. Well, I, I'm not an activist who's going to found an organisation, or, well, I can help, I think the link with organisations is very important because this feeds into you. But, but you shouldn't expect this from me, and uhm, the thing I do best, with, with an 'academic' role between quotation marks, ... the best thing you can do, you are best positioned to contribute by bringing people together, linking contacts, and playing a kind of facilitating role ... . Well, this is basically what I prefer to do. And, and, and also, trying to create more spaces. But, ... but well, ... this is, ... so, yes, we'll see how that's going to evolve further. But I do consider it to be important to make a mark in the public forum, to grant more visibility with respect to the things that are happening, at this moment.
excerpt 142 – 22/08/2008

As the interview with Nadia Fadil demonstrates, political engagement can function as a self-technique. For many of my interviewees, political engagement iimplies that they reshape their lives into ethical and/or aesthetical projects whereby their actions upon the world carve out the flexible boundaries that delimit their selves.

6

Conclusion

The way actors articulate discursive elements with each other impacts on their sense of self, on their sense of politics and on their sense of meaningful political engagement. The analyses presented in this book demonstrate that the articulation of critique involves more than the development of a critical stance with respect to isolated political practices, concepts or identities. It involves the articulation of a dynamic network of signifiers according to an interpretive logic that challenges established patterns in social reality. The establishment of innovative links between subject positions, political discourse topics and discursive practices can be forged through discourse. At the heart of any debate lies a practice of articulation through which social actors determine the contexts with which they make sense of abstract categories such as identity, community, culture, politics or integration.

Social actors value such signifiers by articulating them in discourses structured through particular social, political and fantasmatic logics that provide means for making sense of self and society. Concepts such as integration are valued positively or negatively depending on the voices, topics, narratives and debates they articulated with. Such categories acquire meaning as they are put in functional and interpretive relationships with subject positions one may or may not identify with. They function as social values to the extent that they can be inscribed in the large-scale interpretive logics that structure self and society. The fact that relationships between discursive forms and functions can only be partially fixed in concrete contexts of enunciation guarantees conflict over such signifiers. This becomes especially clear in processes of ideological misrecognition.

A misrecognition of the way social actors deploy abstract categories and identities can easily be interpreted as a non- or misrecognition of one's system of values. It is a folk wisdom that the topics of money and politics should be avoided in order to safeguard civil interactions among friends and family. This principle is by no means limited to the minority debate or to the discourse of the intellectuals and activists I talked to. A lack of metapragmatic awareness with respect to the way interlocutors contextualise socio-political categories such as culture or identity easily leads to modes of interaction and to discursive statements that trigger feelings of misrecognition among interlocutors. The feelings of misrecognition articulated by my interviewees became meaningful to them as they were named and explained with reference to elaborate discourses on the dynamics that constitute the public spheres we live in.

Their feelings of misrecognition were often triggered by interactions in which contextual boundaries marked by conflicting processes of interpellation and interpretation clashed. Context is the flexible and temporal result of a discursive process that contributes to interactional clarity and/or to the establishment of and imagined common ground. This is not a relativist slogan. The power to exert control over the definition of context determines the discursive ground on which one moves. A lack of control over symbolic, material and institutional resources for establishing interpretive common ground provides a fertile condition for the reproduction of unequal and anti-emancipatory power relationships. This principle is by no means limited to the Flemish minority debates. Political struggle takes place because the power to establish contextual boundaries for interpreting political discourse is not distributed equally among social actors

Ethnic, cultural, religious and political categories can function as empty signifiers. However, labels and notions such as Marxist, liberal, freedom or Arab are not necessarily empty to concrete individuals or groups. In fact, a non- or misrecognition of the values attached to such categories can lead to intense emotional turmoil. Concrete actors associate such categories with personal experiences and narratives. This is why debates involving such categories can be counted among the most emotionally challenging speech events subjects may engage in. The intellectuals and activists I talked to exhibited very high degrees of metapragmatic awareness with respect to the usage of such categories. Their frequent usage of linguistic and non-linguistic hedges when using notions such as 'allochthon', 'Muslim' or 'integration' was indicative of this fact. At the same time, many interviewees articulated such notions into complex interpretive logics in order to make sense of themselves and of the political processes that structure (their sense of) self and society.

From a radically democratic point of view, participants in politicised interactional settings share a responsibility to delineate contextual boundaries in emancipating rather than in dominating ways. They share a responsibility to allow each other sufficient room for interpretation, especially where a preferred sense of self is at stake. This is an argument not for a power-free dialogue but for a mode of interaction that allows for modes of empowerment that foster democratic rather than patronising modes of politics. Limitations to the articulation of a counter-discourse marked by alternative logics of critical explanation create an ideal context for processes of misrecognition to occur. In situations where people have limited interpretive and articulatory options to counter forms of address that do not correspond to preferred modes of subjectivity, feelings of alienation are bound to flourish. The narratives of the activists and intellectuals involved in the Flemish minority debates testify to this fact.

Fortunately, human beings have a powerful set of tools at their disposal to deal with feelings of misrecognition and with the political discourse that triggers them. Such tools include empathy, theory and metapragmatic awareness. Empathy allows us to identify ourselves emotionally with others. But without the ability to articulate one's experiences at a higher level of abstraction, subjects run the risk of being reduced to mere bodies entrapped in a never-ending emotional chain of stimuli and responses. The more we become aware of the way abstract categories and values function with respect to politics as well as with respect to one's sense of self, the more we can loosen the interpretive and ideological hold others have over us and vice versa. For this reason, I believe education and theory are invaluable to any mode of political awareness. Moreover, a critical awareness of the socio-political hegemonies that surround us cannot be achieved without an awareness of the way ideological values are discursively constructed in and through discourse.

All intellectuals and activists I talked to used concepts such as identity, culture and politics with varying degrees of critical awareness. They frequently proved to be aware of the fact that such notions perform ideological functions in science and in politics. Such observations force discourse analysts to recognise the political dimension of their own categories and to consider how they can link their own interpretive frameworks with those of others. I have tried to do so by taking the notion of research as articulatory practice seriously. By carefully dissecting how discursive elements operate in relation to the sense of self and politics articulated by my respondents, I have tried to remain sensitive to the multiplicity of interpretations that structure the minority debates as discussed by activist minority members themselves. The analyses of my interviewees varied significantly depending on the conceptual frameworks they deployed when articulating preferred and disavowed modes of politics and subjectivity.

I have argued for a notion of articulation that highlights the interpretive and functional dimensions of discourse and subjectivity. The various theories of discourse and subjectivity discussed in this book can be framed as interpretive and functional theories of articulation, discourse and the self. Linguistic pragmatic, pragmatist and poststructuralist frameworks are alike in the fact that they emphasise the process-based, inter-subjective, differential and indexical functions of language and subjectivity. They provide useful insights into the way human beings come to interpret and shape their discursive reality through an unceasing rearticulation of semiotic forms and functions. An interpretive and functional approach for analysing discourse involves a rearticulation of the functional relatedness of linguistic forms to each other, to the practice(s) of interaction and to the metapragmatic positioning of the interlocutors and voices involved in the speech events under investigation.

Doing research on minorities is a precarious and hazardous thing to do. It is especially precarious and hazardous for minority members themselves, since they run the risk of becoming objects of scientific control. An important part of my motivation to construct an interpretive and functionalist heuristic for analysing political engagement was informed by a need to reduce the risk of overpowering the voices of my respondents. Even though I obviously objectified the discourse of my respondents, and even though I used a great deal of theoretical concepts my interviewees were not aware of, I hope to have rearticulated their discourse(s) in such a way that their words remain functional with respect to their preferred sense of self and sense of politics. As such, the analyses presented in this book constitute a humble attempt to stimulate the debate and to provide an academic forum for the voices of the activists and intellectuals that were prepared to share their insights, their time and their ideas with me.

Glossary

Adaptability refers to the property of language and discourse that enables human beings to make negotiable choices from a variable range of possibilities in a way that allows them to address contextually established communicative needs (see Verschueren, Verschueren).

Articulations of signifiers, identities, narratives and/or political identities rely upon linguistic and/or non-linguistic performances that render them material and allow them to emancipate themselves from the domain of interpretive and discursive imagination. By means of the practice and principle of articulation, we can index semiotic forms and performances as traces of wider interpretive and political processes that allow for reflexive modes of subjectivity. These performances establish pragmatic boundaries for (self-) interpretation. They establish temporary fixations of discursive forms and functions. Any articulation of two or more discursive elements alters the meaning of the elements involved (see Glynos and Zienkowski 2013).

Centring Institutions impact on the way we evaluate and interpret discursive practice. All institutions—for example, families, schools, states, non-governmental organizations (NGOs), or social networks—function as centring institutions. Centring institutions authorise and sanction discursive norms and values. Our social world hosts many centring institutions and is therefore a polycentric phenomenon. It is also stratified because different actors have different possibilities for dealing with centring institutions. Politics involves attempts to rearticulate the value-infused relationships between discursive forms and functions sanctioned by centring institutions (see Blommaert 2005, 75–78).

Context is an interpretive phenomenon. It is generated in a discursive process whereby interlocutors metapragmatically delineate boundaries for interpretation. This orientation process operates through discursive indexes that indicate potentially relevant aspects of mental, spatial, temporal, social and/or intertextual aspects of reality. These indexes need to be taken into account in order to make sense of a statement. Context is the flexible and temporary result of an interpretive process through which social actors imagine some degree of interactional clarity and the possibility of common ground (see Verschueren et al. 2003).

Contextualisation is (the result of) a metapragmatic process that triggers interpretive efforts whereby spatial, temporal, social and/or (inter)textual coordinates of reality are indexed by interlocutors in order to contribute to interactional clarity and imagine common ground (see Bauman and Briggs 1990, Verschueren 1999, 77, Blommaert 2005, 251).

Contextualisation Cues are linguistic or non-linguistic forms that trigger a contextualisation process by means of indexical processes of inference and interpretation. They are used in order to indicate a need for our interlocutors to articulate particular statements with specific aspects of contextual reality in order to draw an inference and generate a meaning that is not explicitly marked in discourse (see Levinson 2003; Prevignano and di Luzio 2003; Gumperz).

Critique is a quintessential political practice that requires reflexivity and metapragmatic awareness with respect to the power-infused ideological and hegemonic dimensions of discourse and subjectivity. It is a label for discursive practices that challenge the presuppositions and conditions of established social norms and relationships in public settings.

Debates are public intertextual networks in which actors articulate their identities in a political struggle over the functions of signifiers that fix the meanings defining the boundaries of self, politics and society. Debates are discursive struggles for hegemony whereby actors seek to fix the meanings of words, norms, values, practices and/or entire policy domains. They are ever-shifting networks in which agents rearticulate and re-imagine their relationships to each other, to themselves and to the practices they are engaged in. They can restructure our sense of self and society.

Glossary 401

Discourse cannot be reduced to language use alone. It is a multi-layered, context-dependent and socially constitutive practice of articulation. Discourse analytical data can include verbal and/or textual language use but may also include multimodal data and observations about the practices that allow for their articulation. The category of discourse can also be used in order to describe various levels of linguistic, textual, semiotic and/or socio-political organisation. The boundaries of what is meant by 'discourse' shift and change because its basic elements are defined by their functions rather than by their forms. The study of discourse focuses on the way we ride ideas as marked and constituted in and through language and other semiotic systems.

Empty Signifiers are signifiers that are so over-coded with meaning that they mean everything and nothing at the same time. They propel us towards political action. They mean everything in the sense that our identities seem to depend on values such as love, freedom and equality. They mean nothing in the sense that they signify ideals that can never be completely realised. The vagueness of terms such as citizenship or freedom is what allows empty signifiers to function as hegemonic nodal points that connect a multiplicity of political identities and projects. Empty signifiers play a key role in the expansion and delineation of chains of equivalence. They function as normative values that allow actors to distinguish between preferred and disavowed modes of politics (see Torfing 1999, 301; Laclau 1994c, 44–45)

Ethics can be considered as a reflexive practice for acting upon the self and upon reality. Ethics and ideology are two sides of the same coin. They refer to different but overlapping modes of investment in identity, discourse and politics. To engage in an ethical mode of subjectivity means that one takes a critical stance with respect to essentialist and reductionist ways of imagining the world. It also entails the development of a reflexive engagement with the discursive practices that fix the meanings of life. Ethics and ideology are not mutually exclusive phenomena but can be thought of in terms of two poles on a continuum of reflexivity. Ethical modes of engagement involve a degree of awareness with respect to the contingencies of discursive reality (see Glynos 2014).

Fantasy and Fantasmatic Logics operate through discursive practices that ensure that the radical contingency of social relationships between actors, signifiers, practices and institutions continues to operate in the background. They allow people to invest emotionally in the values and aspects of identity they consider to be lacking or to be threatened in their lives and/or in society in general. The logic of fantasy generates ideals, as well as obstacles for their realisation. It propels actors to transgress established norms, and it purports to offer some degree of protection from the anxieties associated with a direct confrontation with the radical contingency of social relations. Fantasy structures our emotional relation with social norms and values, as well as the force with which we pursue them (see Glynos and Stavrakakis 2008, 258–259, Glynos 2008, 289).

Hedging   is a linguistic or paralinguistic strategy that makes messages indeterminate and conveys impreciseness in order to mitigate or to reduce the strength of assertions. *Hedges* highlight the fuzziness, vagueness, emptiness or polysemy of statements. They can affect the truth conditions of a proposition (e.g. 'sort of', 'about' and 'roughly') and/or introduce fuzziness about the speaker's commitment with respect to the propositional content of what is conveyed. A hedge can therefore function as a shielding device that protects the speaker from potentially risky claims or speech acts that might violate conversational maxims. Hedges are the opposite of *boosters* that mark what one believes to be correct and that indicate some degree of metapragmatic awareness with respect to the normativity of what one is saying (see McLaren-Hankin 2008, 639; Hyland 2000, 179; 2005, Verschueren 1999, 193).

Hegemony   is a status of common sense that may be acquired by a particular ideological project. The hegemonic status of a particular identity or discourse can only be assessed comparatively. Hegemony is a mode of intellectual leadership involving a dispersion of statements and signifiers across the discourse of competing social and political actors. Only when discursive elements perform similar ideological functions across a variety of discourses can one establish the hegemonic status of a particular idea, identity or practice. No hegemony can be complete because this would presuppose a perfect fixation of discursive forms and meanings for all actors within the public sphere in a totalising chain of equivalence (see Barret 1994, Howarth 2004, Blommaert et al. 2003, Howarth, Norval, and Stavrakakis 2000).

Hegemonic Claims and Projects   should be distinguished from actually established hegemonies. Even though no hegemony can be complete, many political discourses claim a hegemonic status by making absolute claims to common sense and/or to the will of the people. Hegemonic claims are made by political actors that seek to fix the meanings of discursive elements such as subject positions, statements or narratives for as many social actors as possible. Hegemonic projects always attempt to expand chains of equivalence through an engagement with empty signifiers.

Ideology is an interpretive function of articulatory practice. It is a mode of political awareness that allows subjects to embrace and pursue particular hegemonic projects. It is the dimension of discourse that allows people to imagine social reality. It impacts on our ability to imagine alternative worlds and modes of subjectivity. Ideological discourse can be described in terms of social, political and fantasmatic logics of critical explanation. Even though one cannot escape ideology, it is possible to use discourse metapragmatically in order to loosen its hold over us. Ideology is an important aspect of our imperfect forms of sociopolitical and metapragmatic awareness. It can be observed in reflexive and discursive processes of argumentation, framing, legitimation and narration that structure our relationships to identities, attitudes, statements, practices, norms and values (see Torfing 1999, Verschueren 2011, Glynos and Howarth 2007).

Indexicality is a semiotic process whereby shifters, indexes, discourse markers and/or contextualisation cues provide us with spatial, temporal, social and/or (inter)textual coordinates that allow us to delineate relevant contexts for interpreting discursive reality. Indexical meanings are ordered in hierarchically organised and institutionalised regimes of discourse that allow social actors to judge, to include and to exclude each other (Blommaert 2005, 73–75, Silverstein 2003).

Indexicals or Indexical Expressions are linguistic and paralinguistic forms that serve as contextualisation cues. They indicate a need to connect particular statements and enunciations with some aspect of spatial, social and/or (inter)textual reality. They usually function at the linguistic level of morphemes, words and word groups (e.g. pronouns, anaphora and nouns) but may also include paralinguistic and non-verbal signifiers (e.g. intonation, pointing and gaze). These phenomena are also discussed under the header of *deixis* (Silverstein 2003; Sidnell 2009; Levinson 2003).

Interpellation is the discursive process whereby individuals are hailed into specific subject positions and corresponding ideologies. This process of hailing is a metapragmatic process whereby individuals recognise and/or misrecognise themselves in particular forms of address. Feelings of ideological misrecognition caused by misfiring interpellations frequently lie at the basis of heightened modes of political awareness.

Interpretive Functionalism is an approach to discourse that involves an investigation of the functional relatedness of linguistic forms to one another, to the practice(s) of interaction, and to the metapragmatic positioning of the interlocutors and voices involved in the speech event under investigation. The approach to articulation put forward in this book is grounded on interpretive and functional principles.

Lack is a psychoanalytical concept that refers to the impossible fullness of any type of meaning and identity. According to Lacan, lack lies at the heart of signification. As a result of their entry into the Symbolic, human beings attempt to ground their sense of self in identification processes that can never provide a solid ground for identity. In this sense, the main function of the ego is to misrecognise the impossibility of fullness. Experiences of ideological misrecognition drive people towards attempts to fill this lack by means of practices of articulation (see Laclau and Zac 1994, Stavrakakis 1999).

Logic The discourse theoretical notion of *logic* refers to the rules that regulate practices of articulation. One can distinguish between social, political and fantasmatic logics of critical explanation. These logics configure the relationships between subject positions, statements, practices, topics and other discursive elements. By naming and describing logics, researchers and other critical actors can explain and criticise how meanings are fixed in specific social and political contexts. Logics inform the self-interpretations through which social actors establish particular modes of engagement with themselves and with others. They shape social and political subjectivity and allow people to distinguish between preferred and disavowed modes of self, society and politics (Glynos and Howarth 2007, Zienkowski 2013, 2014).

Metapragmatics can be understood as the study of indicators of reflexive awareness that can be found in the choices made by language users. It can also be understood as a cover term for the interpretive practices through which people negotiate meanings in concrete contexts of enunciation. In this sense, there is a metapragmatic dimension to all language use (see Bublitz and Hübler 2007; Hübler 2011; Verschueren 1999, 188).

Metapragmatic Awareness can be described as a flawed, incomplete and normative awareness of the way interlocutors communicate in order to achieve interpretive and communicative effects. Discourse and language use involve at least some degree of metapragmatic awareness with respect to the way interlocutors adapt themselves to and negotiate about the variable contexts through which they move. Metapragmatic awareness may be marked explicitly or may be left to operate implicitly in discourse. It is a key condition for the development and articulation of political awareness and subjectivity. Like any other reflexive process related to language use, it may or may not be marked explicitly in discourse (see Verschueren 1999, 187–188).

Glossary   405

Metapragmatic Markers   indicate a mental awareness and a normative stance with respect to the way an aspect of discourse is or ought to be used. They allow us to trace subjectivity in discourse. They can be found in explicit metalanguage in the form of metapragmatic descriptions, discourse markers, shifters, hedges, sentence adverbs, explicit intertextual links, reported speech and so on. They may also function more implicitly through uses of mood, modality, deictic expressions, code-switching and other features of enunciation that mark the presence of implicit voices in discourse (see Hübler and Bublitz 2007, Verschueren 2004, Zienkowski 2013).

Negotiability   is the property of language responsible for the fact that there are no strict rules that fix the relationship between discursive forms and functions. It highlights the fact that discursive choices are made on the basis of highly flexible principles and strategies that can be deployed with varying degrees of metapragmatic awareness. Negotiability implies indeterminacy in choice making in the production and interpretation of discourse. The principle of negotiability guarantees that these interpretive choices can always be renegotiated (see Verschueren).

Nodal Points   are privileged discursive elements (e.g. images, people, names and abstract categories) within a chain of equivalence. They are key signifiers (e.g. a flag or a notion such as democracy) within the discourse of specific social actors, genres and/or institutions. They quilt signifiers into chains of equivalence and perform a cohesive function in discourse. Nodal points signify some type of lack on which people can project their desires (e.g. freedom, order or community). A nodal point can attain the hegemonic status of an empty signifier when it becomes the focal point of political struggle (see Torfing 1999, Stavrakakis 1999, Howarth and Stavrakakis 2000).

Politics   is a dimension of social and discursive reality. The political character of social reality is rendered explicit whenever social actors challenge and rearticulate established norms, practices and discourses in society. Politics emerges whenever subjects engage in attempts to reimagine society by calling sedimented relationships between social actors, signifiers, statements, practices and institutions into question. It refers to the process of organising (in-) equality and to the multiplicity of attempts to regulate the distribution of different forms of capital in society.

Political Awareness   refers to reflexive and metapragmatic modes of awareness with respect to the contingent ways in which (the meanings of) identities, practices, institutions and discourses are fixed. It involves an awareness of ideological processes that establish or sustain inequalities, power relationships and hegemonic claims.

Political Engagement is an umbrella term for the practices through which social actors publicly (re-)imagine, (re-)articulate and negotiate social and political relationships through imagined collective action. It consists of heterogeneous sets of practices through which people rearticulate and negotiate fantasy-infused ideals and emotional relationships with each other and with the practices and institutions that populate the public realm.

Political Logics of Equivalence and Difference highlight the contingency of discursive relationships. Logics of equivalence simplify social and political space through the establishment of equivalences between discursive elements (e.g. identities, subject positions, narratives, practices and institutions). Logics of difference expand and complicate political space by decomposing existing chains of equivalence. Logics of equivalence and difference are integral to the construction and contestation of social and political practices and the fixation of meaning through practices of (re-)articulation (Laclau and Mouffe 1985, Glynos and Howarth 2007).

Power cannot be analysed in the abstract. It is a functional relationship that operates in historically contingent ways on social actors, shaping them in the process. The power of a feudal tribesman from the middle ages operates differently than the power exercised by an NGO in late capitalism. Power relationships operate through discursive rationalities that structure the way we act upon ourselves, upon others and upon the world. The exercise of power requires freedom. Power relationships should therefore be distinguished from relationships of domination that can be described as perpetually continued asymmetrical relationships that severely restrict the ability of actors to engage with themselves and with the world as they see fit.

Pragmatics can be understood as the interdisciplinary study of linguistic and communicative phenomena from the point of view of their usage properties and processes. It is a perspective on language use that highlights the functional, reflexive and process-based features of empirically observable language use. Linguistic pragmatics can be considered in terms of a poststructuralist perspective on language and communication that has moved beyond the idea of language as a closed and centred system. Many approaches within pragmatics embrace dynamic, reflexive and heterogeneous concepts of subjectivity (see Verschueren, Zienkowski, Östman and Verschueren).

Public Spheres function as imagined communities that allow for a sense of continuity and discontinuity with times, places and people who are not necessarily present at the same time and place. They cannot be reduced to specific times and places. The concept of the public sphere is a spatial metaphor for a heterogeneous set of practices through which social actors rearticulate social and political relationships in democratic ways. The public realm consists of a multiplicity of language games and speech events in which actors use discourse in order to cast a net that allows them to fix the meanings of particular identities, experiences and/or practices. The casting of this net implies that these actors position themselves in relation to others as well as in relation to themselves.

Recognition and Misrecognition are ideological effects of discourse. Recognition occurs when forms of address interpellate subjects on the basis of subject positions that correspond to their sense of self. Feelings of misrecognition can be triggered when such claims about and over identity conflict with one's preferred mode of subjectivity. Subjects may politicise feelings of misrecognition through metapragmatic articulatory practices that allow them to publicly address the logics that inform such interpellations.

Selves are social, decentred and process-based frameworks or assemblies. As such, the self operates as a reification of the processes that allow us to act reflexively upon ourselves and upon others. It is a reification of the processes that allow us to position ourselves as more or less coherent minds/bodies in relation to spatial, temporal, social and (inter)textual aspects of contextual reality. Selves are ideas we ride and objects that can be shaped through historically contingent self-techniques. The self is only as stable as the performances we enact in order to give ourselves the semblance of substance. Our selves may be relatively unified and centred, but only to the extent that our interpretive logics and self-techniques allow us to be.

Subjectivity can be understood as a reflexive mode of engagement with discursive reality. It is an opaque phenomenon that may or may not be marked in discourse. When marked, it can be observed at any level of discursive structure. Subjectivity involves an imperfect awareness of the aspects, processes and practices constitutive of our sense of self. It can be described in terms of large-scale interpretive logics that articulate subject positions, discourses and practices with each other.

Subject Positions are discursive functions of statements from which authoritative utterances and identity claims can be made. They are valued by centring institutions but need to be activated in discourse. They function through spatial, temporal, social and/or intertextual forms of indexicality. Our relationships towards subject positions shift and change as we activate different contexts of enunciation. An individual may (partially) identify his or her self with any subject position articulated in discourse. However, selves and subjectivities can never be reduced to subject positions without running the risk of triggering feelings of misrecognition or forms of ideological overinvestment.

Self-Interpretations cannot be accessed directly. Subjectivity will always remain a rather opaque phenomenon. But even though we cannot literally 'pass through' the self-interpretations of subjects, we can assess self-interpretations as marked in discourse. Metalanguage and markers of metapragmatic awareness provide us with traces of subjectivity that can be used for interpretive purposes.

Social The *social* consists of hegemonic practices, identities, institutions and relationships that provide a relatively stable ground for our ideological presuppositions and practices. Because of the primacy of the political, every aspect of the social is open for rearticulation and politicisation. The social consists of the sum total of political decisions and discourses that have crystallised into hegemonic normalcy.

Social Logics operate at a relatively low level of abstraction in comparison to fantasmatic and political logics of critical explanation. One may talk about bureaucratic, systemic or neoliberal logics that articulate a multiplicity of subject positions, practices and institutions into complex discursive networks. In order to identify social logics, researchers need to pass metapragmatically through the self-interpretations of the subjects on which these logics operate. By naming and describing the social logics of a discursive practice, researchers engage in acts of critical explanation.

Structure can be understood as a reification of the range of options we have at our disposal for making sense of and acting upon the world. Discursive elements such as words, sentences, narratives and languages can be understood as *structural objects of adaptability* that simultaneously operate at different levels of discursive structure. These structures do not exist as static or closed totalities. The production of discourse implies acts of articulation whereby social actors combine such structural objects of adaptability in meaningful ways (see Verschueren 2008).

Topics of discourse are expressible as noun phrases and can be named with reference to key lexical items that can be found in the discourse under investigation. The identification and negotiation of discourse topics play a crucial role in the establishment of interpretive coherence. Discourse topics may consist of several levels of subtopics. Discourse topics that span large stretches of discourse can be distinguished from more local topics that operate at the level of sentences, utterances and other short segments of language use (Watson Todd 2005, 94; Wanska and Bedrosian 1985).

Variability is an important principle for thinking diversity and change in discourse. It defines the structures of discourse (e.g. morphology, grammar, discourse strategy, textual structure or genre) and describes the way we deal with them. The structures of discourse are never stable (Verschueren 1999, 56–59). The choice of a particular discursive element (e.g. a sound, a word, a prosodic form, a metaphor, a narrative structure, a genre, a discourse strategy or a sociolect) alters the range of possibilities for consequent choices for communication. Variability operates at every level of discursive structure (see Verschueren 1999, 2004, Verschueren and Brisard 2009).

Bibliography

Abicht, Ludo, Lucas Catherine, Patrick Develtere, Nadia Fadil, Ico Maly, Rik Pinxten, Nigel Williams, Sami Zemni, and Walter Zinzen. 2011. "Het multiculturele debat is failliet." 20/05/2011. http://www.demorgen.be/dm/nl/2461/De-Gedachte/article/detail/1267064/2011/05/20/Het-multiculturele-debat-is-failliet.dhtml

Allen, Amy. 2000. The anti-subjective hypothesis: Michel Foucault and the death of the subject. *The Philosophical Forum XXXI* 2: 113–130.

Alsulaiman, Abied. 1998. De bestuurlijke randvoorwaarden voor de toepassing van het integratieconcept. In *Nieuwe burgers in de samenleving: burgerschap en inburgering in België en Nederland*, ed. Bernard Hubeau and Marie-Claire Foblets, 183–201. Antwerpen: Acco.

Althusser, Louis. 1970. Ideology and ideological state apparatuses: Notes towards an investigation. In *On ideology*, 1–60. London: Verso.

Anderson, Benedict. 1983. *Imagined communities: Reflections on the origin and spread of nationalism*, 2006th ed. London: Verso.

Angermuller, Johannes. 2011. From the many vocies to the subject positions in anti-globalization discourse: Enunciative pragmatics and the polyphonic organization of subjectivity. *Journal of Pragmatics* 43: 29992–3000.

Angermuller, Johannes. 2014a. Einleitung: Diskursforschung als Theorie und Analyse: Umrisse eines interdisziplinären und internationalen Feldes. In *Diskursforschung: ein interdisziplinäres Handbuch*, ed. Johannes Angermuller,

Martin Nonhoff, Eva Herschinger, Felicitas Macgilchrist, Martin Reisigl, Juliette Wedl, Daniel Wrana and Alexander Ziem. Bielefeld: Transcript Verlag.

Angermuller, Johannes. 2014. *Poststructuralist discourse analysis: Subjectivity in enunciative pragmatics*. Houndmills: Palgrave Macmillan.

Angermuller, Johannes, Dominique Maingueneau, and Ruth Wodak (eds.). 2014a. *The discourse studies reader*. Amsterdam: John Benjamins.

Angermuller, Johannes, Dominique Maingueneau, and Ruth Wodak. 2014b. An introduction. In *The discourse studies reader*, ed. Johannes Angermuller, Dominique Maingueneau, and Ruth Wodak, 1–14. Amsterdam: John Benjamins.

Angermuller, Johannes, Dominique Maingueneau, and Ruth Wodak. 2014c. Introduction. In *The discourse studies reader*, ed. Johannes Angermuller, Dominique Maingueneau, and Ruth Wodak, 17–20. Amsterdam: John Benjamins.

Angermuller, Johannes, Dominique Maingueneau, and Ruth Wodak. 2014d. Introduction. In *The discourse studies reader*, ed. Johannes Angermuller, Dominique Maingueneau, and Ruth Wodak, 136–139. Amsterdam: John Benjamins.

Anscombre, Jean-Claude. 2009. La comédie de la polyphonie et ses personnages. *Langue Française* 164: 11–31.

Arnaut, Karel, and Bambi Ceuppens. 2009. De ondiepe gronden en de vage grenzen van de raciale verbeelding in Vlaanderen. In *Een leeuw in een kooi: de grenzen van het multiculturele Vlaanderen*, ed. Karel Arnaut, Sarah Bracke, Bambi Ceuppens, Sarah De Mul, and Meryem Kanmaz, 28–47. Antwerpen: Meulenhoff.

Arnaut, Karel, Sarah Bracke, Bambi Ceuppens, Nadia Fadil, and Meryem Kanmaz (eds.). 2009. *Een leeuw in een kooi: de grenzen van het multiculturele Vlaanderen*. Antwerpen: Meulenhoff/Manteau.

Atkins, Kim. 2005. Commentary on Descartes. In *Self and subjectivity*, ed. Kim Atkins, 7–11. Oxford: Blackwell Publishing Ltd.

Auer, Peter. 1992. Introduction: John Gumperz' approach to contextualization. In *The contextualization of language*, ed. Peter Auer and Aldo di Luzio, 1–37. Amsterdam: John Benjamins.

Auer, Peter. 2009. Context and contextualisation. In *Key notions for pragmatics*, ed. Jef Verschueren and Jan-Ola Östman, 86–101. Amsterdam: John Benjamins Publishing Company.

Austin, John L. 2011. How to do things with words. In *The pragmatics reader*, ed. Dawn Archer and Peter Grundy, 19–26. London/New York: Routlegde.

Authier-Revuz, Jacqueline. 1995a. *Ces mots qui ne vont pas de soi: boucles réflexives et non-coïncidences du dire*. 2 vols. vol. 2. Paris: Larousse.
Authier-Revuz, Jacqueline. 1995b. *Ces mots qui ne vont pas de soi: boucles réflexives et non-coïncidences du dire*. 2 vols. Vol. 1. Paris: Larousse.
Bachmann-Medick, Doris. 2016. *Cultural turns: New orientations in the study of culture*. Berlin: De Gruyter.
Bacon, Michael. 2012. *Pragmatism: An introduction*. Cambridge: Polity Press.
Baker, Paul. 2013. *Discourse analysis and media attitudes: The representation of Islam in the British Press*. Cambridge/New York: Cambridge University Press.
Balibar, Etienne. 1991. Is there a neo-racism? In *Race, nation, class: Ambiguous identities*, ed. Etienne Balibar and Immanuel Wallerstein, 17–28. London: Verso.
Bamberg, Michael, Anna De Fina, and Deborah Schiffrin (eds.). 2007. *Selves and identities in narrative and discourse*. Amsterdam: John Benjamins.
Barret, Michèle. 1994. Ideology, politics, hegemony: From Gramsci to Laclau and Mouffe. In *Mapping ideology*, ed. Slavoj Žižek, 235–277. London/New York: Verso. Original edition, 1991.
Barros, Sebastian, and Gustavo Castagnola. 2000. The political frontiers of the social: Argentine politics after Peronist populism (1955–1973). In *Discourse theory and political analysis: Identities, hegemonies and social change*, ed. David Howarth, Aletta Norval and Yannis Stavrakakis, 24–37. London/New York: Manchester University Press.
Baudrillard, Jean. 1995. *The Gulf ward did not take place*. Bloomington: Indiana University Press.
Bauman, Richard, and Charles Briggs. 1990. Poetics and performance as critical perspectives on language and social life. *Annual Review of Anthropology* 19: 59–88.
Belga. 2002. Verhofstadt bereid AEL eventueel te laten verbieden. *De Standaard*, 28/11/2002. http://www.standaard.be/cnt/nflh28112002_001
Benveniste, Emile. 1970. L'appareil formel de l'énonciation. *Langages* 17: 12–18.
Benveniste, Emile. 1974. *Problèmes de linguistique générale*. Paris: Gallimard.
Benveniste, Emile. 2014. The formal apparatus of enunciation. In *The discourse studies reader*, ed. Johannes Angermuller, Dominique Maingueneau, and Ruth Wodak, 141–145. Amsterdam: John Benjamins.
Bernstein, Richard J. 2010. *The pragmatic turn*. Cambridge: Polity Press.
Bertucelli Papi, Marcella. 2009. Implicitness. In *Key notions for pragmatics*, ed. Jef Verschueren and Jan-Ola Östman, 139–162. Amsterdam: John Benjamins Publishing Company.
Bhabha, Homi K. 1994. *The location of culture*. London/New York: Routledge.

Billig, Michael. 1999a. Conversation analysis and the claims of naivety. *Discourse and Society* 10(4): 572–576.
Billig, Michael. 1999b. Whose terms? Whose ordinariness? Rhetoric and ideology in conversation analysis. *Discourse and Society* 10(4): 543–582.
Billig, Michael, Susan Condor, Derek Edwards, Mike Gane, and David Middleton. 1988. *Ideological dilemmas: A social psychology of everyday thinking.* London: Sage.
Blommaert, Jan. 2001. Context is/as critique. *Journal of Anthropology* 21(1): 13–32.
Blommaert, Jan. 2005. *Discourse.* Cambridge: Cambridge University Press.
Blommaert, Jan. 2006. Het politieke discours over minderheden. In *Immigratie en integratie anders denken: een Belgisch interuniversitair initiatief,* ed. Bichara Khader, Marco Martiniello, Andrea Rea, and Christiane Timmerman, 203–212. Brussel: Bruylant.
Blommaert, Jan. 2010. *Burgerschap, integratie en ander fraais: drie problemen.* Den Haag: Burgerschap en integratie.
Blommaert, Jan. 2010b. *Vrijheid, meningen, en schelden: de déjà vu van Benno Barnard.* DeWereldMorgen. http://www.dewereldmorgen.be/artikels/2010/04/07/vrijheid-meningen-en-schelden-de-déja-vu-van-benno-barnard Published: 07/04/2010; Last accessed: 20/09/2016
Blommaert, Jan. 2011. Pragmatics and discourse. In *Cambridge handbook of sociolinguistics,* ed. Rajend Meshtrie, 122–137. Cambridge: Cambridge University Press.
Blommaert, Jan, and Jef Verschueren. 1992. *Het Belgische Migrantendebat: de pragmatiek van de abnormalisering.* Antwerp: International Pragmatics Association.
Blommaert, Jan, and Jef Verschueren. 1998. *Debating diversity: Analysing the discourse of tolerance.* London: Routledge.
Blommaert, Jan, James Collins, Monica Heller, Ben Rampton, Stef Slembrouck, and Jef Verschueren. 2001. Discourse and critique: Part one. *Critique of Anthropology* 21(1): 5–12.
Blommaert, Jan, James Collins, Monica Heller, Ben Rampton, Stef Slembrouck, and Jef Verschueren. 2003. Introduction. In *Pragmatics: Quarterly publication of the international pragmatics association,* Vol. 13, Special issue: Ethnography, discourse and hegemony, 1–10.
Bossche, Mario. 2008. Integratie. In *Knack,* 127.
Bourdieu, Pierre. 1986. The forms of capital. In *Handbook of theory and research for the sociology of education,* ed. J. Richardson, 241–258. New York: Greenwood.

Bousetta, Hassan (ed.). 2003. *Breek de stilte: een burgerlijk standpunt van Belgische intellectuelen van Maghrebijnse afkomst over de gebeurtenissen sinds 11 september 2001*. Brussel: VUBPress.
Bousetta, Hassan. 2001. Immigration, post-immigration politics and the political mobilisation of ethnic minorities: A comparative case-study of Moroccans in four European studies. Ph.d., Political and Social Sciences, Katholieke Universiteit Brussel.
Bouzarmat, Imane. 2010. Speech 10 jaar SAMV. Accessed 7 Nov 2011.
Bouzerda, Abdou. 2009. Vervang integratie door emancipatie. In *Een leeuw in een kooi: de grenzen van het multiculturele Vlaanderen*, ed. Karel Arnaut, Sarah Bracke, Bambi Ceuppens, Sarah De Mul, and Meryem Kanmaz, 130–135. Antwerpen: Meulenhoff/manteau.
Bowman, Glenn. 1994. 'A country of words': Conceiving the Palestinian nation from the position of exile. In *The making of political identities*, ed. Ernesto Laclau, 138–170. London: Verso.
Breeze, Ruth. 2011. Critical discourse analysis and its critics. *Pragmatics* 21(4): 493–525.
Brenner, Neil. 1994. Foucault's new functionalism. *Theory and Society* 23: 679–709.
Briggs, Charles. 2003. Interviewing, power/knowledge and social inequality. In *Postmodern interviewing*, ed. Jaber F. Gubrium and James A. Holstein, 243–254. London: Sage.
Briggs, Charles. 2007. The Gallup poll, democracy and the *vox pupuli*: Ideologies of interviewing and the communicability of modern life. *Text & Talk* 27(5/6): 681–704.
Bublitz, Wolfram, and Axel Hübler (eds.). 2007. *Metapragmatics in use*. Amsterdam: John Benjamins.
Bublitz, Wolfram, and Neal R. Norrick. 2011. Introduction: The burgeoning field of pragmatics. In *Foundations of pragmatics*, ed. Wolfram Bublitz and Neal R. Norrick, 1–22. Berlin: De Gruyter Mouton.
Buekens, Filip. 1995. Pragmatism. *Handbook of pragmatics online*. Accessed 9 Sept 2010.
Butler, Judith, and Ernesto Laclau. 2004. Appendix I: The uses of equality. In *Laclau: A critical reader*, ed. Simon Critchley and Oliver Marchart, 329–344. London/New York: Routledge.
Butler, Judith. 1990. *Gender trouble: Feminism and the subversion of identity*. New York/London: Routledge. Reprint, 2006.
Butler, Judith. 1999. Preface. In *Gender trouble: Feminism and the subversion of identity*, ed. Judith Butler, vii–xxviii. New York/London: Routledge.

Caffi, C. 1993. Metapragmatics. In *Encyclopedia of language and linguistics*, ed. Ron Ahser, 2461–2466. Oxford: pergamon.

Caffi, C. 1998. Metapragmatics. In *Concise encyclopedia of pragmatics*, ed. Jacob L. Mey, 581–586. Amsterdam: Elsevier.

Calhoun, Craig. 1992. Introduction: Habermas in the public sphere. In *Habermas and the public sphere*, ed. Craig Calhoun, 1–48. Cambridge: MIT Press.

Campbell, James. 2011. A history of pragmatism. In *The continuum companion to pragmatism*, ed. Sami Philström, 69–80. London: Continuum.

Carpentier, Nathalie. 2011. Wilders gooit Vlaming uit partij. *De Morgen*, 19/07/2011, 7.

Cattebeke, Hannes. 2008. Niets dan Allah en zijn profeet. *Knack*, 17/12/2008, 32.

Chandler, Daniel. 2002. *Semiotics: The basics*. London: Routledge.

Charmaz, Kathy. 2008. Constructionism and the grounded theory method. In *Handbook of constructionist research*, ed. J.A. Holstein and J.F. Gubrium, 397–412. New York: Guilldford Press.

Choenni, C. 1992. Allochtonen en burgerschap. In *Burgerschap in praktijken*, ed. H.R. Gunsteren and P. Hoed, 57–98. Den Haag: Standaard Uitgeverij.

Concentra. 2007. Integratie is achterhaald. *Gazet van Antwerpen*, 10/12/2005, 65.

Connolly, W. E. 2002. *Identity/Difference*, 2nd Edition, Ithaca: CornellUniversity Press.

Culioli, Antoine. 2002. *Variations sur la linguistique: entretiens avec Frédéric Fau*. Paris: Klincksieck.

Cummings, Louise. 2005. *Pragmatics: A multidisciplinary perspective*. Edinburgh: Edinburgh University Press.

Cutting, Joan. 2007. *Pragmatics and discourse: A resource book for students*. London: Routledge.

d'Hondt, Paula. 1989. *Integratie(beleid): een werk van lange adem*. Brussel: Koninklijk Commissariaat voor het Migrantenbeleid.

Dahlberg, Lincoln, and Sean Phelan (eds.). 2011. *Discourse theory and critical media politics*. Houndmills: Palgrave Macmillan.

Daryl Slack, Jennifer. 1996. The theory and method of articulation in cultural studies. In *Stuart Hall: Critical dialogues in cultural studies*, 112–130. London/New York: Routledge.

De Mul, Sarah. 2007. Oproerkraaiers in het culturele landschap: de AEL en de identiteitspolitiek voor etnische minderheden in Vlaanderen. *Freespace Nieuw-zuid* 3(10): 60–75.

De Wit, John. 2008. Hof van beroep spreekt AEL-kopstukken vrij. *Gazet van Antwerpen*, 21/10/2008.
Van den Broeck, Ann. 2013. Gent schrapt het woord allochtoon. *De Morgen*, 14/02/2013, 1.
Dijk, Van, and A. Teun. 1999. Critical discourse analysis and conversation analysis. *Discourse and Society* 10(4): 459–460.
Domke, Christine, and Werner Holly. 2011. Foundations: Ethnomethodology and Erving Goffman. In *Foundations of pragmatics*, ed. Wolfram Bublitz and Neal R. Norrick, 261–288. Berlin: De Gruyter Mouton.
Ducrot, Oswald. 1984. *Le dire et le dit*. Paris: Les éditions de minuit.
Duranti, Alessandro, and Charles Goodwin (eds.). 1992. *Rethinking context: Language as an interactive phenomenon*. Cambridge: Cambridge University Press.
Edley, Nigel. 2001. Analysing masculinity: Interpretative repertoires, ideological dilemmas and subject positions. In *Discourse as data*, ed. Maragaret Wetherell, Stephanie Taylor, and Simeon Yates, 189–228. London: Sage.
Edwards, Derek. 2005. Discursive psychology. In *Handbook of language and social interaction*, ed. Kristine L. Fitch and Robert E. Sanders, 257–273. Mahwah: Lawrence Erlbaum Associates.
Eerdmans, Susan L., Carlo L. Prevignano, and Paul J. Thibault (eds.). 2003. *Language and interaction: Discussions with John J. Gumperz*. Amsterdam: John Benjamins.
Eldridge, Michael, and Sami Philström. 2011. Glossary. In *The continuum companion to pragmatism*, ed. Sami Philström, 29–45. London: Continuum.
Elliott, Anthony. 2009. *Concepts of the self*, 2nd ed. Cambridge: Polity Press. Original edition.
Ellis, Carolyn, and Leigh Berger. 2003. Their story/my story/our story. In *Postmodern interviewing*, ed. Jaber F. Gubrium and James A. Holstein, 157–183. London: Sage.
Entzinger, Han. 1998. Inburgeren met én zonder concessies. In *Nieuwe burgers in de samenleving? Burgerschap en inburgering in België en Nederland*, ed. Marie-Claire Foblets and Bernard Hubeau, 29–42. Antwerpen: Acco.
Esser, Hartmut. 2006. Migration, language and integration. In *AKI research review 4*. Berlin: Social Science Research Center.
Fadil, Nadia, and Meryem Kanmaz. 2009. Identiteitspolitiek en burgerschap in Vlaanderen: een meervoudige kritiek. In *Een leeuw in een kooi: de grenzen van het multiculturele Vlaanderen*, ed. Karel Arnaut, Sarah Bracke, Bambi Ceuppens, Sarah De Mul, Nadia Fadil, and Meryem Kanmaz, 111–127. Antwerpen: Meulenhoff.

Fadil, Nadia. 2008a. Submitting to God, submitting to the self: Secular and religious trajectories of second generation Maghrebi in Belgium. Ph.d., Social Sciences, Katholieke Universiteit Leuven.

Fadil, Nadia. 2008b. Wij behoren tot de AEL-generatie. *De Morgen*, 26/05/2008.

Fadil, Nadia, Dirk Jacobs, Axel Marx, Herman De Ley, Jan Blommaert, and Meryem Kanmaz. 2002. Open brief aan alle beleidsverantwoordelijken. *De Morgen*, 03/12/2002.

Fairclough, Norman. 1992. *Discourse and social change*. Cambridge: Blackwell Publishers.

Fairclough, Norman, and Lilie Chouliaraki. 1999. *Discourse in late modernity*. Edinburgh: Edinburgh University Press.

Fairclough, Norman, and Ruth Wodak. 1997. Critical discourse analysis. In *Discourse as social interaction*, ed. Teun A. Van Dijk, 258–284. London: Sage.

Faubion, James. 1994. Introduction. In *Michel Foucault: Power: essential works of Foucault 1954–1984*, ed. James Faubion, xi–xlii. London: Penguin Books.

Fetzer, Anita. 2011. Pragmatics as a linguistic concept. In *Foundations of pragmatics*, ed. Wolfram Bublitz and Neal R. Norrick, 23–50. Berlin: De Gruyter Mouton.

Fludernik, Monika. 1991. Shifters and deixis: Some reflections on Jespersen, Jakobson and reference. *Semiotica* 86(3–4): 193–230.

Flyvbjerg, Bent. 1998. Habermas and Foucault: Thinkers for civil society? *British Journal for Sociology* 49(2): 210–233.

Flyvbjerg, Bent. 2001. *Making social science matter: Why social inquiry fails and how it can succeed again*, 2008th ed. Cambridge: Cambridge University Press.

Foblets, Marie-Claire. 2008. Moroccan women in Europe: Bargaining for autonomy. *Washington and Lee Law Review* 64(4): 1385–1414.

Foblets, Marie-Claire, and Bernard Hubeau. 1997. Burgerschap en inburgering als nieuwe integratieconcepten? In *Nieuwe burgers in de samenleving? Burgerschap en inburgering in België en Nederland*, ed. Marie-Claire Foblets and Bernard Hubeau, 17–28. Antwerpen: Acco.

Forchtner, Bernhard. 2011. Critique, the discourse-historical approach, and the Frankfurt School. *Critical Discourse Studies* 8(1): 1–14.

Forchtner, Bernard, and Ana Tominc. 2012. Critique and argumentation: On the relation between the discourse-historical approach and pragma-dialectics. *Journal of Language and Politics* 11(1): 31–50.

Foucault, Michel. 1969. *The archaeology of knowledge*. 2007 ed, *Routledge Classics*. London: Routledge.

Foucault, Michel. 1972. *The archaeology of knowledge*. London: Routledge.

Foucault, Michel. 1976. *The will to knowledge, The history of sexuality*, vol. 1. London: Penguin Books. Reprint 1998.
Foucault, Michel. 1979a. The birth of biopolitics. In *Michel Foucault: Ethics: subjectivity and truth*, ed. Paul Rabinow, 73–79. London: Penguin Books.
Foucault, Michel. 1979b. Omnes et singulatim. In *Michel Foucault: Power*, ed. James Faubion, 298–325. London: Penguin Books.
Foucault, Michel. 1982a. Sex, power, and the politics of identity. In *Michel Foucault: Ethics: subjectivity and truth*, ed. Paul Rabinow, 164–173. London: Penguin Books.
Foucault, Michel. 1982b. The subject and power. In *Michel Foucault: Power*, ed. James Faubion. London: Penguin Books.
Foucault, Michel. 1989. The ethics of the concern for self as a practice of freedom. In *Michel Foucault: Ethics: subjectivity and truth*, ed. Paul Rabinow, 281–301. London: Penguin Books.
Foucault, Michel, and Paul Rabinow. 1982. Space, knowledge and power. In *Michel Foucault: Essential works of Foucault 1954–1984*, ed. James Faubion, 349–364. London: Penguin Books.
Foucault, Michel, Mauro Bertani, and Alessandro Fontana (eds.). 1997. *Society must be defended: Lectures at the collège de France, 1975–76*. London: Penguin books.
Fraihi, Tarik. 2000. Het failliet van de integratie-industrie. *De Morgen*, 08/05/2011. http://www.flw.ugent.be/cie/CIE/fraihi.htm
Fraihi, Tarik. 2002. Dimensies van minorisering en ongelijkheid bij het minderhedenbeleid. In *Het failliet van de integratie? Het multiculturalismedebat in Vlaanderen*, ed. Bob Van den Broeck and Marie-Claire Foblets, 103–109. Leuven: Acco.
Fraser, Nancy. 1992. Rethinking the public sphere: A contribution to the critique of actually existing democracy. In *Habermas and the public sphere*, ed. Craig Calhoun, 109–142. Cambridge: Cambridge University Press.
Fried, Mirjam. 2010. Introduction: From instances of change to explanations of change. In *Variation and change: Pragmatic perspectives*, ed. Mirjam Fried, Jan-Ola Östaman, and Jef Verschueren, 1–16. Amsterdam: John Benjamins.
Fried, Mirjam, Jan-Ola Östman, and Jef Verschueren (eds.). 2010. *Variation and change: Pragmatic perspectives*. Amsterdam: John Benjamins.
Gal, Susan, and Kathryn Woolard. 1995. Constructing languages and publics: Authority and representation. *Pragmatics: Quarterly Publication of the International Pragmatics Association* 5(2): 129–138.
Gasteiger, Ludwig, and Schneider Werner. 2014. Die Modernisierung der Hochschule im Spannungsfeld von politischer Steuerung und Autonomie: interpretativ-rekonstruktive Diskursforschung und grounded Theory Methodologie.

In *Diskursforschung: ein interdisziplinäres Handbuch, Band 2: Methoden und Analysepraxis: Perspectiven auf Hoschulreformdiskurse*, ed. Nonhoff Martin, Herschinger Eva, Angermuller Johannes, Macgilchrist Felicitas, Reisigl Martin, Wedl Juliette, Wrana Daniel, and Ziem Alexander, 140–163. Bielefeld: Transcript.

Gasteiger, Ludwig, and Werner Schneider. 2014b. Diskursanalyse und die Verwending von CAQDA-software: zur Herausforderung der Instrumentalisierung von technischen Programmen. In *Diskursforschung: ein interdisziplinäres Handbuch, Band 2: Methoden und Analysepraxis: Perspectiven auf Hoschulreformdiskurse*, ed. Martin Nonhoff, Eva Herschinger, Johannes Angermuller, Felicitas Macgilchrist, Martin Reisigl, Juliette Wedl, Daniel Wrana and Alexander Ziem. Bielefeld: Transcript.

Gee, James Paul, and Michael Handford (eds.). 2012. *The Routledge handbook of discourse analysis*. Abingdon: Routledge.

Gibbs, Braham R. 2007. *Qualitative data analysis: Explorations with NVIVO*. In *Understanding social research*, ed. Alan Bryman. Berkshire: Open University Press.

Glynos, Jason. 2008. Ideological fantasy at work. *Journal of Political Ideologies* 13(3): 275–296.

Glynos, Jason. 2011. On the ideological and political significance of fantasy in the organization of work. *Psychoanalysis, Culture & Society* 16(4): 373–393.

Glynos, Jason. 2014. Neoliberalism, markets, fantasy: The case of health and social care. *Psychoanalysis, Culture & Society* 19(1): 5–12.

Glynos, Jason, and David Howarth. 2007. *Logics of critical explanation in social and political theory*. London: Routledge.

Glynos, Jason, and David Howarth. 2008. Structure, agency and power in political analysis: Beyond contextualised self-interpretations. *Political Studies Review* 6: 155–169.

Glynos, Jason, and Yannis Stavrakakis. 2008. Lacan and political subjectivity: Fantasy and enjoyment in psychoanalysis and political theory. *Subjectivity* 2008(24): 256–274.

Glynos, Jason, and Yannis Stavrakakis. 2004. Encounters of the real kind: Sussing out the limits of Laclau's embrace of Lacan. In *Laclau: A critical reader*, ed. Simon Critchley and Oliver Marchart, 201–216. London/New York: Routledge.

Glynos, Jason, David Howarth, Aletta Norval, and Ewen Speed. 2009. Discourse analysis: Varieties and methods. In *ESRC National Centre for Research Methods Review Paper*: ESRC National Centre for Research Methods.

Glynos, Jason, Robin Klimecki, and Hugh Wilmott. 2012. Cooling out the marks: The ideology and politics of the financial crisis. *Journal of Cultural Economy* 5(3): 297–320.
Goatly, Andrew. 1997. *The language of metaphors*. London: Routledge.
Goffman, Erving. 1959. *The presentation of self in everyday life*. New York: Doubleday Anchor.
Goffman, Erving. 1969. *The presentation of self in everyday life*. London: Penguin Books.
Goodwin, Charles, and Alessandro Duranti. 1992. Rethinking context: An introduction. In *Rethinking context: Language as an interactive phenomenon*, ed. Alessandro Duranti and Charles Goodwin, 1–42. Cambridge: Cambridge University Press.
Gottdiener, M. 1995. *Postmodern semiotics*. Oxford: Blackwell Publishers.
Grice, H.P. 2011. Logic and conversation. In *The pragmatics reader*, ed. Dawn Archer and Peter Grundy, 43–54. London/New York: Routledge.
Griggs, Steven, and David Howarth. 2000. New environmental movements and direct action protest: The campaign against Manchester Airport's second runway. In *Discourse theory and political analysis: Identities, hegemonies, and social change*, ed. David Howarth, Aletta Norval, and Yannis Stavrakakis, 52–69. Manchester/New York: Manchester University Press.
Grillo, Eric. 2005. Two dogmas of discourse analysis. In *Power without domination*, ed. Eric Grillo, 3–41. Amsterdam: John Benjamins.
Grossberg, Lawrence. 1986. On postmodernism and articulation: An interview with Stuart Hall. In *Stuart Hall: Critical dialogues in cultural studies*, ed. David Morley and Kuan-Hsing Chen, 131–150. London/New York: Routledge.
Gubrium, Jaber F., and James A. Holstein. 2003a. Active interviewing. In *Postmodern interviewing*, ed. Jaber F. Gubrium and James A. Holstein, 67–80. London: Sage.
Gubrium, Jaber F., and James A. Holstein. 2003b. From the individual interview to the interview society. In *Postmodern interviewing*, ed. Jaber F. Gubrium and James A. Holstein, 21–50. London: Sage.
Gubrium, Jaber F., and James A. Holstein (eds.). 2003c. *Postmodern interviewing*. London: Sage.
Gubrium, Jaber F., and James A. Holstein. 2003d. Postmodern sensibilities. In *Postmodern interviewing*, ed. Jaber F. Gubrium and James A. Holstein, 3–18. London: Sage.
Gumperz, John J. 1982. *Discourse strategies*. Cambridge: Cambridge University Press.

Gumperz, John J. 1992a. Contextualization and understanding. In *Rethinking context: Language as an interactive phenomenon*, ed. Alessandro Duranti and Charles Goodwin, 292–252. Cambridge: Cambridge University Press.

Gumperz, John J. 1992b. Contextualization revisited. In *The contextualization of language*, ed. Peter Auer and Aldo di Luzio, 39–53. Amsterdam: John Benjamins.

Gumperz, John J., and Dell Hymes (eds.). 1972. *Directions in sociolinguistics: The ethnography of communication*. New York: Holt.

GVA. 2010. Extremisten verhinderen islamdebat in Antwerpen. *Gazet Van Antwerpen*, 01/04/2010.

Habermas, Jürgen. 1989. The public sphere: An encyclopedia article. In *Media and cultural studies: Keyworks*, ed. Meenakshi Gigi Durham and Douglas Kellner, 102–107. Oxford: Blackwell Publishers Ltd.

Hak, Tony, and Niels Helsloot (eds.). 1995. *Michel Pêcheux: Automatic discourse analysis*. Amsterdam: Rodopi.

Hall, Donald E. 2004. *Subjectivity, the new critical idiom*. London: Routledge.

Hanks, William F. 1992. The indexical ground of deictic reference. In *Rethinking context: Language as an interactive phenomenon*, ed. Alessandro Duranti and Charles Goodwin, 43–76. Cambridge: Cambridge University Press.

Hawkes, David. 1996. *Ideology*, The new critical idiom, 2nd ed. London: Routledge.

Henneman, Jelle, and Dries Bervoet. 2008. Eerst werk, dan cultuur. *De Metro* (16/09/2008).

Heritage, John, and Steven Clayman. 2010. *Talk in action: Interactions, identities, and institutions*. Oxford: Wiley-Blackwell.

Hesters, Delphine. 2011. Identity, culture talk & culture. Ph.d., Faculteit sociale wetenschappen, KULeuven.

Hogan-Brun, Gabrielle, Clare Mar-Molinero, and Patrick Stevenson. 2009. Testing regimes: Introducing cross-national perspectives on language, migration and citizenship. In *Discourse on language and integration*, ed. Gabrielle Hogan-Brun, Clare Mar-Molinero, and Patrick Stevenson, 1–13. Amsterdam: John Benjamins.

Holstein, James A., and Jaber F. Gubrium. 2000. *The self we live by: Narrative identity in a postmodern world*. New York: Oxford University Press.

Hongladarom, Krisadawan. 2007. "Don't Blame me for criticizing you …": A study of metapragmatic comments in Thai. In *Metapragmatics in use*, ed. Wolfram Bublitz and Axel Hübler, 29–48. Amsterdam/Philadelphia: J. Benjamins Pub. Co.

Howarth, David. 2000. *Discourse*. Buckingham: Open University Press.

Howarth, David. 2005. Applying discourse theory: The method of articulation. In *Discourse theory in European politics: Identity, policy and governance*, ed. David Howarth and Jacob Torfing, 316–349. New York: Palgrave/Macmillan.

Howarth, David. 2004. Hegemony, political subjectivity, and radical democracy. In *Laclau: A critical reader*, ed. Simon Critchley and Oliver Marchart, 256–276. London/New York: Routledge.

Howarth, David, and Yannis Stavrakakis. 2000. Introducing discourse theory and political analysis. In *Discourse theory and political analysis: Identities, hegemonies and social change*, ed. David Howarth, Aletta Norval, and Yannis Stavrakakis, 1–23. Manchester: Manchester University Press.

Howarth, David, and Jacob Torfing (eds.). 2005. *Discourse theory in European politics: Identity, policy and governance*. New York: Palgrave/Macmillan.

Howarth, David, Aletta Norval, and Yannis Stavrakakis (eds.). 2000. *Discourse theory and political analysis: Identities, hegemonies and social change*. Manchester: Manchester University Press.

Huang, Yan. 2007. *Pragmatics*. Oxford: Oxford University Press.

Hübler, Axel. 2011. Metapragmatics. In *Foundations of pragmatics*, ed. Wolfram Bublitz and Neal R. Norrick, 107–136. Berlin: De Gruyter Mouton.

Hübler, Axel, and Wolfram Bublitz. 2007. Introducing metapragmatics in use. In *Metapragmatics in use*, ed. Wolfram Bublitz and Axel Hübler, 1–26. Amsterdam: John Benjamins.

Huntington, Samuel. 1998. *The clash of civilizations and the remaking of world order*. London: Touchstone.

Hyland, Ken. 2000. Hedges, boosters and lexical invisibility: Noticing modifiers in academic texts. *Language Awareness* 9(4): 179–197.

Hyland, Ken. 2005. *Metadiscourse: Exploring interaction in writing*. Continuum: London/New York.

Jacobs, Dirk. 2005. Arab European Legue (AEL): The rapid rise of a radical immigrant movement. *Journal of Muslim Minority Affairs* 25(1): 99–117.

Jacobs, Dirk, and Andrea Rea. 2006. Construction and import of ethnic categorisations: Allochthones in the Netherlands and Belgium. Working paper, 29, Fondazione Eni Enrico Mattei, Milano

Jahjah, Dyab Abou. 2002. Wij zijn hier en we blijven hier. In *Het failliet van de integratie? Het multiculturalismedebat in Vlaanderen*, ed. Bob Van den Broeck and Marie-Claire Foblets, 118–120. Leuven: Acco.

Jakobson, Roman. 1971. Shifters, verbal categories, and the Russian verb. In *Roman Jakobson: Selected writings II: word and language*, ed. Roman Jakobson, 130–147. The Hague/Paris: Mouton.

James, William. 1947. What pragmatism means. In *Selected papers on philosophy*, ed. Wiliam James, 198–217. London: J.M. Dent & Sons Ltd.

James, Wiliam. 1981. *The principles of psychology*, vol. 1. Cambridge/London: Harvard University Press.

James, Wiliam, ed. 2003. *The correspondence of William James: William and Henry, April 1905–March 1908*. Edited by J.J. McDermott. 12 vols. Vol. 11. Charlottesville: University Press of Virginia.

Jaworski, Adam, Nikolas Coupland, and Dariusz Galasinski (eds.). 2004. *Metalanguage: Social and ideological perspectives*. Mouton de Gruyter: Berlin/New York.

Johansson, Marjut, and Eija Suomela-Salmi. 2011. Enonciation. In *Discursive pragmatics*, ed. Jan Zienkowski, Jef Verschueren, and Jan-Ola Östman, 71–101. Amsterdam: John Benjamins Publishing Company.

Jørgensen, Marianne Winther, and Louise J. Philips. 2002. *Discourse analysis as theory and method*. London: Sage.

JVI. 2009. Islam. *Knack*, 07/01/2009, 126.

Kanmaz, Meryem. 2007. Moskeeën in Gent: tussen subcultuur en sociale beweging: emancipatiedynamieken van moslimminderheden in de diaspora. Ph.d., Political and social sciences, University of Ghent.

Kerbrat-Orecchioni, Catherine. 1980. *L'énonciation de la subjectivité dans la langage*. Paris: Armand Colin.

Koller, Veronika, and Ruth Wodak. 2010. Introduction: Shifting boundaries and emergent public spheres. In *Handbook of communication in the public sphere*, ed. Ruth Wodak and Veronika Koller, 1–17. Berlin: De Gruyter Mouton.

Kompa, Nikola, and Georg Meggle. 2011. Pragmatics in modern philosophy of language. In *Foundations of pragmatics*, ed. Wolfram Bublitz and Neal R. Norrick, 203–228. Berlin: De Gruyter Mouton.

Kopytko, Roman. 2000. From Cartesian towards non-Cartesian pragmatics. *Journal of Pragmatics* 33: 783–804.

Kopytko, Roman. 2007. Philosophy and pragmatics: A language-game with Ludwig Wittgenstein. *Journal of Pragmatics* 39: 792–812.

Korta, Kepa. 2007. Malinowski and pragmatics: Claim making in the history of linguistics. *Journal of Pragmatics* 40: 1645–1660.

Koyama, Wataru. 2011. The rise of pragmatics: A historiographic overview. In *Foundations of pragmatics*, ed. Wolfram Bublitz and Neal R. Norrick, 139–165. Berlin: De Gruyter Mouton.

Kress, Gunther. 2001. From Saussure to critical sociolinguistics: The turn towards a social view of language. In *Discourse theory and practice: A reader*,

ed. Maragaret Wetherell, Stephanie Taylor, and Simeon Yates, 29–38. London: Sage.
Kruipsunt M-I. 2009. Voorstellingsbrochure. 31.
Kruispunt M-I. 2011. Inburgerings- en integratiesector. http://www.kruispuntmi.be/detail.aspx?id=187. Accessed 28 Aug 2011.
Lacan, Jacques. 1994. The mirror-phase as formative of the function of the I. In *Mapping ideology*, ed. Slavoj Žižek, 93–99. London/New York: Verso. Original edition, 1968.
Laclau, Ernesto. 1994a. Introduction. In *The making of political identities*, ed. Ernesto Laclau, 1–8. London: Verso.
Laclau, Ernesto (ed.). 1994b. *The making of political identities*. London: Verso.
Laclau, Ernesto. 1994c. Why do empty signifiers matter to politics? In *Emancipation(s)*, ed. Ernesto Laclau, 36–46. London: Verso.
Laclau, Ernesto. 2000. Foreword. In *Discourse theory and political analysis: Identities, hegemonies and social change*, ed. Howarth David, Aletta J. Norval, and Stavrakakis Yannis, x–xi. Manchester/New York: Manchester University Press.
Laclau, Ernesto, and Chantal Mouffe. 1985. *Hegemony and socialist strategy: Towards a radical democratic politics*. London: Verso.
Laclau, Ernesto, and Chantal Mouffe. 1990. Post-marxism without apologies. In *New reflections on the revolution of our time*, ed. Ernesto Laclau, 97–132. London: Verso.
Laclau, Ernesto, and Lilian Zac. 1994. Minding the gap: The subject of politics. In *The making of political identities*, ed. Ernesto Laclau, 11–39. London/New York: Verso.
Laclau, Ernesto, and Chantal Mouffe. 2001. Preface to the second edition. In *Hegemony and socialist strategy: Towards a radical democratic politics*, ed. Ernesto Laclau and Chantal Mouffe, vii–xix. London: Verso.
Ladd, Robert D. 2012. What *is* duality of patterning, anyway? *Language and Cognition* 4: 261–273.
Lakoff, George, and Mark Johnson. 1980. *Metaphors we live by*. Chicago: University of Chicago Press.
Leilich, Joachim. 2011. Ludwig Wittgenstein. In *Philosophical perspectives for pragmatics*, ed. Marina Sbisà, Jan-Ola Östaman, and Jef Verschueren, 297–308. Amsterdam: John Benjamins.
Lemke, Thomas. 2002. Foucault, governmentality, and critique. *Rethinking Marxism* 14(3): 49–64.
Levinson, Stephen C. 1983. *Pragmatics*. Cambridge: Cambridge University Press.

Levinson, Stephen C. 2003. Contextualizing 'contextualization cues'. In *Language and interaction: Discussions with John J. Gumperz*, ed. Susan L. Eerdmans, Carlo L. Prevignano, and Paul J. Thibault, 31–39. Amsterdam: John Benjamins.

MacMillan, Katie. 2005. More than just coding? Evaluating CAQDAS in a dicourse analysis of news texts. *Forum Qualitative Sozialforschung/Forum: Qualitative Social Research* 6. Accessed 11 May 2015.

Maingueneau, Dominique. 1991. *L'analyse du discours: Introduction aux lectures de l'archive*. Amiens: Hachette Supérieur.

Maingueneau, Dominique, and Johannes Angermuller. 2007. Discourse analysis in France: A conversation. *Forum Qualitative Sozialforschung* 8 (2). Accessed 3 Jan 2009.

Maly, Ico. 2007a. Collaboratie in abnormalisering. In *Cultu(u)r(en)politiek: Over media globalisering en culturele identiteiten*, ed. Ico Maly, 183–200. Antwerp: Garant.

Maly, Ico. 2007b. Culturenpolitiek, media en verrechtsing. In *Cultu(u)r(en)politiek: Over media, globalisering en culturele identiteiten*, ed. Ico Maly, 243–247. Antwerpen: Garant.

Maly, Ico. 2007c. De botsing der beschavingen. In *Cultu(u)r(en)politiek*, ed. Ico Maly, 93–108. Antwerpen: Garant.

Maly, Ico. 2007d. De culturalisatie van het politiek discours. In *Cultu(u)renpolitiek*, ed. Ico Maly, 109–126. Antwerpen: Garant.

Maly, Ico, Jan Blommaert, and Joachim Ben Yakkoub (eds.). 2014. *Superdiversiteit en democratie*. Berchem: EPO.

Mansfeld, Nick. 2000. *Subjectivity: Theories of the self from Freud to Haraway*. New York: New York Univeristy Press.

Manz, Stefan. 2013. Constructing a normative national identity: The Leitkultur Debate in Germany, 2000–2001. *Journal of Multilingual and Multicultural Development* 25(5–6): 481–496.

Marchart, Oliver. 2004. Politics and the ontological difference: On the 'strictly philosophical' in Laclau's work. In *Laclau: A critical reader*, ed. Simon Critchley and Oliver Marchart, 54–72. London: Routledge.

Martens, Albert. 1997. Burgerschap en inburgering in België: de caleidoscoop als perspectief – de onanie als vuistregel. In *Nieuwe burgers in de samenleving? Burgerschap en inburgering in België en Nederland*, ed. Foblets Marie-Claire and Hubeau Bernard. Leuven: Acco.

McLaren-Hankin, Yvonne. 2008. "We expect to report on significant progress in our product pipeline in the coming year": Hedging forward-looking statements in corporate press releases. *Discourse Studies* 10(5): 635–654.

Mead, George Herbert. 1967. *Mind, self, and society: From the standpoint of a social behaviorist*. Chicago/London: The University of Chicago Press.
Meeks, John. 2003. In the wake of Edward Said. *Journal for Cultural and Religious Theory* 5(1): 130–138.
Meltzer, Bernard N., John W. Petras, and Larry T. Reynolds. 1975. *Symbolic interactionism: Genesis, varieties and criticism*. London and Boston: Routledge & Kegan Paul.
Melucci, Alberto. 1989. *Nomads of the presesnt: Social movements and individual needs in contemporary societies*. London: Hutchinson Radius.
Mey, Jacob L. 1998. Pragmatics. In *Concise encyclopedia of pragmatics*, ed. Jacob L. Mey, 716–737. Amsterdam: Elsevier.
Mey, Jacob L. 1999. *Pragmatics: An introduction*. Oxford: Blackwell Publishers ltd.
Moleman, Hans. 2013. Amsterdam schrapt als eerste stad in Nederland. *De Morgen*, 14/02/2013.
Morris, Charles W. 1963. Introduction. In *Mind, self & society: From the standpoint of a social behaviorist*, ed. George W. Mead, ix–xxxv. Chicago/London: The University of Chicago Press.
Mouffe, Chantal. 1993. *The return of the political*. London: Verso.
Mouffe, Chantal. 1979. Hegemony and ideology in Gramsci. In *Gramsci and marxist theory*, ed. Chantal Mouffe, 168–204. London/New York: Routledge.
Nerlich, Brigitte, and David C. Clarke. 1996. *Language, action, context: The early history of pragmatics in Europe and America, 1780–1930*. John Benjamins: Amsterdam/Philadelphia.
O'Driscoll, Jim. 2009. Erving Goffman. In *The pragmatics of interaction*, ed. Sigurd D'Hondt, Jan-Ola Östman, and Jef Verschueren, 79–95. Amsteradm: John Benjamins.
OED. 2010. Articulation. In *Oxford English dictionary*, ed. John Simpson. Oxford: Oxford University Press.
Omlo, Jurriaan. 2011. *Integratie én uit de gratie?* Delft: Uitgeverij Eburon.
Papafragou, Anna, Peggy Li, Yungon Choi, and Chung-hye Han. 2007. Evidentiality in language and cognition. *Cognition* 103: 253–299.
Pêcheux, Michel. 1994. The mechanism of ideological (mis)recognition. In *Mapping ideology*, ed. Slavoj Žižek, 141–151. London/New York: Verso. Original edition, 1982.
Peirce, Charles Sanders. 1970a. The fixation of belief. In *Pragmatism: The classic writings*, ed. H. Standish Thayer, 61–78. New York: The New American Library.
Peirce, Charles Sanders. 1970b. How to make our ideas clear. In *Pragmatism: The classic writings*, ed. H. Standish Thayer, 79–100. New York: New American Library.

Pfohl, Stephen. 1997. Review: The Gulf War did not take place, by Jean Baudrillard. *Contemporary Sociology* 26(2): 138–141.
Powell, Ronald R. 1997. *Basic research methods for librarians*. Greenwich: Ablex.
Prevignano, Carlo, and Aldo di Luzio. 2003. A discussion with John J. Gumperz by Carlo Prevignano and Aldo Di Luzio. In *Language and interaction: Discussions with John J. Gumperz*, ed. Susan L. Eerdmans, Carlo L. Prevignano, and Paul J. Thibault, 7–29. Amsterdam: John Benjamins.
Putnam, Hilary. 1995. *Pragmatism: an open question*. Oxford: Blackwell.
Reisigl, Martin, and Ruth Wodak. 2001. *Discourse and discrimination: Rhetorics of racism and antisemitism*. London: Routledge.
Robinson, Douglas. 2006. *Introducing performative pragmatics*. London/New York: Routledge.
Rose, Nikolas. 1998. *Inventing our selves*. Cambridge: Cambridge University Press.
Rothenberg, Molly Anne. 2006. Embodied political performativity in *Excitable speech*: Butler's psychoanalytic revision of historicism. *Theory, Culture and Society* 23(4): 71–93.
Roulet, Eddy. 2011. Polyphony. In *Discursive pragmatics*, ed. Jan Zienkowski, Jef Verschueren, and Jan-Ola Östman, 208–222. Amsterdam: John Benjamins.
Said, Edward. 1981. *Covering Islam: How the media and the experts determine how we see the rest of the world*. London: Routledge and Kegan Paul.
Said, Edward. 2005. *Oriëntalisten*. Amsterdam: Mets & Schilt Uitgevers.
Saldaña, Johny. 2013. *The coding manual for qualitative researchers*. London: Sage.
Saleel, Renata. 1994. The crisis of identity and the struggle for new hegemony in the former Yugoslavia. In *The making of political identities*, ed. Ernesto Laclau, 205–232. London: Verso.
Sbisà, Marina. 2009. Speech act theory. In *Key notions for pragmatics*, ed. Jef Verschueren and Jan-Ola Östman, 229–244. Amsterdam: John Benjamins Publishing Company.
Sbisà, Marina. 2011a. Analytical philosophy: Ordinary language philosophy. In *Philosophical perspectives for pragmatics*, ed. Marina Sbisà, Jan-Ola Östman, and Jef Verschueren, 11–25. Amsterdam: John Benjamin.
Sbisà, Marina. 2011b. Introduction. In *Philosophical perspectives for pragmatics*, ed. Marina Sbisà, 1–10. Amsterdam: John Benjamins.
Scheepers, Sarah. 2011. Equality for those who are competent: Discourses on competencies, diversity and equality in the public sector. In *Displaying competence in organizations: A discourse perspective*, ed. Priscilla Heynderickx, Katja Pelsmaekers, Craig Rollo, and Tom Van Hout, 36–60. Hampshire: Palgrave.

Schegloff, Emanuel A. 1997. Whose text? Whose context? *Discourse and Society* 8(2): 165–187.
Schegloff, Emanuel A. 1998. Reply to Wetherell. *Discourse and Society* 9(3): 413–416.
Schegloff, Emanuel A. 1999a. Naivity vs sophistication or discipline vs self-indulgence: A rejoinder to Billig. *Discourse and Society* 10(4): 577–582.
Schegloff, Emanuel A. 1999b. 'Schegloff's texts' as 'Billig's data': A critical reply. *Discourse and Society* 10(4): 558–572.
Schiffrin, Deborah. 2000. *Narrative identity*. Amsterdam: John Benjamins.
Schinkel, Willem. 2008. *Denken in een tijd van sociale hypochondrie: aanzet tot een theorie voorbij de maatschappij*. Kampen: Klement.
Searle, John R. 2011. Indirect speech acts. In *The pragmatics reader*, ed. Dawn Archer and Peter Grundy, 27–42. London/New York: Routledge.
Shapiro, I. 2002. Problems, methods and theories in the study of politics. *Political Theory* 30(4): 596–619.
Sidnell, Jack. 2009. Deixis. In *Key notions for pragmatics*, ed. Jef Verschueren and Jan-Ola Östman, 114–138. Amsterdam: John Benjamins Publishing Company.
Sidnell, Jack, and Tanya Stivers (eds.). 2013. *The handbook of conversation analysis*. Oxford: Wiley-Blackwell.
Silverstein, Michael. 2003. Indexical order and the dialectics of sociolinguistic life. *Language and Communication* 23: 193–229.
Slembrouck, Stef. 2001. Explanation, interpretation and critique in the analysis of discourse. *Critique of Anthropology* 21(1): 33–57.
Sokal, Alain D. 1996a. A physicist experiments with cultural studies. *Lingua Franca* May/June: 1–6.
Sokal, Alain D. 1996b. Transgressing the boundaries: Towards a transformative hermeneutics of quantum gravity. *Social Text* (46/47):217–252.
Sokal, Alain D., and Jean Bricmont. 1997. *Impostures intellectuelles*. Paris: Jacob.
Solomon, Robert C. 1988. *Continental philosophy since 1750: The rise and fall of the self*. Oxford: Oxford University Press.
Stavrakakis, Yannis. 1999. *Lacan and the political*. London: Routledge.
Stouthuysen, Patrick. 1995. De vredes- en antiracismebeweging: de ontmoeting van de oude en nieuwe sociale bewegingen. In *Van "mei 68" tot "Hand in Hand": nieuwe sociale bewegingen in België 1965–1995*, ed. Hellemans Stef and Hooghe Marc. Leuven: Garant.
Strauss, Anselm, and Juliet Corbin. 1990. *Basics of qualitative research: Grounded theory procedures and techniques*. Newbury Park: Sage.

Talhaoui, Fauzaya. 1998. Burgerschap en integratie in het Belgische samenlevingsmodel: een evaluatie van gangbare beleidsconcepten en een pleidooi voor een nieuwe benadering. In *Nieuwe burgers in de samenleving? Burgerschap en inburgering in België en Nederland*, ed. Marie-Claire Foblets and Bernard Hubeau, 73–85. Antwerpen: Acco.

Thayer, H.S. 1970. Introduction: George Herbert Mead. In *Pragmatism: The classical writings*, ed. H.S. Thayer, 337–340. New York/Toronto: New American Library.

Titscher, Stefan, Michael Meyer, Ruth Wodak, and Eva Vetter. 2000. *Methods of text and discourse analysis*. London: Sage.

Torfing, Jacob. 1999. *New theories of discourse: Laclau, Mouffe and Žižek*. Oxford: Blackwell.

Torfing, Jacob. 2005. Discourse theory: Achievements, arguments, and challenges. In *Discourse theory in European politics: Identity, policy and governance*, ed. David Howarth and Jacob Torfing, 1–32. New York: Palgrave/Macmillan.

Trombadori, D., and Michel Foucault. 1980. Interview with Michel Foucault. In *Michel Foucault: Power: essential works of Foucault 1954–1984*, ed. James Faubion, 239–297. London: Penguin Books.

Turner, Bryan. 2004. Edward W. Said: Overcoming orientalism. *Theory, Culture and Society* 21(1): 173–177.

Van Avermaet, Piet. 2009. Fortress Europe? Language policy regimes for immigration and citizenship. In *Discourses on language and integration*, ed. Gabrielle Hogan-Brun, Clare Mar-Molinero, and Patrick Stevenson, 15–43. Amsterdam: John Benjamins.

Van den Eede, Steven, Johan Wets, and François Levrau. 2009. De Vlaamse integratiekaart deel II: exploratieve literatuurstudie van het concept integratie. Steunpunt Gelijkekansenbeleid.

Van Dijk, Teun A. 1999. Critical discourse analysis and conversation analysis. *Discourse and Society* 10 (4):459–460.

Van Dijk, Teun. 2007. Comments on context and conversation. In *Discourse and contemporary social change*, eds. Norman Fairclough, Giuseppina Cortese and Patrizia Ardizzone, 281–316. Bern: Peter Lang.

Van Dijk, Teun. 2008. *Discourse and context: a sociocognitive approach*. Cambridge: Cambridge University Press.

Van Puymbroeck, Jihad. 2014. Er is politieke onwil om daadkrachtig tegen racisme op te treden: interview met Zohra Othman (PVDA). Accessed 12/06/2015.

Veenman, J. 1994. *Participatie in perspectief: ontwikkelingen in de sociaal-economische positie van zes allochtone groepen in Nederland*. Houten/Zaventem: Bohn Stafleu Van Loghum.
Vergauwen, Roger. 1995. Logical analysis. *Handbook of pragmatics online*.
Verhoeven, H., J. Anthierens, D. Neudt, and Albert Martens. 2003. *Het Vlaams minderhedenbeleid gewikt en gewogen: evaluatie van het Vlaams minderhedenbeleid (1996–2002): rapport voor de Vlaamse regering mei 2003*. Leuven: Katholieke Universiteit Leuven.
Verhofstadt, Guy. 1991. *Burgermanifest*: s.n.
Verhofstadt, Guy. 1992. *De weg naar politieke vernieuwing: het tweede burgermanifest*. Antwerpen: Hadewijch.
Vermeulen, Hans, and Rinus Penninx. 1994. *Het democratisch ongeduld: de emancipatie en integratie van zes doelgroepen van het minderhedenbeleid*. Amsterdam: Het Spinhuis.
Verschelden, Wouter. 2012. Waarom wij, De Morgen, 'allochtoon' niet meer gebruiken. *De Morgen*, 20/09/2012, 1.
Verschueren, Jef. 1999. *Understanding pragmatics*, 2003rd ed. London: Arnold.
Verschueren, Jef. 2001. Predicaments of criticism. *Critique of Anthropology* 21(1): 59–81.
Verschueren, Jef. 2004. Notes on the role of metapragmatic awareness in language use. In *Metalanguage: Social and ideological perspectives*, ed. Adam Jaworski, Nikolas Coupland and Dariusz Galasinski, 53–74. Berlin/New York: Mouton de Gruyter.
Verschueren, Jef. 2008. Context and structure in a theory of pragmatics. *Studies in Pragmatics* 10: 13–23.
Verschueren, Jef. 2009. Introduction: The pragmatic perspective. In *Key notions for pragmatics*, ed. Jef Verschueren and Jan-Ola Östman, 1–27. Amsterdam: John Benjamins Publishing Company.
Verschueren, Jef. 2011. *Ideology in language use: Pragmatic guidelines for empirical research*. Cambridge: Cambridge University Press.
Verschueren, Jef, and Frank Brisard. 2009. Adaptability. In *Key notions for pragmatics*, ed. Jef Verschueren and Jan-Ola Östman, 28–47. Amsterdam: John Benjamins Publishing Company.
Verschueren, Jef, and Jan-Ola Östman (eds.). 2009. *Key notions for pragmatics, Handbook of pragmatics highlights*, vol. 1. Amsterdam: John Benjamins Publishing Company.
Vlaams belang. 2011. Abou Imram choqueert op debat in Antwerpen, 20/09/2016. https://www.youtube.com/watch?v=1V5Fx1dMk0g

Vlierinck, Jogchum. 2010. Van haat gesproken? Een rechtsantropologisch onderzoek naar de bestrijding van rasgerelateerde uitingsdelicten in België. Ph.d., Faculteit Rechtsgeleerdheid, Katholieke Universiteit Leuven.
VOEM. 2015. Wat is VOEM? http://www.voem-vzw.be/VOEM.htm. Accessed 01 June 2015
Wanska, Susan, and Jan Bedrosian. 1985. Conversational structure and topic performance in mother-child interaction. *Journal of Speech and Hearing Research* 28: 579–584.
Watson, Rod. 2010. Symbolic interactionism. In *Society and language use*, ed. Jürgen Jaspers, Jan-Ola Östman, and Jef Verschueren, 304–313. Amsterdam: John Benjamins.
Watson Todd, Richard. 2005. A fuzzy approach to discourse topics. *Semiotica* 155(1): 93–123.
Weir, J.M. 1998. Bakthin, Michail M. (1895–1975). In *Concise encyclopedia of pragmatics*, ed. Jacob L. Mey, 1052–1053. Amsterdam: Elsevier.
Wetherell, Maragaret. 1998. Positioning and interpretative repertoires: Conversation analysis and post-structuralism in dialogue. *Discourse and Society* 9(3): 387–412.
Wetherell, Maragaret. 2007. A step too far: Discursive psychology, linguistic ethnography and questions of identity. *Journal of Sociolinguistics* 11(5): 661–681.
Wetherell, Maragaret, Stephanie Taylor, and Simeon Yates (eds.). 2003. *Discourse as data: A guide for analysis*. Milton Keynes: Open University.
Wiley, Norbert. 2006. Pragmatism and the dialogical self. *International Journal for Dialogical Science* 1(1): 5–21.
Williams, Raymond. 1983. *Keywords: A vocabulary of culture and society: revised edition*. New York: Oxford University Press.
Williams, Glyn. 1999. *French discourse analysis: The method of post-structuralism*. London: Routledge.
Windels, Kristof. 2012. Regering: 'gebruik 'allochtoon' niet meer'. *De Morgen*, 21/09/2012.
Wittgenstein, Ludwig. 1967. *Philosophical investigations*. Oxford: Blackwell.
Wodak, Ruth. 1997. Critical discourse analysis and the study of doctor-patient interaction. In *The construction of professional discourse*, ed. Britt-Louise Gunnarson, Per Linell, and Bengt Nordberg, 173–200. London: Longman.
Wodak, Ruth. 2007. Pragmatics and critical discourse analysis: A cross-disciplinary inquiry. *Pragmatics & Cognition* 15(1): 203–225.
Wodak, Ruth, ed. 2013a. *Critical discourse analysis: Concept, history, theory*. Edited by Ruth Wodak. 4 vols. Vol. 1, *Critical discourse analysis*. London: Sage.

Wodak, Ruth, ed. 2013b. *Critical discourse analysis: Doing CDA/case studies*. 4 vols. Vol. 3, *Critical discourse analysis*. London: Sage.
Wright, Scott. 2010. Language, communication and the public sphere: Definitions. In *Handbook of communication in the public sphere*, ed. Ruth Wodak and Veronika Koller, 21–43. Berlin: De Gruyter Mouton.
Young, Robert J. 2006. Preface: Sartre: The 'African Philosopher'. In *Colonialism and neocolonialism*, edited by Jean-Paul Sartre, ix–xxviii. London/New York: Routledge.
Zemni, Sami. 2009. *Het Islam Debat*. Berchem: EPO.
Zienkowski, Jan. 2011a. Analysing political engagement: an interpretive and functionalist discourse analysis of evolving political subjectivities among public activists and intellectuals with a Moroccan background in Flanders. Ph.d., Department of Linguistics, University of Antwerp.
Zienkowski, Jan. 2013. Marking subjectivity in interviews on political engagement: Interpretive logics and the metapragmatics of identity. In *Was machen Marker? Logik, Materialität und Politik von Differenzierungsprozessen*, ed. Eva Bonn, Christian Knöppler, and Miguel Souza, 85–112. Berlin: Transcript.
Zienkowski, Jan. 2014. Articulating metalinguistic and political awareness in Flemish discourses on integration and allochthony. *Journal of Political Ideologies* 19(3): 283–306.
Zienkowski, Jan. 2015. Marking a sense of self and politics in interviews on political engagement: Interpretive logics and the metapragmatics of identity. *Journal of Language and Politics* 14(4).
Zienkowski, Jan, and Ico Maly. 2007. Tussen natuur en verbeelding. In *Cultu(u)r(en)politiek*, ed. Ico Maly, 25–62. Antwerpen: Garant.
Zienkowski, Jan, Joan Leeflang, Jessy D. De Maeyer, and Ico Maly. 2007. Over there. In *Cultu(u)r(en)politiek: Over media, globalisering, en culturele identiteiten*, ed. Ico Maly. Antwerpen: Garant.
Zienkowski, Jan, Jan-Ola Östman, and Jef Verschueren (eds.). 2011a. *Discursive pragmatics, Handbook of pragmatics highlights*. Amsterdam: John Benjamins.
Zienkowski, Jan, et al. 2011b. Discursive pragmatics: A platform for the pragmatic study of discourse. In *Discursive pragmatics*, ed. Jan Zienkowski, Jef Verschueren, and Jan-Ola Östman, 296. Amsterdam: John benjamins.
Žižek, Slavoj. 1995. *The sublime object of ideology*. London: Verso.
Zoglin, Katie. 2009. Morocco's family code: Improving equality for women. *Human Rights Quarterly* 31(4): 964–984.

Index

A
Abou Jahjah, Dyab, 13, 26, 195, 215, 216, 245, 257, 384, 385
abstract categories, 3, 9–19, 30, 37, 53, 83, 93, 157, 175, 178, 211, 214, 224, 239, 262, 329, 350, 393–5, 405
academic discourse, 9, 11, 12, 16, 18, 25, 29, 35, 37, 38, 109, 114, 158, 164, 176–80, 199, 203, 207, 262, 271, 280, 283–5, 288–9, 296, 298, 304, 307–8, 357, 369, 375, 381, 382, 390, 397
Actiecomité Moslim Vrouwen (AMV), 212, 232, 233
activism, 290, 292–4, 338, 342. *See also* political engagement
  definition, 368
  as a value, 244

adaptability, 108, 110, 112–14, 156, 161–3, 302, 371, 399, 408
  definition, 399
AEL. *See* Arab European League (AEL)
affect, 57, 58, 165, 267, 268, 328, 334, 337, 338, 347, 348, 395
agency, 75, 97, 116, 131, 137, 237, 361
agonism, 56, 151, 172
allochthony, 2, 5, 16, 24, 29, 176, 179, 186–7, 189, 194–204, 206–10, 215, 217–19, 221, 224, 225, 229, 230, 234, 242, 247, 249–51, 253, 254, 256, 258–62, 264, 278, 283–5, 298–301, 304–7, 310–13, 315, 326, 329, 331–2, 334, 335, 337–9, 341, 342, 349, 395

© The Author(s) 2017
J. Zienkowski, *Articulations of Self and Politics in Activist Discourse*,
DOI 10.1007/978-3-319-40703-6

435

allochthony (*cont.*)
  debates on, 196–8
  definition, 199, 200
  etymology, 199–201
allocutions, 147
ambivalence, 267, 280–3, 289
AMV. *See* Actiecomité Moslim Vrouwen (AMV)
Anderson, Benedict, 164, 170
Angermuller, Johannes, 91, 92, 95, 97, 103, 104, 144–6, 148, 150–1
animator, 132
antagonism, 33, 54–6, 59, 150, 151, 188, 209, 217, 220, 225
anti-essentialism, 72, 95, 115, 134, 218
anti-subjective hypothesis, 70
Arab European League (AEL), 12, 14–18, 26, 27, 195, 212, 214–17, 219, 222, 223, 237, 243, 245, 257–9, 301, 302, 313–14, 317, 329, 352, 364, 373, 378, 384–9
Arabic, 221, 222, 257, 373, 374, 384
archaeology, 68, 70, 71, 145
articulation
  as a connection, 35, 54
  definition, 94, 399
  etymology, 35–7
  and indexicality, 148, 166
  Laclau and Mouffe on, 45
  and language use, 147
  linguistic dimension of, 88
  as performance, 35
  and political awareness, 338
  pragmatic dimension of, 95, 101, 271
  and recognition, 334
  and subjectivity, 303, 338, 368
assimilation, 28, 180, 189, 191, 205, 206, 209, 217, 221, 223–5, 227, 240, 250, 257, 264, 302, 312–17, 349
asylum seekers, 198
Austin, John, 73, 103, 133, 135–7, 139, 144
Authier-Revuz, Jacqueline, 145, 149
author, 132
autochthony, 179, 186, 187, 196–8, 200–3, 206–10, 216, 219, 224, 250, 253, 258, 259, 261, 262, 310, 332–5, 337, 385

B

Bakhtin, Mikhail, 149
Barnard, Benno, 287
Baudrillard, Jean, 292
behaviourism, 111, 112
Belgium, 6, 10, 19, 26, 27, 56, 65, 67, 98, 176, 186–9, 195, 197–201, 211, 216, 225–7, 237, 239, 248, 249, 252, 257–9, 264, 283, 305, 314, 323, 328, 339–41, 344, 349, 351–4, 359–60, 362, 364–6, 370, 381, 383, 384, 390
Benveniste, Emile, 144–9
Berber, 209, 317
Bernstein, Richard, 70, 115–17, 120, 133
Bhabha, Homi, 294, 295

binary pairs, 179, 196–8, 202, 206, 210, 262
Blommaert, Jan, 56, 92, 104, 144, 153, 158, 159, 164–5, 168, 184, 185, 189–91, 198, 201–4, 206, 207, 209, 283, 285, 381, 385, 400, 402, 403
BOEH!, 5–7, 212, 219, 244
Bricmont, Jean, 293–4
Briggs, Charles, 81, 82, 160, 167, 169, 400
Butler, Judith, 72, 73, 94, 97, 137, 138, 152

C

capital, 125, 172, 187, 268, 346, 377, 405
centring institutions, 164, 179, 185, 206, 232, 238, 328, 400
CGKR, 190, 193
chains of equivalence, 51, 54–6, 191, 209, 395, 403, 405
Charmaz, Kathy, 273, 275
choice, 2, 108, 113
Chomsky, Noam, 109, 142
citizenship, 12, 25, 26, 28, 44, 66, 173, 188, 202–4, 215, 217, 218, 243, 310, 317, 347, 401
clash of civilisations, 207
clash of cultures, 207
class, 357, 375–8
code switching, 96, 154, 161, 405
coding, 110, 158, 269, 271–8, 374, 376
   as articulation, 274, 275

cogito, 117, 120, 127
coherence, 2–9, 32, 53, 61, 67, 72, 83, 93, 107, 110, 123, 132, 170, 231, 276, 280, 302, 325, 338, 340, 347, 349, 351, 408
cohesion, 179, 181, 182, 188, 229, 276
common ground, 111, 113, 163, 169, 394, 400
communicative needs, 113, 399
community, 11, 21, 25, 27–9, 31, 55, 82, 117–19, 128, 187, 195, 202, 211, 222, 226, 228, 235–9, 247, 250, 251, 254, 256, 257, 261, 281–2, 297, 315, 317, 329, 334, 339, 343–5, 369, 373, 378, 390, 393, 405
community of inquirers, 117, 118
computer-assisted qualitative data analysis (CAQDAS), 212, 271, 274
constatives, 135
constituent subject, 71
constitutive heterogeneity, 149
constructivism, 115, 122, 182, 273, 275
context, 94
   as 'brought along,' 160
   in CA and CDA, 157–9
   container model of, 156
   definition, 400
   delineating, 62, 94, 102, 104, 152, 163, 172, 238

context (*cont.*)
  as figure and ground, 160
  and ideology, 158
  as imagined common ground, 113, 163
  and indexicality, 160, 164
  and lines of vision, 161
  as lines of vision, 338, 379, 382
  in linguistic pragmatics, 152–66, 160, 167
  Malinowski on, 112
  as 'out there', 152
  and power, 158
  pre-theoretical notions of, 156
  as a yellow brick road, 157
contextual correlates of adaptability, 162
contextualisation, 82
  and debates, 168
  definition, 400
contextualisation cues, 113, 137, 154, 160–1, 279, 400, 402, 403
  definition, 400
conversational implicatures, 112, 138, 143
conversational logic, 139
conversational maxims, 139
conversation analysis, 42, 92, 114, 157–9
Cooley, Charles, 103, 123, 125, 126, 128, 129
co-operative principle, 139, 141, 142
Corbin, Juliet, 272, 273
counterlogics, 178, 188, 210, 213, 224, 255, 290, 346–50
  definition, 205

critical awareness, 7, 63, 97, 98, 166, 177, 202, 210, 386, 396
critical discourse analysis (CDA), 43, 63, 97, 157, 159, 218
critique, 66, 167, 172, 178, 228, 231, 245, 247, 256, 264, 297–8, 303, 313, 393
  concepts of, 63
  defintion, 400
  Frankfurt school on, 63
  Glynos and Howarth on, 64
  Kant on, 63
  Reisigl and Wodak on, 64
Crosspoint MI, 193
cultural relativism, 287, 289

D

data selection, 211, 212
death of the subject, 68, 70, 74
debates, 121, 137, 173, 230
  definition, 167, 168, 400
  and subjectivity, 173
deconstruction, 288, 289
definition of the situation, 131
deixis, 105, 144, 155, 261, 312, 403
democracy, 32, 43, 44, 53, 54, 56, 65, 170, 172, 209, 281, 304, 317, 329, 387–9, 405
Derrida, Jacques, 72, 137, 288, 290, 292–5
Descartes, René, 80, 106, 115–20, 122, 135, 137, 144, 149
Dewey, John, 119
DHA, 63
dialogism, 129, 149
Dienst Integratie Antwerpen (DIA), 98, 212, 234, 236, 239,

240, 247, 253, 260, 330, 334, 335
difference, 51–6, 151, 267, 406
discourse, 1–89, 91, 96
    definition, 91, 96, 401
    and interpretive logics, 223
    Laclau and Mouffe on, 47
    and power, 387
    and the self, 223, 387
discourse studies, 37, 88, 91, 97, 121, 137, 149, 156–8, 175, 272, 274, 276
discourse theory, 30, 35–89, 91, 94, 103, 108, 114, 122, 273
    as theory and method, 85
discrimination, 6, 8, 12, 63, 96, 97, 158, 187, 194, 195, 197, 205, 232, 250, 256, 297–8, 326, 347, 356, 380–3, 385, 390
discursive structure, 2, 107, 108, 162, 214, 286, 407–9
dispersion of statements, 47, 403
diversity, 3, 9, 13, 19, 28, 30, 33, 65, 69, 99, 100, 109, 167, 176, 177, 179–82, 184, 189–92, 196, 198, 202, 204–6, 209, 215, 216, 218, 220–1, 224, 234, 238, 240, 247, 260–2, 270, 317–19, 334, 409
doubling, 127
Ducrot, Oswald, 145, 149, 150
Duranti, Alessandro, 135
Dutch, 5, 7, 184, 186, 187, 190, 191, 196, 198–202, 209, 212, 214, 215, 221, 224, 232, 248, 249, 254, 256, 311, 313

E

ego, 49, 124, 404
eigenheid, 15, 214, 215, 223, 313
Ella, 237, 338, 339, 345
emancipation, 23–4, 63, 81, 97, 159, 171, 189, 194–5, 205, 210, 217, 220, 233, 241, 243, 247, 251, 262, 296, 304, 311–13, 317, 339, 341–7, 350, 373, 394
embodiment, 72, 347–8, 354
embrayeurs, 148
emotions, 1, 13, 16, 36, 57, 77, 99, 239, 262, 268, 280, 301, 308, 328–30, 333–8, 347–8, 351, 362, 395, 402, 406
empowerment, 80, 82, 195, 205, 339, 395
empty signifiers, 13, 54–7, 178, 182, 227, 249, 329, 394, 401, 403, 405
    definition, 401
enjoyment, 55, 58
énoncé, 68, 147
enunciateur, 150
enunciation, 61, 104, 107, 144–52, 146, 152, 192, 275, 302, 328, 346, 347, 350, 394, 404, 405, 407
enunciative linguistics, 98, 139, 144, 148
enunciative pragmatics, 132, 145, 149
    language in, 146
    meaning in, 146
    subjectivity in, 147
    subject positions in, 151

enunciators, 150
equivalence, 39, 44, 51, 52, 54–6, 61, 95, 191, 209, 267, 401, 403, 405, 406
essentialism, 43, 308
Essex school of discourse theory, 36–8, 42–3, 45, 47–8, 50–1, 56–7, 61–2, 64, 72, 84, 85, 87, 89, 94, 103, 165, 172
ethics, 58, 223
  definition, 401
ethnicity, 17, 27, 44, 176, 180, 182, 186, 187, 192, 193, 198–201, 204, 205, 208, 210, 215, 216, 220, 300, 312, 313, 317, 340, 373, 374, 377
ethnography of communication, 63, 92, 104
ethnomethodology, 114, 130
Europe, 176, 179, 180, 207, 208, 239, 256, 257, 281, 329, 369, 370, 377, 387, 388, 390
exclusion, 164, 193, 196, 208, 220, 254, 256, 307, 312, 315, 330–7

F
face, 132
Fairclough, Norman, 157
fantasmatic, 393
fantasy, 56–61, 72, 131, 179, 183, 188, 209, 268, 271, 282, 297, 315, 319, 329, 368, 401, 402, 406
  beatific, 57, 58, 210, 282, 315
  definition, 402
  ethical detachment of, 58
  horrific, 57, 58, 183, 209, 210, 236, 271, 297, 315–16
  ideological, 131
feminism, 6, 7, 46, 53, 212, 232, 341, 342, 382, 383
fixation of meaning, 38, 41, 45–8, 51–6, 57, 59, 62, 67, 74, 76, 89, 92, 95, 102, 103, 106, 110, 114, 117, 118, 120, 121, 137, 145, 148, 163, 167, 179, 211, 239, 264, 265, 275, 278, 303, 328, 346, 347, 350, 351, 368, 371, 391, 394, 400, 401, 403–6
  through equivalence and difference, 51–6
  through technologies of the self, 77–83
Flanders, 3, 6, 8, 10, 12, 18, 21, 24, 28–30, 33, 55, 56, 65, 66, 86, 97, 98, 100–2, 108, 123, 151, 176–81, 183, 186, 188–98, 200–2, 204–13, 215, 217–21, 224–5, 227–9, 232, 235, 239, 241, 243, 246, 247, 250, 254, 256, 257, 260, 262, 264, 265, 278, 279, 285, 286, 289, 290, 296, 298, 305, 309–10, 313, 314, 316–18, 321–5, 327, 328, 331, 333–5, 338–42, 344–6, 349, 350, 352, 355, 358, 361, 370, 374, 379, 384, 385, 388–90, 394, 395

Flyvbjerg, Bent, 65, 170
FMV, 23–6, 212, 245, 250, 319
form, 102, 110–12
formal apparatus of
  language, 146
Foucault, Michel, 26, 39, 47, 48, 64,
  68–78, 96, 111, 144–7,
  236, 288, 290, 292, 293
function, 69, 95, 110, 112
  definition of, 69
functionalism, 69, 104, 111, 403

G
game, 128
gender, 6, 85, 97, 157, 159, 176,
  205, 209, 211, 278, 338–9,
  341, 342, 346
generalised other, 128
Gestalt, 40, 49
Glaser, Barney, 272
Glynos, Jason, 38, 39, 48, 51, 52,
  55, 57–61, 64, 84–5, 88,
  131, 134, 158, 165, 185,
  205, 274–5, 329, 399, 401,
  402, 404, 406
Gramsci, Antonio, 45, 46
Grice, Paul, 133, 135, 138–44
Groen, 260, 261
grounded theory, 272–5
  classic, 273
  constructivist, 275
  and discourse studies, 272,
    274–5
  and poststructuralism, 273
Gubrium, Jaber, F., 80, 81, 275
guest workers, 198, 200
Gumperz, John, 92–4, 109, 154,
  160, 161, 400

H
Habermas, Jürgen, 70, 168–70,
  282
habitus, 374–7
Hand in Hand, 283
headscarf, 221
hedges, 25, 229
hedging, 218
  definition, 402
hegemonic claim
  definition, 403
hegemony, 10, 44–6, 51, 54, 55, 58,
  60, 63, 65, 66, 81, 84, 87,
  94, 98, 100, 101, 121, 158,
  164–7, 173, 176, 177, 179,
  180, 186, 188, 196, 200,
  205, 206, 208, 210, 213,
  215, 217, 223, 224, 229,
  237, 244, 255, 257,
  262–4, 290, 297, 298, 313,
  322, 383, 400–3, 405, 407,
  408
  definition, 403
heuristic, 31, 77, 83, 85, 145, 177,
  178, 211, 213, 263, 269,
  272, 273, 276–8, 397
Holstein, James, 31, 78–81, 122,
  125, 126, 131, 275, 351
Howarth, David, 38, 39, 44–6, 52,
  55, 58, 61, 68, 84–6, 134,
  158, 274, 403, 405
Huntington, Samuel, 208
hybridity, 180

I
I (the), 123, 125, 126, 128, 148
identification, 267, 268, 280, 316,
  337

identity, 1, 2, 8–13, 15–18, 27, 29,
31, 32, 35, 37, 38, 40, 46,
48–53, 55–7, 65, 68, 75,
84, 87, 102, 109, 121,
132, 137, 164, 173, 185,
188, 202, 206, 210, 214,
215, 218, 235, 236, 240,
242, 247, 256, 258, 267,
285, 295–7, 301, 315–17,
324, 326, 329, 337,
340–2, 346, 367, 372–4,
377, 380–1, 393, 394,
396, 401, 403, 404,
406, 407
ideological dilemmas, 165
ideology, 7, 8, 97, 99, 165, 167, 341,
381
 and creativity, 268
 definition, 402
 ethical detachment of, 58
 grip of, 56, 268, 290, 337
 investment in, 58, 67, 101, 267
illocutionary force, 136
illocutions, 136
Imaginary, the, 48–9
imagined communities, 164, 170,
237, 239, 390, 406
imperialism, 358, 365, 366
implications, 143
implicit meaning, 143
impression management, 130
inburgering, 202, 203, 245, 247,
305, 310, 311
indexical expressions
 definition, 403
indexicality, 102, 104, 144–8, 153,
164, 166, 267, 407
 definition, 402, 403

indexicals, 82, 105, 112, 118, 145,
148, 149, 151–3, 155, 161,
163, 164, 166, 178, 261,
278, 351, 368, 396, 400,
403
individualism, 227, 247
individuality, 6, 7, 12–17, 40, 69,
72, 78, 131, 214, 215, 217,
220–3, 236, 240, 313, 316,
328, 329, 334
inference, 51, 77, 97, 106, 130,
139, 141, 142, 144, 160,
400
inquiry, 114, 117, 119
integration
 as an accomplishment, 249–61
 as an imperative, 250
 as an unfinished process, 334,
249–61
 and articulation, 262
 bankruptcy of, 193, 195, 242–4,
246, 247
 as a boundary concept, 183, 185
 centres, 193
 and citizenship, 204
 in classic sociology, 181
 debates on, 190, 191, 195, 196
 definition, 189, 191, 250, 251,
255
 and diversity, 204
 expectations about, 99, 231, 254
 failure of, 186–96, 242, 243, 247,
248, 285
 far right on, 191
 hegemonic discourse on, 186,
205
 and heterogeneity, 182
 as a hypochondric obsession, 83

and imagined communities, 237
indexing the location of, 255–61
indicators of, 186, 187
industry, 192
lack of, 55, 243
logics of, 66, 176, 177, 214–23, 228, 253, 257, 263, 313, 317
in the media, 232, 234, 298
modes of, 220, 226, 244, 259
as a myth, 249
myth of, 239
as a natural phenomenon, 239–43
objects of, 184
obstacles for, 234
paradox of, 187, 188
policy, 98–102, 151, 189–96, 212, 215, 217, 220, 229, 231, 244, 250, 253
as a political process, 239–43
polycentric concept of, 185, 186, 255, 261
and the public sphere, 236
and recognition, 334
and reification, 185
sector, 194
as social cohesion, 179, 181
and speaking Dutch, 248
status of, 239
and subjectivity, 217, 222, 235, 236, 239, 258, 263
talk on, 176, 183
trajectory, 219
as a value, 177, 188, 224, 262, 393
as a verb, 184, 185
Integration Between Science and Politics, 179–88

intellectuals, 286, 290, 293, 294, 300, 307, 333, 356, 357, 387
and the media, 298
interculturalism, 192
interpellation, 219, 267, 283, 299–300, 304, 328, 330, 337–48, 350, 365, 394, 403, 406, 407
definition, 403
interpretive functionalism, 94, 125, 129, 132, 178, 213, 224, 264, 271, 351, 369, 396, 402
definition, 403
intertextuality, 7, 26, 29, 31, 93, 96, 107, 148–9, 152, 160, 167, 211, 274, 279, 293, 294, 307, 381, 400, 405, 407
interviewing, 77–83
active, 80
and authenticity, 81
and the public realm, 83
as a self-technique, 83
Islam, 3, 4. 6, 8, 10–18, 24–6, 29, 55, 65, 66, 100, 101, 176, 180, 184, 201, 208–10, 220, 222, 232, 233, 236, 258–60, 278, 283–6, 289, 290, 296–8, 301, 308–10, 314–18, 321, 322, 325, 326, 328–9, 339, 340, 352, 353, 357, 371–4, 386, 395

J

James, William, 103, 112, 114, 116, 119–21, 123, 125, 126, 128–30, 135, 137, 139, 351

K

KCM, 189–91, 193, 200, 201
Kif Kif, 212, 217–19, 228, 237–9, 242, 244–6, 253, 289, 290, 319, 326
Kopytko, Roman, 122, 134

L

labelling, 130, 200, 229, 275, 276, 311, 326, 349
labels, 9, 25, 61, 87, 94, 129, 152, 154, 229, 230, 261, 267, 272, 274, 278, 280, 326, 369, 394
Lacan, Jacques, 48–50, 57, 72, 149, 404
lack, 50, 55, 227, 243, 318
 definition, 404
Laclau, Ernesto, 38, 42–8, 55, 56, 62, 72, 84, 87, 95, 182, 183, 401, 404, 406
language, 2
language games, 47, 81, 87, 94, 99, 103, 107, 108, 113, 133–44, 170, 188, 231, 299, 301, 303, 329, 339, 341, 350, 406
langue, 46, 104, 111, 144, 146, 149, 262
Leitkultur, 208
Lemke, Thomas, 76
Lévi-Strauss, Claude, 72, 207, 292, 295
liberalism, 2, 6, 13, 14, 23, 24, 31, 44, 56, 63, 65, 66, 168, 204, 205, 224, 225, 227, 228, 236, 237, 245–7, 276, 282, 349, 378, 394

Lilla, Mark, 293
linguistic anthropology, 104, 114
linguistic pragmatics, 42, 63, 95, 97, 98, 103, 105, 114, 115, 120, 122, 129, 133, 160
linguistic turn, 106
locuteur, 147, 150–1
locutions, 136, 147
logics
 of assimilation, 206, 209, 317
 of capitalism, 357–61, 364
 of closure, 326, 327, 349
 of critical explanation, 50
 of culturalisation, 101, 177, 196, 206–8, 255, 287, 295–8, 307, 309, 313, 358
 definition, 50, 60, 67, 404
 dialectic, 324
 of dialogism, 321
 of difference, 51, 52, 101, 406
 of disclosure, 326, 327, 349, 363
 of dissent, 324
 of emancipation, 304
 of embodiment, 347, 348, 354
 of enunciation, 347
 enunciative, 344, 346, 347, 350, 370
 of equivalence, 101, 406
 essentialist, 307, 309
 fantasmatic, 51, 59, 65, 97, 100, 101, 113, 171, 173, 205, 206, 209, 210, 227, 239, 240, 243, 263, 264, 330, 393, 408
 and games, 134
 of homogenisation, 65, 66, 96, 177, 181, 190, 206, 240, 255, 257, 282, 297, 301, 313, 314

of integration, 65, 173, 217, 220, 223, 227, 233, 255
interpretive, 83, 89, 152, 154, 165, 167, 178, 188, 197, 213, 223, 231, 262, 263, 267, 269, 271, 277, 278, 280, 301–3, 308, 329, 339, 340, 346–50, 393, 395, 407
naming of, 61, 62
of neoliberalism, 295, 296
patronising, 304, 306–7, 310, 350
political, 51, 56, 406
pragmatic enactment of, 101
and rules, 134
social, 408
spatial, 349
systemic, 359, 360, 364
tactile, 347–8
visual, 347, 348, 354, 370

M

Malinowski, Bronislaw, 111, 112
Maly, Ico, 185, 186, 198, 207–9, 290, 358
markers of metapragmatic awareness, 155
markers of subjectivity, 152, 155
marxism, 43, 45, 46, 63, 65, 144, 165, 269, 292, 296, 297, 326, 351–3, 357–8, 360, 366, 394
maxims, 142
  breaching of, 142
  flouting of, 142
  observation of, 140
Me (the), 123, 125, 128
Mead, George-Herbert, 31, 103, 116, 123, 125–30, 207

metadiscourse, 153, 167
metalinguistic awareness, 165
metalinguistics, 13, 18, 27, 32, 80, 89, 99, 149, 153, 158, 165–7, 177, 178, 219
metaphors, 31, 42, 55, 94, 156, 168, 169, 181, 225, 228, 261, 290, 312, 320, 326, 340, 342–4, 347–9, 361, 370, 409
metapragmatic awareness, 89, 102, 153, 154, 156, 167, 330, 404
  definition, 404
metapragmatic markers, 145, 147, 151, 152, 154–6, 160, 161, 219, 262, 404, 407
  definition, 405
metapragmatics, 80, 82, 137, 138, 152–6, 164, 167, 206, 211, 213–14, 219, 246, 262, 264, 268, 271, 279–80, 286, 320, 323, 328, 330, 337, 338, 346, 349–52, 357, 369, 394–6, 400, 402–5, 407
  definition, 404
methodological deficit, 87, 88, 95
migrants, 176, 180, 189–91, 193, 198, 205, 215, 224, 226, 229, 242, 249, 309, 321, 354, 355, 359, 364–6, 372, 390
migration, 3, 28, 30, 56, 65, 101, 171, 179–81, 185, 186, 189, 190, 194, 199, 202, 203, 206, 207, 209, 216, 225, 241, 278, 339, 365, 381, 390
mind in society, 113, 162

minorities, 257
  organisations of, 193
  visibility of, 238
minorities, 306
minority debate, 30, 175–265,
  348, 369–72, 374, 377,
  379, 386
Minority Forum, 193, 283, 301,
  303–7, 310–11, 330,
  332, 347
mirror stage, 48
misrecognition, 241, 242, 269, 300,
  301, 308, 328–30, 332,
  335–8, 342, 345–50, 394,
  395, 403, 404, 406, 407
  definition, 406
Moroccan, 2, 3, 5, 9–11, 16–18, 82,
  86, 108, 176, 177, 179,
  186–8, 200, 202, 209, 211,
  217, 220–2, 225, 244, 245,
  250–3, 261, 265, 269, 279,
  299, 317, 319, 336, 338,
  340–1, 344, 349, 354, 355,
  365, 376, 379–83
Morris, Charles, 114
Mouffe, Chantal, 38, 39, 42–8, 53,
  56, 167, 172
MSC Ahlan, 212
multiculturalism, 138, 192, 195,
  202
  failure of, 195

N

naming, 55, 60–2, 64, 65, 68, 85,
  93, 217, 404, 408
narratives, 2, 13, 16, 27, 31, 37, 42,
  57, 58, 79, 93, 94, 96, 104,
  107, 109, 111, 113, 115,
  129, 163, 167, 172, 178,
  214, 224, 262, 267, 268,
  270, 276, 280, 283, 285,
  289, 290, 302, 338, 358,
  361, 371, 372, 379, 393,
  395, 399, 403, 406, 408,
  409
nationalism, 52, 56, 179–80, 206,
  208, 257, 258, 264, 278,
  281–2, 297, 373, 374
negation, 52, 143, 149
negotiability, 108, 110, 112, 114,
  132, 161, 163, 302, 405
  definition, 405
neoliberalism, 203, 276, 295–8, 301,
  408
Netherlands, 179, 181, 183, 186,
  196, 198–201, 208, 220,
  314
neutrality, 6–8, 28, 78, 169, 329
nodal points, 52–4, 57, 401, 405
  definition, 405
norms, 65, 142, 167, 180, 185, 186,
  202, 206, 208, 209, 222,
  241, 267, 270, 305, 306,
  322, 323, 329, 338, 399,
  400, 402, 405
NVIVO, 212, 269, 271, 272

O

Objectief, 354
ontology, 44, 46–51, 74, 87, 152,
  223, 224, 228, 239, 242,
  249, 264
orders of discourse, 96
orders of indexicality, 164
othering, 100, 225, 305, 307,
  309, 331

P

PAJ, 212
parole, 46, 104, 111, 144, 146, 149
participation frameworks, 132
Pêcheux, Michel, 144, 145
Peirce, Charles S, 114, 116–20, 145
performances, 19, 51, 72, 73, 77, 94–7, 101, 106, 137, 155, 171, 214, 237, 239, 245, 246, 271, 319, 376, 399, 407
performatives, 135
performativity, 35–7, 65, 67–73, 106, 130–44, 257
perlocutions, 112, 136
philosophy of language, 104, 133–44
play, 127
political awareness, 13, 18, 24, 27, 31–3, 37, 67, 99, 154, 166–73, 178, 181, 217, 237, 264, 268, 280, 289, 303, 312, 313, 315, 328–30, 338, 347–8, 350, 352–4, 356, 362, 366, 382, 396, 402–4
 definition, 405
political correctness, 197, 201
political engagement, 3, 8, 29, 30, 32, 33, 35, 81, 121, 172, 175, 179, 211, 227, 228, 230, 234, 238, 256–63, 271, 283, 285, 290, 293–5, 297–8, 303, 304, 315, 316, 318, 331, 341, 342, 346, 348, 349, 361, 364, 368, 370, 371, 393, 397
 definition, 172, 262, 368, 391, 406
political logics, 51, 101, 310, 408
political subjectivity, 386
politics
 as articulation, 281
 as the art of the possible, 280
 definition, 167, 405
 modes of, 268, 269, 280, 293, 297, 301, 322, 323, 325
 preferred mode of, 175, 177, 225, 269, 270, 281, 282, 321, 325, 349, 361, 363, 364, 378
polyphony, 9, 104, 149–51, 217, 243, 261–5, 262, 270
post-colonialism, 288, 289
postmodernism, 293–6
poststructuralism, 18, 30, 36, 37, 39, 40, 42–51, 57, 65, 68, 71, 79, 83–9, 92, 94, 95, 103, 107, 108, 114–16, 122, 123, 134, 135, 144–6, 152, 165, 170, 181, 214, 262, 273, 278, 289–91, 293–6, 396, 406
power, 26, 36, 39, 42, 52–3, 63–5, 68, 70, 72–6, 78, 79, 81, 83, 92, 96, 97, 101, 104, 137, 157, 158, 167, 169–71, 190, 197, 207, 227, 247, 282, 297, 303, 319, 363, 378, 381–3, 386–9, 394, 395, 400, 405, 408
 as conduct of conduct, 75
 definition, 408
 as domination, 64, 65, 73–83, 165, 170, 195, 304, 395, 408
 as freedom, 75

power (*cont.*)
  and knowledge, 70
  as rationality, 74
  reified notions of, 74
  as a relationship, 75
pragmatic dam-burst, 104
pragmatic maxim, 116, 118, 120, 137, 351
pragmatics, 132
  as a component of linguistics, 143
  definition, 105, 106, 115, 406
  and discourse analysis, 121
  everyday meanings of, 116
  and ideology, 106
  on language, 107
  as a perspective, 103, 143
  poststructuralism, 103, 108, 109
  as a rag-bag, 105
pragmatic turn, 104, 106, 145, 148
pragmatism, 64, 79, 89, 98, 104, 111–16, 118–21, 123, 126, 129, 130, 132, 133, 135, 145, 325, 396
  and discourse analysis, 132
  and knowledge, 117
  as a source for pragmatics, 115
presuppositions, 143
primacy of the political, 408
principal, 132
pronouns, 7, 94, 123, 125, 145, 148, 155, 161, 403
prosody, 161
psychoanalysis, 48, 131, 404
public sphere, 167–72, 180, 231, 261–5, 270, 283, 394
  and articulation, 171
  definition, 170–2, 231, 406
  imagining the, 171, 172, 231

  logics of, 231, 270
PvdA, 326, 351, 354, 356–7, 364–8

R

race, 207
racism, 15, 44, 53, 62, 66, 96, 138, 166, 179, 180, 184, 188, 190, 194–6, 206, 207, 216, 218, 239, 247, 251, 257, 278, 283, 285, 297, 298, 324, 326, 334–5, 337, 352–62, 364–6, 371, 378–83
radical democracy, 43, 44, 172
radical empiricism, 120
reality, 57, 72, 163
  contextual, 93, 102, 113, 114, 148, 152, 156, 163, 351, 400, 407
Real, the, 48–50, 59, 303
recognition, 14, 102, 172, 176, 193, 194, 201, 236, 269, 301, 325, 328–38, 354, 355, 384
  definition, 406
reflexivity, 14, 26, 27, 32, 59, 63, 65, 68, 70–3, 77, 79–80, 93, 94, 98, 102, 103, 106–8, 114–16, 125–7, 130, 137, 144, 151–4, 158, 159, 163, 165, 167, 173, 178, 186, 188, 206, 210, 211, 213, 214, 219, 223, 227, 263, 264, 267, 268, 271–4, 303, 308, 323, 337, 346–8, 350–1, 368, 369, 371, 379, 399–401, 404–7

refugees, 198, 264, 292
regularities of dispersion, 47, 274, 403
reification, 74, 77, 82, 106, 109, 114, 162, 170, 185, 207, 208, 231, 270, 351, 358, 361, 407, 408
relativism, 278, 288, 291, 295, 301, 308–10, 347, 394
religion, 4–6, 8, 12, 13, 15–17, 24–8, 52, 97, 128, 173, 192, 193, 195, 198, 200, 206, 208, 209, 211, 215, 220, 222, 225, 236, 237, 240–2, 258, 260, 267, 281, 282, 284, 286, 287, 297, 300, 313–15, 317, 320, 326, 327, 334, 339, 340, 352–3, 370–8, 394
religious, 186, 210
reported speech, 8, 144, 149, 154, 218, 219, 405
repression, 131
research questions, 213, 269–71
research topic, 3, 28–9, 86, 175, 176, 178, 211, 263
Resist, 352, 364
roles, 1, 3, 4, 31, 40, 52, 60, 63, 78, 79, 109, 113, 120, 121, 123, 127, 129–32, 135, 161, 162, 173, 178, 206, 216, 222, 232, 242, 247, 251, 276, 307, 308, 313, 314, 334–6, 339, 343, 345, 357, 373, 385, 389–90, 401, 408
Rorty, Richard, 119
rules, 134

S
Said, Edward, 208, 290–1
Samenlevingsopbouw, 244
SAMV, 212, 237, 338–45
Sartre, Jean-Paul, 292
Saussure, Ferdinand, 40, 41, 46, 49, 71, 72, 109, 118, 149
Schinkel, Willem, 181–3, 186, 198, 207, 208
Searle, John, 103, 138, 139, 144
self
  as an assemblage, 77, 78, 80, 351
  as an assembly, 80, 351
  as an idea we ride, 351, 370
  as an internalised conversation of gestures, 127
  concepts of, 30
  Cooley on, 126, 128
  decentred, 123
  definition, 351, 407
  dialogical, 115
  and ehtics, 223
  empirical, 123, 126, 132, 351
  feeling, 126
  as fluctuating material, 124
  as form, 129
  Goffman on the, 130
  interpretations, 59–62, 68, 77, 81, 83, 86, 87
  James on the, 123
  looking glass, 126
  material, 124
  Mead on the, 126
  mortification of the, 131
  multiplicity of, 2, 123, 124, 128
  as object and subject, 126
  as a performance, 131
  performance of, 130

self (*cont.*)
   and political debates, 173
   and politics, 268
   preferred sense of, 11, 175, 269, 280, 326, 328, 329, 334, 338, 341–3, 353, 395, 397
   reduction of the, 82, 131
   as a reification, 77
   as a scam, 131
   spiritual, 124
   staying true to one's, 312–17
   techniques, 26, 77, 83–4, 122
   technologies of the, 76, 83
   as Thought, 125
   transcendental, 123
   as a working framework, 351
self-interpretations, 93, 106, 123, 131, 196, 205–6, 211, 239, 240, 267, 268, 302, 303, 308, 316, 329, 337, 348, 351, 356, 362, 404, 407, 408
   defintion, 407
self-techniques, 351, 372, 407
semantics, 105, 114, 135, 142, 143, 150
semiotics, 43, 104, 105, 114, 115
Sharia4Belgium, 77
Shifters, 148
shown heterogeneity, 149
signs, 46, 95, 114, 118, 119, 125, 148, 161, 171
social logics, 51, 59–68, 85, 206, 209, 217, 302, 408
   definition, 408
   naming of, 61
social mobility, 374–7
social, the, 408
Sokal, Alain, 293–4

soul, 125
speaker meaning, 138
speech acts, 37, 68, 73, 93, 97, 103, 104, 106, 113, 133, 135–8, 301, 402
Spirit of Cartesianism, 116, 122
statements, 47, 69, 96, 111
Stavrakakis, Yannis, 39, 49, 50, 53, 57, 404, 405
stereotypes, 82, 328
stigma, 131
Strauss, Anselm, 272
stream of consciousness, 125
structuralism, 39–41, 46, 69, 72, 104, 133, 144
structural objects of adaptability, 110, 113, 162
structure, 108–10, 162, 223, 229, 283, 289, 408
subject
   as an effect of discourse and power, 73
   decentred, 145
   in poststructuralism, 68
subjectivity, 1, 114, 329
   as an effect of language use, 144
   and debate, 173
   definition, 407
   in enuciative pragmatics, 146
   Lacan on, 49
   markers of, 147
   modes of, 283, 285, 301, 303, 316, 335, 336, 340
   multiplicity of, 107
   preferred mode of, 16, 22, 285, 300, 301, 335, 336, 340, 344, 348–50, 352, 363, 378, 406
   unity of, 148

subject positions, 67–9, 80, 87, 97, 98, 113, 145, 151, 163, 178, 219, 224, 229, 247, 261, 267–70, 272, 275, 277–80, 285, 289, 293, 301, 325, 328, 334, 337, 354, 357, 371, 374, 382, 386, 393, 394, 403, 404, 406–8
   definition, 278, 407
   Foucault on, 69
   investment in, 268, 280
   metapragmatics of, 180
sujet parlant, 150, 151
symbolic interactionism, 122, 125, 130
Symbolic, the, 48–50, 404
syntax, 105, 135

T

technologies
   of the self, 368
tolerant majority, 183, 184, 206
topics
   definition, 276, 408
totalising institutions, 131
truth, 268
turns, 105, 120

U

unities of discourse, 31, 47, 96, 106
utopia, 317, 319, 327

V

values, 3–5, 11, 13, 27, 31, 41, 46, 51, 56, 99–101, 152, 167, 170, 172, 178, 180, 182, 186–8, 202, 206, 208, 209, 217, 224, 241, 254, 258, 267, 268, 270, 281, 282, 305, 306, 320, 322, 323, 325, 329, 344, 352–3, 393–5, 399–402
Van Dijk, Teun, 156, 157, 159, 160
van Rooy, Wim, 287
variability, 108, 109, 114, 132, 302
   definition, 409
variation, 109
veiling, 6–8, 100, 151, 176, 191, 209, 210, 220–2, 232–4, 237, 260, 261, 314, 315, 322–4, 342, 378
Verschueren, Jef, 93–5, 97, 102, 105, 107–14, 133, 137, 139–43, 153–5, 158–62, 166, 190, 191, 202, 206, 208, 381, 385, 399, 400, 402, 404–6, 408, 409
Vlaams Belang, 66, 191, 194, 215, 259, 281, 288, 300, 354
Vlaams Blok, 189–191, 194, 215, 354
VMC, 192, 193
VOEM, 318
voice, 7, 80, 145, 150, 154, 217, 219, 225, 230, 268, 298, 328, 332, 371, 380
Vygotsky, Lev, 113

W

Wittgenstein, Ludwig, 87, 103, 133–5, 138

Z

Žižek, Slavoj, 53, 54

The manufacturer's authorised representative in the EU is Springer Nature Customer Service Centre GmbH, Europaplatz 3, 69115 Heidelberg, Germany. If you have any concerns regarding our products, please contact ProductSafety@springernature.com

Printed and bound by CPI Group (UK) Ltd, Croydon, CR0 4YY
23/03/2026
02076736-0015